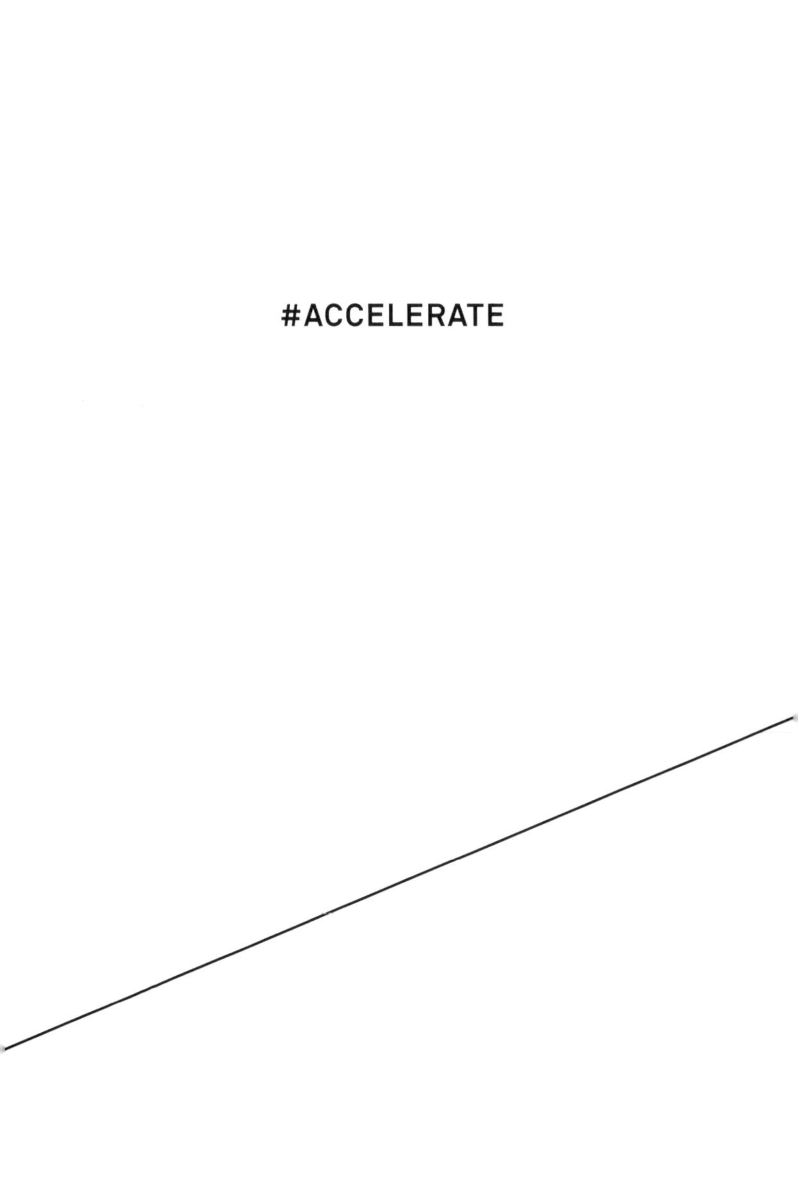
#ACCELERATE

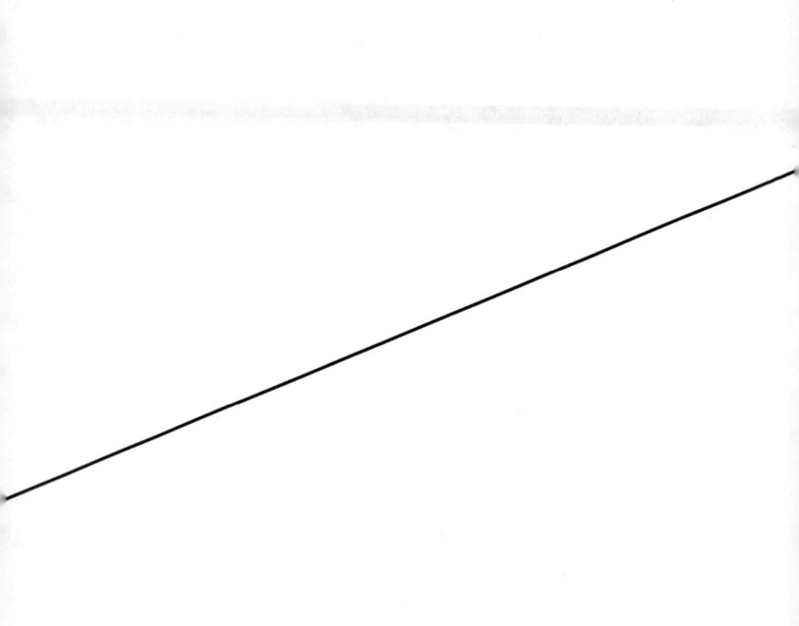

Merve
Verlag

#ACCELERATE#

editors

ROBIN MACKAY +

ARMEN AVANESSIAN

URBANOMIC

First published in 2014 by
URBANOMIC MEDIA LTD,
THE OLD LEMONADE FACTORY,
WINDSOR QUARRY,
FALMOUTH TR11 3EX,
UNITED KINGDOM

in association with
MERVE
CRELLESTRASSE 22
10827, BERLIN

Second edition 2017
Third edition 2019
Fourth edition (print on demand) 2021

BRITISH LIBRARY CATALOGUING-IN-PUBLICATION DATA
A full catalogue record of this book is available
from the British Library

ISBN 978-0-9575295-5-7

Distributed by the MIT Press,
Cambridge Massachusetts and London, England

Type by Norm, Zurich

www.urbanomic.com
www.merve.de

CONTENTS

LIST OF SOURCES

Marx 'Fragment on Machines', edited extract from *Grundrisse*, tr. M. Nicolaus, by kind permission of the translator; **Butler** 'The Book of the Machines', edited extract from *Erewhon* (1871); **Fedorov** 'The Common Task', edited extract from *What Was Man Created For? The Philosophy of the Common Task*, trans. E. Koutaissoff and M. Minto (London: Honeyglen, 1990), by permission of Honeyglen Publishing; **Veblen** 'The Machine Process', edited extract from *The Theory of Business Enterprise* (New York: Mentor, 1958); **Firestone** 'Two Modes of Cultural History', extract from *The Dialectics of Sex*. Copyright © 1970 by Shulamith Firestone. Reprinted by permission of Farrar, Straus and Giroux, LLC; **Camatte** 'Decline of Humanity?', edited extract from *The Wandering of Humanity* tr. F. Perlman (Detroit: Black and Red, 1975); **Deleuze+Guattari** 'The Civilized Capitalist Machine', edited extract from *Anti-Oedipus: Capitalism and Schizophrenia,* tr. R. Hurley, M. Seem and H.R. Lane (London and New York: Continuum 2004). Copyright © 1972 Gilles Deleuze and Félix Guattari, by permission of Continuum, an imprint of Bloomsbury Publishing PLC; **Lyotard** 'Energumen Capitalism', review in *Critique* 306 (Nov. 1972), tr. R. Mackay for this volume; 'Every Political Economy is a Libidinal Economy', *from Économie Libidinale* (Paris: Minuit, 1974), by permission of Éditions Minuit, tr. Iain Hamilton Grant in *Libidinal Economy* (London: Athlone, 1993); 'Desirevolution', from *Dérive à partir de Marx et Freud* (Paris: UGE, 1973), tr. Iain Hamilton Grant for this volume; **Lipovetsky** 'Power of Repetition', from *L'Arc* 64 (1976), tr. Robin Mackay for this volume, by permission of the author. **Ballard** 'Fictions of Every Kind', from *Books and Bookmen* 1971, Copyright © 1971, J. G. Ballard, used by permission of The Wylie Agency (UK) Limited.; **Land** 'Circuitries', from *Pli* 4:1/2 (1992), republished in *Fanged*

Noumena: Collected Writings 1987–2007 (Falmouth, UK and New York: Urbanomic and Sequence Press, 2011); **Grant** 'LA 2019', previously unpublished conference paper presented at 'Justice and Post-Politics' conference, University of Bristol, 1996; **CCRU** 'Cybernetic Culture', previously unpublished; 'Swarmachines', from *Abstract Culture* Swarm 1, 1996; **Plant+Land** 'Cyberpositive', from M. Fuller (ed), *Unnatural: Techno-Theory for a Contaminated Culture* (London: Underground, 1994); **Fisher** 'Terminator vs Avatar', previously unpublished, presentation at 'Accelerationism' symposium at Goldsmiths University of London, 2012; **Williams+Srnicek** '#Accelerate', first published online, 2013; **Negri** 'Reflections', first published online by Euronomade at euronomade.info, 2014, tr. M. Pasquinelli; **Parisi** 'Automated Architecture', previously unpublished; **Terranova** 'Red Stack Attack!', first published online by Euronomade at euronomade.info, 2014; **Negarestani** 'The Labor of the Inhuman', earlier version published online by E-Flux at e-flux.com, 2014; **Brassier** 'Prometheanism', developed from a presentation at PS1, New York, 2013; **Singleton**, 'Maximum Jailbreak', earlier version published online by E-Flux at e-flux.com; **Land** 'Teleoplexy', previously unpublished; **Reed** 'Seven Prescriptions', previously unpublished. **Bauer** includes layered images as follows: *Anticipations:* patent diagram for wireless telegraphy (1915); *Ferment:* central core of HAL9000 from *2001: A Space Odyssey* (1968); *Cyberculture:* Lebbeus Woods's *War and Architecture* (1996); *Acceleration:* computer simulation depicting a solar neutrino event at Sudbury Neutrino Observatory (2011).

Introduction

Robin Mackay
+
Armen Avanessian

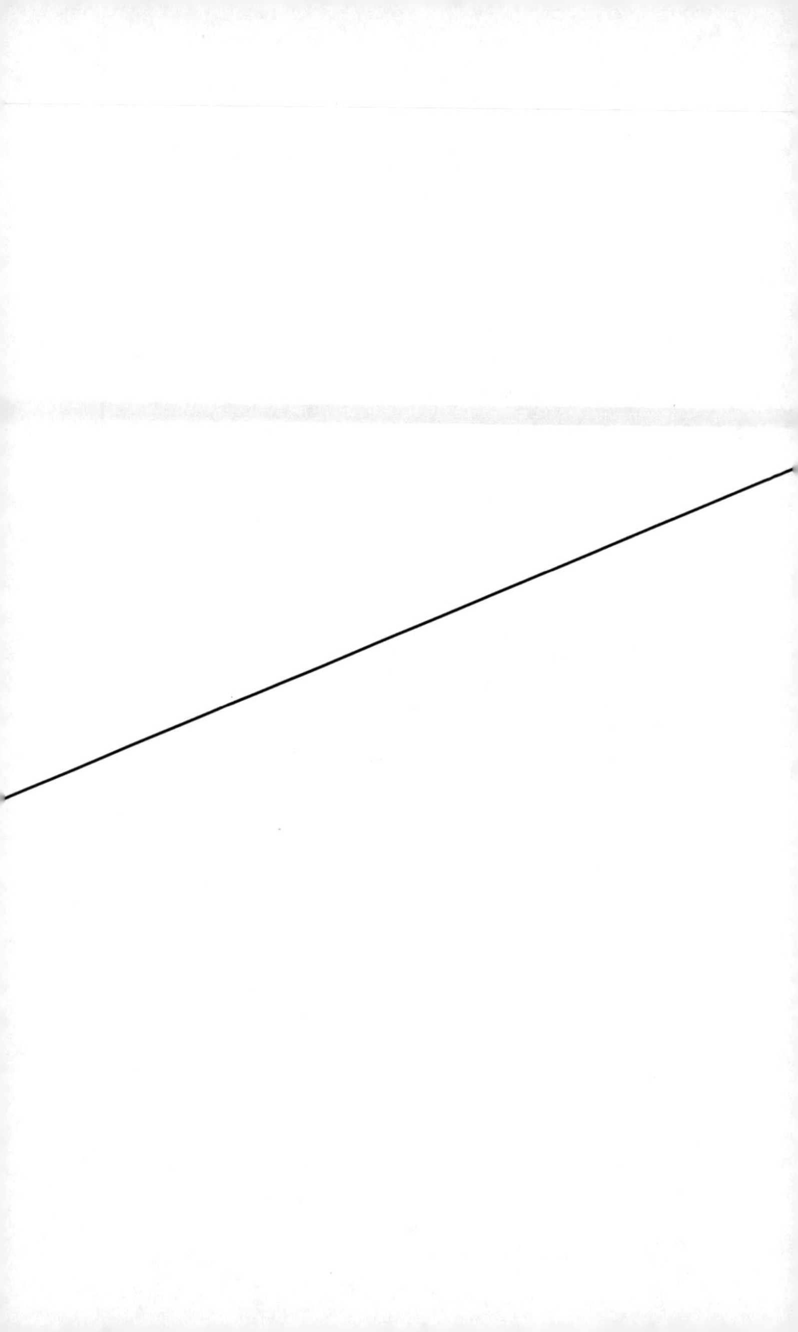

1858

The science which compels the inanimate limbs of the machinery, by their construction, to act purposefully, as an automaton, does not exist in the worker's consciousness, but rather acts upon him through the machine as an alien power.

Karl Marx

1970

Just as the merging of the divided sexual, racial, and economic classes is a precondition for sexual, racial, or economic revolution respectively, so the merging of the aesthetic with the technological culture is the precondition of a cultural revolution.

Shulamith Firestone

1994

Catastrophe is the past coming apart. Anastrophe is the future coming together. Seen from within history, divergence is reaching critical proportions. From the matrix, crisis is a convergence misinterpreted by mankind.

Sadie Plant + Nick Land

2013

The most important division in today's Left is between those that hold to a folk politics of localism, direct action, and relentless horizontalism, and those that outline what must become called an accelerationist politics at ease with a modernity of abstraction, complexity, globality, and technology.

Alex Williams + Nick Srnicek

Accelerationism is a political heresy: the insistence that the only radical political response to capitalism is not to protest, disrupt, or critique, nor to await its demise at the hands of its own contradictions, but to accelerate its uprooting, alienating, decoding, abstractive tendencies. The term was introduced into political theory to designate a certain nihilistic alignment of philosophical thought with the excesses of capitalist culture (or anticulture), embodied in writings that sought an immanence with this process of alienation. The uneasy status of this impulse, between subversion and acquiescence, between realist analysis and poetic exacerbation, has made accelerationism a fiercely-contested theoretical stance.

At the basis of all accelerationist thought lies the assertion that the crimes, contradictions, and absurdities of capitalism have to be countered with a politically and theoretically progressive attitude towards its constituent elements. Accelerationism seeks to side with the emancipatory dynamic that broke the chains of feudalism and ushered in the constantly ramifying range of practical possibilities characteristic of modernity. The focus of much accelerationist thinking is the examination of the supposedly intrinsic link between these transformative forces and the axiomatics of exchange value and capital accumulation that format contemporary planetary society.

This stance apparently courts two major risks: on the one hand, a cynical resignation to a *politique du pire*, a politics that must hope for the worst and can think the future only as apocalypse and tabula rasa; on the other, the replacement of the insistence that capitalism will die of its internal contradictions with a championing of the market whose supposed radicalism is indistinguishable from the passive acquiescence into which political power has devolved. Such convenient extremist caricatures, however, obstruct the consideration of a diverse set of ideas united in the claim that a truly progressive political thought—a thought that is not beholden to inherited authority, ideology or institutions—is possible only by way of a future-oriented and realist philosophy; and that only a politics constructed on this basis can open up new perspectives on the human project, and on social and political adventures yet to come. This assumption that we are at the *beginning* of a political project, rather than at the bleak terminus of history, seems crucial today in order to avoid endemic social depression and lowering of expectations in the face of global cultural homogenization, climate change and ongoing financial crisis. Confronting such developments, and the indifference of markets to their human consequences, even the keenest liberals are hard-pressed to argue that capitalism remains the vehicle and sine qua non of modernity and progress; and yet the political response to this situation often seems to face backwards rather than forwards.

Despair seems to be the dominant sentiment of the contemporary Left, whose crisis perversely mimics its foe, consoling itself either with the minor pleasures of shrill denunciation, mediatised protest, and ludic disruptions, or with the scarcely credible notion that maintaining a grim 'critical' vigilance on the total subsumption of human life under capital, from the safehouse of theory, or from within contemporary art's self-congratulatory fog of 'indeterminacy', constitutes resistance. Hegemonic neoliberalism claims there is no alternative, and established Left political thinking, careful to desist from Enlightenment 'grand narratives', wary of any truck with a technological infrastructure tainted by capital, and allergic to an entire civilizational heritage that it lumps together and discards as 'instrumental thinking', patently fails to offer the alternative it insists must be possible, except in the form of counterfactual histories and all-too-local interventions into a decentred, globally-integrated system that is at best indifferent to them. The general reasoning is that if modernity=progress=capitalism=acceleration, then the only possible resistance amounts to deceleration, whether through a fantasy of collective organic self-sufficiency or a solo retreat into miserablism and sagacious warnings against the treacherous counterfinalities of rational thought.

Needless to say, a well-to-do liberal Left, convinced that technology equates to instrumental mastery and that capitalist economics amounts to a heap of numbers, in most cases leaves concrete technological nous and economic arguments to its adversary—something it shares with its more radical but equally technologically illiterate academic counterparts, who confront capitalism with theoretical constructs so completely at odds with its concrete workings that the most they can offer is a faith in miraculous events to come, scarcely more effectual than organic folk politics. In some quarters, a Heideggerian *Gelassenheit* or 'letting be' is called for, suggesting that the best we can hope for is to desist entirely from destructive development and attempts to subdue or control nature—an option that, needless to say, is also the prerogative of an individualised privileged spectator who is the subjective product of global capital.

From critical social democrats to revolutionary Maoists, from Occupy mic checks to post-Frankfurt-School mutterings, the ideological slogan goes: There must be an outside! And yet, given the real subsumption of life under capitalist relations, what is missing, precluded by reactionary obsessions with purity, humility, and sentimental attachment to the personally gratifying rituals of critique and protest and their brittle and fleeting forms of collectivity? Precisely any pragmatic criteria for the identification and selection of elements of this system that might be effective in a concrete transition to another life beyond the iniquities and impediments of capital.

It is in the context of such a predicament that accelerationism has recently emerged again as a leftist option. Since the 2013 publication of Alex Williams and Nick Srnicek's '#Accelerate: Manifesto for an Accelerationist Politics' [MAP], the term has been adopted to name a convergent group of new theoretical enterprises that aim to conceptualise the future outside of traditional critiques and regressive, decelerative, or restorative 'solutions'. In the wake of the new philosophical realisms of recent years, they do so through a recusal of the rhetoric of human finitude in favour of a renewed Prometheanism and rationalism, an affirmation that the increasing immanence of the social and technical is irreversible and indeed desirable, and a commitment to developing new understandings of the complexity this brings to contemporary politics. This new movement has already given rise to lively international debate, but is also the object of many misunderstandings and rancorous antagonism on the part of those entrenched positions whose dogmatic slumbers it disturbs. Through a reconstruction of the historical trajectory of accelerationism, this book aims to set out its core problematics, to explore its historical and conceptual genealogy, and to exhibit the gamut of possibilities it presents, so as to assess the potentials of accelerationism as both philosophical configuration and political proposition.

But what does it mean to present the history of a philosophical tendency that exists only in the form of isolated eruptions which each time sink without trace under a sea of unanimous censure and/or dismissive scorn? Like the 'broken, explosive, volcanic line' of thinkers Gilles Deleuze sought to activate, the scattered episodes of accelerationism exhibit only incomplete continuities which have until now been rendered indiscernible by their heterogeneous influences and by long intervening silences. At the time of writing we find a contemporary accelerationism in the process of mapping out a common terrain of problems, but it describes diverse trajectories through this landscape. These paths adjust and reorient themselves daily in a dialogue structured by the very sociotechnologies they thematize, the strategic adoption of the tag #accelerate having provided a global address through which to track their progress and the new orientations they suggest.

If a printed book (and even more so one of this length) inevitably seems to constitute a deceleration in relation to such a burgeoning field, it should be noted that this reflective moment is entirely in keeping with much recent accelerationist thought. The explicit adoption of an initially rather pejoratively used term[1] indicates a certain defiance towards anticipated attacks. But it also indicates that a revisionary process is underway—one of refining, selecting, modifying, and consolidating earlier tendencies, rebooting accelerationism as an evolving theoretical program, but simultaneously reclaiming it as an untimely provocation, an irritant that returns implacably from the future to bedevil the official sanctioned discourse of institutional politics and political theory. This book therefore aims to participate in the writing of a philosophical counterhistory, the construction of a genealogy of accelerationism (not the only possible one—other texts could have been included, other stories will be told), at the same time producing accelerationism 'itself' as a fictional or hyperstitional anticipation of intelligence to come.

This revisionary montage proceeds in four phases, first setting out three sets of historical texts to be appropriated and reenergized by the undecided future of accelerationism following the appearance of the MAP, and subsequently bringing together a sequence of contemporary accelerationist texts galvanized by the Manifesto's call.

ANTICIPATIONS

The first section features late-nineteenth and early-twentieth-century thinkers who, confronted with the rapid emergence of an integrated globalised industrial complex and the usurpation

1. The term 'accelerationism' was initially coined by Roger Zelazny in his 1967 SF novel *Lord of Light*, and taken up as a critical term by Benjamin Noys in *The Persistence of the Negative* (Edinburgh: Edinburgh University Press, 2010), 4–9. Noys continues his meditation on accelerationism in *Malign Velocities: Acceleration and Capitalism* (London: Zer0, 2014).

of inherited value-systems by exchange value, attempted to understand the precise nature of the relation between technical edifice and economic system, and speculated as to their potential future consequences for human society and culture.

Karl Marx is represented in perhaps his most openly accelerationist writing, the *Grundrisse*'s 'Fragment on Machines'. Here Marx documents the momentous shift between the worker's use of tools as prosthetic organs to amplify and augment human cognitive and physical abilities (labour power), and machine production properly speaking, dating the latter to the emergence of an integrated 'automatic system of machines' wherein knowledge and control of nature leveraged as industrial process supplant direct means of labour. Within this system, the worker increasingly becomes a prosthesis: rather than the worker animating the machine, the machine animates the worker, making him a part of its 'mighty organism', a 'conscious organ' subject to its virtuosity or 'alien power'. Individuals are incorporated into a new, machinic culture, taking on habits and patterns of thought appropriate to its world, and are irreversibly resubjectivized as social beings.

In *Erewhon*'s 'Book of the Machines', **Samuel Butler** develops Marx's extrapolations of the machine system into a full-scale machinic delirium, extending an intrinsic science-fictional aspect of his theoretical project which also entails a speculative anthropology: if technology is bound up with the capitalist decanting of primitive and feudal man into a new mode of social being, then a speculation on what machines will become is also a speculation on what the human is and might be. In line with the integration that at once fascinates Marx and yet which he must denounce as a fantasy of capital, Butler's vision, a panmachinism that will later be inspirational for Deleuze and Guattari, refuses any special natural or originary privilege to human labour: Seen from the future, might the human prove nothing but a pollinator of a machine civilization to come?

Refusing such machinic fatalism, **Nicolai Fedorov**'s utopian vision reserves within a 'cosmist' vision of expansion a Promethean role for man, whose scientific prowess he sees as capable of introducing purposefulness into an otherwise indifferent and hostile nature. Fedorov exhorts mankind to have the audacity to collectively invest in the unlimited and unknown possibilities this mastery of nature affords him: to abandon the modesty of earthly concerns, to defy mortality and transcend the parochial planetary habitat. It is only by reaching beyond their given habitat, according to Fedorov, that humans can fulfill their collective destiny, rallying to a 'common task'.

Thorstein Veblen, famously the author of *The Theory of the Leisure Class*, takes up the question of the insurrectionary nature of scientific and technical change as part of his evolutionary analysis of developments in modern capitalism (the emergence of monopolies and trusts). For Veblen it is not the proletariat but the technical class, the scientists and engineers, who ultimately promise to be the locus of revolutionary agency; he sees the tendencies of the machine system as being at odds with the ethos of business enterprise, which, ultimately, is just one more institutional archaism to be sloughed off in the course of its development. Significant also is Veblen's refusal to conceive 'culture' narrowly in an ameliorative role, offering compensation for the 'social problems' triggered by the reshaping of individuals and social relations in accordance with the automatism and standardization of the machine system: instead he insists that this process be understood as a radical transformation of human culture, and one that will outlive its occasional cause—an assumption shared by Fedorov in his vision of a 'multi-unity' allied in the 'common task' and armed with a confidence in the capacity of science and engineering to reshape the human life-world.

All of the core themes of accelerationism appear in germ in the projects of these writers, along with the variety of forms—

descriptive, prescriptive, utopian, fictional, theoretical, scientific, realist—in which they will later be developed. The speculative extrapolation of the machine process, the affirmation that this process is inextricably social, technical, and epistemic; the questioning of its relation to capitalism, the indifferent form of exchange-value and its corrosion of all previous social formations and subjective habits; and its effect upon culture and the new possibilities it opens up for the human conceived not as an eternal given, fated to suffer the vicissitudes of nature, but as a historical being whose relation to nature (including its own), increasingly mediated through technical means, is mutable and in motion.

FERMENT

The second section belongs predominantly to a moment in modern French philosophy that sought to integrate a theoretical analysis of political economy with an understanding of the social construction of human desire. Galvanized by the still uncomprehended events of May '68 and driven to a wholesale rejection of the stagnant cataracts of orthodox party politics, these thinkers of the 'Marx-Freud synthesis' suggest that emancipation from capitalism be sought not through the dialectic, but by way of the polymorphous perversion set free by the capitalist machine itself. In the works of Deleuze and Guattari, Lyotard, and Lipovetsky, the indifference of the value-form, the machine composition of labour, and their merciless reformatting of all previous social relations is seen as the engine for the creation of a new fluid social body. It is the immanence with universal schizophrenia toward which capital draws social relations that promises emancipation here, rather than the party politics that, no doubt, paled by comparison with the oneiric escapades of '68. It is at this point that the credo of accelerationism is for the first time openly formulated—most explicitly by Gilles Lipovetsky: '"[R]evolutionary actions" are not those which aim to overthrow the system of Capital, which has never ceased to be revolutionary, but those which complete its rhythm in all its radicality, that is to say actions which accelerate the metamorphic process of bodies'.

In 'Decline of Humanity?', **Jacques Camatte** extends the reflections of Marx and Veblen on the 'autonomization of capital', arguing that, in testing to the limit certain ambivalent analyses in Marx's thought, it reveals shortcomings in his thinking of capital. Marx claims that capital blocks its own 'self-realization' process, the way in which its 'revolutionary' unconditional development of production promises eventually to subvert capitalist relations of production. Capital is thus at once a revolutionary force (as evidenced by its destruction of all previous social formations) *and* a barrier, a limited form or mere transitional moment on the way to this force's ultimate triumph in another mode of social relation.

According to Camatte, Marx here underestimates the extent to which, particularly through the runaway acceleration of the 'secondary' productive forces of the autonomic form of machine capital, the revolutionary role of the proletariat is taken over by capitalism itself. Manifestly it leads to no crisis of contradiction: rather than the productive forces of humans having been developed by capital to the point where they exceed its relations of production, productive forces (including human labour power) now exist only for capital and not for humans. Thus Camatte suggests we can read Marx not as a 'prophet of the decline of capital' but instead as a Cassandra auguring the decadence of the human. Capital can and has become truly independent of human will, and any opportunity for an intervention that would develop its newly-reformatted sociotechnological beings into communist subjects is definitively lost.

Along similar lines to contemporaries such as Althusser and Colletti, Camatte concludes: no contradiction, therefore no dialectic. 'On this we agree: the human being is dead': more exactly, the human being has been transformed by capital into a passive machine part, no longer possessed of any 'irreducible element' that would allow it to revolt against capital. For Camatte the only response to this consummate integration of humans is absolute revolt. The entire historical product of capitalism is to be condemned; indeed we must reject production itself as a basis for the analysis of social relations. Revolutionary thought for Camatte, therefore, urges a refusal of Marx's valorization of productivism, and counsels absolute retreat—we can only 'leave this world' (Camatte's work was thus a strong influence on anarcho-primitivist trends in political thought).[2]

Anything but an accelerationist, then, Camatte nevertheless sets the scene for accelerationism by describing this extreme predicament: Faced with real subsumption, is there any alternative to pointless piecemeal reformism apart from total secession? Can the relation between revolutionary force, human agency, and capitalism be thought differently? Where does alienation end and domestication begin? Is growth in productive force necessarily convertible into a socialized wealth? Camatte's trenchant pessimism outlines accelerationism in negative: He commits himself to a belief that subsumption into the 'community of capital' is a definitive endpoint in capital's transformation of the human. Still in search of a revolutionary thought, however, and despite his own analysis, he also commits himself to a faith in some underlying human essence that may yet resist, and that may be realised in an 'elsewhere' of capital—a position underlying many radical political alternatives imagined today. In contrast, accelerationism, making a different analysis of the ambivalent forces at work in capital, will insist on the continuing dynamism and transformation of the human wrought by the unleashing of productive forces, arguing that it is possible to align *with* their revolutionary force but *against* domestication, and indeed that the only way 'out' is to plunge further in.

2. For more on Camatte in relation to accelerationism, see R. Brassier, 'Wandering Abstraction', <http://www.metamute.org/editorial/articles/wandering-abstraction>.

Gilles Deleuze + Félix Guattari's *Anti-Oedipus* developed precisely the ambivalences noted by Camatte, modelling capitalism as a movement at once revolutionary—decoding and deterritorializing—and constantly reterritorializing and indifferently reinstalling old codes as 'neoarchaic' simulations of culture to contain the fluxes it releases. It is within this dynamic that a genuine accelerationist strategy explicitly emerges, in order to reformulate the question that haunts every Left political discourse, namely whether there is a 'revolutionary path' at all. It is not by chance that probably the most famous 'accelerationist' passage in Deleuze and Guattari's work, included in the extract from *Anti-Oedipus* here, plays out against the backdrop of the dichotomy between a folk-political approach (in this case Samir Amin's Third-Worldist separatism) and the exact opposite direction, 'to go still further, that is, in the movement of the market, of decoding and deterritorialization? For perhaps the flows are not yet deterritorialized enough, not decoded enough, from the viewpoint of a theory and a practice of a highly schizophrenic character. Not to withdraw from the process, but to go further, to "accelerate the process".' Famously Deleuze and Guattari, at least in 1972, opt for the latter. Rather than contradictions precipitating collapse, on the contrary, ongoing crises remain an immanent source of capitalist productivity, and this also implies the production of ever new axioms capable of digesting any arising contradictions. For Deleuze and Guattari, there is no necessary conclusion to these processes, indeed the absence of any limit is their primary assumption; and yet they suggest that, as the capitalist socius draws into an ever-closer immanence with universal schizophrenia, (further deterritorializing) lines of flight are a real prospect.

In his writings from the early 70s, **Jean-François Lyotard** amplifies Deleuze and Guattari's heresies, at the same time as he joins *Anti-Oedipus*'s struggle against reflective deceleration in theoretical writing and critique. In a series of extraordinary texts the claim of the immanence of the political and libidinal is enacted within writing itself. In *Libidinal Economy* Lyotard uncovers a set of repressed themes in Marx, with the latter's oeuvre itself seen as a libidinal 'dispositif' split between an enjoyment of the extrapolation and imaginary acceleration of capitalism's liquefying tendencies, and the ever-deferred will to prosecute it for its iniquities (embodied in the dramatis personae of 'Little Girl Marx' and 'Old Bearded Prosecutor Marx').

Lyotard strikingly reads *Anti-Oedipus* not primarily as a polemical anti-psychoanalytical tract, but as a stealth weapon that subverts and transforms Marxism through the tacit retirement of those parts of its critical apparatus that merely nourish *ressentiment* and the petty power structures of party politics. He denounces the Marxist sad passion of remonstrating and harping at the system to pay back what it owes to the proletariat while simultaneously decrying the dislocations brought about by capitalism—the *liberation* of generalised cynicism, the *freedom* from internalised guilt, the *throwing off* of inherited mores and obligations—as 'illusory' and 'alienated'. From the viewpoint of a schizoanalytics informed by the decoding processes of 'Kapital', there are only perversions, libidinal bodies and their liquid investments, and no 'natural' position. Yet critique invests its energies in striving to produce the existence of an alienated proletariat as a wrong, a contradiction upon which it can exercise its moral authority. Instead, Lyotard, from the point of view of an immanence of technical, social, and libidinal bodies, asks: How can living labour be dismembered, how can the body be fragmented by capitalism's exchangeable value-form, if bodies are already fragments and if the will to unity is just one perversion among others? Thus he proposes an energetics that not only voluntarily risks anarchic irrationalism, but issues in a scandalous advocacy of the industrial proletariat's *enjoyment* of their machinic dissection at the hands of capital. Lyotard dares us to 'admit it...': the deracinating affect of capitalism, also, is a source of *jouissance*, a mobilization of desire.

Saluting *Anti-Oedipus* as 'one of the most intense products of the new libidinal configuration that is beginning to gel inside capitalism, Lyotard summons a 'new dispositif' that is like a virus thriving in the stomach of capital: in the restless yet undirected youth movements of the late 60s and early 70s 'another figure is rising' which will not be stifled by any pedantic theoretical critique. As Deleuze and Guattari assert, 'nothing ever died of contradictions', and the only thing that will kill capitalism is its own 'excess' and the 'unserviceability' loosed by it, an excess of wandering desire over the regulating mechanisms of antiproduction.

Eschewing critique, then, here writing forms a pact with the demon energy liberated by Kapital that liquidates all inheritance and solidity, staking everything on the unknown future it is unlocking. Few can read Lyotard's deliberately scandalous celebration of the prostitution of the proletariat without discomfort. Yet it succeeds in uncovering the deepest stakes of unstated Marxist dogma as to the human and labour power: If there never was any human, any primary economic productivity, but only libidinal bodies along with their investments, their fetishes, where does theory find the moral leverage to claim to 'save' the worker from the machines, the proletariat from capital—or to exhort them to save themselves?

In 'Power of Repetition' **Gilles Lipovetsky** gives a broad exposition of the ungrounded metaphysics of desire underpinning *Libidinal Economy*'s analyses (a metaphysics Lyotard simultaneously disclaims as just another fiction or libidinal device). In laying out very clearly a dichotomy between the powers of repetition and reinstatement of identity, and the errant metamorphic tendencies of capital, Lipovetsky makes a crucial distinction: Although capitalism may appear to depend upon powers of antiproduction which police it and ensure the minimal stability necessary for the extraction of profit, in fact these 'guard-dogs' are obstacles to the core tendency of capital qua 'precipitate experimentation' in the 'recombination of bodies'—and this latter tendency is the side that must be taken by emancipatory discourse and practice. Resisting the 'Marxist reflex' to critique 'capitalist power', Lipovetsky states that there is no such thing, but only and always a multiplicity of powers, which in fact restrain capital's advance. He thus repeats Lyotard's call for chaos and permanent revolution: there is no way to prevent new alien recombinations settling back into new forms of power; we must match and exceed capital's inhuman speeds, 'keep moving' in 'a permanent and accelerated metamorphic errancy'.

Lipovetsky also draws further attention to one of the important departures from Marx that Lyotard had expanded upon: For Deleuze and Guattari, more basic to an analysis of capitalism than human labour power is the way in which capitalism mobilizes time itself through the function of credit. (As Marx himself declares in *Grundrisse*, 'economy of time, to this all economy ultimately reduces itself'). Lipovetsky confirms that the supposed 'contradictions' of capital are a question of configurations of *time*, and accordingly his accelerationism pits capital's essentially destabilizing temporal looping of the present through the future against all stabilising reinstantiations of the past.

This futural orientation is also at work in Lyotard's attempt at an indistinction between description and prescription, between the theoretical and the exhortatory, something that will be extended in later accelerationisms—as Nick Land will write, there is 'no real option between a cybernetics of theory and a theory of cybernetics': The subject of theory can no longer affect to stand outside the process it describes: it is integrated as an immanent machine part in an open ended experimentation that is inextricable from capital's continuous scrambling of its own limits—which operates via the reprocessing of the actual through its virtual futures, dissolving all bulwarks that would preserve the past. In hooking itself up to this haywire time-machine, theory seeks to cast off its own inert obstacles.

It would indeed be churlish to deny the enduring rhetorical power of these texts; and yet the hopes of their call to permanent revolution are poignant from a contemporary viewpoint: As we can glimpse in the starkness of Lipovetsky's exposition, beneath the desperate joy with which they dance upon the ruins of politics and critique, there is a certain 'Camattian' note of despair (acceleration 'for lack of anything better', as Lipovetsky says); and an unwitting anticipation of the integral part that the spirit of permanent creative festivity would come to play in the neoconservative landscape of late twentieth-century consumer capitalism.

Those writers included in the 'Anticipations' section had emphasised in their analyses that the incursion of the value-form and of machine production are not a 'merely economic' question, but one of the transformation of human culture and indeed of what it means to be human. As can clearly be seen in the mercurial topicality of Lyotard's 'Energumen Capitalism', under different cultural and sociotechnological conditions the same goes for the texts of this second phase of accelerationism. The position is set out in exemplary fashion by radical feminist activist and theorist **Shulamith Firestone**. Beyond Fedorov's arguably shortsighted dismissal of the aesthetic response to the world as a squandering of energy that could be directed into the technological achievement of real transcendence, Firestone insists that the separation of these two modes of 'realizing the conceivable in the possible' is an artefact of the same constraints as class barriers and sex dualism. She envisages an 'anticultural' revolution that would fuse them, arguing that 'the body of scientific discovery (the new productive modes) must finally outgrow the empirical (capitalistic) mode of using them'. In Firestone's call for this cultural revolution the question is no longer, as in Fedorov, that of *replacing* imaginary transcendence with a practical project of transcendence, but of erasing the separation between imaginary vision and practical action.

If we accept Firestone's definition of culture as 'the attempt by man to realize the conceivable in the possible', we can see at once that (as Veblen had indicated) the application of culture as a salve for the corrosive effects of machine culture on the subject merely indicates a split within culture itself: the Promethean potentiality of the human, evidenced in 'the accumulation of skills for controlling the environment, technology' is hobbled by the obstruction of the dialogue between aesthetic and scientific modes of thinking. With industry, science, and technology subsumed into commerce and exchange value, the question of other, aesthetic values becomes a matter of a compensatory 'outside' of the market, a retreat into private (and marketized) pleasures.

Closing this section of the volume, novelist **J.G. Ballard** echoes Firestone's call for a merging of artistic and technological modes, advocating the role of science fiction not only as 'the only possible realism in an increasingly artificialized society', but as an ingredient in its acceleration. SF dissolves fear into excited anticipation, implicitly preparing readers for a 'life radically different from their own'. Accepting that 'the future is a better guide to the present than the past', SF is not involved in the elaboration of the *meaning* of the present, but instead participates in the construction of the future through its speculative recombination: the only meaning it registers is the as yet uncomprehended 'significance of the gleam on an automobile instrument panel'. Like Firestone, Ballard cheerfully jettisons the genius cult of the individual artist and high culture, instead imagining the future of SF along the lines of an unceremonious integration of fiction into global industry and communications that is already underway.

Punctuating the end of this phase of accelerationism, Ballard's world of 'the gleam of refrigerator cabinets, the conjunction of musculature and chromium artefact' is echoed in the cut-up text 'Desirevolution' where Lyotard refuses to cede the dream-work of '68 to institutional politics and Party shysters, countering its inevitable recuperation through an acceleration of the cut-up reality of the spectacle, an accelerated collage of 'fragments of alienation' launching one last salvo against political and aesthetic representation.

CYBERCULTURE

In the 90s the demonic alliance with capital's deterritorializing forces and the formal ferment it provoked in writing was pursued yet further by a small group of thinkers in the UK. Following Lyotard's lead, the authors of this third section attempt not simply to diagnose, but to propagate and accelerate the destitution of the human subject and its integration into the artificial mechanosphere. It is immediately apparent from the opening of **Nick Land**'s 'Circuitries' that a darkness has descended over the festive atmosphere of desiring-production envisaged by the likes of Deleuze and Guattari, Lyotard and Lipovetsky. At the dawn of the emergence of the global digital technology network, these thinkers, rediscovering and reinterpreting the work of the latter, develop it into an antihumanist *anastrophism*. Their texts relish its most violent and dark implications, and espouse radical alienation as the only escape from a human inheritance that amounts to imprisonment in a biodespotic security compound to which only capital has the access code. From this point of view, it seems that the terminal stages of libidinal economics (as affirmation) mistook the transfer of all motive force from human subjects to capital as the inauguration of an aleatory drift, an emancipation *for* the human; while postmodernism can do no more than mourn this miscognition, accelerationism now gleefully explores what is escaping *from* human civilization,[3] viewing modernity as an 'anastrophic' collapse into the future, as outlined in **Sadie Plant + Nick Land**'s 'Cyberpositive'.

---

3. For more on this strain of accelerationism see the editorial introduction to N. Land, *Fanged Noumena* (Falmouth and New York: Urbanomic/Sequence Press, 2011).

The radical shift in tone and thematics, despite conceptual continuities, can be related to the intervening hiatus: What differed from the situation in France one or two decades earlier? Precisely that, particularly in popular culture in the UK, a certain relish for the 'inconceivable alienations' outputted by the monstrous machine-organism built by capital had emerged—along with a manifest disinterest in being 'saved' from it by intellectuals or politicians, Marxist or otherwise. Of particular note here as major factors in the development of this new brand of accelerationism were the collective pharmaco-socio-sensory-technological adventure of rave and drugs culture, and the concurrent invasion of the home environment by media technologies (VCRs, videogames, computers) and popular investment in dystopian cyberpunk SF, including William Gibson's *Neuromancer* trilogy and the *Terminator*, *Predator*, and *Bladerunner* movies (which all became key 'texts' for these writers). As Ballard had predicted, SF had become the only medium capable of addressing the disorienting reality of the present: *everything is SF, spreading like cancer.*

90s cyberculture employed these sonic, filmic and novelistic fictions to turbocharge libidinal economics, attaching it primarily to the interlocking regimes of commerce and digitization, and thanatizing Lyotard's *jouissance* by valorizing a set of aesthetic affects that locked the human sensorium into a catastrophic desire for its dispersal into machinic delirium. The dystopian strains of darkside and jungle intensified alienation by sampling and looping the disturbing invocations of SF movie narratives; accordingly, the cyberculture authors side not with the human but with the Terminator, the cyborg prosecuting a future war on the battleground of now, travelling back in time to eliminate human resistance to the rise of the machines; with *Terminator II*'s future hyperfluid *commercium* figured as a 'mimetic polyalloy' capable of camouflaging itself as any object in order to infiltrate the present; and against the Bladerunner, ally of Old Bearded Prosecutor Marx, agent of biodespotic defense, charged with preventing the authentic, the human, from irreversible contamination (machinic incest), tasked with securing the 'retention of [the fictitious figure of] natural humanity' or organic labour.

Rediscovering Lipovetsky's repetitious production of interiority and identity on the libidinal surface in the figure of a 'negative cybernetics' dedicated to 'command and control', cyberculture counters it with a 'positive cybernetics' embodied in the runaway circuits of modernity, in which 'time itself is looped' and the only command is that of the feverishly churning virtual futurity of capital as it disassembles the past and rewrites the present. Against an 'immunopolitics' that insists on continually reinscribing the prophylactic boundary between the human and its technological other in a futile attempt to shore up the 'Human Security System', it scans the darkest vistas of earlier machinic deliriums, echoing Butler in anticipating the end of 'the human dominion of terrestrial culture', welcoming the fatal inevitability of a looming nonhuman intelligence: *Terminator*'s Skynet, Marx's fantastic 'virtuous soul' refigured as a malign global AI from the future whose fictioning is the only perspective from which contemporary reality makes sense.

This jungle war fought between immunopolitics and cyborg insurgency, evacuating the stage of politics, realises within theory the literal welding of the *punk* No with the looped-up machinic positivity of the *cyber*—'No demands. No hint of strategy. No logic. No hopes. No end...No community. No dialectics. No plans for an alternative state' (CCRU)—in a deliberate culmination of the most 'evil' tendencies of accelerationism. Beyond a mere description of these processes, this provocation employs theory and fiction interchangeably, according to a remix-and-sample regime, as devices to construct the future it invokes. Thus the performance-assemblages of the collective Cybernetic Culture Research Unit (CCRU), of which the hypersemically overloaded texts here ('text at sample velocity') were only partial components.[4]

4.See CCRU, *Writings 1997–2003* (Falmouth: Urbanomic, 2017).

ACCELERATION

The final section documents the contemporary convergence toward which the volume as a whole is oriented. While distancing itself from mere technological optimism, contemporary accelerationism retains an antipathy, a disgust even, for retreatist solutions, and an ambitious interest in reshaping and repurposing (rather than refusing) the technologies that are the historical product of capitalism. What is most conspicuously jettisoned from 70s and 90s accelerationism is the tendency to reduce theoretical positions to libidinal figures. Gone is the attempt to write *with* rather than *about* the contemporary moment, and a call for Enlightenment values and an apparently imperious rationalism make an unexpected appearance. If prima facie at odds with the enthusiastic nihilism of its forerunners, however, today's accelerationisms can be seen as a refinement and rethinking of them through the prism of the decades that spanned the end of the twentieth century and the birth of the twenty-first. Broadly speaking, today the anarchistic tendencies of 'French Theory' are tempered by a concern with the appropriation of sociotechnological infrastructure and the design of post-capitalist economic platforms, and the antihumanism of the cyberculture era is transformed, through its synthesis with the Promethean humanism found in the likes of Marx and Fedorov, into a rationalist inhumanism.

Once again this apparent rupture can be understood through consideration of the intervening period, which had seen the wholesale digestion by the capitalist spectacle of the yearning for extra-capitalistic spaces, from 'creativity' to ethical consumerism to political horizontalism, all of which capitalism had cheerfully supplied. In a strange reversal of cyberculture's prognostications, technology and the new modes of monetization now inseparable from it ushered in a banal resocialisation process, a reinstalling of the most confining and identitarian 'neo-archaisms' of the human operating system. Even as they do the integrative work of Skynet, the very brand names of this ascendent regime—iPod, Myspace, Facebook—ridicule cyberculture's aspiration to vicariously participate in a dehumanising adventure: instead, we (indistinguishably) work for and consume it *as* a new breed of autospectacularized all-too-human being. At the same time as these social neo-archaisms lock in, the depredations of capital pose an existential risk to humanity, while finance capital itself is in crisis, unable to bank on the future yet continuing to colonise it through instruments whose operations far outstrip human cognition. All the while, an apparently irreversible market cannibalization of what is left of the public sector and the absorption of the state into a corporate form continues worldwide, to the troubling absence of any coherent alternative. In short, it is not that the decoding and deterritoralization processes envisioned in the 70s, and the digital subsumption relished in the 90s, did not take place: only that the promise of enjoyment, the rise of an 'unserviceable' youth, new fields of dehumanised experience, 'more dancing and less piety', were efficiently rerouted back into the very identitarian attractors of repetition-without-difference they were supposed to disperse and abolish, in sole favour of capital's investment in a stable future for its major beneficiaries.

When **Mark Fisher**, former member of CCRU, returned in 2012 to the questions of accelerationism, outlining the current inconsistency and disarray in left political thought, the notion of a 'left accelerationism' seemed an absurdity. And yet, as Fisher asks, who wants or truly believes in some kind of return to a past that can only be an artefact of the imaginary of capitalism itself? As Plant and Land had asked: 'To what could we wish to return?' The intensification of sociotechnological integration has gone hand in hand with a negative theology of an outside of capital; as Fisher remarks, the escapist nostalgia for a precapitalist world that mars political protest is also embedded in popular culture's simulations of the past. The accelerationist dystopia of *Terminator* has been replaced by the primitivist yearnings of *Avatar*. Fisher therefore states that, in so far as we seek egress from the immiseration of capitalist realism, 'we are all accelerationists'; and yet, he challenges, 'accelerationism has never happened' as a real political force. That is, insofar as we do not fall into a number of downright inconsistent and impossible positions, we must indeed, be 'all accelerationists', and this heresy must form part of any anticapitalist strategy.

A renewed accelerationism, then, would have to work through the fact that the energumen capital stirred up by Lyotard and co. ultimately delivered what Fisher has famously called 'capitalist realism'.[5] And that, if one were to maintain the accelerationist gambit à la cyberculture at this point, it would simply amount to taking up arms for capitalist realism itself, rebuffing the complaint that capitalism did not deliver as sheer miserablism (*Compared to what? And after all, what is the alternative?*) and retracting the promises of *jouissance* and 'inconceivable alienations' as narcissistic demands that have no place in an inhuman process (*Isn't it enough that you're working for the Terminator, you want to enjoy it too?*)—a dilemma that opens up a wider debate regarding the relation between aesthetic enjoyment and theoretical purchase in earlier accelerationism.

Alex Williams + Nick Srnicek's '#Accelerate: Manifesto for an Accelerationist Politics' can be read as an attempt to honour Fisher's demand for a contemporary left accelerationist position. In provocation of the contemporary Left's often endemic technological illiteracy, Srnicek and Williams insist on the necessity of precise cognitive mapping, and thus epistemic acceleration, for any progressive political theory and action today. With full confidence that alternatives are thinkable, they state the obvious, namely that neoliberal capitalism is not just unfair or unjust as a system, but is no longer a guarantor of dynamism or progress.

---

5. M. Fisher, *Capitalist Realism: Is There No Alternative?* (London: Zer0, 2009).

Intended as a first draft of a longer theoretical and political project, MAP found immediate notoriety (being translated into numerous languages within months of appearing online) but was also criticised for not yet offering new solutions beyond focussing on three general demands: firstly for the creation of a new intellectual infrastructure, secondly for far-reaching media reform, and thirdly for the reconstitution of new forms of class power. Following the example of Marx—according to them a 'paradigmatic accelerationist thinker'—Wiliams and Srnicek attempt to overcome the mistrust of technology on the left in the last decades. And closely affiliated to the rationalist wing of current speculative philosophy, they adopt the topos of 'folk psychology' for their polemic against a *folk politics*, opposing a politics based on inherited and intuitively ready-to-hand categories with an accelerationist politics that conceives its program on the basis of 'a modernity of abstraction, complexity, globality, and technology' that outstrips such categories.

A key element of any left Promethean politics must be a conviction in a transformative potential of technology, including the 'transformative anthropology' it entails, and an eagerness to further accelerate technological evolution. Thus this new accelerationism is largely dependent on maturing our understanding of the current regime of technology and value. Even though **Antonio Negri**'s response is critical of what he calls the 'technological determinism' of the Manifesto, he agrees that the most crucial passage of the manifesto—concerning the relation between machinic surplus value and social cooperation—cannot really be understood independently of the technological dimension implied. Clearly it is not enough to valorize the 'real' human force of labour over the perversions of technocapital or to attempt to recover it: if 'the surplus added in production is derived primarily from socially productive cooperation', as Negri says, and if it must be admitted that this cooperation is technically mediated, then the project of reappropriation cannot circumvent the necessity to deal with the specific 'material and technical qualities' that characterise this fixed capital today.

With Negri's response, the first of several contributions by Italian authors linked to 'post-operaismo' who address precisely this point, we are dealing with a tradition that is already heretical to official Marxism. Both in theory and in political practice the 'operaismo' (workerism) of the 1960s and 70s was opposed to official party politics and its focus on the state. Operaism's molecular politics, focused on concrete activities in factories, is also the background for recent (post-operaistic) investigations of immaterial labour and biopower. In the present context this tradition contributes towards a greater insight into the nature of technological change (an insight which also owes something to the bitter experience following early optimism with regard to the Internet's liberatory possibilities). This allows a much subtler reading of the relation between technology and acceleration than cyberculture's championing of positive feedback and networks, which in certain ways reiterates the horizontalism of Lyotard's metaphysics of the flat 'libidinal band'. Not only has this horizontalism (as MAP indicates) been an ineffective paradigm for political intervention, it also significantly misrepresents the mode of operation of 'network technology' in general. For the latter's technological and subjectivizing power (as substantially anticipated in Veblen) resides in the progressive and hierarchical 'locking in' of standardized hardware and software protocols each of which cannot be understood as means to a particular end, but rather present an open set of possibilities.

Tiziana Terranova suggests a reappropriation of this logic in the form of a 'red stack' bringing together the types of autonomous electronic currencies that are currently emerging outside the bounds of nation-state or corporate governance, social media technology, and the 'bio-hypermedia' that is thriving in the interference zone between digital and bodily identities. This vision of a digital infrastructure of the common enacts MAP's shift from abstract political theory ('this is not a utopia') to an experimental collaboration with design, engineering, and programming so as to activate the latent potential of these technologies in the direction of another *socius*.

In 'finally grasp[ing] the shift from the hegemony of material labour to the hegemony of immaterial labour' (Negri), a particular focus is the increased importance of the algorithm as the general machine regime in the information economy, which takes the baton from Marx and Veblen's 'machine system' in continually accumulating, integrating, linking, and synergizing 'informational fixed capital' at every level of collective production, commercial circulation and consumption. As has been widely discussed, the rise of the algorithm runs parallel to the visible absorption into the integrated machine system of human cognitive and affective capacities, which are also now (in Marx's words) 'set in motion by an automaton'—or rather, a global swarm of abstract automata. The algorithms at work in social media technologies and beyond present an acute test case for reappropriation. Unlike heavy metal machines, algorithms do not themselves embody a value, but rather are valuable in so far as they allow value to be extracted from social interaction: the real fixed capital today, as Negri suggests, is the value produced through intensive technically coordinated cooperation, producing a 'surplus beyond the sum' of its parts (the 'network externalities' which economists agree are the source of value in a 'connected economy').

To reduce of the value of software to its capacity for monetization, as Terranova suggests, leaves unspoken the enthusiasm and creativity in evidence in open source software movements. Perhaps the latter are better thought of as a collective practice of supererogation seizing on the wealth of opportunities already produced by capitalism as a historical product, in the form of hardware and software platforms, and which breaks the loop whereby this wealth is reabsorbed into the cycles of exchange value. This invocation of the open-source movement is a powerful reminder that there are indeed other motivating value systems that may provide the 'libidinizing impulse' that Fisher calls for in the search for alternative constructions; it also recalls Firestone's call for a cultural revolution in which the distinction between aesthetic imagination and technical construction is effaced.

Next **Luciana Parisi** turns to computational design to ask what we can learn from the new cutting-edge modes of production that are developing today. Carefully paring apart the computational processes from their ideological representations, Parisi suggests that these new computational processes do indeed present a significant break from a model of rationality that seeks command and control through the top-down imposition of universal laws, aiming to symbolically condense and circumscribe a system's behaviour and organization. And yet computation driven by material organization cannot be regarded as simply entering into a dynamic immanence with the 'intelligence of matter'. Rather, these algorithmic operations have their own logic, and open up an artificial space of functions, a 'second nature'. For Parisi these developments in design figure the more general movement toward systems whose accelerated and extended search and evaluation capabilities (for example in 'big data' applications) suggest a profound shift within the conception of computation itself.

It is often claimed that through such advanced methods accelerated technocapital invests the entire field of material nature, completely beyond the human field of perception. Such a strict dichotomy, Parisi argues, loses sight of the reality of abstraction in the order of algorithmic reason itself, moving too quickly from the Laplacean universe of mechanism governed by absolute laws to a vitalist universe of emergent materiality. Instead, as Parisi argues, the action of algorithms opens up a space of speculative reason as a Whiteheadian 'adventure of ideas' in which the counter-agency of reason is present as a motor for experimentation and the extraction of novelty.

Reza Negarestani addresses a related dichotomy to the one Parisi critiques, and which lies behind contemporary political defeatism and inertia—namely, the choice between either equating rationality with a discredited and malign notion of absolute mastery, or abandoning all claim for the special status of human sapience and rationality. In the grip of this dichotomy, any possible platform for political claims is nullified. Rather than an abdication of politics, for Negarestani accelerationism must be understood precisely as the making possible of politics through the refusal of such a false alternative. In 'The Labor of the Inhuman', he sets out a precise argument to counter the general trend to identify the overcoming of anthropomorphism and human arrogance with a negation of the special status of the human and the capacities of reason.

The predicament of a politics after the death of god and in the face of real subsumption—and the temptation either to destitute subjectivity, leaving the human as a mere cybernetic relay, or to cling to obsolete political prescriptions made on the basis of obsolete folk models of agency—is stripped down by Negarestani to its epistemic and functional kernel. Drawing on the normative functionalism of Wilfrid Sellars and Robert Brandom, he criticizes the antihumanism of earlier accelerationisms as an overreaction no less nihilistically impotent than a yearning for substantial definitions of the human. In its place Negarestani proposes an 'inhumanism' that emerges once the question of what it means to be human is correctly posed, 'in the context of uses and practices'.

What is specific to the human is its access to the symbolic and sociotechnological means to participate in the construction and revision of norms; the task of exploring what 'we' are is therefore an ongoing labour whose iterative loops of concept and action yield 'non-monotonic' outcomes. In this sense, understanding and committing to the human is synonymous with revising and constructing the human. Far from involving a voluntaristic impulse to 'freedom', this labour entails the navigation of a constraining field of collateral commitments and ramifications, through which the human responds to the demands of an agency (reason) that has no interest in preserving the initial self-image of the human, but whose unforeseeable ramifications are unfolded *through* the human—'a future that writes its own past' in so far as one views present commitments from the perspective of their future ramifications, yielding each time a new understanding of past actions.

In other words, whereas the human cannot 'accelerate' within the strictures of its inherited image, in merely rejecting reason it abdicates the possibility of revising this image at all. Acceleration takes place when and in so far as the human repeatedly affirms its commitment to being impersonally piloted, not by capital, but by a program which demands that it cede control to collective revision, and which draws it towards an inhuman future that will prove to have 'always' been the meaning of the human. 'A commitment works its way back from the future', and inconceivable vistas of intelligence open up through the 'common task' or duty of the labour of the inhuman.[6]

In the absence of this indispensable platform of commitment and revision, Negarestani insists, no politics, however shrill its protestations and however severe its prescriptions, has the necessary motor with which to carry a project forward—indeed it is this inability to 'cope with the consequences of committing to the real content of humanity' that is according to him at the root of today's political inertia. In effect, then, Negarestani re-places the infinite will-without-finality within reason rather than capital, and rethinks the inhuman futural feedback process through which it conducts human history not as a thanatropic compulsion but as social participation in the progressive and self-cultivating anastrophism of in/humanity.

6. Negarestani further develops all of these themes in his *Intelligence and Spirit* (Falmouth and New York: Urbanomic/Sequence Press, 2018).

Design strategist **Benedict Singleton**, in a contemporary return to Fedorov's project, rethinks the question of the mastery of nature through the question of perhaps humankind's most Promethean project: space exploration. Continuing Negarestani's examination of the pragmatic momentum that drives a continual opening up of new frontiers of action, he finds in the logic of design a way to think this 'escape' otherwise than in the form of a creative 'leap of faith': as an 'escapology not an escapism', a twisted path in which the stabilisation of new invariants provides the basis for new modes of action, and, reciprocally, new modes of action and new instruments for cognition enable new perspectives on where we have come from and where we are going: design is a dense and ramified leveraging of the environment that makes possible the startling clarity of *new observables*, as well as enabling the transformation of apparently natural constants into manipulable variables required for constructing new worlds.

Drawing out a language of *scheming*, *crafting*, and *plotting* that declares itself quite clearly in the vocabulary surrounding design, but which has been studiously ignored by a design theory rather too keen to ingratiate itself with humanist circles, Singleton elaborates a counter-history of design that affirms this plotting or manipulative mode of thought, and even its connotations of deception, drawing on Marcel Detienne and Jean-Pierre Vernant's unearthing of the Greek notion of *mêtis*—'cunning intelligence'. As Singleton suggests, mêtis is exemplified in the *trap*, which sees the predator adopting the point of view of the prey so that its own behaviour is harnessed to ensure its extinction. Mêtis thus equates to a practice in which, in the absence of complete information, the adoption of hypothetical perspectives enables a transformation of the environment—which in turn provides opportunities for further ruses, seeking to power its advance by craftily harnessing the factors of the environment and its expected behaviours to its own advantage.

Important here is the distinguishing of this 'platform logic' from a means-end 'planning' model of design. In altering the parameters of the environment in order to create new spaces upon which yet more invention can be brought to bear, cunning intelligence gradually twists free of the conditions in which it finds itself 'naturally' ensnared, generating paths to an outside that does not conform to the infinite homothetism of 'more of the same' but instead opens up onto a series of convoluted plot twists—precisely the ramifying paths of the 'labour of the inhuman' described by Negarestani. Ultimately this escapology, Singleton insists, requires an abduction of *ourselves* by perspectives that relativize our spontaneous phenomenal grasp of the environment. Echoing Fedorov, he calls for a return to an audacity that, far from seeking to 'live in harmony with nature', seeks to spring man out of his proper place in the natural order so as to accelerate toward ever more alien spaces.

Taking up this Promethean theme, **Ray Brassier** launches a swingeing critique of some of the absurd consequences entailed by the countervailing call to humility, and uncovers their ultimately theological justification. Whence the antipathy toward any project of *remaking* the world, the hostility to the normative claim that not only *ought* things to be different but that they ought to be *made* different? Examining Jean-Pierre Dupuy's critique of human enhancement, Brassier shows how the inflation of human difference into ontological difference necessitates the same transcendental policing that Iain Hamilton Grant explores in his reading of *Bladerunner*: what is *given*—the inherited image of the human and human society assumed as transcendental bond—shall by no means be *made* or indeed *remade.* Certain limits must be placed on the ability of the human to revise its own definition, on pain of disturbing a certain 'fragile equilibrium'. As Brassier remarks, since the conception of what a human can be and should tolerate is demonstrably historical, it is only possible to understand this invocation of a proper balance or limit as a theological sentiment. This reservation of an unconceptualisable transcendence beyond the limits of manipulation devolves into a farcical discourse on the 'reasonableness' of the suffering inflicted by nature's indifference to the human—a suffering, subjection, and finitude which is understood to provide a precious resource of meaning for human life. However Prometheanism consists precisely both in the refusal of this incoherency and in the affirmation that the core of the human project consists in generating *new* orientations and ends—as in Negarestani's account of the production and consumption of norms, echoed here in the 'subjectivism without selfhood [...] autonomy without voluntarism' that Brassier intimates must lie at the core of Prometheanism. The productivism of Marx, too, as Brassier reminds us, holds mankind capable of forging its own truth, of knowing and controlling that which is given to it, and of remaking it. Like Negarestani, Brassier holds that the essential project here is one of integrating a descriptive account of the objective (not transcendental) constitution of rational subjectivation with an advocacy of the rational subject's accession to self-mastery.

Against these new approaches, **Nick Land**, in 'Teleoplexy', insists that it is the practice of forward-looking capitalization alone that can produce the futural dynamic of acceleration. Against Williams and Srnicek, for whom 'capitalism cannot be identified as the agent of true acceleration', and Negarestani, for whom the space of reasons is the future source from which intelligence assembles itself, Land argues that the complex positive feedback instantiated in market pricing mechanisms is the only possible referent for acceleration. And since it is capitalization alone that gives onto the future, the very question W*hat do we want*—the very conception of a *conditional* accelerationism and the concomitant assertion, made by both MAP and Negri, that 'planning is necessary' in order to instrumentalise knowledge into action—for Land amounts to nothing but a call for a compensatory movement to *counteract* acceleration. For him it is the state and politics per se that constitute constraints, not 'capital'; and therefore the claim that 'capitalism has begun to constrain the productive forces of technology' is senseless. Land's 'right accelerationism' appears here as an inverted counterpart to the communitarian retreat in the face of real subsumption: like the latter, it accepts that the historical genesis of technology in capitalism precludes the latter from any role in a postcapitalist future. If at its most radical accelerationism claims, in Camatte's words, that 'there can be a revolution that is not for the human' and draws the consequences of this, then one can either take the side of an inherited image of the human against the universal history of capital and dream of 'leaving this world'; or one can accept that 'the means of production are going for a revolution on their own'. This reappearance of accelerationism in its form as a foil for the Left (even left-accelerationism), with Land still fulfilling his role as 'the kind of antagonist that the left needs' (Fisher), rightly places the onus on the new accelerationisms to show how, between a prescription for nothing but despair and a excitable description that, at most, contributes infinitesimally to Skynet's burgeoning self-awareness, a space for action can be constructed.

If 'left accelerationism' is to succeed in 'unleashing latent productive forces', and if its putative use of 'existing infrastructure as a springboard to launch towards postcapitalism' is to issue (even speculatively) in anything but a centralized bureaucracy administering the decaying empty shell of the historical product of capitalism, then the question of incentives and of an alternative feedback loop to that of capitalization will be central. This is one of the 'prescriptions' that **Patricia Reed** makes in her review of the potentials and lacunae of the Manifesto that concludes our volume. Among her other interventions is the suggestion that a corrective may be in order to address the more unpalatable undertones of its relaunch of the modern—a new, less violent model of universalisation.

It also does not pass unnoticed by Reed that the MAP's rhetoric is rather modest in comparison to earlier accelerationism's enthusiastic invocations and exhortations ('maximum slogan density'). A tacit aim in the work of Plant, Land, Grant, and CCRU is an attempt to find a place for human agency once the motor of transformation that drives modernity is understood to be inhuman and indeed indifferent to the human. The attempt to *participate* vicariously in its positive feedback loop by fictioning or even mimicking it can be understood as an answer to this dilemma. The conspicuous fact that, shunned by the mainstream of both the 'continental philosophy' and cultural studies disciplines which it hybridized, the Cyberculture material had more subterranean influence on musicians, artists, and fiction writers than on traditional forms of political theory or action, indicates how its stance proved more appropriable as an *aesthetic* than effective as a political force. The new accelerationisms instead concentrate primarily on constructing a conceptual space in which we can once again ask *what to do* with the tendencies and machines identified by the analysis; and yet Fisher's initial return to accelerationism turned upon the importance of an 'instrumentalisation of the libido' for a future accelerationist politics. Reed accordingly takes MAP to task in its failure to minister to the positive 'production of desire', limiting itself to diagnostics and prognostics too vague to immediately impel participation. She rightly raises the question of the power of belief and of motivation: Whatever happened to *jouissance*? Where is the motor that will drive commitment to eccentric acceleration? Where is the 'libidinal dispositif' that will recircuit the compelling incentives of consumer capitalism, so deeply embedded in popular imagination, and the bewildered enjoyment of the collective fantasies of temporary autonomous zones? As Negri says, 'rational imagination must be accompanied by the collective fantasy of new worlds'. Certainly however much one might 'rationalise' the logic of speculation, it still maintains a certain bond with fiction; yet earlier accelerationisms had attempted to mobilize the force of imaginative fictions so as to adjust the human perspective to otherwise dizzying speculative vistas.

In addition, as Reed notes, Accelerationism, far from entailing a short-termism, involves taking a long view on history that traditional politics is unable to encompass in its 'procedures... based on finitude, and the timescale of the individual human'; and equally needs to engage with algorithmic processes that happen beneath the perceptual thresholds of human cognition (Terranova, Parisi). Therefore a part of the anthropological transformation at stake here involves the appropriation and development of a conceptual and affective apparatus that allows human perception and action some kind of purchase upon this 'Promethean scale'—new science-fictional practices, if not necessarily in literary form; and once again, Firestone's 'merging of the aesthetic with the technological culture'.

RETURN TO OR DEPARTURE FROM MARX?

Before closing this introduction, it is worth returning in more detail to Marx, since much of the volume contends with his contributions, whether implicitly or explicitly. The disarray of the Left fundamentally stems from 'the failure of a future that was thought inevitable' (Camatte) by Marxism—the failure of capitalism to self-destruct as part of history's 'intrinsic organic development', for the conflict between productive forces and capitalist relations of production to reach a moment of dialectical sublation, or for the proletariat to constitute itself into a revolutionary agent. And theoretical analysis of the resulting situation (real subsumption into the spectacle) seems to offer no positive possibility of opposition, yielding only modes of opposition frozen in cognitive dissonance between the 'disruptions' they stage and the inevitability of their recuperation. Accelerationism is significant in the way in which it confronts this plight through a return to a few fundamental questions posed by Marx upstream from various Marxist orthodoxies such as the dialectic, alienation, and the labour theory of value. Indeed one feature of accelerationism is a repeated return to these fundamental insights each time under a set of stringent conditions related to the prevailing political conditions of the epoch, a radical repetition that sometimes demands violent rejections. For, as the MAP contends, there is an accelerationist strand to Marx's work which is far from being the result of a tendentious reading.

According to the 'Fragment', then, the development of large-scale integrated machine production is a sine qua non of Capital's universal ascendency ('not an accidental moment', says Marx, later positing that intensity of machinic objectification=intensity of capital). Machine production follows directly from, maximally effects, and enters into synergy with capital's exigency to reduce the need for human labour and to continually increase levels of production. Undoubtedly the absorption of the worker into the burgeoning machine organism more clearly than ever reduces the worker to a tool of capital. And yet, crucially, Marx makes it clear that these two forms of subsumption—under capital, and into a technical system of production—are neither identical nor inseparable in principle.

In the machine system, the unity of labour qua collectivity of living workers as foundation of production is shattered, with human labour appearing as a 'mere moment [...] infinitesimal and vanishing' of an apparently autonomous production process. And although it reprocesses its original human material into a more satisfactory format for Capital, for Marx the machine system does not preclude the possibility of other relations of production under which it may be employed. It is, however, inseparable from a certain metamorphosis of the human, embedded in a system that is at once social, epistemic (depending on the scientific understanding and control of nature), and technological. Man no longer has a direct connection to production, but one that is mediated by a ramified, accumulated objective social apparatus constructed through the communication, technological embodiment, replication and enhancement of knowledge and skills—what Marx calls the 'elevation of direct labour into social labour' wherein 'general social knowledge [...] become[s] a direct force of production'. Once again, however, this estrangement is not *identical* with alienation through capital; nor is the former, considered apart from the strictures of the latter, necessarily a deplorable consequence. It is precisely at this point that Marx enters the speculative terrain of accelerationism: for in separating these two tendencies—the expanded field of production and the continuing metamorphoses of the human within it, and the monotonous regime of capital as the meta-machine that appropriates and governs this production process and its development—the question arises of whether, and how, the colossal sophistication, use value, and transformative power of one could be effectively freed of the limitations and iniquities of the other.

Such is the kernel of the MAP's problematic and a point of divergence between the various strains of accelerationism: Williams and Srnicek, for example, urge us to devise means for a practical realization of this separability, whereas for Nick Land and Iain Hamilton Grant writing in the 90s, Deleuze and Guattari's immanentization of social and technical machines was to be consummated by rejecting their distinction between technical machines and the capitalist axiomatic.

Since the 'new foundation' created by integrated machine industry is dependent not upon direct labour but upon the application of technique and knowledge, according to Marx it usurps capitalism's primary foundation of production upon the extortion of surplus labour. Indeed, through it capital 'works toward its own dissolution': the total system of production qua complex ramified product of collective social labour tends to counteract the system that produced it. The vast increase in productivity made possible through the compaction of labour into the machine system, of course, ought also to free up time, making it possible for individuals to produce themselves as new subjects. How then to reconcile this emancipatory vision of the sociotechnological process with the fact that the worker increasingly becomes a mere abstraction of activity, acted on by an 'alien power' that machinically vivisects its body, ruining its unity and tendentially replacing it (a power which, as Marx also notes, is 'non-correlated'—that is, the worker finds it impossible to cognitively encompass it)?

Once again, Marx distinguishes between the machine system as manifestation of capital's illusory autonomy, confronting the worker as an alien soul whose wishes they must facilitate (just as the worker's wages confront them as the apparent source of their livelihood), and the machine system seen as a concrete historical product. Even as the process of the subsumption of labour into machine production provides an index of the development of capital, it also indicates the extent to which social production becomes an immediate force in the transformation of social practice. The monstrous power of the industrial assemblage is indissociable from the 'development of the social individual': General social knowledge is absorbed as a force of production and thus begins to shape society: 'the conditions of the process of social life itself [...] come under the control of the general intellect and [are] transformed in accordance with it'. Labour then only exists as subordinated to the general interlocking *social* enterprise into which capital introduces it: Capital produces new subjects, and the development of the social individual is inextricable from the development of the system of mechanised capital.

This suggests that the plasticity of the human and the social nature of technology can be understood as a benchmark for progressive acceleration. Marx's contention was that Capitalism's abstraction of the socius generates an undifferentiated social being that can be subjectivated into the proletariat. That is, a situation where the machinic system remained in place and yet human producers no longer faced these means of production as alienating would necessarily entail a further transformation of the human, since, according to Marx, in the machine system humans face the product of their labour through a ramified and complex network of mediation that is cognitively and practically debilitating and disempowering.

This 'transformative anthropology' (Negri) is what every communist or commonist (Negri's or Terranova's post-*operaismo*) programme has to take into account. Granted the in-principle separability of machinic production and its capitalist appropriation, the 'helplessness' of the worker in the face of social production, would have to be resolved through a new social configuration: the worker would still be confronted with this technical edifice and unable to reconcile it with the 'unity of natural labour'; and yet humans would 'enter into the direct production process as [a] different subject', ceasing to suffer from it because they would have attained a collective mastery over the process, the common objectified in the machine system no longer being appropriated by the axiomatic of capital. This participation would thus be a true social project or common task, rather than the endurance of a supposedly natural order of things with which the worker abstractly interfaces through the medium of monetary circulation, the 'metabolism of capital', while the capitalist, operating in a completely discontinuous sphere, draws off and accumulates its surplus.

However, as Marx observes (and as Deleuze and Guattari emphasise), capitalism continues to operate *as if* its necessary assumption were still the 'miserable' basis of 'the theft of labour time', even as the 'new foundation' of machine production provides 'the material conditions to blow this foundation sky-high'.

The extortion of human labour still lies at the basis of capitalist production despite the 'machinic surplus value' (Deleuze and Guattari) of fixed capital, since the social axiomatic of capital is disinterested in innovation for itself and is under the necessity to extract surplus value as conveniently as possible, and to maintain a reserve army of labour and free-floating capital.

The central questions of accelerationism follow: What is the relation between the socially alienating effects of technology and the capitalist value-system? Why and how are the emancipatory effects of the 'new foundation' of machine production counteracted by the economic system of capital? What could the social human be if fixed capital were reappropriated within a new postcapitalist socius?

FORWARD

At the core of new accelerationisms, and responding in depth to these questions so as to fill out the MAP's outlines, new philosophical frameworks suggested by Negarestani, Singleton, and Brassier reaffirm Prometheanism, and bring together a transformative anthropology, a new conception of speculative and practical reason, and a set of schemas through which to understand the inextricably social, symbolic, and technological materials from which any postcapitalist order will have to be constructed. They advocate not accelerationism in a supposedly known direction, and even less sheer speed, but, as Reed suggests, 'eccentrication' and, as Negarestani, Brassier, and Singleton emphasise in various ways, *navigation* within the spaces opened up through a commitment to the future that truly understands itself as such and acknowledges the nature of its own agency.

In earlier accelerationisms, 'exploratory mutation' (Land) was only opened up through the search-space of capital's forward investment in the future. As Land tells us, 'long range processes are self-designing, but only in such a way that the self is perpetuated as something redesigned'. However, for cybercultural acceleration, this 'self' can be none other than capital's 'infinite will' as it absorbs modernity into its 'infinite augmentation', its non-finality. In the account of Negarestani, this non-finality is displaced into the space of reason progressively constructed by the advent of symbolic social technologies and the space of norms they make possible and continually transform, thus providing an underpinning to the MAP's aims and a framework within which its technological and social questions can be treated. In Singleton's understanding of design, the opportunistic and cunning appropriation of the powers of nature progressively ratchets open an uncircumscribable space of freedom, springing human intelligence from its parochial cage and extending it through prostheses and platforms.

Whereas earlier moments of accelerationism had been a matter of a conviction in utopian projects or in the possible imminent collapse of capitalism, and subsequently a delirious summoning of revolutionary forces at work *within* it, today's accelerationism, no less optimistic in certain respects, is undoubtedly more sober; a fact that cannot be unconnected to the fact that it emerges in a climate of combined crisis-and-stagnation for capitalism. It is indeed interesting to note that accelerationism reappears at moments when the powers of capitalism appear to be in crisis and alternatives appear thin on the ground. As Fisher insists, today's crisis provides an opportune point at which to reassess those previous moments.

The destiny of the authors included in the 'Ferment' section is instructive here: Deleuze and Guattari arguably diluted the stance of *Anti-Oedipus* in *A Thousand Plateaus* with calls for caution in deterritorialization and a more circumspect analysis of capitalism. As Iain Grant recounts, Lyotard was soon to openly deplore his 'evil' accelerationist moment, and instead—in effect concurring with Camatte's pessimism—set out to develop minor strategies of aesthetic resistance. In similar fashion, Lipovetsky's

1983 collection tellingly entitled *The Era of Emptiness*[7] modulates the revolutionary tone to one of acquiescent approbation: although still concerned with an 'accelerating destabilisation', he now sees it largely operating through a 'process of personalisation' whose overall liberatory vector is balanced by a contraction into narcissism and the spectacular consumption of ubiquitous 'communication'.

The cyberculture phase, in extending Lyotard's own 'branching-off' from Deleuze and Guattari, arguably reproduced his failure to reckon with the powers of *antiproduction*: Deleuze and Guattari drew attention not just to the 'positive' schizophrenia of decoding and deterritorialization but to a certain schizophrenic *dissociation* within the technical or scientific worker himself, who 'is so absorbed in capital that the reflux of organized, axiomatized stupidity coincides with him' ('Dear, I discovered how to clone people at the lab today. Now we can go skiing in Aspen', as Firestone puts it). The transformation of surplus value of code into surplus value of flux necessitates that, just as technical knowledge is separated from aesthetics, so the potentially insurrectionary social import of machinically-potentiated errant intelligence is itself 'split' and its surplus drawn off safely by capital.

Thus, under capital, individuals are sequestered from the immense forces of production they make possible qua social beings, and feedback is limited to a minimal 'reflux', a purchasing 'power' qualitatively incommensurable with the massive flows of capital. In 'Teleoplexy' Land continues to set store by the crossover between consumer devices and economically-mobilizable technologies within consumer capitalism itself. Yet the earlier expectation that technology would of itself disrupt antiproduction was overoptimistic—in line with the contemporary Thatcherite spirit of free enterprise, which promised to empower every citizen with opportunities for self-realization through access to the market.

---

7. *L'Ère du vide: essais sur l'individualisme contemporain* (Paris: Gallimard, 1983).

The explosion in share ownership, consumer credit, and the burgeoning of consumer media and information technology did little to dislodge this dissociative mechanism that, for Deleuze and Guattari, constitutes 'capitalism's true police'. Projects such as those of Terranova and Parisi, of examining and rebuilding technological platforms outside this value-system and its ideological assumptions, benefit today from a greater appreciation of the subtlety of antiproduction, and complement the new philosophical resources emerging within contemporary accelerationisms.

Herein lies the real divergence between Land's consolidated right-accelerationism and the burgeoning left-accelerationisms: whereas one continues to see an ever increasing accumulation of both collective intelligence and collective freedom, bound together in the monstrous form of Capital itself, the other, as it develops, is proving more speculative and more ambitious in its conception of both 'intelligence' and 'freedom', seeing Capital as neither an inhuman hyperintelligence nor the one true agent of history, but rather as an idiot savant driven to squander collective cognitive potential by redirecting it from any nascent process of collective self-determination back into the self-reinforcing libidinal dynamics of market mechanisms. In this respect, the work of Negarestani and Brassier forms the conceptual bulwark preventing left-accelerationism from collapsing back into schizoid anarchy or technocapitalist fatalism. By reviving the constitutive link between freedom and reason at the heart of German idealism (Kant and Hegel), reconfigured and repurposed by pragmatist functionalism (Sellars and Brandom), they not only provide a dynamic measure of the emancipatory promise of modernity at odds with Capital's own monotonous modes of valuation, but equally demonstrate how its progressive realization implies, in contrast to the blind idiot cyborgod of Kapital, the constitution of a genuine collective political agency.

This dialectic parallels that played out in artificial intelligence research between dominant strains developing AI capable of parochial problem solving and those increasingly concerned with characterising artificial general intelligence (AGI). The shift from conceiving intelligence as a quantitatively homogeneous measure of adaptive problem solving to conceiving it as a qualitatively differentiated typology of reasoning capacities is the properly philosophical condition of the shift from the hyperstitional invocation of machinic intelligence of the Cyberculture era to the active design of new systems of collective intelligence proposed by MAP.

The labour of constructing an accelerationist politics, its machines and its humans, is a matter, as Marx says, of 'both discipline, as regards the human being in the process of becoming... [and] at the same time, practice, experimental science, materially creative and objectifying science, as regards the human being who has become, in whose head exists the accumulated knowledge of society'. If this space of speculation outside of capital is not a mirage, if 'we surely do not yet know what a modern technosocial body can do', isn't this labour of the inhuman not just a rationalist, but also a vitalist one in the Spinozist sense, concerning the indissolubly technical and social human—*homo sive machina*—in the two aspects of its collective labour upon its world and itself: *Homo hominans* and *homo hominata*?

ROBIN MACKAY + ARMEN AVANESSIAN
TRURO + BERLIN, APRIL 2014

ACKNOWLEDGEMENTS

As should already be clear, the conception and production of this volume has been a group effort (the editors, needless to say, take responsibility for its failings). Aside from the authors and translators who have contributed to the volume (several of whom also gave invaluable help in the preparation of this introduction), the editors would specifically like to thank, for their discussion, suggestions, and support: Louise McDermott, Peter Wolfendale (whose contributions to the introduction were crucial), Helen Hester, Tom Lamberty, Bernd Klöckener, Tavi Meraud, Matteo Pasquinelli, Max Weber, Mohammad Salemy, Diana Khamis, Florian Hecker, Terry Kernow Chilli, Nadja Poderegin (Honeyglen), Nick Beck (Wylie), Claire Weatherhead (Bloomsbury), Magdalena Pieta (TJ International), Debbie Wyatt (BJ Press), Simon Sellars, and all the participants in the Accelerationism symposia and workshops in 2012–13; and Laphroaig.

ADDENDUM, 2019: L/ACC, R/ACC, G/ACC, U/ACC...

Over a period during which the nature and possibility of politics has been in continual crisis, apocalypticism has become a baseline norm, traditional left/right dualisms have been scrambled, and meme culture has rescinded any limit on the extent to which formerly esoteric notions may leak into the public sphere, the term 'accelerationism' has seen a startling increase in currency. True, in some circles—echoing the simplifications challenged in the above introduction—it has been adopted as popular shorthand for any provocation designed to help push existing political structures to the point of collapse. But elsewhere more nuanced interventions have continued to appear, informed in part by the reconstructions and projections presented here, and a thousand accelerationisms have bloomed—enough to fill another book, which however would risk being out of date before it was printed. To mention just a few, Laboria Cuboniks's *Xenofeminist Manifesto*, n1x's 'Gender Acceleration: A Blackpaper', Aria Dean's 'Notes on Blaccelerationism', Vincent Garton and Ed Berger's discussions on 'Unconditional Accelerationism', and the continuing provocations of Nick Land can all be easily located online, leading the reader into a still mutating field of thought in which the question of accelerationism continues to provoke hope, dread, enthusiasm, and fear. RM

Fig 4

Fragment on Machines

Karl Marx

1858

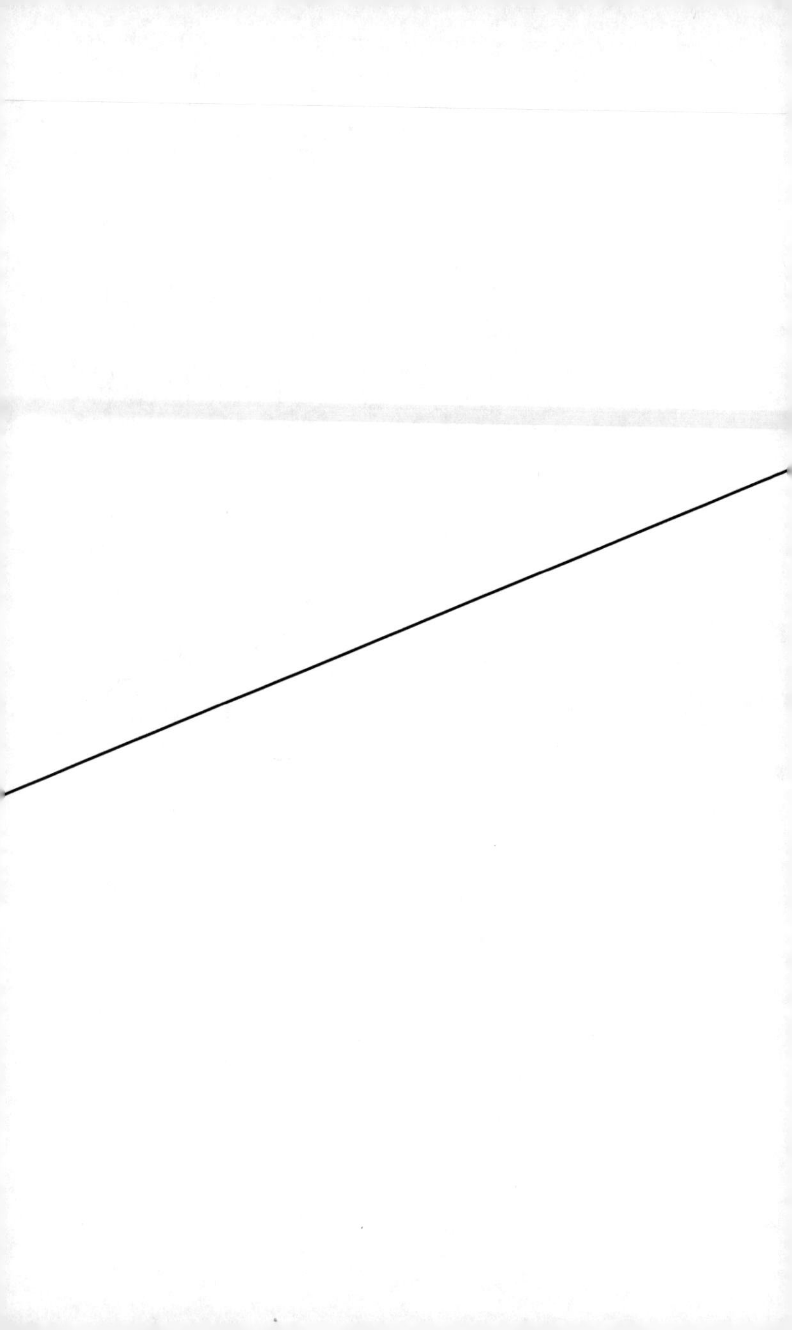

Once adopted into the production process of capital, the means of labour passes through different metamorphoses, whose culmination is the machine, or rather, an automatic system of machinery (system of machinery: the automatic one is merely its most complete, most adequate form, and alone transforms machinery into a system), set in motion by an automaton, a moving power that moves itself; this automaton consisting of numerous mechanical and intellectual organs, so that the workers themselves are cast merely as its conscious linkages.

In the machine, and even more in machinery as an automatic system, the use value, i.e. the material quality of the means of labour, is transformed into an existence adequate to fixed capital and to capital as such; and the form in which it was adopted into the production process of capital, the direct means of labour, is superseded by a form posited by capital itself and corresponding to it. In no way does the machine appear as the individual worker's means of labour. Its distinguishing characteristic is not in the least, as with the means of labour, to transmit the worker's activity to the object; this activity, rather, is posited in such a way that it merely transmits the machine's work, the machine's action, on to the raw material—supervises it and guards against interruptions. Not as with the instrument, which the worker animates and makes into his organ with his skill and strength, and whose handling therefore depends on his virtuosity. Rather, it is the machine which possesses skill and strength in place of the worker, is itself the virtuoso, with a soul of its own in the mechanical laws acting through it; and it consumes coal, oil etc., just as the worker consumes food, to keep up its perpetual motion. The worker's activity, reduced to a mere abstraction of activity, is determined and regulated on all sides by the movement of the machinery, and not the opposite. The science which compels the inanimate limbs of the machinery, by their construction, to act purposefully, as an automaton, does not exist in the worker's consciousness, but rather acts upon him through the machine as an alien power, as the power of the machine itself.

The appropriation of living labour by objectified labour—of the power or activity which creates value by value existing for-itself—which lies in the concept of capital, is posited, in production resting on machinery, as the character of the production process itself, including its material elements and its material motion. The production process has ceased to be a labour process in the sense of a process dominated by labour as its governing unity. Labour appears, rather, merely as a conscious organ, scattered among the individual living workers at numerous points of the mechanical system; subsumed under the total process of the machinery itself, as itself only a link of the system, whose unity exists not in the living workers, but rather in the living (active) machinery, which confronts his individual, insignificant doings as a mighty organism. In machinery, objectified labour confronts living labour within the labour process itself as the power which rules it; a power which, as the appropriation of living labour, is the form of capital. The transformation of the means of labour into machinery, and of living labour into a mere living accessory of this machinery, as the means of its action, also posits the absorption of the labour process in its material character as a mere moment of the realization process of capital. The increase of the productive force of labour and the greatest possible negation of necessary labour is the necessary tendency of capital, as we have seen. The transformation of the means of labour into machinery is the realization of this tendency. In machinery, objectified labour materially confronts living labour as a ruling power and as an active subsumption of the latter under itself, not only by appropriating it, but in the real production process itself; the relation of capital as value which appropriates value-creating activity is, in fixed capital existing as machinery, posited at the same time as the relation of the use value of capital to the use value of labour capacity; further, the value objectified in machinery appears as a presupposition against which the value-creating power of the individual labour capacity is an infinitesimal, vanishing magnitude; the production in enormous mass quantities which is posited with machinery destroys every connection of the product with the direct need of the producer, and hence with direct use value; it is already posited in the form of the product's production and in the relations in which it is produced that it is produced only as a conveyor of value, and its use value only as condition to that end. In machinery, objectified labour itself appears not only in the form of product or of the product employed as means of labour, but in the form of the force of production itself.

The development of the means of labour into machinery is not an accidental moment of capital, but is rather the historical reshaping of the traditional, inherited means of labour into a form adequate to capital. The accumulation of knowledge and skills, of the general productive forces of the social brain, is thus absorbed into capital, as opposed to labour, and hence appears as an attribute of capital, and more specifically of fixed capital, in so far as it enters into the production process as a means of production proper. Machinery appears, then, as the most adequate form of fixed capital, and fixed capital, in so far as capital's relations with itself are concerned, appears as the most adequate form of capital as such. In another respect, however, in so far as fixed capital is condemned to an existence within the confines of a specific use value, it does not correspond to the concept of capital, which, as value, is indifferent to every specific form of use value, and can adopt or shed any of them as equivalent incarnations. In this respect, as regards capital's external relations, it is circulating capital which appears as the adequate form of capital, and not fixed capital.

Further, in so far as machinery develops with the accumulation of society's science, of productive force generally, general social labour presents itself not in labour but in capital. The productive force of society is measured in fixed capital, exists there in its objective form; and, inversely, the productive force of capital grows with this general progress, which capital appropriates free of charge. This is not the place to go into the development of machinery in detail; rather only in its general aspect; in so far as the means of labour, as a physical thing, loses its direct form, becomes fixed capital, and confronts the worker physically as capital. In machinery, knowledge appears as alien, external to him; and living labour [as] subsumed under self-activating objectified labour. The worker appears as superfluous to the extent that his action is not determined by [capital's] requirements.

*

The full development of capital, therefore, takes place—or capital has posited the mode of production corresponding to it—only when the means of labour has not only taken the economic form of fixed capital, but has also been suspended in its immediate form, and when fixed capital appears as machine within the production process, opposite labour; and the entire production process appears as not subsumed under the direct skilfulness of the worker, but rather as the technological application of science. [It is,] hence, the tendency of capital to give production a scientific character; direct labour [is] reduced to a mere moment of this process. As with the transformation of value into capital, so does it appear in the further development of capital, that it presupposes a certain given historical development of the productive forces on one side—science too [is] among these productive forces—and, on the other, drives and forces them further onwards.

Thus the quantitative extent and the effectiveness (intensity) to which capital is developed as fixed capital indicate the general degree to which capital is developed as capital, as power over living labour, and to which it has conquered the production process as such. Also, in the sense that it expresses the accumulation of objectified productive forces, and likewise of objectified labour. However, while capital gives itself its adequate form as use value within the production process only in the form of machinery and other material manifestations of fixed capital, such as railways etc., this in no way means that this use value—machinery as such—is capital, or that its existence as machinery is identical with its existence as capital; any more than gold would cease to have use value as gold if it were no longer money. Machinery does not lose its use value as soon as it ceases to be capital. While machinery is the most appropriate form of the use value of fixed capital, it does not at all follow that therefore subsumption under the social relation of capital is the most appropriate and ultimate social relation of production for the application of machinery.

To the degree that labour time—the mere quantity of labour—is posited by capital as the sole determinant element, to that degree does direct labour and its quantity disappear as the determinant principle of production—of the creation of use values—and is reduced both quantitatively, to a smaller proportion, and qualitatively, as an, of course, indispensable but subordinate moment, compared to general scientific labour, technological application of natural sciences, on one side, and to the general productive force arising from social combination in total production on the other side—a combination which appears as a natural fruit of social labour (although it is a historical product). Capital thus works towards its own dissolution as the form dominating production.

While, then, in one respect the transformation of the production process from the simple labour process into a scientific process, which subjugates the forces of nature and compels them to work in the service of human needs, appears as a quality of fixed capital in contrast to living labour; while individual labour as such has ceased altogether to appear as productive, is productive, rather, only in these common labours which subordinate the forces of nature to themselves, and while this elevation of direct labour into social labour appears as a reduction of individual labour to the level of helplessness in face of the communality represented by and concentrated in capital; so does it now appear, in another respect, as a quality of circulating capital, to maintain labour in one branch of production by means of coexisting labour in another. In small-scale circulation, capital advances the worker the wages which the latter exchanges for products necessary for his consumption. The money he obtains has this power only because others are working alongside him at the same time; and capital can give him claims on alien labour, in the form of money, only because it has appropriated his own labour. This exchange of one's own labour with alien labour appears here not as mediated and determined by the simultaneous existence of the labour of others, but rather by the advance which capital makes. The worker's ability to engage in the exchange of substances necessary for his consumption during production appears as due to an attribute of the part of circulating capital which is paid to the worker, and of circulating capital generally. It appears not as an exchange of substances between the simultaneous labour powers, but as the metabolism [*Stoffwechsel*] of capital; as the existence of circulating capital. Thus all powers of labour are transposed into powers of capital; the productive power of labour into fixed capital (posited as external to labour and as existing independently of it (as object [*sachlich*]); and, in circulating capital, the fact that the worker himself has created the conditions for the repetition of his labour, and that the exchange of this, his labour, is mediated by the coexisting labour of others, appears in such a way that capital gives him an advance and posits the simultaneity of the branches of labour. (These last two aspects actually belong to accumulation.) Capital in the form of circulating capital posits itself as mediator between the different workers.

Fixed capital, in its character as means of production, whose most adequate form [is] machinery, produces value, i.e. increases the value of the product, in only two respects: (1) in so far as it has value; i.e. is itself the product of labour, a certain quantity of labour in objectified form; (2) in so far as it increases the relation of surplus labour to necessary labour, by enabling labour, through an increase of its productive power, to create a greater mass of the products required for the maintenance of living labour capacity in a shorter time. It is therefore a highly absurd bourgeois assertion that the worker shares with the capitalist, because the latter, with fixed capital (which is, as far as that goes, itself a product of labour, and of alien labour merely appropriated by capital) makes labour easier for him (rather, he robs it of all independence and attractive character, by means of the machine), or makes his labour shorter. Capital employs machinery, rather, only to the extent that it enables the worker to work a larger part of his time for capital, to relate to a larger part of his time as time which does not belong to him, to work longer for another. Through this process, the amount of labour necessary for the production of a given object is indeed reduced to a minimum, but only in order to realize a maximum of labour in the maximum number of such objects. The first aspect is important, because capital here—quite unintentionally—reduces human labour, expenditure of energy, to a minimum. This will redound to the benefit of emancipated labour, and is the condition of its emancipation. From what has been said, it is clear how absurd Lauderdale is when he wants to make fixed capital into an independent source of value, independent of labour time. It is such a source only in so far as it is itself objectified labour time, and in so far as it posits surplus labour time. The employment of machinery itself historically presupposes [...] superfluous hands. Machinery inserts itself to replace labour only where there is an overflow of labour powers. Only in the imagination of economists does it leap to the aid of the individual worker. It can be effective only with masses of workers, whose concentration relative to capital is one of its historic presuppositions, as we have seen. It enters not in order to replace labour power where this is lacking, but rather in order to reduce massively available labour power to its necessary measure. Machinery enters only where labour capacity is on hand in masses.

[...] From the moment [...] when fixed capital has developed to a certain extent—and this extent, as we indicated, is the measure of the development of large industry generally—hence fixed capital increases in proportion to the development of large industry's productive forces—it is itself the objectification of these productive forces, as presupposed product—from this instant on, every interruption of the production process acts as a direct reduction of capital itself, of its initial value. The value of fixed capital is reproduced only in so far as it is used up in the production process. Through disuse it loses its use value without its value passing on to the product. Hence, the greater the scale on which fixed capital develops, in the sense in which we regard it here, the more does the continuity of the production process or the constant flow of reproduction become an externally compelling condition for the mode of production founded on capital.

In machinery, the appropriation of living labour by capital achieves a direct reality in this respect as well: It is, firstly, the analysis and application of mechanical and chemical laws, arising directly out of science, which enables the machine to perform the same labour as that previously performed by the worker. However, the development of machinery along this path occurs only when large industry has already reached a higher stage, and all the sciences have been pressed into the service of capital; and when, secondly, the available machinery itself already provides great capabilities. Invention then becomes a business, and the application of science to direct production itself becomes a prospect which determines and solicits it. But this is not the road along which machinery, by and large, arose, and even less the road on which it progresses in detail. This road is, rather, dissection [*Analyse*]—through the division of labour, which gradually transforms the workers' operations into more and more mechanical ones, so that at a certain point a mechanism can step into their places. [...] Thus, the specific mode of working here appears directly as becoming transferred from the worker to capital in the form of the machine, and his own labour capacity devalued thereby. Hence the workers' struggle against machinery. What was the living worker's activity becomes the activity of the machine. Thus the appropriation of labour by capital confronts the worker in a coarsely sensuous form; capital absorbs labour into itself—'as though its body were by love possessed'.[1]

[...] The exchange of living labour for objectified labour—i.e. the positing of social labour in the form of the contradiction of capital and wage labour—is the ultimate development of the value-relation and of production resting on value. Its presupposition is—and remains—the mass of direct labour time, the quantity of labour employed, as the determinant factor in the production of wealth. But to the degree that large industry develops, the creation of real wealth comes to depend less on labour time and on the amount of labour employed than on the power of the agencies set in motion during labour time, whose 'powerful effectiveness' is itself in turn out of all proportion to the direct labour time spent on their production, but depends rather on the general state of science and on the progress of technology, or the application of this science to production. (The development of this science, especially natural science, and all

1. 'Als hätt es Lieb im Leibe', Goethe, *Faust*, Pt I, Act 5, Auerbach's Cellar in Leipzig.

others with the latter, is itself in turn related to the development of material production.) Agriculture, e.g., becomes merely the application of the science of material metabolism, its regulation for the greatest advantage of the entire body of society. Real wealth manifests itself, rather—and large industry reveals this—in the monstrous disproportion between the labour time applied, and its product, as well as in the qualitative imbalance between labour, reduced to a pure abstraction, and the power of the production process it superintends. Labour no longer appears so much to be included within the production process; rather, the human being comes to relate more as watchman and regulator to the production process itself. (What holds for machinery holds likewise for the combination of human activities and the development of human intercourse.) No longer does the worker insert a modified natural thing [*Naturgegenstand*] as middle link between the object [*Objekt*] and himself; rather, he inserts the process of nature, transformed into an industrial process, as a means between himself and inorganic nature, mastering it. He steps to the side of the production process instead of being its chief actor. In this transformation, it is neither the direct human labour he himself performs, nor the time during which he works, but rather the appropriation of his own general productive power, his understanding of nature and his mastery over it by virtue of his presence as a social body—it is, in a word, the development of the social individual which appears as the great foundation-stone of production and of wealth.

The theft of alien labour time, on which the present wealth is based, appears a miserable foundation in face of this new one, created by large-scale industry itself. As soon as labour in the direct form has ceased to be the great well-spring of wealth, labour time ceases and must cease to be its measure, and hence exchange value [must cease to be the measure] of use value. The surplus labour of the mass has ceased to be the condition for the development of general wealth, just as the non-labour of the few, for the development of the general powers of the human head. With that, production based on exchange value breaks down, and the direct, material production process is stripped of the form of penury and antithesis. The free development of individualities, and hence not the reduction of necessary labour time so as to posit surplus labour, but rather the general reduction of the necessary labour of society to a minimum, which then corresponds to the artistic, scientific etc. development of the individuals in the time set free, and with the means created, for all of them. Capital itself is the moving contradiction, [in] that it presses to reduce labour time to a minimum, while it posits labour time, on the other side, as sole measure and source of wealth. Hence it diminishes labour time in the necessary form so as to increase it in the superfluous form; hence posits the superfluous in growing measure as a condition—question of life or death—for the necessary. On the one side, then, it calls to life all the powers of science and of nature, as of social combination and of social intercourse, in order to make the creation of wealth independent (relatively) of the labour time employed on it. On the other side, it wants to use labour time as the measuring rod for the giant social forces thereby created, and to confine them within the limits required to maintain the already created value as value. Forces of production and social relations—two different sides of the development of the social individual—appear to capital as mere means, and are merely means for it to produce on its limited foundation. In fact, however, they are the material conditions to blow this foundation sky-high. 'Truly wealthy a nation, when the working day is six rather than twelve hours. Wealth is not command over surplus labour time' (real wealth), 'but rather, disposable time outside that needed in direct production, for every individual and the whole society.'[2]

2. C. W. Dilke, *The Source and Remedy of the National Difficulties* (1821), 6.

Nature builds no machines, no locomotives, railways, electric telegraphs, self-acting mules etc. These are products of human industry; natural material transformed into organs of the human will over nature, or of human participation in nature. They are organs of the human brain, created by the human hand; the power of knowledge, objectified. The development of fixed capital indicates to what degree general social knowledge has become a direct force of production, and to what degree, hence, the conditions of the process of social life itself have come under the control of the general intellect and been transformed in accordance with it. To what degree the powers of social production have been produced, not only in the form of knowledge, but also as immediate organs of social practice, of the real life process.

[...] The creation of a large quantity of disposable time apart from necessary labour time for society generally and each of its members (i.e. room for the development of the individuals' full productive forces, hence those of society also), this creation of not-labour time appears in the stage of capital, as of all earlier ones, as not-labour time, free time, for a few. What capital adds is that it increases the surplus labour time of the mass by all the means of art and science, because its wealth consists directly in the appropriation of surplus labour time; since value is directly its purpose, not use value. It is thus, despite itself, instrumental in creating the means of social disposable time, in order to reduce labour time for the whole society to a diminishing minimum, and thus to free everyone's time for their own development. But its tendency always, on the one side, to create disposable time, on the other, to convert it into surplus labour. If it succeeds too well at the first, then it suffers from surplus production, and then necessary labour is interrupted, because no surplus labour can be realized by capital. The more this contradiction develops, the more does it become evident that the growth of the forces of production can no longer be bound up with the appropriation of alien labour, but that the mass of workers must themselves appropriate their own surplus labour. Once they have done so—and disposable time thereby ceases to have an antithetical existence—then, on one side, necessary labour time will be measured by the needs of the social individual, and, on the other, the development of the power of social production will grow so rapidly that, even though production is now calculated for the wealth of all, disposable time will grow for all. For real wealth is the developed productive power of all individuals. The measure of wealth is then not any longer, in any way, labour time, but rather disposable time. Labour time as the measure of value posits wealth itself as founded on poverty, and disposable time as existing in and because of the antithesis to surplus labour time; or, the positing of an individual's entire time as labour time, and his degradation therefore to mere worker, subsumption under labour. The most developed machinery thus forces the worker to work longer than the savage does, or than he himself did with the simplest, crudest tools.

> If the entire labour of a country were sufficient only to raise the support of the whole population, there would be no surplus labour, consequently nothing that could be allowed to accumulate as capital If in one year the people raises enough for the support of two years, one year's consumption must perish, or for one year men must cease from productive labour. But the possessors of [the] surplus produce or capital [...] employ people upon something not directly and immediately productive, e.g. in the erection of machinery. So it goes on.[3]

[...] Real economy—saving—consists of the saving of labour time (minimum [and minimization] of production costs); but this

3. Dilke, *The Source and Remedy of the National Difficulties*, 4.

saving is identical with development of the productive force. Hence in no way abstinence from consumption, but rather the development of power, of capabilities of production, and hence both of the capabilities as well as the means of consumption. The capability to consume is a condition of consumption, hence its primary means, and this capability is the development of an individual potential, a force of production. The saving of labour time [is] equal to an increase of free time, i.e. time for the full development of the individual, which in turn reacts back upon the productive power of labour as itself the greatest productive power. From the standpoint of the direct production process it can be regarded as the production of fixed capital, this fixed capital being man himself. It goes without saying, by the way, that direct labour time itself cannot remain in the abstract antithesis to free time in which it appears from the perspective of bourgeois economy. Labour cannot become play, as Fourier would like,[4] although it remains his great contribution to have expressed the suspension not of distribution, but of the mode of production itself, in a higher form, as the ultimate object. Free time—which is both idle time and time for higher activity—has naturally transformed its possessor into a different subject, and he then enters into the direct production process as this different subject. This process is then both discipline, as regards the human being in the process of becoming; and, at the same time, practice [*Ausübung*], experimental science, materially creative and objectifying science, as regards the human being who has become, in whose head exists the accumulated knowledge of society.

---

4. Fourier, *Le Nouveau Monde industriel et sociétaire* (1829), Vol. VI, 242–52.

The Book of the Machines

Samuel Butler

1872

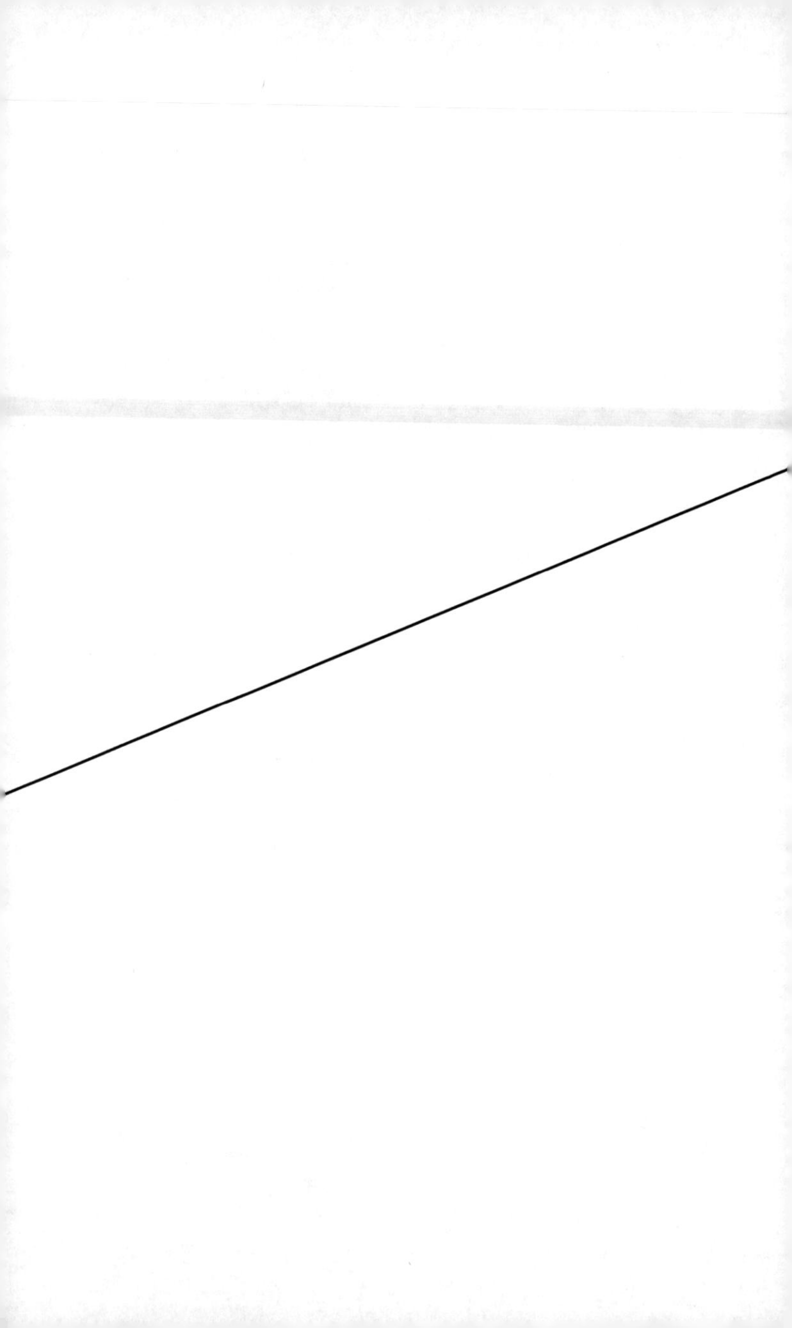

The writer commences:—'There was a time, when the earth was to all appearance utterly destitute both of animal and vegetable life, and when according to the opinion of our best philosophers it was simply a hot round ball with a crust gradually cooling. Now if a human being had existed while the earth was in this state and had been allowed to see it as though it were some other world with which he had no concern, and if at the same time he were entirely ignorant of all physical science, would he not have pronounced it impossible that creatures possessed of anything like consciousness should be evolved from the seeming cinder which he was beholding? Would he not have denied that it contained any potentiality of consciousness? Yet in the course of time consciousness came. Is it not possible then that there may be even yet new channels dug out for consciousness, though we can detect no signs of them at present?'

[...] The writer, after enlarging on the above for several pages, proceeded to inquire whether traces of the approach of such a new phase of life could be perceived at present; whether we could see any tenements preparing which might in a remote futurity be adapted for it; whether, in fact, the primordial cell of such a kind of life could be now detected upon earth. In the course of his work he answered this question in the affirmative and pointed to the higher machines.

'There is no security'—to quote his own words—'against the ultimate development of mechanical consciousness, in the fact of machines possessing little consciousness now. A mollusc has not much consciousness. Reflect upon the extraordinary advance which machines have made during the last few hundred years, and note how slowly the animal and vegetable kingdoms are advancing. The more highly organised machines are creatures not so much of yesterday, as of the last five minutes, so to speak, in comparison with past time. Assume for the sake of argument that conscious beings have existed for some twenty million years: see what strides machines have made in the last thousand! May not the world last twenty million years longer? If so, what will they not in the end become? Is it not safer to nip the mischief in the bud and to forbid them further progress?

'But who can say that the vapour engine has not a kind of consciousness? Where does consciousness begin, and where end? Who can draw the line? Who can draw any line? Is not everything interwoven with everything? Is not machinery linked with animal life in an infinite variety of ways? The shell of a hen's egg is made of a delicate white ware and is a machine as much as an egg-cup is: the shell is a device for holding the egg, as much as the egg-cup for holding the shell: both are phases of the same function; the hen makes the shell in her inside, but it is pure pottery. She makes her nest outside of herself for convenience' sake, but the nest is not more of a machine than the egg-shell is. A "machine" is only a "device".'

Then returning to consciousness, and endeavouring to detect its earliest manifestations, the writer continued:—

'There is a kind of plant that eats organic food with its flowers: when a fly settles upon the blossom, the petals close upon it and hold it fast till the plant has absorbed the insect into its system; but they will close on nothing but what is good to eat; of a drop of rain or a piece of stick they will take no notice. Curious! that so unconscious a thing should have such a keen eye to its own interest. If this is unconsciousness, where is the use of consciousness?

'Shall we say that the plant does not know what it is doing merely because it has no eyes, or ears, or brains? If we say that it acts mechanically, and mechanically only, shall we not be forced to admit that sundry other and apparently very deliberate actions are also mechanical? If it seems to us that the plant kills and eats a fly mechanically, may it not seem to the plant that a man must kill and eat a sheep mechanically?

[...] 'Either', he proceeds, 'a great deal of action that has been called purely mechanical and unconscious must be admitted to contain more elements of consciousness than has been allowed hitherto (and in this case germs of consciousness will be found in many actions of the higher machines)—Or (assuming the theory of evolution but at the same time denying the consciousness of vegetable and crystalline action) the race of man has descended from things which had no consciousness at all. In this case there is no a priori improbability in the descent of conscious (and more than conscious) machines from those which now exist, except that which is suggested by the apparent absence of anything like a reproductive system in the mechanical kingdom. This absence however is only apparent, as I shall presently show.

'Do not let me be misunderstood as living in fear of any actually existing machine; there is probably no known machine which is more than a prototype of future mechanical life. The present machines are to the future as the early Saurians to man. The largest of them will probably greatly diminish in size. Some of the lowest vertebrate attained a much greater bulk than has descended to their more highly organised living representatives, and in like manner a diminution in the size of machines has often attended their development and progress.

'Take the watch, for example; examine its beautiful structure; observe the intelligent play of the minute members which compose it: yet this little creature is but a development of the cumbrous clocks that preceded it; it is no deterioration from them. A day may come when clocks, which certainly at the present time are not diminishing in bulk, will be superseded owing to the universal use of watches, in which case they will become as extinct as ichthyosauri, while the watch, whose tendency has for some years been to decrease in size rather than the contrary, will remain the only existing type of an extinct race.

'But returning to the argument, I would repeat that I fear none of the existing machines; what I fear is the extraordinary rapidity with which they are becoming something very different to what they are at present. No class of beings have in any time past made so rapid a movement forward. Should not that movement be jealously watched, and checked while we can still check it? And is it not necessary for this end to destroy the more advanced of the machines which are in use at present, though it is admitted that they are in themselves harmless?

'As yet the machines receive their impressions through the agency of man's senses: one travelling machine calls to another in a shrill accent of alarm and the other instantly retires; but it is through the ears of the driver that the voice of the one has acted upon the other. Had there been no driver, the callee would have been deaf to the caller. There was a time when it must have seemed highly improbable that machines should learn to make their wants known by sound, even through the ears of man; may we not conceive, then, that a day will come when those ears will be no longer needed, and the hearing will be done by the delicacy of the machine's own construction?—when its language shall have been developed from the cry of animals to a speech as intricate as our own?

'It is possible that by that time children will learn the differential calculus—as they learn now to speak—from their mothers and nurses, or that they may talk in the hypothetical language, and work rule of three sums, as soon as they are born; but this is not probable; we cannot calculate on any corresponding advance in man's intellectual or physical powers which shall be a set-off against the far greater development which seems in store for the machines. Some people may say that man's moral influence will suffice to rule them; but I cannot think it will ever be safe to repose much trust in the moral sense of any machine.

'Again, might not the glory of the machines consist in their being without this same boasted gift of language? "Silence", it has been said by one writer, "is a virtue which renders us agreeable to our fellow-creatures."

'But other questions come upon us. What is a man's eye but a machine for the little creature that sits behind in his brain to look through? A dead eye is nearly as good as a living one for some time after the man is dead. It is not the eye that cannot see, but the restless one that cannot see through it. Is it man's eyes, or is it the big seeing-engine which has revealed to us the existence of worlds beyond worlds into infinity? What has made man familiar with the scenery of the moon, the spots on the sun, or the geography of the planets? He is at the mercy of the seeing-engine for these things, and is powerless unless he tack it on to his own identity, and make it part and parcel of himself. Or, again, is it the eye, or the little see-engine, which has shown us the existence of infinitely minute organisms which swarm unsuspected around us?

'And take man's vaunted power of calculation. Have we not engines which can do all manner of sums more quickly and correctly than we can? What prizeman in Hypothetics at any of our Colleges of Unreason can compare with some of these machines in their own line? In fact, wherever precision is required man flies to the machine at once, as far preferable to himself. Our sum-engines never drop a figure, nor our looms a stitch; the machine is brisk and active, when the man is weary; it is clear-headed and collected, when the man is stupid and dull; it needs no slumber, when man must sleep or drop; ever at its post, ever ready for work, its alacrity never flags, its patience never gives in; its might is stronger than combined hundreds, and swifter than the flight of birds; it can burrow beneath the earth, and walk upon the largest rivers and sink not. This is the green tree; what then shall be done in the dry?

'Who shall say that a man does see or hear? He is such a hive and swarm of parasites that it is doubtful whether his body is not more theirs than his, and whether he is anything but another kind of ant-heap after all. May not man himself become a sort of parasite upon the machines? An affectionate machine-tickling aphid?

'It is said by some that our blood is composed of infinite living agents which go up and down the highways and byways of our bodies as people in the streets of a city. When we look down from a high place upon crowded thoroughfares, is it possible not to think of corpuscles of blood travelling through veins and nourishing the heart of the town? No mention shall be made of sewers, nor of the hidden nerves which serve to communicate sensations from one part of the town's body to another; nor of the yawning jaws of the railway stations, whereby the circulation is carried directly into the heart,—which receive the venous lines, and disgorge the arterial, with an eternal pulse of people. And the sleep of the town, how life-like! with its change in the circulation.'

Here the writer became again so hopelessly obscure that I was obliged to miss several pages. He resumed:—

'It can be answered that even though machines should hear never so well and speak never so wisely, they will still always do the one or the other for our advantage, not their own; that man will be the ruling spirit and the machine the servant; that as soon as a machine fails to discharge the service which man expects from it, it is doomed to extinction; that the machines stand to man simply in the relation of lower animals, the vapour-engine itself being only a more economical kind of horse; so that instead of being likely to be developed into a higher kind of life than man's, they owe their very existence and progress to their power of ministering to human wants, and must therefore both now and ever be man's inferiors.

'This is all very well. But the servant glides by imperceptible approaches into the master; and we have come to such a pass that, even now, man must suffer terribly on ceasing to benefit the machines. If all machines were to be annihilated at one moment, so that not a knife nor lever nor rag of clothing nor anything whatsoever were left to man but his bare body alone that he was born with, and if all knowledge of mechanical laws were taken from him so that he could make no more machines, and all machine-made food destroyed so that the race of man should be left as it were naked upon a desert island, we should become extinct in six weeks. A few miserable individuals might linger, but even these in a year or two would become worse than monkeys. Man's very soul is due to the machines; it is a machine-made thing: he thinks as he thinks, and feels as he feels, through the work that machines have wrought upon him, and their existence is quite as much a sine qua non for his, as his for theirs. This fact precludes us from proposing the complete annihilation of machinery, but surely it indicates that we should destroy as many of them as we can possibly dispense with, lest they should tyrannise over us even more completely.

'True, from a low materialistic point of view, it would seem that those thrive best who use machinery wherever its use is possible with profit; but this is the art of the machines—they serve that they may rule. They bear no malice towards man for destroying a whole race of them provided he creates a better instead; on the contrary, they reward him liberally for having hastened their development. It is for neglecting them that he incurs their wrath, or for using inferior machines, or for not making sufficient exertions to invent new ones, or for destroying them without replacing them; yet these are the very things we ought to do, and do quickly; for though our rebellion against their infant power will cause infinite suffering, what will not things come to, if that rebellion is delayed?

'They have preyed upon man's grovelling preference for his material over his spiritual interests, and have betrayed him into supplying that element of struggle and warfare without which no race can advance. The lower animals progress because they struggle with one another; the weaker die, the stronger breed and transmit their strength. The machines being of themselves unable to struggle, have got man to do their struggling for them: as long as he fulfils this function duly, all goes well with him—at least he thinks so; but the moment he fails to do his best for the advancement of machinery by encouraging the good and destroying the bad, he is left behind in the race of competition; and this means that he will be made uncomfortable in a variety of ways, and perhaps die.

'So that even now the machines will only serve on condition of being served, and that too upon their own terms; the moment their terms are not complied with, they jib, and either smash both themselves and all whom they can reach, or turn churlish and refuse to work at all. How many men at this hour are living in a state of bondage to the machines? How many spend their whole lives, from the cradle to the grave, in tending them by night and day? Is it not plain that the machines are gaining ground upon us, when we reflect on the increasing number of those who are bound down to them as slaves, and of those who devote their whole souls to the advancement of the mechanical kingdom?

'The vapour-engine must be fed with food and consume it by fire even as man consumes it; it supports its combustion by air as man supports it; it has a pulse and circulation as man has. It may be granted that man's body is as yet the more versatile of the two, but then man's body is an older thing; give the vapour-engine but half the time that man has had, give it also a continuance of our present infatuation, and what may it not ere long attain to?

'There are certain functions indeed of the vapour-engine which will probably remain unchanged for myriads of years—which in fact will perhaps survive when the use of vapour has been superseded: the piston and cylinder, the beam, the fly-wheel, and other parts of the machine will probably be permanent, just as we see that man and many of the lower animals share like modes of eating, drinking, and sleeping; thus they have hearts which beat as ours, veins and arteries, eyes, ears, and noses; they sigh even in their sleep, and weep and yawn; they are affected by their children; they feel pleasure and pain, hope, fear, anger, shame; they have memory and prescience; they know that if certain things happen to them they will die, and they fear death as much as we do; they communicate their thoughts to one another, and some of them deliberately act in concert. The comparison of similarities is endless: I only make it because some may say that since the vapour-engine is not likely to be improved in the main particulars, it is unlikely to be henceforward extensively modified at all. This is too good to be true: it will be modified and suited for an infinite variety of purposes, as much as man has been modified so as to exceed the brutes in skill.

'In the meantime the stoker is almost as much a cook for his engine as our own cooks for ourselves. Consider also the colliers and pitmen and coal merchants and coal trains, and the men who drive them, and the ships that carry coals—what an army of servants do the machines thus employ! Are there not probably more men engaged in tending machinery than in tending men? Do not machines eat as it were by mannery? Are we not ourselves creating our successors in the supremacy of the earth? daily adding to the beauty and delicacy of their organisation, daily giving them greater skill and supplying more and more of that self-regulating self-acting power which will be better than any intellect?

'What a new thing it is for a machine to feed at all! The plough, the spade, and the cart must eat through man's stomach; the fuel that sets them going must burn in the furnace of a man or of horses. Man must consume bread and meat or he cannot dig; the bread and meat are the fuel which drive the spade. If a plough be drawn by horses, the power is supplied by grass or beans or oats, which being burnt in the belly of the cattle give the power of working: without this fuel the work would cease, as an engine would stop if its furnaces were to go out.

'A man of science has demonstrated "that no animal has the power of originating mechanical energy, but that all the work done in its life by any animal, and all the heat that has been emitted from it, and the heat which would be obtained by burning the combustible matter which has been lost from its body during life, and by burning its body after death, make up altogether an exact equivalent to the heat which would be obtained by burning as much food as it has used during its life, and an amount of fuel which would generate as much heat as its body if burned immediately after death." I do not know how he has found this out, but he is a man of science—how then can it be objected against the future vitality of the machines that they are, in their present infancy, at the beck and call of beings who are themselves incapable of originating mechanical energy?

'The main point, however, to be observed as affording cause for alarm is, that whereas animals were formerly the only stomachs of the machines, there are now many which have stomachs of their own, and consume their food themselves. This is a great step towards their becoming, if not animate, yet something so near akin to it, as not to differ more widely from our own life than animals do from vegetables. And though man should remain, in some respects, the higher creature, is not this in accordance with the practice of nature, which allows superiority in some things to animals which have, on the whole, been long surpassed? Has she not allowed the ant and the bee to retain superiority over man in the organisation of their communities and social arrangements, the bird in traversing the air, the fish in swimming, the horse in strength and fleetness, and the dog in self-sacrifice?

'It is said by some with whom I have conversed upon this subject, that the machines can never be developed into animate or quasi-animate existences, inasmuch as they have no reproductive system, nor seem ever likely to possess one. If this be taken to mean that they cannot marry, and that we are never likely to see a fertile union between two vapour-engines with the young ones playing about the door of the shed, however greatly we might desire to do so, I will readily grant it. But the objection is not a very profound one. No one expects that all the features of the now existing organisations will be absolutely repeated in an entirely new class of life. The reproductive system of animals differs widely from that of plants, but both are reproductive systems. Has nature exhausted her phases of this power?

'Surely if a machine is able to reproduce another machine systematically, we may say that it has a reproductive system. What is a reproductive system, if it be not a system for reproduction? And how few of the machines are there which have not been produced systematically by other machines? But it is man that makes them do so. Yes; but is it not insects that make many of the plants reproductive, and would not whole families of plants die out if their fertilisation was not effected by a class of agents utterly foreign to themselves? Does any one say that the red clover has no reproductive system because the humble bee (and the humble bee only) must aid and abet it before it can reproduce? No one. The humble bee is a part of the reproductive system of the clover. Each one of ourselves has sprung from minute animalcules whose entity was entirely distinct from our own, and which acted after their kind with no thought or heed of what we might think about it. These little creatures are part of our own reproductive system; then why not we part of that of the machines?

[...] 'The misery is that man has been blind so long already. In his reliance upon the use of steam he has been betrayed into increasing and multiplying. To withdraw steam power suddenly will not have the effect of reducing us to the state in which we were before its introduction; there will be a general break-up and time of anarchy such as has never been known; it will be as though our population were suddenly doubled, with no additional means of feeding the increased number. The air we breathe is hardly more necessary for our animal life than the use of any machine, on the strength of which we have increased our numbers, is to our civilisation; it is the machines which act upon man and make him man, as much as man who has acted upon and made the machines; but we must choose between the alternative of undergoing much present suffering, or seeing ourselves gradually superseded by our own creatures, till we rank no higher in comparison with them, than the beasts of the field with ourselves.

'Herein lies our danger. For many seem inclined to acquiesce in so dishonourable a future. They say that although man should become to the machines what the horse and dog are to us, yet that he will continue to exist, and will probably be better off in a state of domestication under the beneficent rule of the machines than in his present wild condition. We treat our domestic animals with much kindness. We give them whatever we believe to be the best for them; and there can be no doubt that our use of meat has increased their happiness rather than detracted from it. In like manner there is reason to hope that the machines will use us kindly, for their existence will be in a great measure dependent upon ours; they will rule us with a rod of iron, but they will not eat us; they will not only require our services in the reproduction and education of their young, but also in waiting upon them as servants; in gathering food for them, and feeding them; in restoring them to health when they are sick; and in either burying their dead or working up their deceased members into new forms of mechanical existence.

'The very nature of the motive power which works the advancement of the machines precludes the possibility of man's life being rendered miserable as well as enslaved. Slaves are tolerably happy if they have good masters, and the revolution will not occur in our time, nor hardly in ten thousand years, or ten times that. Is it wise to be uneasy about a contingency which is so remote? Man is not a sentimental animal where his material interests are concerned, and though here and there some ardent soul may look upon himself and curse his fate that he was not born a vapour-engine, yet the mass of mankind will acquiesce in any arrangement which gives them better food and clothing at a cheaper rate, and will refrain from yielding to unreasonable jealousy merely because there are other destinies more glorious than their own.

'The power of custom is enormous, and so gradual will be the change, that man's sense of what is due to himself will be at no time rudely shocked; our bondage will steal upon us noiselessly and by imperceptible approaches; nor will there ever be such a clashing of desires between man and the machines as will lead to an encounter between them. Among themselves the machines will war eternally, but they will still require man as the being through whose agency the struggle will be principally conducted. In point of fact there is no occasion for anxiety about the future happiness of man so long as he continues to be in any way profitable to the machines; he may become the inferior race, but he will be infinitely better off than he is now. Is it not then both absurd and unreasonable to be envious of our benefactors? And should we not be guilty of consummate folly if we were to reject advantages which we cannot obtain otherwise, merely because they involve a greater gain to others than to ourselves?'

The Common Task

Nicolai Fedorov

1906

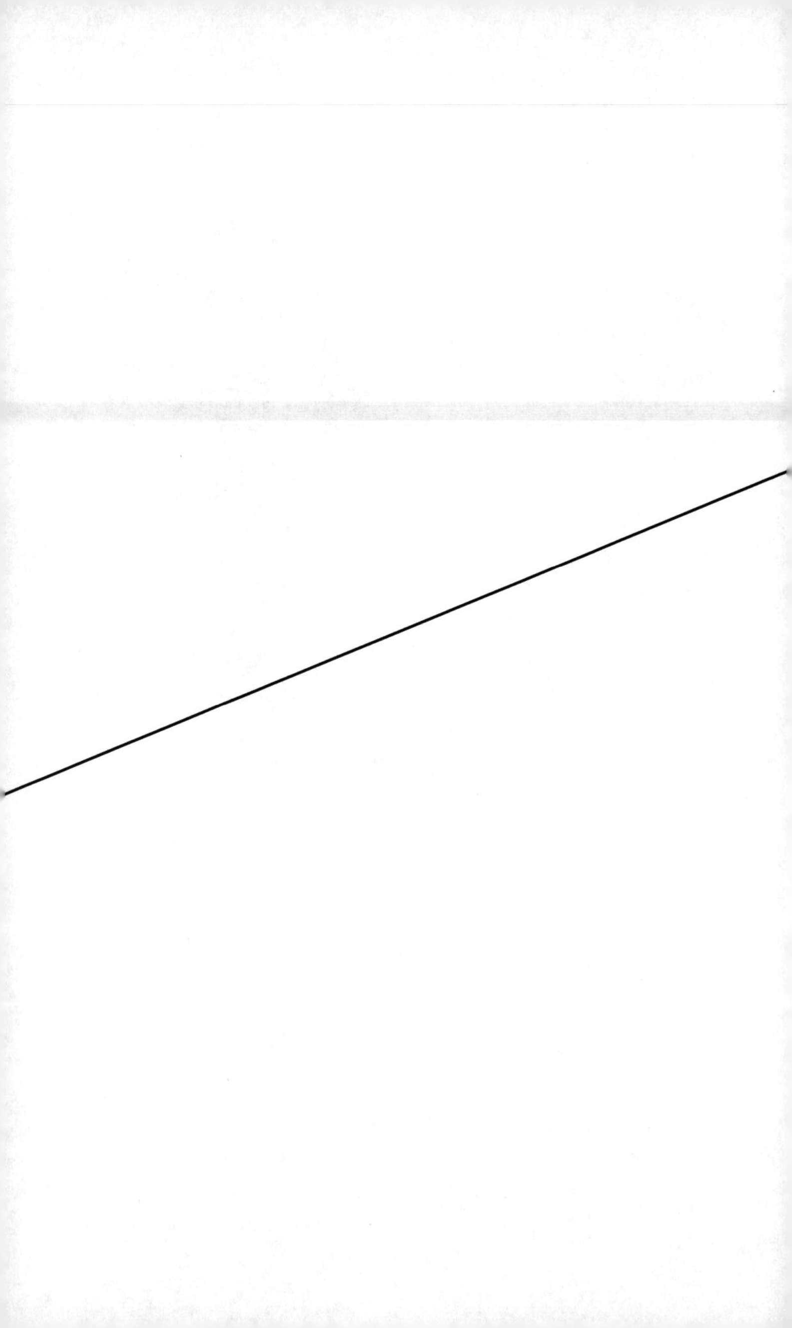

A classless agricultural commune, where the intellectuals would be the teachers and where cottage industries would be carried on during the winter months, would end competition, speculation, social unrest, revolutions and even international wars, because all those vital forces now squandered on quarrelling would find a boundless field of application. In the worldwide activity of the classless rural communes there would be scope for peaceful labour and also for daring courage, the spirit of adventure, the thirst for sacrifice, novelty and exploits. And any commune is likely to have a percentage of such innate abilities. Out of such stuff were made knights errant, the ascetics who opened up the forests of the far north, Cossacks, runaway serfs, and the like. Now they would be the explorers, the new explorers of celestial space.

The prejudice that the celestial expanse is unattainable to man has grown gradually over the centuries, but cannot have existed ab initio. Only the loss of tradition and the separation of men of thought from men of action gave birth to this prejudice. However, for the sons of man the celestial worlds are the future homes of the ancestors, since the skies will be attainable only to the resurrected and the resurrecting. The exploration of outer space is only the preparation for these future dwelling places.

The spread of humanity over the planet was accompanied by the creation of new (artificial) organs and coverings. The purpose of humanity is to change all that is natural, a free gift of nature, into what is created by work. Outer space, expansion beyond the limits of the planet, demands precisely such radical change. The great feat of courage now confronting humanity requires the highest martial virtues such as daring and self-sacrifice, while excluding that which is most horrible in war—taking the lives of people like oneself.

The destiny of the Earth convinces us that human activity cannot be bounded by the limits of the planet. We must ask whether our knowledge of its likely fate, its inevitable extinction, obliges us to do something or not. Can knowledge be useful, or is it a useless frill? In the first case we can say that Earth itself has become conscious of its fate through man, and this consciousness is evidently active—the path of salvation. The mechanic has appeared just as the mechanism has started to deteriorate. It is absurd to say that nature created both the mechanism and the mechanic; one must admit that God is educating man through his own human experience. God is the king who does everything for man but also through man. There is no purposefulness in nature—it is for man to introduce it, and this is his supreme raison d'être. The Creator restores the world through us and brings back to life all that has perished. That is why nature has been left to its blindness, and mankind to its lusts. Through the labour of resuscitation, man as an independent, self-created, free creature freely responds to the call of divine love. Therefore humanity must not be idle passengers, but the crew of its terrestrial craft propelled by forces the nature of which we do not even know—is it photo-, thermo- or electro-powered? We will remain unable to discover what force propels it until we are able to control it. In the second case, that is to say, if the knowledge of the final destiny of our Earth is unnatural, alien and useless to it, then there is nothing else to do than to become passively fossilised in contemplating the slow destruction of our home and graveyard.

The possibility of a real transcendence from one world to another only seems fantastic. The necessity of such movements is self-evident to those who dare take a sober look at the difficulties of creating a truly moral society, in order to remedy all social ills and evils, because to forgo the possession of celestial space is to forgo the solution of the economic problem posed by Malthus and, more generally, of a moral human existence. What is more of a fantasy—to think how to realise a moral ideal while closing one's eyes to the tremendous obstacles in the way, or to boldly recognise these obstacles? Of course, one can give up morality, but that implies giving up being human. What is more fantastic—to create a moral society by postulating the existence of other beings in other worlds and envisioning the emigration thither of souls, the existence of which cannot be proven, or to transform this transcendental migration into an immanent one—that is, to make such a migration the goal of human activity?

The obstacle to the building of a moral society is the absence of a cause or task great enough to absorb all the energies of those who spend them at present on discord. In world history we know of no event which, although threatening the end of the society in question, could unite all its forces and stop all quarrels and hostilities within that society. All periods of history have witnessed aspirations that reveal humanity as unwilling to remain confined within the narrow limits of our Earth. The so-called states of ecstasy and ravishments into heaven were manifestations of such aspirations. Is this not a proof that unless mankind finds a wider field of activity, eras of common sense, or rather of fatigue and disillusionment with fruitless longings, will be succeeded by eras of enthusiasm, ecstatic visions, and so on? Throughout history these moods have alternated. Our era confirms all this, for we see alongside 'the kingdom of this world', with its filthy reality, a 'Kingdom of God' in the form of revivalist movements, spiritualistic table-turning, and the like. So long as there are no real translations to other worlds, people will resort to fantasies, ecstatic rapture and drug abuse. Even common drunkenness is apparently caused by the absence of a wider, purer, all-absorbing activity.

The three particular problems—the regulation of atmospheric phenomena, the control of the motion of the Earth and the search for 'new lands' (to colonise) form one general problem, that of survival or, more precisely, the return to life of our ancestors. Death can be called real only when all means of restoring life, at least all those that exist in nature and have been discovered by the human race, have been tried and have failed. It should not be assumed that we hope that a special force will be discovered for this purpose. What we should assume is that the transformation of the blind force of nature into a conscious force will be that agent. Mortality is an inductive conclusion. We know that we are the offspring of a multitude of deceased ancestors. But however great the number of the deceased, this cannot be the basis for an incontrovertible acceptance of death because it would entail an abdication of our filial duty. Death is a property, a state conditioned by causes; it is not a quality which determines what a human being is and must be.

[...] To ensure good harvests, agriculture must extend beyond the boundaries of the Earth, since the conditions which determine harvests and, in general, plant and animal life do not depend on soil alone. If the hypotheses are correct that the solar system is a galaxy with an eleven-year electromagnetic cycle during which the quantity of sunspots and magnetic (the Northern Lights) and electric storms reach in turn their maximum and minimum, and that the meteorological process depends on these fluctuations, it follows that good and bad harvests do so too. Consequently, the entire telluric-solar process must be brought into the field of agriculture. If, moreover, it is true that interactions between phenomena are of an electrical nature and that this force is akin to or even identical with that of the nervous impulses which serve will and consciousness, then it follows that the present state of the solar system can be compared to an organism in which the nervous system has not yet fully developed and has not yet become differentiated from its muscular and other systems.

Man's economic needs require the organisation of just such a regulatory apparatus, without which the solar system would remain a blind, untrammelled, death-bearing entity. The problem consists, on the one hand, in elaborating the paths which would transmit to human consciousness everything going on in the solar system and, on the other, in establishing the conductors by means of which all that is happening in it, all that is procreating, could become an activity of restoration. So long as no such paths for informing consciousness exist, so long as we have no more than conductors directing activity—mere revolutions and upheavals—the world will present a strange, distorted order, which could better be described as disorder, 'indifferent nature', unfeeling and unconscious, will continue 'to shine with eternal beauty',[1] while a being conscious of the beauty of incorruption will feel both excluded and excluding. Could a Being which is neither excluded nor excluding be the Creator of what is a chaos rather than a cosmos?

Of course we cannot know what the world was like in the beginning because we only know it as it is. However, judging by the Creator, we can to some extent presume or imagine what a world of innocence and purity could have been. Could we not envision, too, that the relations of the first humans with the world were similar to those of an infant not yet in control of his organs, who has not yet learned to manage them—in other words, could the first humans have been beings who should (and could, without suffering or pain) have created such organs as would have been capable of living in other worlds, in all environments? But man preferred pleasure and failed to develop, to create organs adapted to all environments, and these organs (namely, cosmic forces) became atrophied and paralysed, and the Earth became an isolated planet. Thought and being became distinct. Man's creative activity of developing organs corresponding to various environments was reduced to feeding and then to devouring.

Man placed himself at the mercy of fate (that is to say, the annual rotation of the Earth), he submitted to the Earth; childbirth

---

1. From Pushkin's poem 'Brozhu li ya vdol' ulits shumnykh...', 1829.

replaced the artistry of reproducing oneself in other beings, a process comparable to the birth of the Son from the Father, or the procession of the Holy Ghost. Later, proliferation increased the struggle, which was fostered by an unbridled surge of procreation; and with the increase in birth, mortality increased too. The conditions which could have regulated this concatenation of phenomena disappeared, and gradually there came revolutions, storms, drought and earthquakes; the solar system became an uncontrolled world, a star with an eleven-year cycle or some other periodicity of various catastrophes. Such is the system we know. One way or another, to confirm us in our knowledge, the solar system must be transformed into a controlled economic entity.

The immensity of the solar system is sufficient to inspire awe and, naturally, objectors will stress our smallness. When we turn our attention to small particles which consist of an enormous number of even smaller ones and which should also be brought within human economic management, then the objection will be our own size; indeed, for infusoria these tiny particles seem very great, and yet they are more accessible to them than to us.

The problem is obviously not one of size, and our relative smallness or bigness only indicates the difficulty—a severe difficulty, but not an impossibility. For a vast intellect able to encompass in one formula the motions both of the largest celestial bodies in the Universe and of the tiniest atoms, nothing would remain unknown; the future as well as the past would be accessible to him. The collective mind of all humans working for many generations together would of course be vast enough—all that is needed is concord, multi-unity.

The Machine Process and the Natural Decay of the Business Enterprise

Thorstein Veblen

1904

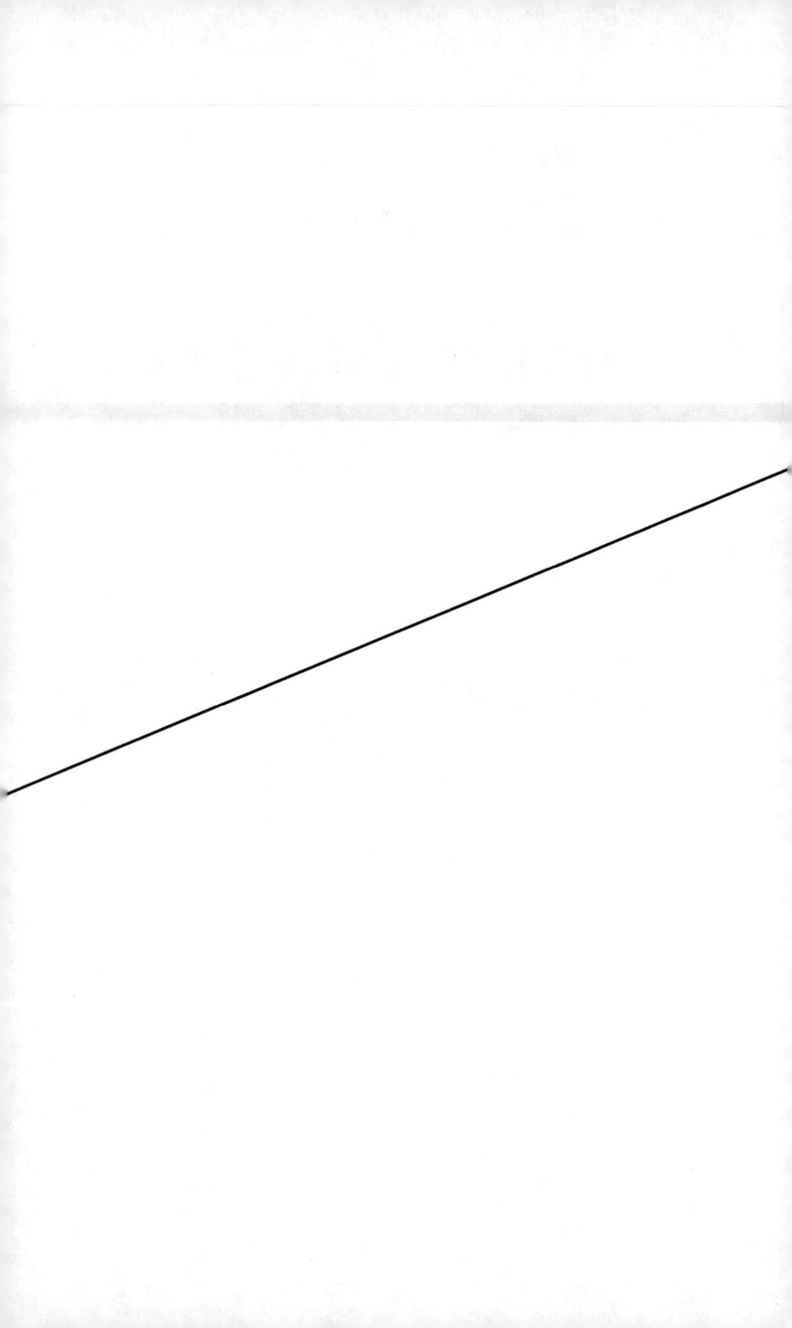

THE MACHINE PROCESS

In its bearing on modern life and modern business, the 'machine process' means something more comprehensive and less external than a mere aggregate of mechanical appliances for the mediation of human labor. It means that, but it means something more than that. The civil engineer, the mechanical engineer, the navigator, the mining expert, the industrial chemist and mineralogist, the electrician—the work of all these falls within the lines of the modern machine process, as well as the work of the inventor who devises the appliances of the process and that of the mechanician who puts the inventions into effect and oversees their working. The scope of the process is larger than the machine.[1] In those branches of industry in which machine methods have been introduced, many agencies which are not to be classed as mechanical appliances, simply, have been drawn into the process, and have become integral factors in it. Chemical properties of minerals, e.g., are counted on in the carrying out of metallurgical processes with much the same certainty and calculable effect as are the motions of those mechanical appliances by whose use the minerals are handled.

The sequence of the process involves both the one and the other, both the apparatus and the materials, in such intimate interaction that the process cannot be spoken of simply as an action of the apparatus upon the materials. It is not simply that the apparatus reshapes the materials; the materials reshape themselves by the help of the apparatus. Similarly in such other processes as the refining of petroleum, oil, or sugar; in the work of the industrial chemical laboratories; in the use of wind, water, or electricity, etc.

Wherever manual dexterity, the rule of thumb, and the fortuitous conjunctures of the seasons have been supplanted by a

---

1. Cf. C. Taylor, *Modern Factory System* (London, 1891), 74–7.

reasoned procedure on the basis of a systematic knowledge of the forces employed, there the mechanical industry is to be found, even in the absence of intricate mechanical contrivances. It is a question of the character of the process rater than a question of the complexity of the contrivances employed. Chemical, agricultural, and animal industries, as carried on by the characteristically modern methods and in due touch with the market, are to be included in the modern complex of mechanical industry.[2]

No one of the mechanical processes carried on by the use of a given outfit of appliances is independent of other processes going on elsewhere. Each draws upon and presupposes the proper working of many other processes of a similarly mechanical character. None of the processes in the mechanical industries is self-sufficing. Each follows some and precedes other processes in an endless sequence, into which each fits and to the requirements of which each must adapt its own working. The whole concert of industrial operations is to be taken as a machine process, made up of interlocking detail processes, rather than as a multiplicity of mechanical appliances each doing its particular work in severalty. This comprehensive industrial process draws into its scope and

---

2. Even in work that lies so near the fortuities of animate nature as dairying, stock-breeding, and the improvement of crop plants, a determinate, reasoned routine replaces the rule of thumb. By mechanical control of his materials the dairyman, e.g., selectively determines the rate and kind of the biological processes that change his raw material into finished product. The stock-breeder's aim is to reduce the details of the laws of heredity, as they apply within his field, to such definite terms as will afford him a technologically accurate routine of breeding, and then to apply this technological breeding process to the production of such varieties of stock as will, with the nearest approach to mechanical exactness and expedition, turn the raw materials of field and meadow into certain specified kinds and grades of finished product. The like is true of the plant-breeders. Agricultural experiment stations and bureaus, in all civilized countries, are laboratories working toward an effective technological control of biological factors, with a view to eliminating fortuitous, disserviceable, and useless elements from the processes of agricultural production, and so reducing these processes to a calculable, expeditious, and wasteless routine.

turns to account all branches of knowledge that have to do with the material sciences, and the whole makes a more or less delicately balanced complex of sub-processes.[3]

Looked at in this way the industrial process shows two well-marked general characteristics: (a) the running maintenance of interstitial adjustments between the several sub-processes or branches of industry, wherever in their working they touch one another in the sequence of industrial elaboration; and (b) an unremitting requirement of quantitative precision, accuracy in point of time and sequence, in the proper inclusion and exclusion of forces affecting the outcome, in the magnitude of the various physical characteristics (weight, size, density, hardness, tensile strength, elasticity, temperature, chemical reaction, actinic sensitiveness, etc.) of the materials handled as well as of the appliances employed. This requirement of mechanical accuracy and nice adaptation to specific uses has led to a gradual pervading enforcement of uniformity to a reduction to staple grades and staple character in the materials handled, and to a thorough standardizing of tools and units of measurement. Standard physical measurements are of the essence of the machine's regime.[4]

[...] The like is true of the finished products. Modern consumers in great part supply their wants with commodities that conform to certain staple specifications of size, weight, and grade. The consumer (that is to say the vulgar consumer) furnishes his hose, his table, and his person with supplies of standard weight and measure, and he can to an appreciable degree specify his needs and his consumption in the notation of the standard gauge. As regards the mass of civilized mankind, the idiosyncrasies of the individual consumers are required to conform to the uniform gradations imposed upon consumable goods by the comprehensive

---

3. Cf. Sombart, *Moderne Kapitalismus*, vol. II, ch. III.

4. Twelfth Census (US): 'Manufactures,' pt. I, xxxvi.

mechanical processes of industry. 'Local color' it is said, is falling into abeyance in modern life, and where it is still found it tends to assert itself in units of the standard gauge.

[...] The machine process pervades the modern life and dominates it in a mechanical sense. Its dominance is seen in the enforcement of precise mechanical measurements and adjustment and the reduction of all manner of things, purposes and acts, necessities, conveniences, and amenities of life, to standard units. [...] The point of immediate interest here is the further bearing of the machine process upon the growth of culture, the disciplinary effect which this movement for standardization and mechanical equivalence has upon the human material.

This discipline falls more immediately on the workmen engaged in the mechanical industries, and only less immediately on the rest of the community which lives in contact with this sweeping machine process. Wherever the machine process extends, it sets the pace for the workmen, great and small. The pace is set, not wholly by the particular processes in the details of which the given workman is immediately engaged, but in some degree by the more comprehensive process at large into which the given detail process fits. It is no longer simply that the individual workman makes use of one or more mechanical contrivances for effecting certain results. Such used to be his office in the earlier phases of the use of machines, and the work which he now has in hand still has much of that character. But such a characterization of the workman's part in industry misses the peculiarly modern feature of the case. He now does this work as a factor involved in a mechanical process whose movement controls his motions. It remains true, of course, as it always has been true, that he is the intelligent agent concerned in the process, while the machine, furnace, roadway, or retort are inanimate structures devised by man and subject to the workman's supervision. But the process comprises him and his intelligent motions, and it is by virtue of his necessarily taking an intelligent part in what is going forward that the mechanical process has its chief effect upon him. The process standardizes his supervision and guidance of the machine. Mechanically speaking, the machine is not his to do with it as his fancy may suggest. His place is to take thought of the machine and its work in terms given him by the process that is going forward. His thinking in the premises is reduced to standard units of gauge and grade. If he fails of the precise measure, by more or less, the exigencies of the process check the aberration and drive home the absolute need of conformity.

There results a standardization of the workman's intellectual life in terms of mechanical process, which is more unmitigated and precise the more comprehensive and consummate the industrial process in which he plays a part. This must not be taken to mean that such work need lower the degree of intelligence of the workman. No doubt the contrary is nearer the truth. He is a more efficient workman the more intelligent he is, and the discipline of the machine process ordinarily increases his efficiency even for work in a different line from that by which the discipline is given. But the intelligence required and inculcated in the machine industry is of a peculiar character. The machine process is a severe and insistent disciplinarian in point of intelligence. It requires close and unremitting thought, but it is thought which runs in standard terms of quantitative precision. Broadly, other intelligence on the part of the workman is useless; or it is even worse than useless, for a habit of thinking in other than quantitative terms blurs the workman's quantitative apprehension of the facts with which he has to do.[5]

---

5. If, e.g., he takes to myth making and personifies the machine or the process and imputes and benevolence to the mechanical applications, after the manner of current nursery tales and pulpit oratory, he is sure to go wrong.

In so far as he is a rightly gifted and fully disciplined workman, the final term of his habitual thinking is mechanical efficiency, understanding 'mechanical' in the sense in which it is used above. But mechanical efficiency is a matter of precisely adjusted cause and effect. What the discipline of the machine industry inculcates, therefore, in the habits of life and of thought of the workman, is regularity of sequence and mechanical precision; and the intellectual outcome is an habitual resort to terms of measurable cause and effect, together with a relative neglect and disparagement of such exercise of the intellectual faculties as does not run on these lines.

Of course, in no case and with no class does the discipline of the machine process mould the habits of life and of thought fully into its own image. There is present in the human nature of all classes too large a residue of the propensities and aptitudes carried over from the past and working to a different result. The machine's regime has been of too short duration, strict as its discipline may be, and the body of inherited traits and traditions is too comprehensive and consistent to admit of anything more than a remote approach to such a consummation.

The machine process compels a more or less unremitting attention to phenomena of an impersonal character and to sequences and correlations not dependent for their force upon human predilection nor created by habit and custom. The machine throws out anthropomorphic habits of thought. It compels the adaptation of the workman to his work, rather than the adaptation of the work to the workman. The machine technology rests on a knowledge of impersonal, material cause and effect, not on the dexterity, diligence, or personal force of the workman, still less on the habits and propensities of the workman's superiors. Within the range of this machine-guided work, and within the range of modern life so far as it is guided by the machine process, the course of things is given mechanically, impersonally, and the resultant discipline is a discipline in the handling of impersonal facts for mechanical effect. It inculcates thinking in terms of opaque, impersonal cause and effect, to the neglect of those norms of validity that rest on usage and on the conventional standards handed down by usage. Usage counts for little in shaping the processes of work of this kind or in shaping the modes of thought induced by work of this kind.

The machine process gives no insight into questions of good and evil, merit and demerit, except in point of material causation, nor into the foundations or the constraining force of law and order, except such mechanically enforced law and order as may be stated in terms of pressure, temperature, velocity, tensile strength, etc.[6] The machine technology takes no cognizance of conventionally established rules of precedence; it knows neither manners nor breeding and can make no use of any of the attributes of worth. Its scheme of knowledge and of inference is based on the laws of material causation, not on those of immemorial custom, authenticity, or authoritative enactment. Its metaphysical basis is the law of cause and effect, which in the thinking of its adepts has displaced even the law of sufficient reason.[7]

The range of conventional truths, or of institutional legacies, which it traverses is very comprehensive, being, indeed, all-inclusive. It is but little more in accord with the newer, eighteenth century conventional truths of natural rights, natural liberty, natural

6. Such expressions as 'good and ill,' 'merit and demerit,' 'law and order,' when applied to technological facts or to the outcome of material science, are evidently only metaphorical expressions, borrowed from older usage and serviceable only as figures of speech.

7. Tarde, *Psychologie Économique* (Paris: Alcan, 1902), vol. I. 122–31, offers a characterization of the psychology of modern work, contrasting, among other things, the work of the machine workman with that of the handicraftsman in respect of its psychological requirements and effects. It may be taken as a temperate formulation of the cent commonplaces on this topic, and seems to be fairly wide of the mark.

law, or natural religion, than with the older norms of the true, the beautiful, and the good which these displaced. Anthropomorphism, under whatever disguise, is of no use and of no force here.

[...] The discipline of the modern industrial employments is relatively free from the bias of conventionality, but the difference between the mechanical and the business occupations in this respect is a difference of degree. It is not simply that conventional standards of certainty fall into abeyance for lack of exercise, among the industrial classes. The positive discipline exercised by their work in good part runs counter to the habit of thinking in conventional, anthropomorphic terms, whether the conventionality is that of natural rights or any other. And in respect of this positive training away from conventional norms, there is a large divergence between the several lines of industrial employment. In proportion as a given line of employment has more of the character of a machine process and less of the character of handicraft, the matter-of-fact training which it gives is more pronounced. In a sense more intimate than the inventors of the phrase seem to have appreciated, the machine has become the master of the man who works with it and an arbiter in the cultural fortunes of the community into whose life it has entered.

The intellectual and spiritual training of the machine in modern life, therefore, is very far-reaching. It leaves but a small proportion of the community untouched; but while its constraint is ramified throughout the body of the population, and constrains virtually all classes at some points in their daily life, it falls with the most direct, intimate, and unmitigated impact upon the skilled mechanical classes, for these have no respite from its mastery, whether they are at work or at play. The ubiquitous presence of the machine, with its spiritual concomitant—workday ideals and scepticism of what is only conventionally valid is the unequivocal mark of the Western culture of to-day as contrasted with the culture of other times and places.

It pervades all classes and strata in a varying degree, but on an average in a greater degree than at any time in the past, and most potently in the advanced industrial communities and in the classes immediately in contact with the mechanical occupations. As the comprehensive mechanical organization of the material side of life has gone on, a heightening of this cultural effect throughout the community has also supervened, and with a farther and faster movement in the same direction a farther accentuation of this 'modern' complexion of culture is fairly to be looked for, unless some remedy be found. And as the concomitant differentiation and specialization of occupations goes on, a still more unmitigated discipline falls upon ever widening classes of the population, resulting in an ever weakening sense of conviction, allegiance, or piety toward the received institutions.

THE NATURAL DECAY OF BUSINESS ENTERPRISE

Broadly, the machine discipline acts to disintegrate the institutional heritage, of all degrees of antiquity and authenticity—whether it be the institutions that embody the principles of natural liberty or those that comprise the residue of more archaic principles of conduct still current in civilized life. It thereby cuts away that ground of law and order on which business enterprise is founded. The further cultural bearing of this disintegration of the received order is no doubt sufficiently serious and far-reaching, but it does not directly concern the present inquiry. It comes in question here only in so far as such a deterioration of the general cultural tissues involves a setback to the continued vigor of business enterprise. But the future of business enterprise is bound up with the future of civilization, since the cultural scheme is, after all, a single one, comprising many interlocking elements, no one of which can be greatly disturbed without disturbing the working of all the rest.

In its bearing on the question in hand, the 'social problem' at large presents this singular situation. The growth of business enterprise rests on the machine technology as its material foundation. The machine industry is indispensable to it; it cannot get along without the machine process, But the discipline of the machine process cuts away the spiritual, institutional foundations of business enterprise; the machine industry is incompatible with its continued growth; it cannot, in the long run, get along with the machine process. In their struggle against the cultural effects of the machine process, therefore, business principles cannot win in the long run; since an effectual mutilation or inhibition of the machine system would gradually push business enterprise to the wall; whereas with a free growth of the machine system business principles would presently fall into abeyance.

The institutional basis of business enterprise—the system of natural rights—appears to be a peculiarly instable affair. There is no way of retaining it under changing circumstances, and there is no way of returning to it after circumstances have changed. It is a hybrid growth, a blend of personal freedom and equality on the one hand and of prescriptive rights on the other hand. The institutions and points of law under the natural-rights scheme appear to be of an essentially provisional character. There is relatively great flexibility and possibility of growth and change; natural rights are singularly insecure under any change of circumstances. The maxim is well approved that eternal vigilance is the price of (natural) liberty. When, as now, this system is endangered by socialistic or anarchistic disaffection there is no recourse that will carry the institutional apparatus back to a secure natural-rights basis. The system of natural liberty was the product of a peaceful regime of handicraft and petty trade; but continued peace and industry presently carried the cultural growth beyond the phase of natural rights by giving rise to the machine process and the large business; and these are breaking down the structure of natural rights by making these rights nugatory on the one hand and by cutting away the spiritual foundations of them on the other hand. Natural rights being a by-product of peaceful industry, they cannot be reinstated by a recourse to warlike habits and a coercive government, since warlike habits and coercion are alien to the natural-rights spirit. Nor can they be reinstated by a recourse to settled peace and freedom, since an era of settled peace and freedom would push on the dominance of the machine process and the large business, which break down the system of natural liberty.

When the question is cast up as to what will come of this conflict of institutional forces—called the Social Problem—it is commonly made a question of remedies: What can be done to save civilized mankind from the vulgarization and disintegration wrought by the machine industry?

Now, business enterprise and the machine process are the two prime movers in modern culture; and the only recourse that holds a promise of being effective, therefore, is a recourse to the workings of business traffic. And this is a question, not of what is conceivably, ideally, idyllically possible for the business community to do if they will take thought and act advisedly and concertedly toward a chosen cultural outcome, but of what is the probable cultural outcome to be achieved through business traffic carried on for business ends, not for cultural ends. It is a question not of what ought to be done, but of what is to take place.

Persons who are solicitous for the cultural future commonly turn to speculative advice as to what ought to be done toward holding fast that which is good in the cultural heritage, and what ought further to be done to increase the talent that has been intrusted to this generation. The practical remedy offered is commonly some proposal for palliative measures, some appeal to philanthropic, aesthetic, or religious sentiment, some endeavor to conjure with the name of one or another of the epiphenomena of modern culture. Something must be done, it is conceived, and this something takes the shape of charity organizations, clubs and societies for social 'purity', for amusement, education, and manual training of the indigent classes, for colonization of the poor, for popularization of churches, for clean politics, for cultural missionary work by social settlements, and the like. These remedial measures whereby it is proposed to save or to rehabilitate certain praiseworthy but obsolescent habits of life and of thought are, all and several, beside the point so far as touches the question in hand. Not that it is hereby intended to cast a slur on these meritorious endeavors to save mankind by treating symptoms. The symptoms treated are no doubt evil, as they are said to be; or if they are not evil, the merits of that particular question do not concern the present inquiry. The endeavors in question are beside the point in that they do not fall into the shape of a business proposition. They are, on the whole, not so profitable a line of investment as certain other ventures that are open to modern enterprise. Hence, if they traverse the course of business enterprise and of industrial exigencies, they are nugatory, being in the same class with the labor of Sisyphus; whereas if they coincide in effect with the line along which business and industrial exigencies move, they are a work of supererogation, except so far as they may be conceived to accelerate a change that is already under way.

The Two Modes of Cultural History

Shulamith Firestone

1970

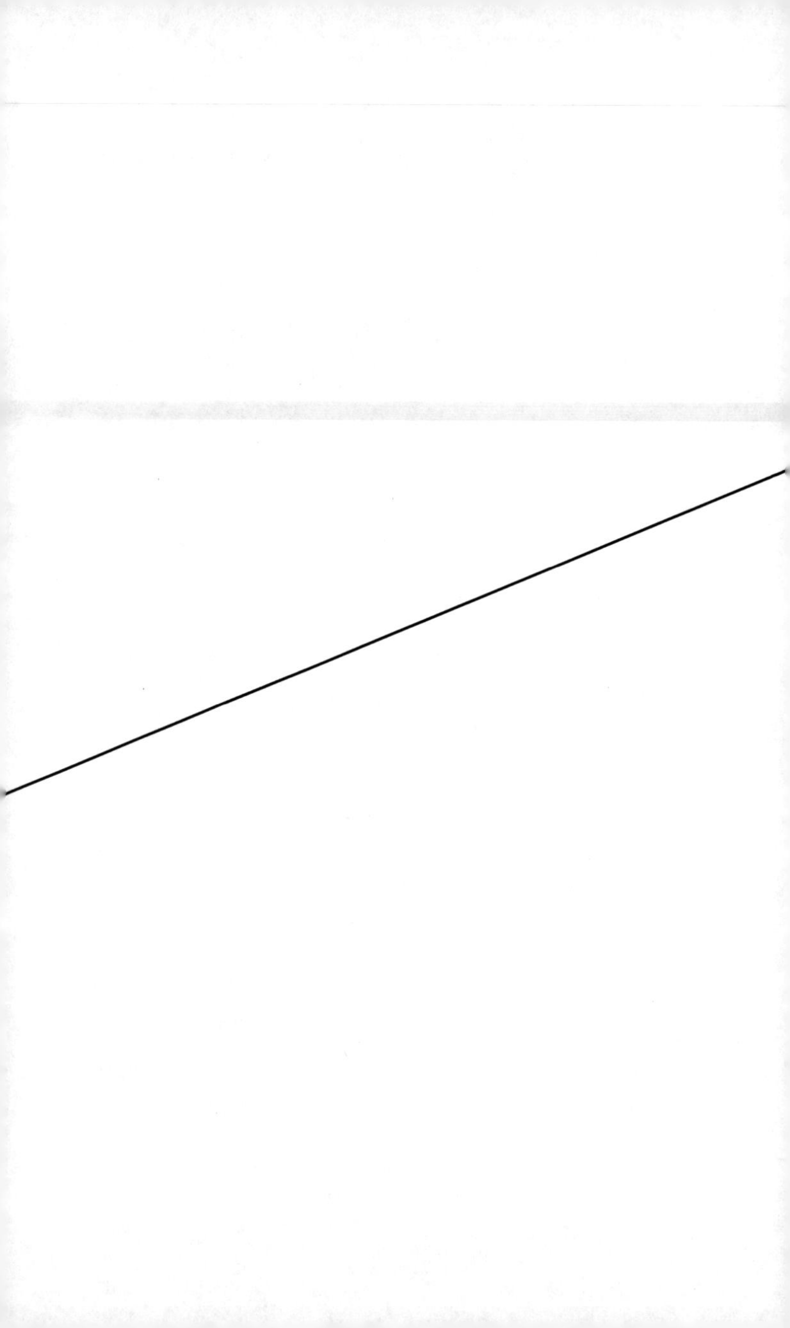

For our analysis we shall define culture in the following way: Culture is the attempt by man to realize the conceivable in the possible. Man's consciousness of himself within his environment distinguishes him from the lower animals, and turns him into the only animal capable of culture. This consciousness, his highest faculty, allows him to project mentally states of being that do not exist at the moment. Able to construct a past and future, he becomes a creature of time—a historian and a prophet. More than this, he can imagine objects and states of being that have never existed and may never exist in the real world—he becomes a maker of art. Thus, for example, though the ancient Greeks did not know how to fly, still they could imagine it. The myth of Icarus was the formulation in fantasy of their conception of the state 'flying'.

But man was not only able to project the conceivable into fantasy. He also learned to impose it on reality: by accumulating knowledge, learning experience, about that reality and how to handle it, he could shape it to his liking. This accumulation of skills for controlling the environment, technology, is another means to reaching the same end, the realization of the conceivable in the possible. Thus, in our example, if, in the BC era, man could fly on the magic carpet of myth or fantasy, by the twentieth century, his technology, the accumulation of his practical skills, had made it possible for him to fly in actuality—he had invented the airplane. Another example: In the Biblical legend, the Jews, an agricultural people stranded for forty years in the desert, were provided by God with Manna, a miraculous substance that could be transformed at will into food of any color, texture, or taste; modern food processing, especially with the 'green revolution', will probably soon create a totally artificial food production, perhaps with this chameleon attribute. Again, in ancient legend, man could imagine mixed species, e.g., the centaur or the unicorn, or hybrid births, like the birth of an animal from a human, or a virgin birth;

the current biological revolution, with its increasing knowledge of the reproductive process, could now—if only the first crude stages—generate these monstrosities in reality. Brownies and elves, the Golem of medieval Jewish lore, Mary Shelley's monster in *Frankenstein*, were the imaginative constructions that preceded by several centuries the corresponding technological acumen. Many other fantastical constructions—ghosts, mental telepathy, Methuselah's age—remain to be realized by modern science.

These two different responses, the idealistic and the scientific, do not merely exist simultaneously: there is a dialogue between the two. The imaginative construction precedes the technological, though often it does not develop until the technological knowhow is 'in the air'. For example, the art of science fiction developed, in the main, only a half-century in advance of, and now coexists with, the scientific revolution that is transforming it into a reality—for example (an innocuous one), the moon flight. The phrases 'way out', 'far out', 'spaced', the observation 'it's like something out of science fiction' are common language. In the aesthetic response, because it always develops in advance, and is thus the product of another age, the same realization may take on a sensational or idealistic cast, e.g., Frankenstein's monster, as opposed to, let us say, General Electric's CAM (Cybernetic Anthropomorphic Machines) Handyman. (An artist can never know in advance just how his vision might be articulated in reality.)

Culture then is the sum of, and the dynamic between, the two modes through which the mind attempts to transcend the limitations and contingencies of reality. These two types of cultural responses entail different methods to achieve the same end, the realization of the conceivable in the possible. In the first,[1] the individual denies the limitations of the given reality by escaping from

---

1. The idealistic mode corresponding roughly to the suprahistorical, nonmaterialist 'metaphysical' mode of thought against which Marx and Engels revolted.

it altogether, to define, create, his own possible. In the provinces of the imagination, objectified in some way—whether through the development of a visual image within some artificial boundary, say four square feet of canvas, through visual images projected through verbal symbols (poetry), with sound ordered into a sequence (music), or with verbal ideas ordered into a progression (theology, philosophy)—he creates an ideal world governed by his own artificially imposed order and harmony, a structure in which he consciously relates each part to the whole, a static (and therefore 'timeless') construction. The degree to which he abstracts his creation from reality is unimportant, for even when he most appears to imitate, he has created an illusion governed by its own—perhaps hidden—set of artificial laws. (Degas said that the artist had to lie in order to tell the truth.) This search for the ideal, realized by means of an artificial medium, we shall call the Aesthetic Mode.

In the second type of cultural response the contingencies of reality are overcome, not through the creation of an alternate reality, but through the mastery of reality's own workings: the laws of nature are exposed, then turned against it, to shape it in accordance with man's conception. If there is a poison, man assumes there is an antidote; if there is a disease, he searches for the cure: every fact of nature that is understood can be used to alter it. But to achieve the ideal through such a procedure takes much longer, and is infinitely more painful, especially in the early stages of knowledge. For the vast and intricate machine of nature must be entirely understood—and there are always fresh and unexpected layers of complexity before it can be thoroughly controlled. Thus before any solution can be found to the deepest contingencies of the human condition, e.g., death, natural processes of growth and decay must be catalogued, smaller laws related to larger ones. This scientific method (also attempted by Marx and Engels in their materialist approach to history) is the attempt by man to master nature through the complete understanding of its mechanics. The coaxing of reality to conform with man's conceptual ideal, through the application of information extrapolated from itself, we shall call the Technological Mode.

We have defined culture as the sum of, and the dialectic between, the two different modes through which man can resolve the tension created by the flexibility of his mental faculties within the limitations of his given environment. The correspondence of these two different cultural modes with the two sexes respectively is unmistakable. We have noted how those few women directly creating culture have gravitated to disciplines within the Aesthetic Mode. There is a good reason for this: the aesthetic response corresponds with 'female' behavior. The same terminology can be applied to either: subjective, intuitive, introverted, wishful, dreamy or fantastic, concerned with the subconscious (the id), emotional, even temperamental (hysterical). Correspondingly, the technological response is the masculine response: objective, logical, extroverted, realistic, concerned with the conscious mind (the ego), rational, mechanical, pragmatic and down-to-earth, stable. Thus the aesthetic is the cultural recreation of that half of the psychological spectrum that has been appropriated to the female, whereas the technological response is the cultural magnification of the male half.

Just as we have assumed the biological division of the sexes for procreation to be the fundamental 'natural' duality from which grows all further division into classes, so we now assume the sex division to be the root of this basic cultural division as well. The interplay between these two cultural responses, the 'male' Technological Mode and the 'female' Aesthetic Mode, recreates at yet another level the dialectic of the sexes—as well as its superstructure, the caste and the economic-class dialectic. And just as the merging of the divided sexual, racial, and economic classes is a precondition for sexual, racial, or economic revolution respectively, so the merging of the aesthetic with the technological culture is the precondition of a cultural revolution. And just as the revolutionary goal of the sexual, racial, and economic revolutions is, rather than a mere leveling of imbalances of class, an elimination of class categories altogether, so the end result of a cultural revolution must be, not merely the integration of the two streams of culture, but the elimination of cultural categories altogether, the elimination of culture itself as we know it. But before we discuss this ultimate cultural revolution or even the state of cultural division in our own time, let us see how this third level of the sex dialectic—the interaction between the Technological and Aesthetic Modes—operated to determine the flow of cultural history.

*

At first technological knowledge accumulated slowly. Gradually man learned to control the crudest aspects of his environment—he discovered the tool, control of fire, the wheel, the melting of ore to make weapons and plows, even, eventually, the alphabet—but these discoveries were few and far between, because as yet he had no systematic way of initiating them. Eventually however, he had gathered enough practical knowledge to build whole systems, e.g., medicine or architecture, to create juridical, political, social, and economic institutions. Civilization developed the primitive hunting horde into an agricultural society, and finally, through progressive stages, into feudalism, capitalism, and the first attempts at socialism.

But in all this time, man's ability to picture an Ideal world was far ahead of his ability to create one. The primary cultural forms of ancient civilizations—religion and its offshoots, mythology, legend, primitive art and magic, prophesy and history—were in the Aesthetic Mode: they imposed only an artificial, imaginary order on a universe still mysterious and chaotic. Even primitive scientific theories were only poetic metaphors for what would later be realized empirically. The science and philosophy and mathematics of classical antiquity, forerunners of modem science, by sheer imaginative prowess, operating in a vacuum independently of material laws, anticipated much of what was later proven: Democritus' atoms and Lucretius' 'substance' foreshadowed by thousands of years the discoveries of modern science. But they were realized only within the realm of the imaginary Aesthetic Mode.

In the Middle Ages the Judaeo-Christian heritage was assimilated with pagan culture, to produce medieval religious art and the metaphysics of Thomas Aquinas and the Scholastics. Though concurrently Arab, science, an outgrowth of the Greek Alexandrian Period (third century BC to seventh century AD), was amassing considerable information in such areas as geography, astronomy, physiology, mathematics—a tabulation essential to the later empiricism—there was little dialogue. Western science with its alchemy, its astrology, the 'humours' of medieval medicine, was still in a 'pseudo-scientific' stage, or in our definition, still operating according to the Aesthetic Mode. This medieval aesthetic culture, composed of the Classical and Christian legacies, culminated in the Humanism of the Renaissance.

Until the Renaissance, then, culture occurred in the Aesthetic Mode because, prior to that time, technology had been so primitive, the body of scientific knowledge so far from complete. In terms of the sex dialectic, this long stage of cultural history corresponds with the matriarchal stage of civilization: The Female Principal—dark, mysterious, uncontrollable—reigned, elevated by man himself, still in awe of unfathomable Nature. Men of culture were its high priests of homage: until and through the Renaissance *all* men of culture were practitioners of the ideal aesthetic mode, thus, in a sense, artists. The Renaissance, the pinnacle of cultural humanism, was the golden age of the Aesthetic (female) Mode.

And also the beginning of its end. By the sixteenth century culture was undergoing a change as profound as the shift from matriarchy to patriarchy in terms of the sex dialectic, and corresponding to the decline of feudalism in the class dialectic. This was the first merging of the aesthetic culture with the technological, in the creation of modern (empirical) science.

In the Renaissance, Aristotelian Scholasticism had remained powerful though the first cracks in the dam were already apparent. But it was not until Francis Bacon, who first proposed to use science to 'extend more widely the limits of the power and the greatnesses of man,' that the marriage of the Modes was consummated. Bacon and Locke transformed philosophy, the attempt to understand life, from abstract speculation detached from the real world (metaphysics, ethics, theology, aesthetics, logic) to an uncovering of the *real* laws of nature, through proof and demonstration (empirical science).

In the empirical method propounded by Francis Bacon, insight and imagination had to be used only at the earliest stage of the inquiry. Tentative hypotheses would be formed by induction from the facts, and then consequences would be deduced logically and tested for consistency among themselves and for agreement with the primary facts and results of *ad hoc* experiments. The hypothesis would become an accepted theory only after all tests had been passed, and would remain, at least until proven wrong, a theory capable of predicting phenomena to a high degree of probability.

The empirical view held that by recording and tabulating all possible observations and experiments in this manner, the Natural Order would emerge automatically. Though at first the question 'why' was still asked as often as the question 'how', after information began to accumulate, each discovery building upon the last to complete the jigsaw, the speculative, the intuitive, and the imaginative gradually became less valuable. When once the initial foundations had been laid by men of the stature of Kepler, Galileo, and Newton, thinkers still in the inspired 'aesthetic' science tradition, hundreds of anonymous technicians could move to fill in the blanks, leading to, in our own time, the dawn of a golden age of science—to the Technological Mode what the Renaissance had been to the Aesthetic Mode.

THE TWO CULTURES TODAY

Now, in 1970, we are experiencing a major scientific breakthrough. The new physics, relativity, and the astrophysical theories of contemporary science had already been realized by the first part of this century. Now, in the latter part, we are arriving, with the help of the electron microscope and other new tools, at similar achievements in biology, biochemistry, and all the life sciences. Important discoveries are made yearly by small, scattered work teams all over the United States, and in other countries as well—of the magnitude of DNA in genetics, or of Urey and Miller's work in the early fifties on the origins of life. Full mastery of the reproductive process is in sight, and there has been significant advance in understanding the basic life and death process. The nature of aging and growth, sleep and hibernation, the chemical functioning of the brain and the development of consciousness and memory are all beginning to be understood in their entirety. This acceleration promises to continue for another century, or however long it takes to achieve the goal of Empiricism: total understanding of the laws of nature.

This amazing accumulation of concrete knowledge in only a few hundred years is the product of philosophy's switch from the Aesthetic to the Technological Mode. The combination of 'pure' science, science in the Aesthetic Mode, with pure technology, caused greater progress toward the goal of technology—the realization of the conceivable in the actual—than had been made in thousands of years of previous history.

Empiricism itself is only the means, a quicker and more effective technique, for achieving technology's ultimate cultural goal: the building of the ideal in the real world. One of its own basic dictates is that a certain amount of material must be collected and arranged into categories before any decisive comparison, analysis, or discovery can be made. In this light, the centuries of empirical science have been little more than the building of foundations for the breakthroughs of our own time and the future. The amassing of information and understanding of the laws and mechanical processes of nature ('pure research') is but a means to a larger end: total understanding of Nature in order, ultimately, to achieve transcendence.

In this view of the development and goals of cultural history, Engels' final goal, quoted above in the context of political revolution, is again worthy of quotation:

> The whole sphere of the conditions of life which environ man, and have hitherto ruled him, now comes under the dominion and control of man, who for the first time becomes the real conscious Lord of Nature.

Empirical science is to culture what the shift to patriarchy was to the sex dialectic, and what the bourgeois period is to the Marxian dialectic—a latter-day stage prior to revolution. Moreover, the three dialectics are integrally related to one another vertically as well as horizontally: The empirical science growing out of the bourgeoisie (the bourgeois period is in itself a stage of the patriarchal period) follows the humanism of the aristocracy (The Female Principle, the matriarchy) and with its development of the empirical method in order to amass real knowledge (development of modern industry in order to amass capital) eventually puts itself out of business. The body of scientific discovery (the new productive modes) must finally outgrow the empirical (capitalistic) mode of using them.

And just as the internal contradictions of capitalism must become increasingly apparent, so must the internal contradictions of empirical science—as in the development of pure knowledge to the point where it assumes a life of its own, e.g., the atomic bomb. As long as man is still engaged only in the means—the charting of the ways of nature, the gathering of 'pure' knowledge—to his final realization, mastery of nature, his knowledge, because it is not complete, is dangerous. So dangerous that many scientists are wondering whether they shouldn't put a lid on certain types of research. But this solution is hopelessly inadequate. The machine of empiricism has its own momentum, and is, for such purposes, completely out of control. Could one actually decide what to discover or not discover? That is, by definition, antithetical to the whole empirical process that Bacon set in motion. Many of the most important discoveries have been practically laboratory accidents, with social implications barely realized by the scientists who stumbled into them. For example, as recently as five years ago Professor F. C. Steward of Cornell discovered a process called 'cloning': by placing a single carrot cell in a rotating nutrient he was able to grow a whole sheet of identical carrot cells, from which he eventually recreated the same carrot. The understanding of a similar process for more developed animal cells, were it to slip out—as did experiments with 'mind-expanding' drugs—could have some awesome implications. Or, again, imagine parthenogenesis, virgin birth, as practiced by the greenfly, actually applied to human fertility.

Another internal contradiction in empirical science: the mechanistic, deterministic, 'soulless' scientific world view, which is the result of the means to, rather than the (inherently noble and often forgotten) ultimate purpose of, Empiricism: the actualization of the ideal in reality.

The cost in humanity is particularly high to the scientist himself, who becomes little more than a cultural technician. For, ironically enough, to properly accumulate knowledge of the universe requires a mentality the very opposite of comprehensive and integrated. Though in the long run the efforts of the individual scientist could lead to domination of the environment in the interest of humanity, temporarily the empirical method demands that its practitioners themselves become 'objective,' mechanistic, overprecise. The public image of the white-coated Dr. Jekyll with no feelings for his subjects, mere guinea pigs, is not entirely false: there is no room for feelings in the scientist's work; he is forced to eliminate or isolate them in what amounts to an occupational hazard. At best he can resolve this problem by separating his professional from his personal self, by compartmentalizing his emotion. Thus, though often well-versed in an academic way about the arts—the frequency of this, at any rate, is higher than of artists who are well-versed in science—the scientist is generally out of touch with his direct emotions and senses, or, at best, he is emotionally divided. His 'private' and 'public' life are out of whack; and because his personality is not well-integrated, he can be surprisingly conventional ('Dear, I discovered how to clone people at the lab today. Now we can go skiing at Aspen.') He feels no contradiction in living by convention, even in attending church, for he has never integrated the amazing material of modern science with his daily life. Often it takes the misuse of his discovery to alert him to that connection which he has long since lost in his own mind.

The catalogue of scientific vices is familiar: it duplicates, exaggerates the catalogue of 'male' vices in general. This is to be expected: if the Technological Mode develops from the male principle then it follows that its practitioners would develop the warpings of the male personality in the extreme. But let us leave science for the moment, winding up for the ultimate cultural revolution, to see what meanwhile had been happening to the aesthetic culture proper.

With philosophy in the broadest classical sense—including 'pure' science—defecting, aesthetic culture became increasingly narrow and ingrown, reduced to the arts and humanities in the refined sense that we now know them. Art (hereafter referring to the 'liberal arts,' especially the arts and letters) had always been, in its very definition, a search for the ideal, removed from the real world. But in primitive days it had been the handmaiden of religion, articulating the common dream, objectifying 'other' worlds of the common fantasy, e.g., the art of the Egyptian tombs, to explain and excuse this one. Thus even though it was removed from the real world, it served an important social function: it satisfied artificially those wishes of society that couldn't yet be realized in reality. Though it was patronized and supported only by the aristocracy, the cultured elite, it was never as detached from life as it later became; for the society of those times was, for all practical purposes, synonymous with its ruling class, whether priesthood, monarchy, or nobility. The masses were never considered by 'society' to be a legitimate part of humanity, they were slaves, nothing more than human animals, drones, or serfs, without whose labor the small cultured elite could not have maintained itself.

The gradual squeezing out of the aristocracy by the new middle class, the bourgeoisie, signalled the erosion of aesthetic culture. We have seen that capitalism intensified the worst attributes of patriarchalism, how, for example, the nuclear family emerged from the large, loose family household of the past, to reinforce the weakening sex class system, oppressing women and children more intimately than ever before. The cultural mode favored by this new, heavily patriarchal bourgeoisie was the 'male' Technological Mode—objective, realistic, factual, 'common sense'—rather than the effeminate, otherworldly, 'romantic idealist' Aesthetic Mode. The bourgeoisie, searching for the ideal in the real, soon developed the empirical science that we have described. To the extent that they had any remaining use for aesthetic culture, it was only for 'realistic' art, as opposed to the 'idealistic' art of classical antiquity, or the abstract religious art of primitive or medieval times. For a time they went in for a literature that described reality—best exemplified by the nineteenth-century novel—and a decorative easel art: still lifes, portraits, family scenes, interiors. Public museums and libraries were built alongside the old salons and private galleries. But with its entrenchment as a secure, primary, class, the bourgeoisie no longer needed to imitate aristocratic cultivation. More important, with the rapid development of their new science and technology, the little practical value they had for art was eclipsed. Take the scientific development of the camera: The bourgeoisie soon had little need for portrait painters; the little that painters or novelists had been able to do for them, the camera could do better.

'Modern' art was a desperate, but finally self-defeating, retaliation ('*épater le bourgeois*') for these injuries: the evaporation of its social function, the severance of the social umbilical cord, the dwindling of the old sources of patronage. The modern art tradition, associated primarily with Picasso and Cézanne, and including all the major schools of the twentieth century—cubism, constructivism futurism expressionism, surrealism, abstract expressionism, and so on—is not an authentic expression of modernity as much as it is a reaction to the realism of the bourgeoisie. Post-impressionism deliberately renounced all reality-affirming conventions—indeed the process began with impressionism itself, which broke down the illusion into its formal values, swallowing reality whole and spitting it up again as art—to lead eventually to an art-for-art's-sake so pure, a negation of reality so complete as to make it ultimately meaningless, sterile, even absurd. (Cab drivers *are* philistine: they know a put-on when they see one.) The deliberate violating, deforming, fracturing of the image, called 'modern' art, was nothing more than a fifty-year idol smashing—eventually leading to our present cultural Impasse.

In the twentieth century, its life blood drained, its social function nullified altogether, art is thrown back on whatever wealthy classes remain, those *nouveaux riches*—particularly in America, still suffering from a cultural inferiority complex—who still need to prove they have 'arrived' by evidencing a taste for culture. The sequestering of intellectuals in ivory tower universities, where, except for the sciences, they have little effect on the outside world, no matter how brilliant (and they aren't, because they no longer have the necessary feedback); the abstruse—often literally unintelligible—jargon of the social sciences; the cliquish literary quarterlies with their esoteric poetry; the posh 57th Street galleries and museums (it is no accident that they are right next door to Saks Fifth Avenue and Bonwit Teller) staffed and supplied by, for the most part, fawning rich-widows'-hairdresser types; and not least the vulturous critical establishment thriving on the remains of what was once a great and vital culture—all testify to the death of aesthetic humanism.

For the centuries that Science climbed to new heights, Art decayed. Its forced inbreeding transformed it into a secret code. By definition escapist from reality, it now turned in upon itself to such degree that it gnawed away its own vitals. It became diseased—neurotically self-pitying, self-conscious, focused on the past (as opposed to the futurist orientation of the technological culture) and thus frozen into conventions and academies—orthodoxies of which 'avant-garde' is only the latest—pining for remembered glories, the Grand Old Days When Beauty Was In Flower; it became pessimistic and nihilistic, increasingly hostile to the society at large, the 'philistines.' And when the cocky young Science attempted to woo Art from its ivory tower—eventually garret—with false promises of the courting lover ('You can come down now, we're making the world a better place every day'), Art refused more vehemently than ever to deal with him, much less accept his corrupt gifts, retreating ever deeper into her daydreams—neoclassicism, romanticism, expressionism, surrealism, existentialism.

The individual artist or intellectual saw himself as either a member of an invisible elite, a 'highbrow,' or as a down-and-outer, mingling with whoever was deemed the dregs of his society. In both cases, whether playing Aristocrat or Bohemian, he was on the margin of the society as a whole. The artist had become a freak. His increasing alienation from the world around him—the new world that science had created was, especially in its primitive stages, an incredible horror, only intensifying his need to escape to the ideal world of art—his lack of an audience, led to a mystique of 'genius.' Like an ascetic Saint Simeon on his pedestal, the Genius in the Garret was expected to create masterpieces in a vacuum. But his artery to the outside world had been severed. His task, increasingly impossible, often forced him into literal madness or suicide.

Painted into a corner with nowhere else to go the artist has got to begin to come to terms with the modern world. He is not too good at it: like an invalid shut away too long, he doesn't know anything about the world anymore, neither politics, not science, nor even how to live or love. Until now, yes, even now, though less and less so, sublimation, that warping of personality, was commendable: it was the only (albeit indirect) way to achieve fulfilment. But the artistic process has—almost—outlived its usefulness. And its price is high.

The first attempts to confront the modem world have been for the most part misguided. The Bauhaus, a famous example, failed at its objective of replacing an irrelevant easel art (only a few optical illusions and designy chairs mark the grave), ending up with a hybrid, neither art nor science, and certainly not the sum of the two. They failed because they didn't understand science on its own terms:

to them, seeing in the old aesthetic way, it was simply a rich new subject matter to be digested whole into the traditional aesthetic system. It is as if one were to see a computer as only a beautifully ordered set of lights and sounds, missing completely the function itself. The scientific experiment is not only beautiful, an elegant structure, another piece of an abstract puzzle, something to be used in the next collage—but scientists, too, in their own way, see science as this abstraction divorced from life—it has a real intrinsic meaning of its own, similar to, but not the same as, the 'presence,' the '*en-soi,*' of modern painting. Many artists have made the mistake of thus trying to annex science, to incorporate it into their own artistic framework, rather than using it to expand that framework.

Is the current state of aesthetic culture all bleak? No, there have been some progressive developments in contemporary art. We have mentioned how the realistic tradition in painting died with the camera. This tradition had developed over centuries to a level of illusionism with the brush—examine a Bouguereau—that was the equal of, better than, the early photography, then considered only another graphic medium, like etching. The beginning of the new art of film and the realistic tradition of painting overlapped, peaked, in artists like Degas, who used a camera in his work. Then realistic art took a new course: Either it became decadent, academic, divorced from any market and meaning, e.g., the nudes that linger on in art classes and second-rate galleries, or it was fractured into the expressionist or surrealist image, posing an alternate internal or fantastical reality. Meanwhile, however, the young art of film, based on a true synthesis of the Aesthetic and Technological Modes (as Empiricism itself had been), carried on the vital realistic tradition. And just as with the marriage of the divided male and female principles, empirical science bore fruit; so did the medium of film. But, unlike other aesthetic media of the past, it broke down the very division between the artificial and the real, between culture and life itself, on which the Aesthetic Mode is based.

Other related developments: the exploration of artificial materials, e.g., plastics; the attempt to confront plastic culture itself (pop art); the breakdown of traditional categories of media (mixed media), and of the distinctions between art and reality itself (happenings, environments). But I find it difficult to unreservedly call these latter developments progressive: as yet they have produced largely puerile and meaningless works. The artist does not yet know what reality is, let alone how to affect it. Paper cups lined up on the street, pieces of paper thrown into an empty lot, no matter how many ponderous reviews they get in *Art News*, are a waste of time. If these clumsy attempts are at all hopeful, it is only insofar as they are signs of the breakdown of 'fine' art.

The merging of the Aesthetic with the Technological Mode will gradually suffocate 'pure' high art altogether. The first breakdown of categories, the remerging of art with a (technologized) reality, indicate that we are now in the transitional pre-revolutionary period, in which the three separate cultural streams, technology ('applied science'), 'pure research,' and 'pure' modern art, will melt together—along with the rigid sex categories they reflect.

The sex-based polarity of culture still causes many casualties. If even the 'pure' scientist, e.g., nuclear physicist (let alone the 'applied', scientist, e.g., engineer), suffers from too much 'male,' becoming authoritarian, conventional, emotionally insensitive, narrowly unable to understand his own work within the scientific—let alone cultural or social—jigsaw, the artist, in terms of the sex division, has embodied all the imbalances and suffering of the female personality: temperamental, insecure, paranoid, defeatist, narrow. And the recent withholding of reinforcements from behind the front (the larger society) has exaggerated all this enormously; his overdeveloped 'id' has nothing left to balance it. Where the pure scientist is 'schiz,' or worse, *ignorant* of emotional reality altogether, the pure artist *rejects* reality because of its lack of perfection, and, in modem centuries, for its ugliness.[2]

And who suffers the most, the blind (scientist) or the lame (artist)? Culturally, we have had only the choice between one sex role or the other: either a social marginality leading to self-consciousness, introversion, defeatism, pessimism, oversensitivity, and lack of touch with reality, or a split 'professionalized' personality, emotional ignorance, the narrow views of the specialist.

CONCLUSION: THE ANTICULTURE REVOLUTION

I have tried to show how the history of culture mirrors the sex dichotomy in its very organization and development. Culture develops not only out of the underlying economic dialectic, but also out of the deeper sex dialectic. Thus, there is not only a horizontal dynamic, but a vertical one as well: each of these three strata forms one more story of the dialectics of history based on the biological dualism. At present we have reached the final stages of Patriarchalism, Capitalism (corporate capitalism), and of the Two Cultures at once. We shall soon have a triplicate set of preconditions for revolution, the absence of which is responsible for the failure of revolutions of the past.

The difference between what is almost possible and what exists is generating revolutionary forces.[3] We are nearing— I believe we shall have, perhaps within a century, if the snowball of empirical knowledge doesn't smash first of its own velocity—a cultural revolution, as well as a sexual and economic one.

---

2. One abstract painter I knew, who had experienced the horrors of North African battlefields in World War II—fields of men (buddies) rotting in the sun with rats darting out of their stomachs—spent years moving a pure beige circle around a pure beige square. In this manner, the 'modern' artist denies the ugliness of reality (rats in the stomachs of buddies) in favor of artificial harmonies (circles in squares).

3. Revolutionaries, by definition, are still visionaries of the Aesthetic Mode, the idealists of pragmatic politics.

The cultural revolution, like the economic revolution, must be predicated on the elimination of the (sex) dualism at the origins not only of class, but also of cultural division.

What might this cultural revolution look like? Unlike 'cultural revolutions' of the past, it would not be merely a quantitative escalation, more and better culture, in the sense that the Renaissance was a high point of the Aesthetic Mode, or that the present technological breakthrough is the accumulation of centuries of practical knowledge about the real world. Great as they were, neither the Aesthetic nor the Technological culture, even at their respective peaks, ever achieved universality—either it was wholistic but divorced from the real world, or it 'achieved progress,' at the price of cultural schizophrenia, and the falseness and dryness of 'objectivity.' What we shall have in the next cultural revolution is the reintegration of the Male (Technological Mode) with the Female (Aesthetic Mode), to create an androgynous culture surpassing the highs of either cultural stream, or even of the sum of their integrations. More than a marriage, rather an abolition of the cultural categories themselves, a mutual cancellation—a matter-antimatter explosion, ending with a poof!—of culture itself.

We shall not miss it. We shall no longer need it: by then humanity will have mastered nature totally, will have realized in *actuality* its dreams. With the full achievement of the conceivable in the actual, the surrogate of culture will no longer be necessary. The sublimation process, a detour to wish fulfilment, will give way to direct satisfaction in experience, as felt now only by children, or adults on drugs. (Though normal adults 'play' to varying degrees, the example that illustrates more immediately to almost everyone the intense level of this future experience, ranking zero on a scale of accomplishment—'nothing to show for it'—but nevertheless somehow always worth everyone's while, is lovemaking.) Control and delay of 'id' satisfaction by the 'ego' will be unnecessary; the *id* can live free. Enjoyment will spring directly from being and acting itself, the process of experience, rather than from the quality of achievement. When the male Technological Mode can at last produce in actuality what the female Aesthetic Mode had envisioned we shall have eliminated the need for either.

Decline of the Capitalist Mode of Production or Decline of Humanity?

Jacques Camatte

1973

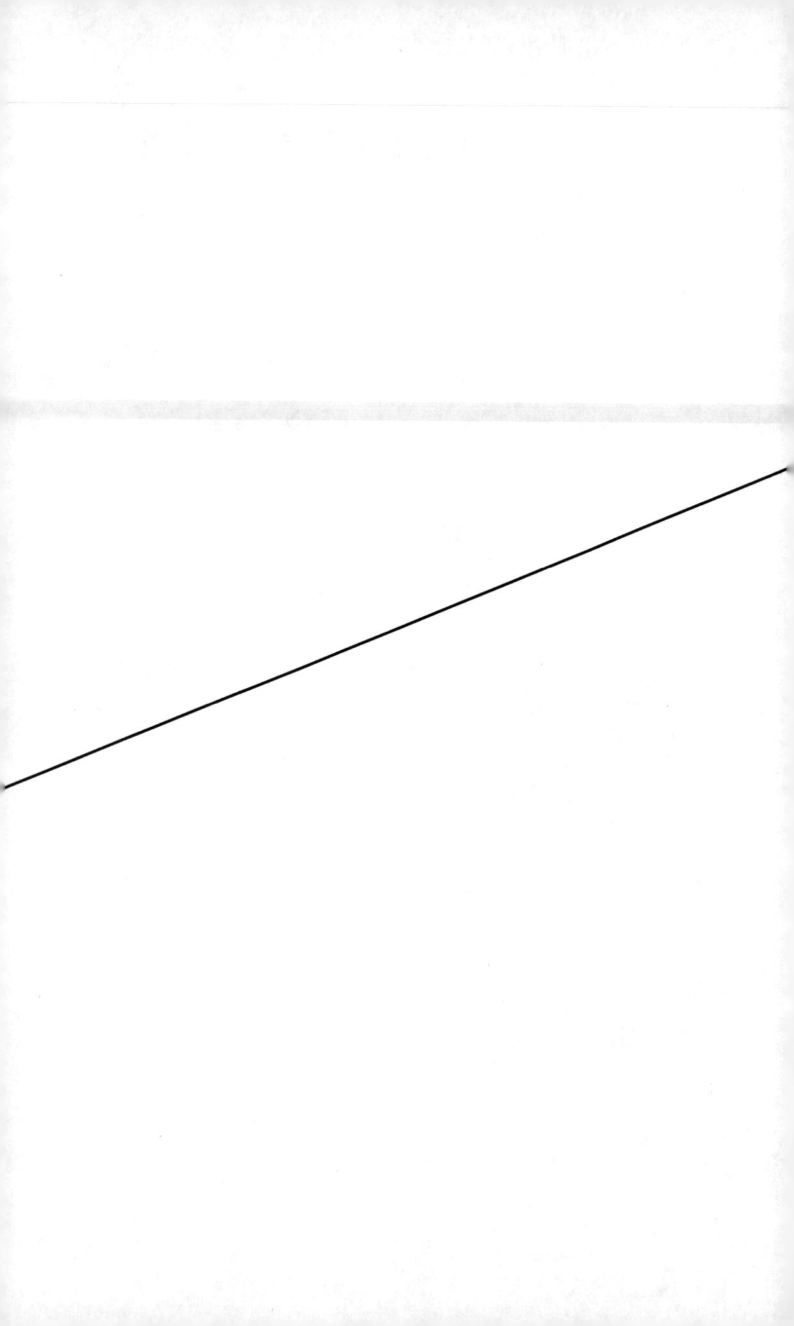

It has often been thought and written that communism would blossom after the destruction of the capitalist mode of production, which would be undermined by such contradictions that its end would be inevitable. But numerous events of this century have unfortunately brought other possibilities into view: the return to 'barbarism', as analyzed by R. Luxemburg and the entire left wing of the German workers' movement, by Adorno and the Frankfurt School; the destruction of the human species, as is evident to each and all today; finally a state of stagnation in which the capitalist mode of production survives by adapting itself to a degenerated humanity which lacks the power to destroy it. In order to understand the failure of a future that was thought inevitable, we must take into account the domestication of human beings implemented by all class societies and mainly by capital, and we must analyze the autonomization of capital.

We do not intend to treat these historical deviations exhaustively in a few pages. By commenting on a passage in Marx's *Grundrisse* we can show that it is possible to understand the autonomization of capital on the basis of Marx's work, and we can also see the contradictions in Marxist thought and its inability to solve the problem. The passage is from the chapter on the process of circulation. To understand it, we should keep in mind what Marx had said shortly before this passage:

> *Circulation time thus appears as a barrier to the productivity of labour* = an increase in necessary labour time = a decrease in surplus labour time = a decrease in surplus value = an obstruction, a barrier to the self-realization process [*Selbstverwertungsprozess*] of capital.[1]

---

1. K. Marx, *Grundrisse* (London: Pelican, 1973), 539.

Here Marx makes an extremely important digression:

> There appears here the universalizing tendency of capital, which distinguishes it from all previous stages of production and thus becomes the presupposition of a new mode of production, which is founded not on the development of the forces of production for the purpose of reproducing or at most expanding a given condition, but where the free, unobstructed, progressive and universal development of the forces of production is itself the presupposition of society and hence of its reproduction; where advance beyond the point of departure is the only presupposition.[2]

What makes capital a barrier is not stated here, whereas its revolutionary, positive aspect is emphasized (this aspect is emphasized on many other pages of the *Grundrisse*, and of *Capital*): the tendency toward universal development of the forces of production. However, and this is what interests us here, capital cannot realize this; it will be the task of another, superior mode of production. The future of society here takes the form of an indefinite, cumulative movement.

> This tendency—which capital possesses, but which at the same time, since capital is a limited form of production, contradicts it and hence drives it towards dissolution—distinguishes capital from all earlier modes of production, and at the same time contains this element, that capital is posited as a mere point of transition.[3]

Hence capital is driven towards dissolution by this contradiction. It is a pity that Marx did not here mention what he understands by 'limited form of production', since this keeps us from 'seeing'

---

2. Ibid., 540.

3. Ibid.

clearly what he means by contradiction in this specific case. This conditions the understanding of the statement that the capitalist mode of production is a transitory form of production. Even without an explanation of the contradiction, we can understand it as follows: the capitalist mode of production is not eternal—Marx's polemical argument against the bourgeois ideologues. This is the content of his main statements. But another argument is embedded in the preceding one: the capitalist mode of production is revolutionary and makes possible the passage to another, superior social form where human beings will no longer be dominated by the sphere of necessity (the sphere of the production of material life) and where alienation will cease to exist.

Today, after the blossoming of Marxism as a theory of development, another part of this sentence appears basic: there is a continuum between the two periods. What is a transition if not the opposite of a break? This continuum consists of the development of the forces of production. From which follows the shameful but real relationship: Marx-Lenin-Stalin! But this is not our topic. Our aim is to determine what constitutes the productive forces and for whom they exist, according to Marx in the *Grundrisse*,

> All previous forms of society—or, what is the same, of the forces of social production—foundered on the development of wealth.[4]

Wealth resides in the productive forces and in the results of their action. There is a contradiction here which, according to Marx, characterizes the totality of human history: wealth is necessary and therefore sought, but it destroys societies. Societies must therefore oppose its development. This is not the case in the capitalist mode of production (it thus destroys all other social formations), which exalts the productive forces, but for whom?

---

4. Ibid.

Those thinkers of antiquity who were possessed of consciousness therefore directly denounced wealth as the dissolution of the community [*Gemeinwesen*]. The feudal system, for its part, foundered on urban industry, trade, modern agriculture (even as a result of individual inventions like gunpowder and the printing press). With the development of wealth—and hence also new powers and expanded intercourse on the part of individuals—the economic conditions on which the community [*Gemeinwesen*] rested were dissolved, along with the political relations of the various constituents of the community which corresponded to those conditions: religion, in which it was viewed in idealized form (and both [religion and political relations] rested in turn on a given relation to nature, into which all productive force resolves itself); the character, outlook, etc. of the individuals. The development of science alone—i.e. the most solid form of wealth, both its product and its producer—was sufficient to dissolve these communities. But the development of science, this ideal and at the same time practical wealth, is only one aspect, one form in which the development of the human productive forces, i.e. of wealth, appears. Considered ideally, the dissolution of a given form of consciousness sufficed to kill a whole epoch. In reality, this barrier to consciousness corresponds to a definite degree of development of the forces of material production and hence of wealth. True, there was not only a development on the old basis, but also a development of this basis itself.[5]

For Marx, the productive forces are human (from the human being) and they are for the human being, for the individual. Science as a productive force (thus also wealth, as was already shown in the 1844 Manuscripts and in *The German Ideology*) is determined by the development of these forces and corresponds to the appearance of a large number of externalizations, a greater

5. Ibid., 540–1.

possibility to appropriate nature. Even if it takes an ambiguous form, the blossoming of the human being is possible; it is the moment when, in the development of the dominant class, individuals can find a model of a fuller life. For Marx, the capitalist mode of production, by pushing the development of productive forces, makes possible a liberating autonomization of the individual. This is its most important revolutionary aspect.

The highest development of this basis itself (the flower into which it transforms itself; but it is always this basis, this plant as flower; hence wilting after the flowering and as a consequence of the flowering) is the point at which it is itself worked out, developed, into the form in which it is compatible with the highest development of the forces of production, hence also the richest development of the individuals. As soon as this point is reached, the further development appears as decay, and the new development begins from a new basis.[6]

There is decay because the development of individuals is blocked. It is not possible to use this sentence to support the theory of the decline of the capitalist mode of production[7] since it would have to be stated that the decline started, not at the beginning of this century, but minimally in the middle of the previous century; or else it would have to be shown that the decline of individuals is simultaneously the decline of capital, which contradicts what can be observed; Marx himself repeatedly explained that the development of capital was accompanied by the destruction of human beings and of nature.

When did the development of productive forces accompany the development of individuals in different societies? When was the capitalist mode of production revolutionary for itself and for

6. Ibid., 541.

7. As is done by Victor in *Révolution Internationale* série 1, No. 7, 'Volontarisme et confusion', fourth page.

human beings? Do the productive forces advance continually, in spite of moments when individuals decay? Marx said: '...the further development appears as decay...'. Do the productive forces stagnate; does the capitalist mode of production decay?[8]

The remainder of Marx's digression confirms that the decay refers to human beings. Individuals blossom when the productive forces allow them to develop, when the evolution of one parallels the evolution of the other. By means of a comparison with the pre-capitalist period, Marx shows that capital is not hostile to wealth but, on the contrary, takes up its production. Thus it takes up the development of productive forces. Previously the development of human beings, of their community, was opposed to the development of wealth; now there is something like symbiosis between them. For this to happen, a certain mutation was necessary: capital had to destroy the limited character of the individual; this is another aspect of its revolutionary character.

> We saw earlier that property in the conditions of production was posited as identical with a limited, definite form of the community [*Gemeinwesen*], hence of the individual with the characteristics—limited characteristics and limited development of his productive forces—required to form such a community [*Gemeinwesen*]. This presupposition was itself in turn the result of a limited historic stage of the development of the productive forces, of wealth as well as the mode of creating it. The purpose of the community [*Gemeinwesen*], of the individual—as well as the condition of production—is the reproduction of these specific conditions of production and of the individuals, both singly and in their social groupings and relations—as living carriers of these conditions.

---

8. Various authors have spoken of stagnation and declining production between the two world wars. Bordiga always rejected the theory of the decline of the capitalist mode of production as a gradualist deformation of Marx's theory (see 'Le renversement de la praxis dans la théorie marxiste,' in *Invariance* 4, série 1).

> Capital posits the production of wealth itself and hence the universal development of the productive forces, the constant overthrow of its prevailing presuppositions, as the presupposition of its reproduction. Value excludes no use value; i.e. includes no particular kind of consumption etc., of intercourse etc. as absolute condition; and likewise every degree of the development of the social forces of production, of intercourse, of knowledge etc. appears to it only as a barrier which it strives to overpower.[9]

This passage has momentous consequences. There is no reference to the proletariat; it is the revolutionary role of capital to overthrow the prevailing presuppositions. Marx had already said this, in a more striking manner:

> It is destructive towards all of this, and constantly revolutionizes it, tearing down all the barriers which hem in the development of the forces of production, the expansion of needs, the all-sided development of production, and the exploitation and exchange of natural and mental forces.[10]

We are forced to take a new approach toward the manner in which Marx situated the proletarian class in the context of the continual upheaval carried out by the capitalist mode of production. What is immediately evident is that the capitalist mode of production is revolutionary in relation to the destruction of ancient social relations, and that the proletariat is defined as revolutionary in relation to capital. But it is at this point that the problem begins: capitalism is revolutionary because it develops the productive forces; the proletariat cannot be revolutionary if, after its revolution, it develops or allows a different development of the productive forces.

---

9. Marx, *Grundrisse*, 541.

10. Ibid., 410.

How can we tangibly distinguish the revolutionary role of one from that of the other? How can we justify the destruction of the capitalist mode of production by the proletariat? This cannot be done in a narrowly economic context. Marx never faced this problem because he was absolutely certain that the proletarians would rise against capital. But we have to confront this problem if we are going to emerge from the impasse created by our acceptance of the theory according to which the production relations come into conflict with the development of the productive forces (forces which were postulated to exist for the human being, since if this were not the case, why would human beings rebel?) If the productive forces do not exist for human beings but for capital, and if they conflict with production relations, then this means that these relations do not provide the proper structure to the capitalist mode of production, and therefore there can be revolution which is not for human beings (for example, the general phenomenon which is called fascism). Consequently capital escapes. In the passage we are examining, Marx makes a remarkable statement about the domination of capital:

> Its own presupposition—value—is posited as product, not as a loftier presupposition hovering over production.[11]

Capital dominates value. Since labor is the substance of value, it follows that capital dominates human beings. Marx refers only indirectly to the presupposition which is also a product: wage labor, namely the existence of a labor force which makes valorization possible:

> The barrier to capital is that this entire development proceeds in a contradictory way, and that the working-out of the productive

---

11. Ibid., 541.

> forces, of general wealth etc., knowledge etc., appears in such a way that the working individual alienates himself [*sich entäußern*]; relates to the conditions brought out of him by his labor as those not of his own but of an alien wealth and of his own poverty.[12]

How can this be a limit for capital? One might suppose that under-consumption by the workers causes crises, and the final crisis. This is one possibility; at least it appears that way at certain times. Marx always refused to ground a theory of crises on this point, but this did not keep him from mentioning this underconsumption. For Marx capital has a barrier because it despoils the working individual. We should keep in mind that he is arguing against apologists for capital and wants to show that the capitalist mode of production is not eternal and does not achieve human emancipation. Yet in the course of his analysis he points to the possibility for capital to escape from human conditions. We perceive that it is not the productive forces that become autonomous, but capital, since at a given moment the productive forces become 'a barrier which it strives to overpower'. This takes place as follows: the productive forces are no longer productive forces of human beings but of capital; they are for capital.[13]

The despoliation (alienation) of the working individual cannot be a barrier for capital, unless Marx means barrier in the sense of a weakness; such a weakness would make capitalism inferior to other modes of production, particularly if we contrast this weakness to the enormous development of productive forces which it impels. In Marx's work there is an ambiguity about the subject to which the productive forces refer: are they for the human being or for capital?

---

12. Ibid.

13. This is what Marx shows when he analyzes fixed capital in the *Grundrisse*, and also in Book I of *Capital*, where he analyzes the transformation of the work process into a process of production of capital (see also *Un chapitre inédit du Capital* [Paris: 10/18, 1971]).

This ambiguity grounds two interpretations of Marx. The ethical interpretation (see especially Rubel) emphasizes the extent to which Marx denounces the destruction of the human being by capital, and vigorously insists that the capitalist mode of production can only be a transitory stage. The interpretation of Althusser and his school holds that Marx does not succeed in eliminating the human being from his economic analyses, which reflects his inability to abandon ideological discourse, from which follows Althusser's problem of correctly locating the epistemological break.

It is possible to get out of this ambiguity. If capital succeeds in overcoming this barrier, it achieves full autonomy. This is why Marx postulates that capital must abolish itself; this abolition follows from the fact that it cannot develop the productive forces for human beings while it makes possible a universal, varied development which can only be realized by a superior mode of production. This contains a contradiction: capital escapes from the grasp of human beings, but it must perish because it cannot develop human productive forces. This also contradicts Marx's analysis of the destruction of human beings by capital. How can destroyed human beings rebel? We can, if we avoid these contradictions, consider Marx a prophet of the decline of capital, but then we will not be able to understand his work or the present situation. The end of Marx's digression clarifies these contradictions.

> But this antithetical form is itself fleeting, and produces the real conditions of its own suspension. The result is: the tendentially and potentially general development of the forces of production—of wealth as such—as a basis; likewise, the universality of intercourse, hence the world market as a basis. The basis as the possibility of the universal development of the individual, and the real development of the individuals from this basis as a constant suspension of its barrier, which is recognized as a barrier, not taken for a sacred limit. Not an ideal or imagined universality

> of the individual, but the universality of his real and ideal relations. Hence also the grasping of his own history as a process, and the recognition of nature (equally present as practical power over nature) as his real body. The process of development itself posited and known as the presupposition of the same. For this, however, necessary above all that the full development of the forces of production has become the condition of production; and not that specific conditions of production are posited as a limit to the development of the productive forces.[14]

If this process is to concern individuals, capital has to be destroyed and the productive forces have to be for human beings. In the article 'La KAPD et le mouvement proletarien,'[15] we referred to this passage to indicate that the human being is a possibility, giving a foundation to the statement: the revolution must be human. This is in no way a discourse on the human being conceived as invariant in every attribute, a conception which would merely be a restatement of the immutability of human nature. But we have to point out that this is still insufficient, since the development of productive forces which, according to Marx, will take place in a superior mode of production, is precisely the same development presently carried out by capital. The limit of Marx is that he conceived communism as a new mode of production where productive forces blossom. These forces are undoubtedly important, but their existence at a certain level does not adequately define communism.

For Marx, capital overcomes its contradictions by engulfing them and by mystifying reality. It can only apparently overcome its narrow base, its limited nature which resides in the exchange of capital-money against labor force. Capital must inevitably come into conflict with this presupposition; thus Marx speaks of the opposition between private appropriation

14. Marx, *Grundrisse*, 541–2.

15. *Invariance*, Série II, No. 1.

and socialization of production. Private appropriation of what? Of surplus value, which presupposes the proletarian, and thus the wage relation. But the entire development of capital (and Marx's own explanations are a precious aid in understanding it) makes the mystification effective, making capital independent of human beings, thus enabling it to avoid the conflict with its presupposition. One might say that the conflict nevertheless persists, as a result of the total process: socialization. This is true. But the socialization of production and of human activity, the universal development of the productive forces and thus the destruction of the limited character of the human being—all this was only a possible ground for communism; it did not pose communism automatically. Furthermore, the action of capital tends constantly to destroy communism, or at least to inhibit its emergence and realization. To transform this possible ground into reality, human intervention is necessary. But Marx himself showed that capitalist production integrates the proletariat. How could the destruction of human beings and of nature fail to have repercussions on the ability of human beings to resist capital and, a fortiori, to rebel?

Some will think we are attributing to Marx a position which is convenient to us. We will cite an extraordinary passage:

> What precisely distinguishes capital from the master-servant relation is that the worker confronts [capital] as consumer and possessor of exchange values, and that in the form of the possessor of money, in the form of money he becomes a simple center of circulation—one of its infinitely many centers, in which his specificity as worker is extinguished.[16]

One of the modalities of the re-absorption of the revolutionary power of the proletariat has been to perfect its character as consumer, thus catching it in the mesh of capital. The proletariat

16. Marx, *Grundrisse*, 420–1.

ceases to be the class that negates; after the formation of the working class it dissolves into the social body. Marx anticipates the poets of the 'consumer society' and, as in other instances, he explains a phenomenon which is observed only later and then falsely, if only in terms of the name given to it.

The preceding observations do not lead to a fatalistic conception (this time negative), such as: whatever we do, there's no way out; it's too late; or any other mindless defeatism which would generate a sickening patchwork reformism. First we have to draw the lesson. Capital has run away from human and natural barriers; human beings have been domesticated: this is their decadence. The revolutionary solution cannot be found in the context of a dialectic of productive forces where the individual would be an element of the contradiction. Present day scientific analyses of capital proclaim a complete disregard for human beings who, for some, are nothing but a residue without consistency. This means that the discourse of science is the discourse of capital, or that science is possible only after the destruction of human beings; it is a discourse on the pathology of the human being. Thus it is insane to ground the hope of liberation on science. The position is all the more insane where, as with Althusser, it cannot make its own break, liquidate its 'archeology', since it remains faithful to a proletariat—a proletariat which in this conception is merely an object of capital, an element of the structure. But this inefficient, destroyed human being is the individual produced by class societies. And on this we agree: the human being is dead. The only possibility for another human being to appear is our struggle against our domestication, our emergence from it. Humanism and scientism (and the followers of 'ethical science' à la Monod are the most absolute slaves of capital) are two expressions of the domestication of humanity. All those who nurse the illusion of the decadence of capital revive ancient humanist conceptions or give birth to new scientific myths. They remain impermeable to the revolutionary phenomenon running through our world.

Until now all sides have argued as if human beings remained unchanged in different class societies and under the domination of capital. This is why the role of the social context was emphasized (man, who was fundamentally good, was seen to be modified positively or negatively by the social context) by the materialist philosophers of the eighteenth century, while Marxists emphasized the role of an environment conditioned by the development of productive forces. Change was not denied, and after Marx it was repeated that history was a continual transformation of human nature. Nevertheless it was held explicitly or implicitly that an irreducible element continued to allow human beings to revolt against the oppression of capital. And capitalism itself was described in a Manichean manner: on one side the positive pole, the proletariat, the liberating class; on the other the negative pole, capital. Capital was affirmed as necessary and as having revolutionized the life of human beings, but it was described as an absolute evil in relation to the good, the proletariat. The phenomenon which emerges today does not in the least destroy the negative evaluation of capital, but forces us to generalize it to the class which was once antagonistic to it and carried within itself all the positive elements of human development and today of humanity itself. This phenomenon is the recomposition of a community and of human beings by capital, reflecting human community like a mirror. The theory of the looking glass could only arise when the human being became a tautology, a reflection of capital. Within the world of the despotism of capital (this is how society appears as of today), neither a good nor an evil can be distinguished. Everything can be condemned. Negating forces can only arise outside of capital. Since capital has absorbed all the old contradictions, the revolutionary movement has to reject the entire product of the development of class societies. This is the crux of its struggle against domestication, against the decadence of the human species. This is the essential moment of the process of formation of revolutionaries, absolutely necessary for the production of revolution.

The Civilized Capitalist Machine

Gilles Deleuze
+
Félix Guattari

1972

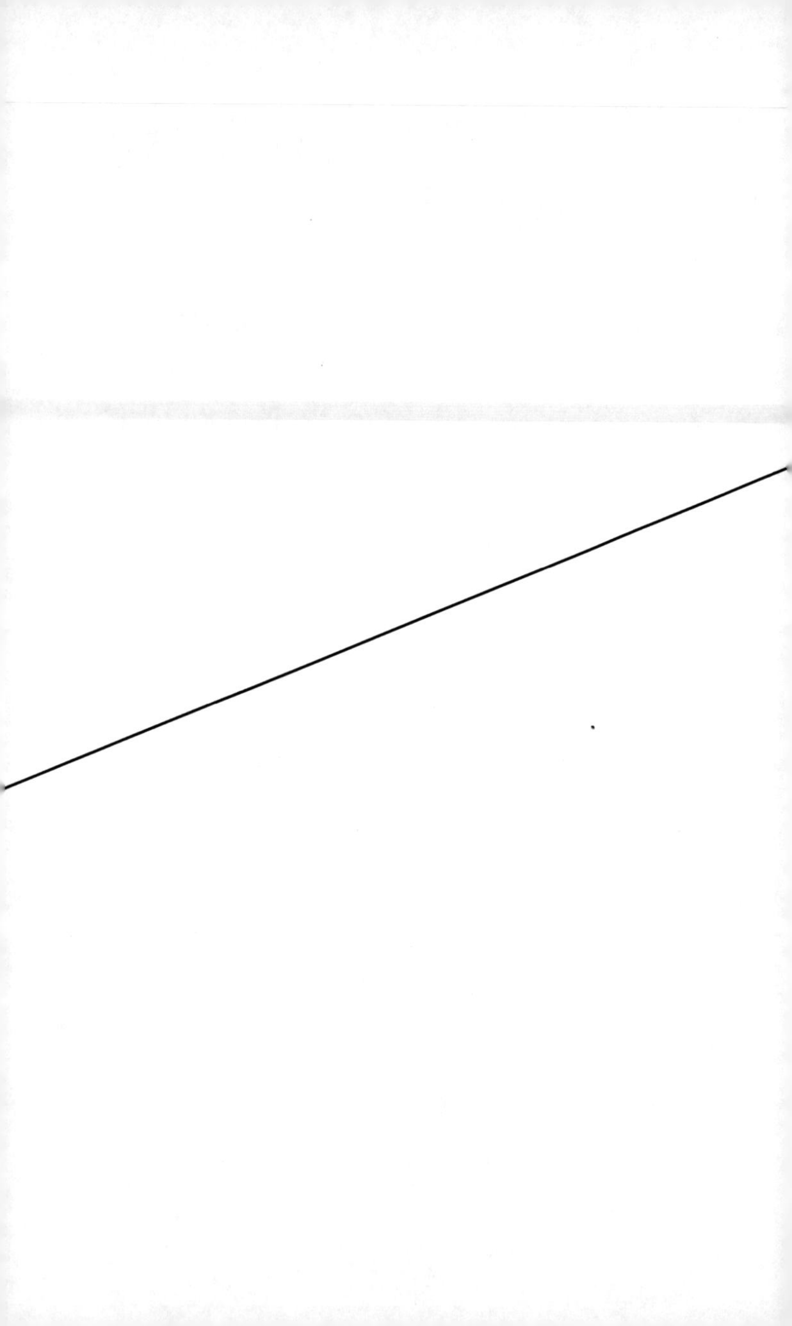

Let us return to the dualism of money, to the two boards, the two inscriptions, the one going into the account of the wage earner, the other into the balance sheet of the enterprise. Measuring the two orders of magnitude in terms of the same analytical unit is a pure fiction, a cosmic swindle, as if one were to measure intergalactic or intra-atomic distances in meters and centimeters. There is no common measure between the value of the enterprises and that of the labor capacity of wage earners. That is why the falling tendency has no conclusion. A quotient of differentials is indeed calculable if it is a matter of the limit of variation of the production flows from the viewpoint of a full output, but it is not calculable if it is a matter of the production flow and the labor flow on which surplus value depends. Thus the difference is not canceled in the relationship that constitutes it as a difference in nature; the 'tendency' has no end, it has no exterior limit that it could reach or even approximate. The tendency's only limit is internal, and it is continually going beyond it, but by displacing this limit—that is, by reconstituting it, by rediscovering it as an internal limit to be surpassed again by means of a displacement; thus the continuity of the capitalist process engenders itself in this break of a break that is always displaced, in this unity of the schiz and the flow. In this respect already the field of social immanence, as revealed under the withdrawal and the transformation of the Urstaat, is continually expanding, and acquires a consistency entirely its own, which shows the manner in which capitalism for its part was able to interpret the general principle according to which things work well only providing they break down, crises being 'the means immanent to the capitalist mode of production'. If capitalism is the exterior limit of all societies, this is because capitalism for its part has no exterior limit, but only an interior limit that is capital itself and that it does not encounter, but reproduces by always displacing it. Jean-Joseph Goux rigorously analyzes the mathematical phenomenon of the curve without a tangent, and the direction it is apt to take in economy as well as linguistics: 'If the movement does not tend toward any limit, if the quotient of differentials is not calculable, the present no longer has any meaning.... The quotient of differentials is not resolved, the differences no longer cancel one another in their relationship. No limit opposes the break [*la brisure*], or the breaking of this break. The tendency finds no end, the thing in motion never quite reaches what the immediate future has in store for it; it is endlessly delayed by accidents and deviations.... Such is the complex notion of a continuity within the absolute break'.[2] In the expanded immanence of the system, the limit tends to reconstitute in its displacement the thing it tended to diminish in its primitive emplacement.

Now this movement of displacement belongs essentially to the deterritorialization of capitalism. As Samir Amin has shown, the process of deterritorialization here goes from the center to the periphery, that is, from the developed countries to the underdeveloped countries, which do not constitute a separate world, but rather an essential component of the world-wide capitalist machine. It must be added, however, that the center itself has its organized enclaves of underdevelopment, its reservations and its ghettos as interior peripheries. (Pierre Moussa has defined the United States as a fragment of the Third World that has succeeded and has preserved its immense zones of underdevelopment.) And if it is true that the tendency to a falling rate of profit or to its equalization asserts itself at least partially at the center, carrying the economy toward the most progressive and the most automated sectors, a veritable 'development of underdevelopment' on the periphery ensures a rise in the rate of surplus value, in the

1. Marx, *Capital*, Vol. 3, tr. E. Untermann (New York: International, 1967), 250 n72: 'Capitalist production seeks continually to overcome these immanent barriers, but overcomes them only by means which again place these barriers in its way and on a more formidable scale. The real barrier of capitalist production is capital itself.'

2. J.-J. Goux, 'Derivable et inderivable', *Critique*, January 1970, 48–9.

form of an increasing exploitation of the peripheral proletariat in relation to that of the center. For it would be a great error to think that exports from the periphery originate primarily in traditional sectors or archaic territorialities: on the contrary, they come from modern industries and plantations that generate an immense surplus value, to a point where it is no longer the developed countries that supply the underdeveloped countries with capital, but quite the opposite. So true is it that primitive accumulation is not produced just once at the dawn of capitalism, but is continually reproducing itself. Capitalism exports filiative capital. At the same time as capitalist deterritorialization is developing from the center to the periphery, the decoding of flows on the periphery develops by means of a 'disarticulation' that ensures the ruin of traditional sectors, the development of extraverted economic circuits, a specific hypertrophy of the tertiary sector, and an extreme inequality in the different areas of productivity and in incomes.[3] Each passage of a flux is a deterritorialization, and each displaced limit, a decoding. Capitalism schizophrenizes more and more on the periphery. It will be said that, even so, at the center the falling tendency retains its restricted sense, i.e., the relative diminution of surplus value in relation to total capital—a diminution that is ensured by the development of productivity, automation, and constant capital.

This problem was raised again recently by Maurice Clavel in a series of decisive and wilfully incompetent questions—that is, questions addressed to Marxist economists by someone who doesn't quite understand how one can maintain human surplus value as the basis for capitalist production, while recognizing that machines too 'work' or produce value, that they have always worked, and that they work more and more in proportion to man, who thus ceases to be a constituent part of the production

---

3. S. Amin, *L'accumulation a l'echelle mondiale* (Paris: Anthropos, 1970), 373ff.

process, in order to become adjacent to this process.[4] Hence there is a machinic surplus value produced by constant capital, which develops along with automation and productivity, and which cannot be explained by factors that counteract the falling tendency—the increasing intensity of the exploitation of human labor, the diminution of the price of the elements of constant capital, etc.—since, on the contrary, these factors depend on it. It seems to us, with the same indispensable incompetence, that these problems can only be viewed under the conditions of the transformation of the surplus value of code into a surplus value of flux. In defining precapitalist regimes by a surplus value of code, and capitalism by a generalized decoding that converted this surplus value of code into a surplus value of flux, we were presenting things in a summary fashion, we were still acting as though the matter were settled once and for all, at the dawn of a capitalism that had lost all code value. This is not the case, however. On the one hand, codes continue to exist—even as an archaism—but they assume a function that is perfectly contemporary and adapted to the situation within personified capital (the capitalist, the worker, the merchant, the banker). But on the other hand, and more profoundly, every technical machine presupposes flows of a particular type: *flows of code* that are both interior and exterior to the machine, forming the elements of a technology and even a science. It is these flows of code that find themselves encasted, coded, or overcoded in the precapitalist societies in such a way that they never achieve any independence (the blacksmith, the astronomer). But the decoding of flows in capitalism has freed, deterritorialized, and decoded the flows of code just as it has the others—to such a degree that the automatic machine has always

---

4. M. Clavel, *Qui est aliené?* (Paris: Flammarion, 1970), 110–24, 320–27. See Marx's great chapter on automation (1857–58) in the *Grundrisse*, 692ff [See Marx, 'Fragment on Machines' in this volume].

increasingly internalized them in its body or its structure as a field of forces, while depending on a science and a technology, on a so-called intellectual labor distinct from the manual labor of the worker (the evolution of the technical object). In this sense, it is not machines that have created capitalism, but capitalism that creates machines, and that is constantly introducing breaks and cleavages through which it revolutionizes its technical modes of production.

But several correctives must be introduced in this regard. These breaks and cleavages take time, and their extension is very wide-ranging. By no means does the diachronic capitalist machine allow itself to be revolutionized by one or more of its synchronous technical machines, and by no means does it confer on its scientists and its technicians an independence that was unknown in the previous regimes. Doubtless it can let a certain number of scientists—mathematicians, for example—'schizophrenize' in their corner, and it can allow the passage of socially decoded flows of code that these scientists organize into axiomatics of research that is said to be basic. But *the true axiomatic* is elsewhere. (Leave the scientists alone to a certain point, let them create their own axiomatic, but when the time comes for serious things...For example, nondeterminist physics, with its corpuscular flows, will have to be brought into line with 'determinism'.) The true axiomatic is that of the social machine itself, which takes the place of the old codings and organizes all the decoded flows, including the flows of scientific and technical code, for the benefit of the capitalist system and in the service of its ends. That is why it has often been remarked that the Industrial Revolution combined an elevated rate of technical progress with the maintenance of a great quantity of 'obsolescent' equipment, along with a great suspicion concerning machines and science. An innovation is adopted only from the perspective of the rate of profit its investment will offer by the lowering of production costs; without this prospect, the capitalist will keep the existing equipment, and stand ready to make a parallel investment in equipment in another area.[5]

Thus the importance of human surplus value remains decisive, even at the center and in highly industrialized sectors. What determines the lowering of costs and the elevation of the rate of profit through machinic surplus value is not innovation itself, whose value is no more measurable than that of human surplus value. It is not even the profitability of the new technique considered in isolation, but its effect on the over-all profitability of the firm in its relationships with the market and with commercial and financial capital. This implies diachronic encounters and countersectings such as one already sees for example in the early part of the nineteenth century, between the steam engine and textile machines or techniques for the production of iron. In general, the introduction of innovations always tends to be delayed beyond the time scientifically necessary, until the moment when the market forecasts justify their exploitation on a large scale. Here again, alliance capital exerts a strong selective pressure on machinic innovations within industrial capital. In brief, there where the flows are decoded, the specific flows of code that have taken a technical and scientific form are subjected to a properly social axiomatic that is much severer than all the scientific axiomatics, much severer too than all the old codes and overcodes that have disappeared: the axiomatic of the world capitalist market. In brief, the flows of code that are 'liberated' in science and technics by the capitalist regime engender a machinic surplus value that does not directly depend on science and technics themselves, but on capital—a surplus value that is added to human surplus value and that comes to correct the relative diminution of the latter, *both of them constituting the whole of the surplus value of flux that characterizes the*

---

5. P. Baran and P. Sweezy, *Monopoly Capital* (New York: Monthly Review Press, 1966), 93–7.

system. Knowledge, information, and specialized education are just as much parts of capital ('knowledge capital') as is the most elementary labor of the worker. And just as we found, on the side of human surplus value insofar as it resulted from decoded flows, an incommensurability or a fundamental asymmetry (no assignable exterior limit) between manual labor and capital, or between two forms of money, here too, on the side of the machinic surplus value resulting from scientific and technical flows of code, we find no commensurability or exterior limit between scientific or technical labor—even when highly remunerated—and the profit of capital that inscribes itself with another sort of writing. In this respect the knowledge flow and the labor flow find themselves in the same situation, determined by capitalist decoding or deterritorialization. But if it is true that innovations are adopted only insofar as they entail a rise in profits through a lowering of costs of production, and if there exists a sufficiently high volume of production to justify them, the corollary that derives from this proposition is that investment in innovations is never sufficient to realize or absorb the surplus value of flux that is produced on the one side as on the other.[6] Marx has clearly demonstrated the importance of the problem: the ever widening circle of capitalism is completed, while reproducing its immanent limits on an ever larger scale, only if the surplus value is not merely produced or extorted, but absorbed or realized.[7] If the capitalist is not defined in terms of enjoyment, the reason is not merely that his aim is the 'production for production's sake' that generates surplus value, it also includes the realization of this surplus value: an unrealized surplus value of flux is as if not produced, and becomes embodied in unemployment and stagnation. It is easy to list the principal modes of absorption of surplus value outside the spheres of consumption and investment:

---

6. Regarding the concept of depreciation implied by this proposition, ibid., 99–102.

7. *Capital*, Vol. 3, 244.

advertising, civil government, militarism, and imperialism. The role of the State in this regard, within the capitalist axiomatic, is the more manifest in that what it absorbs is not sliced from the surplus value of the firms, but added to their surplus value by bringing the capitalist economy closer to full output within the given limits, and by widening these limits in turn—especially within an order of military expenditures that are in no way competitive with private enterprise, quite the contrary (it took a war to accomplish what the New Deal had failed to accomplish). The role of a politico-military-economic complex is the more manifest in that it guarantees the extraction of human surplus value on the periphery and in the appropriated zones of the center, but also because it engenders for its own part an enormous machinic surplus value by mobilizing the resources of knowledge and information capital, and finally because it absorbs the greater part of the surplus value produced.

The State, its police, and its army form a gigantic enterprise of antiproduction, but at the heart of production itself, and conditioning this production. Here we discover a new determination of the properly capitalist field of immanence: not only the interplay of the relations and differential coefficients of decoded flows, not only the nature of the limits that capitalism reproduces on an ever wider scale as interior limits, but the presence of antiproduction within production itself. The apparatus of antiproduction is no longer a transcendent instance that opposes production, limits it, or checks it; on the contrary, it insinuates itself everywhere in the productive machine and becomes firmly wedded to it in order to regulate its productivity and realize surplus value—which explains, for example, the difference between the despotic bureaucracy and the capitalist bureaucracy. This effusion from the apparatus of antiproduction is characteristic of the entire capitalist system; the capitalist effusion is that of antiproduction within production at all levels of the process. On the one hand, it alone is capable of realizing capitalism's supreme goal, which is to produce lack in the large aggregates, to introduce lack where there is always too much, by effecting the absorption of overabundant resources. On the other hand, it alone doubles the capital and the flow of knowledge with a capital and an equivalent flow of *stupidity* that also effects an absorption and a realization, and that ensures the integration of groups and individuals into the system. Not only lack amid overabundance, but stupidity in the midst of knowledge and science; it will be seen in particular how it is at the level of the State and the military that the most progressive sectors of scientific or technical knowledge combine with those feeble archaisms bearing the greatest burden of current functions.

Here Andre Gorz's double portrait of the 'scientific and technical worker' takes on its full meaning. Although he has mastered a flow of knowledge, information, and training, he is so absorbed in capital that the reflux of organized, axiomatized stupidity coincides with him, so that, when he goes home in the evening, he rediscovers his little desiring-machines by tinkering with a television set—O despair.[8] Of course the scientist as such has no revolutionary potential; he is the first integrated agent of integration, a refuge for bad conscience, and the *forced* destroyer of his own creativity. Let us consider the more striking example of a career *à l'americaine*, with abrupt mutations, just as we imagine such a career to be: Gregory Bateson begins by fleeing the civilized world, by becoming an ethnologist and following the primitive codes and the savage flows; then he turns in the direction of flows that are more and more decoded, those of schizophrenia, from which he extracts an interesting psychoanalytic theory; then, still in search of a beyond, of another wall to break through, he turns to dolphins, to the language of dolphins, to flows that are even stranger and more deterritorialized. But where does the dolphin

8. A. Gorz, *Strategy for Labor*, trans. Martin Nicolaus and Victoria Ortiz (Boston: Beacon Press, 1967), 106.

flux end, if not with the basic research projects of the American army, which brings us back to preparations for war and to the absorption of surplus value.

In comparison to the capitalist State, the socialist States are children—but children who learned something from their father concerning the axiomatizing role of the State. But the socialist States have more trouble stopping unexpected flow leakage except by direct violence. What on the contrary is called the co-opting power of capitalism can be explained by the fact that its axiomatic is not more flexible, but wider and more englobing. In such a system no one escapes participation in the activity of antiproduction that drives the entire productive system. 'But it is not only those who man and supply the military machine who are engaged in an anti-human enterprise. The same can be said in varying degrees of many millions of other workers who produce, and create wants for, goods and services which no one needs. And so interdependent are the various sectors and branches of the economy that nearly everyone is involved in one way or another in these anti-human activities: the farmer supplying food to troops fighting in Vietnam, the tool and die makers turning out the intricate machinery needed for a new automobile model, the manufacturers of paper and ink and TV sets whose products are used to control the minds of the people, and so on and so on.'[9]

Thus the three segments of the ever widening capitalist reproduction process are joined, three segments that also define the three aspects of its immanence: (1) the one that extracts human surplus value on the basis of the differential relation between decoded flows of labor and production, and that moves from the center to the periphery while nevertheless maintaining vast residual zones at the center; (2) the one that extracts machinic surplus value, on the basis of an axiomatic of the flows

9. Baran and Sweezy, *Monopoly Capital*, 344.

of scientific and technical code, in the "core" areas of the center; (3) and the one that absorbs or realizes these two forms of surplus value of flux by guaranteeing the emission of both, and by constantly injecting antiproduction into the producing apparatus. Schizophrenization occurs on the periphery, but it occurs at the center and at the core as well.

The definition of surplus value must be modified in terms of the machinic surplus value of constant capital, which distinguishes itself from the human surplus value of variable capital and from the nonmeasurable nature of this aggregate of surplus value of flux. It cannot be defined by the difference between the value of labor capacity and the value created by labor capacity, but by the incommensurability between two flows that are nonetheless immanent to each other, by the disparity between the two aspects of money that express them, and by the absence of a limit exterior to their relationship—the one measuring the true economic force, the other measuring a purchasing power determined as 'income'. The first is the immense deterritorialized flow that constitutes the full body of capital. An economist of the caliber of Bernard Schmitt finds strange lyrical words to characterize this flow of infinite debt: an instantaneous creative flow that the banks create spontaneously as a debt owing to themselves, a creation *ex nihilo* that, instead of transferring a pre-existing currency as means of payment, hollows out at one extreme of the full body a negative money (a debt entered as a liability of the banks), and projects at the other extreme a positive money (a credit granted the productive economy by the banks)—'a flow possessing a power of mutation' *that does not enter into income and is not assigned to purchases*, a pure availability, nonpossession and nonwealth.[10] The other aspect of money represents the reflux, that is, the relationship that it assumes with goods as soon as it acquires a purchasing

10. B. Schmitt, *Monnaie, salaires et profits* (Paris: PUF, 1966), 234–36.

power through its distribution to workers or production factors, through its allotment in the form of incomes—a relationship that it loses as soon as the latter are converted into real goods (at which point everything recommences by means of a new production that will first come under the sway of the first aspect). The incommensurability of the two aspects—the flux and the reflux—shows that nominal wages fail to embrace the totality of the national income, since the wage earners allow a great quantity of revenues to escape. These revenues are tapped by the firms and in turn form an afflux by means of a conjunction; a flow—this time uninterrupted—of raw *profit*, constituting 'at one go' an undivided quantity flowing over the full body, however diverse the uses for which it is allocated (interest, dividends, management salaries, purchase of production goods, etc.).

The incompetent observer has the impression that this whole economic schema, this whole story is profoundly schizo. The aim of the theory is clear—a theory that refrains, however, from employing any moral reference. 'Who is robbed?' is the serious implied question that echoes Clavel's ironic question, 'Who is alienated?' Yet no one is or can be robbed—just as, according to Clavel, one no longer knows who is alienated or who does the alienating. Who steals? Certainly not the finance capitalist as the representative of the great instantaneous creative flow, which is not even a possession and has no purchasing power. Who is robbed? Certainly not the worker who is not even bought, since the reflux or salary distribution creates the purchasing power, instead of presupposing it. Who would be capable of stealing? Certainly not the industrial capitalist as the representative of the afflux of profit, since 'profits do not flow in the reflux, but side by side with, deviating from rather than penalizing the flow that creates incomes'. How much flexibility there is in the axiomatic of capitalism, always ready to widen its own limits so as to add a new axiom to a previously saturated system! You say you want an axiom for wage earners, for the working class and the unions? Well then, let's see what we can do—and thereafter profit will flow alongside wages, side by side, reflux and afflux. An axiom will be found even for the language of dolphins. Marx often alluded to the Golden Age of the capitalist, when the latter didn't hide his own cynicism: in the beginning, at least, he could not be unaware of what he was doing, extorting surplus value. But how this cynicism has grown—to the point where he is able to declare: no, nobody is being robbed! For everything is then based on the disparity between two kinds of flows, as in the fathomless abyss where profit and surplus value are engendered: the flow of merchant capital's economic force and the flow that is derisively named 'purchasing power'—a flow made truly *impotent* that represents the absolute impotence of the wage earner as well as the relative dependence of the industrial capitalist. This is money and the market, capitalism's true police.

In a certain sense, capitalist economists are not mistaken when they present the economy as being perpetually 'in need of monetarization', as if it were always necessary to inject money into the economy from the outside according to a supply and a demand. In this manner the system indeed holds together and functions, and perpetually fulfills its own immanence. In this manner it is indeed the global object of an investment of desire. The wage earner's desire, the capitalist's desire, everything moves to the rhythm of one and the same desire, founded *on the differential relation of flows having no assignable exterior limit, and where capitalism reproduces its immanent limits on an ever widening and more comprehensive scale.* Hence it is at the level of a generalized theory of flows that one is able to reply to the question: how does one come to desire strength while also desiring one's own impotence? How was such a social field able to be invested by desire? And how far does desire go beyond so-called objective interests, when it is a question of flows to set in motion and to break? Doubtless Marxists will remind us that the formation of money as a specific relation within capitalism depends on the mode of production that makes the economy a monetary economy. The fact remains that the apparent objective movement of capital—which is by no means a failure to recognize or an illusion of consciousness—shows that the productive essence of capitalism can itself function only in this necessarily monetary or commodity form that controls it, and whose flows and relations between flows contain the secret of the investment of desire. It is at the level of flows, the monetary flows included, and not at the level of ideology, that the integration of desire is achieved.

So what is the solution? Which is the revolutionary path? Psychoanalysis is of little help, entertaining as it does the most intimate of relations with money, and recording—while refusing to recognize it—an entire system of economic-monetary dependences at the heart of the *desire* of every subject it treats. Psychoanalysis constitutes for its part a gigantic enterprise of absorption of surplus value. But which is the revolutionary path? Is there one?—To withdraw from the world market, as Samir Amin advises Third World countries to do, in a curious revival of the fascist 'economic solution'? Or might it be to go in the opposite direction? To go still further, that is, in the movement of the market, of decoding and deterritorialization? For perhaps the flows are not yet deterritorialized enough, not decoded enough, from the viewpoint of a theory and a practice of a highly schizophrenic character. Not to withdraw from the process, but to go further, to 'accelerate the process', as Nietzsche put it: in this matter, the truth is that we haven't seen anything yet.

Energumen Capitalism

Jean-François Lyotard

1972

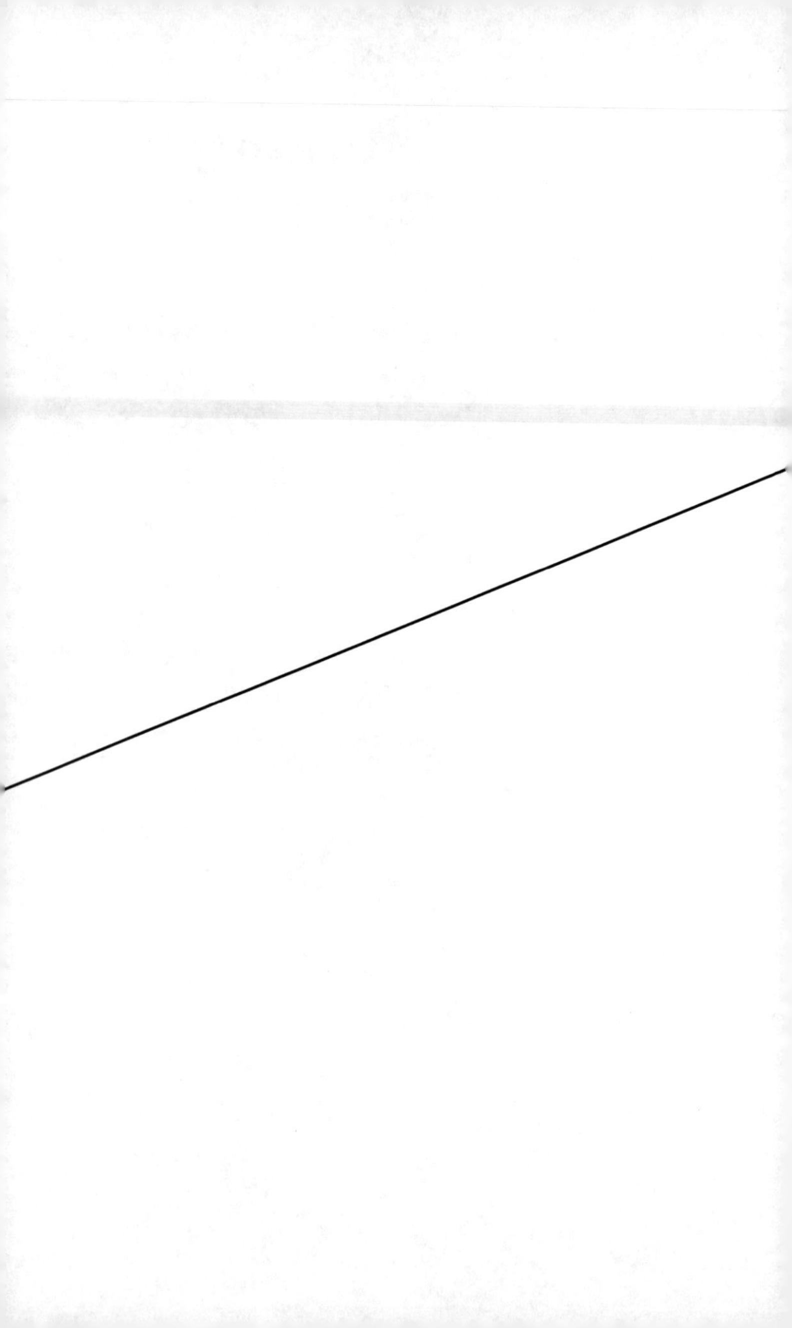

Criticism's not the time to think. Think ahead of time.

—John Cage to Daniel Charles[1]

Bellmer places a mirror perpendicular to a photo of a female nude. And turns it around, observing that, through the abstract split of the contact line, unrecognizable blooms of flesh emerge, or are reabsorbed back into it when the mirror travels in the other direction. The end of representation? Or representation in its modern version, where what is 'interesting' is no longer the full body, now denounced as a poor harmony, a false totality, poor and false because *now impracticable* (or in fact *always* impracticable, notwithstanding the brief collective phantasm of romanticism following the caesura of modernity, Hölderlin, J.-P. Richter and Hegel, and *still* Marx)—but the non-organic, dismembered body, flattened onto itself, folded, entwined, reduced to puddles and shreds, *glued-together* fragments, a non-set of partial objects stitched together in a cacophonous miracle? The end of representation, if to represent is to present, in its absence, *something*—but *still* representation if to represent is to present anyway, to present the *unpresentable*, to represent in the sense of making 'representations' to someone, remonstrances, to *re-monstrate*. For what is remonstrated is disorder. An outmoded sense of the word?

Here it is: is there a rupture of modernity? Is it true that after Cézanne there is no longer anything but shreds? Yes, of course. But this is not the question. What is possible is that before Cézanne, in the baroque, certainly, in 'that which turns', the clear-obscure, shadows efflorescing and cutting up bodies in a kind of bad butchery where the meat is not separated according to its grain but against the grain, as in de la Tour and of course already in Caravaggio (what this system of values means we can see very well once the colour video camera takes

---

1. J. Cage, *M: Writings '67–72* (Middletown, CT: Wesleyan University Press, 1973), 20.

possession of it and prints it on film, in place of the 'spectacle' that Zurich's Living Theatre played for the last time, the evasive liquidity of colours diluting the human into the inhuman, into chemism and chromatics: the 'truth' of the baroque, it is *formless* [*informe*]), thus already in the baroque, and perhaps even already in perspectivist foreshortening (isn't Mantegna's *Lamentation of Christ* Alice, when she shrinks so much that her chin hits her feet?) and in the angular sadism of Brunelleschi's legitimate construction, a box to cut women into pieces, the iron chin-strap into which Dürer fixes his head so as to keep it still facing the woman laid out behind the stretched wicker network, in the impossible perspicacity of Piero, who gives us distances just as *cut out*, just as meticulously linear as his foregrounds—it may be that what is important in this whole representational—and 'primitive' and classical and baroque—dispositif, is not the rule, the synthesis, the beautiful totality, the thing lost or found, the completion of unifying Eros, but distortion, quartering, difference and exteriority to all form. The formless and the disfigured.

Then, according to this hypothesis, the moderns who multiply modalities and inscriptions with their theatres with multiple or transformable scenes (the total theatre of Piscator and Gropius), with the infinite diversity of pictorial inscriptions that they continue to class as 'painting', with the explosion of the music of sonorous intensities drifting in the element of silence-noises, with anti-book and non-book books, travel books—don't they *continue* representation-disfiguration? Believing they were going to have done with it, didn't they displace and *prove* it, opening the box, making the scenic space spread out all around the spectator, below, above, certainly undoing the strict axial relation of the chin-strap, the ramp and the rail and the gate, and even the auditorium/stage division—but retaining the mirrored pane, placing it before the old one? And then it's a deforming mirror, warped, with blind spots, laughter and wrinkles producing distortions, savage, aleatory anamorphoses, like the lenses of the cameras of underground film, and of course already in *Les Demoiselles d'Avignon*, and yet nevertheless the gap between the latter and some nude of Bouguereau, as Gombrich shows, is perhaps no more than that between flat and distorted glass, cubism being certainly a defeated academicism, but cubism and academicism remaining, both, representation.

Here is a depressed thinking, a pious, nihilist thinking: you never have the thing itself, you only ever have its representation, and even when you think you've flushed it out in its original fragmentation, you still only have its representation, the *differed* fragmented thing. It is the thinking that *continues* representation as a complement to piety, as the production of exteriority in the interior. But what if this wasn't the real problem? What if, with modern inscription, it was the exterior/interior limit that was disqualified, spanned? If we must take seriously not representation *once again*, but production tout court; not (representational) effacement but inscription; not re-petition, but difference qua irreparable; not signification, but energetics; not mediation through the building of the stage, but the immediacy of producing no matter where; not localization, but perpetual delocalization? The time is coming no longer to stop at observing the capture and erasure of libidinal fluxes in an order of which representation and its junctive-disjunctive partitionings are, or would be, the last word, for this capture and this erasure are capitalism; the time is coming to serve and to encourage their errant divagation over all the surfaces and splits immediately flooded, with bodies, with history, the earth, language...An attitude that would not even be revolutionary in the sense of an overthrowing, an overturning (or connected to any expertise in these theatrical operations), and thus still a distribution of energy according to the edifice and artifice of representation, but revolutionary in the sense of *Wille*, in the sense of willing that what could be, should be.

To write according to this attitude is to forget. The forgetting of formal propriety first of all, of 'good' style. No longer the French-style canals, parks, groves and ponds of the rarefied writing of yore, no longer the gracious hexagonal epigones of assured taste; nor the thousand *effaced* connotations. When the eye of Deleuze and Guattari blinks, it's massive, like a sluice-gate. Their book is a voluminous displacement of waters, sometimes unleashed in a torrent, sometimes stationary, doing work below, but always moving, with waves, currents and countercurrents. What is involved is not signification, but an energetics. The book adds nothing, but it carries along a great deal, it transports everything. It is a pantograph that conducts electrical energy from the high-voltage line and makes it possible to transform it into the rotation of wheels on rails, for the traveller in landscapes, reveries, musics, in works transformed, destroyed, carried away in their turn. The pantograph itself is moving very fast. It is not a book of philosophy, that is to say a religion. Still less the religion of those who no longer believe in anything, the religion of writing. Rather, writing is treated as a machinery: it absorbs energy and metamorphoses it into a metamorphic potential in the reader.

And then the forgetting of critique. *Anti-Oedipus*, despite its title, is not a book of critique. Instead, like Nietzsche's *Antichrist*, it is a positive, positional book, an energetic position inscribed in discourse, where negation of the enemy takes place not through *Aufhebung*, but through forgetting. Just as atheism is the continuation of religion in negative form—the modern *form* of religion, even, the only form in which modernity could continue to be religious—so critique makes itself the object of its object, establishes itself in the field of the other, accepting the dimensions, directions and space of the other even as it contests them. In Deleuze and Guattari's book you find everywhere a quite explicit contempt for the category of transgression (and thus, implicitly, for all of Bataille): because either *one gets out immediately* without wasting time critiquing, simply because one is elsewhere than the enemy's domain; or else one critiques, keeping one foot inside while stepping outside with the other—positivity of the negative, but in fact nothingness of this positivity. It is this critical non-force that is found in Feuerbach and Adorno. As Marx said in 1844, socialism doesn't need atheism, because the question of atheism is positionally the same as that of religion; it remains a critique. What is important here is not its negativity, but its positioning (the way the problem is posed). From atheism (which Marx saw as utopian communism) to socialism, no frontier is crossed, there is no 'overgrowth', no critique; there is a displacement, desire has wandered nomadically into another space, another dispositif has been activated, it works otherwise, and if it works, it is not by virtue of the other, older machine having been critiqued. For the same reason, all things being equal, the following lines will not be a critique.

Contrary to all expectations, or precisely because the sensational title is an illusory effect, what the book *subverts* most profoundly is what it does not *critique*: Marxism. This does not imply that, symmetrically, it does not subvert psychoanalysis, which it attacks. On the contrary, beneath the different ways in which the *regimes* of this machine that is the book function, depending on whether it operates with Freud or with Marx, there remains an evident identity of *position*. Those parts of Marx that are quietly buried are no less serious or important than those parts of Freud that are flung into the roaring blaze of *Anti-Oedipus*'s counterfire. On one hand, the book-machine unplugs itself from the psychoanalytical dispositif and *exposes* it, forces it to expose itself, just like the man with the tape recorder did, pulling back and projecting all the libidinal energy that was supposed to flow away into the transferential relationship, projecting it onto the paranoiac configuration of the Arche-State which, according to Deleuze and Guattari, underlies the dispositif of psychoanalytical practice; on the other hand, on the contrary, the book pumps out Marxism's theoretical and practical flows, cutting them off here and there, dropping whole parts of the Marxist dispositif without a word. And yet the two Elders are in fact placed under the same sign: all the ways in which libidinal economy communicates with political economy in their works, this is what is truly a transformative force and thus a potential departure; on the contrary, all the ways in which the libidinal conceals the political in Freud or the political the libidinal in Marx must be leapt out of and danced upon. Thus we find that everything that is *unconsciously* political in psychoanalysis is profoundly subverted—such is the visible axis of the book: anti-Oedipus as anti-State, rupture with the despotic configuration unconsciously present in psychoanalysis. But in parallel with this, everything unconsciously libidinal in Marxism must be thawed out, the libido imprisoned in the religious scaffolding of dialectical politics or economic catastrophism, repressed in the suspended analyses of commodity fetishism and the naturality of labour.

Yet the book is anti-Oedipus and not anti-Party (assuming that the Party is, on the socio-political surface of inscription, the analogue of Oedipus on the corporeal surface). Is this not giving too much importance to psychoanalysis in the repressive mechanisms that regulate the circulation of Kapital? Is this critical virulence not too clamorous? Is it not precisely this that will allow the intellectual left to make the book into a gadget, a seasonal commodity, thereby neutralizing it? Is not its true virulence in its silence? By branching off the present short work from the larger work of the book at precisely the point where the latter says nothing, we seek to set off some flows that cannot be exchanged by the merchants and/or the politicians. Thus we reaffirm what the book affirms. We show how it is one of the most intense products of the new libidinal figure that is beginning to 'gel' inside of capitalism.

It doesn't matter whether what we do ends up being melodic.
—C. Wolff to Stockhausen

Marxism says: there is a frontier, a limit beyond which the organization of flows called capital (capitalist relations of production) comes apart, and the whole set of correspondences between money and commodities, capital and labour force, and other parameters besides, is disrupted. And it is the very growth in the productive capacities in the most modern capitalism which, reaching this limit, will cause the dispositif of production and circulation to falter, and cannot fail to let through, to set free more energy flows, allowing to be swept away their system of 'regulation' within capital—that is, the relations of production.

All Marxist politics is built on this assumption; it seeks in this frontier, this limit, this chain, this or that link or stone seemingly ready to give way, the weakest link—or the strongest link, one that is so important that the whole edifice can be brought down with it. This whole politics is a politics of limits and of negativity. There is, or so it requires, some exteriority beyond the reach of capital: at the same time as it extends the law of value to new objects, or rather reformats all the old objects that were formerly 'coded' according to the intricate rules of production of 'trades', according to religious rituals, and according to the customs of older, more 'savage' cultures, so that they may be decoded and made into modern 'objects' stripped of all constraints other than that of exchangeability—at the same time as all that, capital itself approaches a limit it cannot exceed.

What is this limit? The disproportion between flows of credit and flows of production? Between quantities of commodities and quantities of available currency? Between capital invested and the expected rate of profit? The disequilibrium between production capacity and actual production? The disproportion between fixed capital and salaries or variable capital? Between surplus value created by the exploitation of the labour force and its realization or reconversion in production? Or is the limit the decline in the rate of profit? Or the emergence of revolutionary critique within the ranks of a burgeoning proletariat? Or on the contrary, should we observe, bitterly but symmetrically (that is, remaining within the same theoretical and practical field) that the motivation to invest, discouraged by the decline in the rate of profit, is taken over by State interventions; that workers, ever more numerous, are however less and less open to the prospect of revolutionary overthrow (to the extent that Communist parties are obliged to *practically* exclude such a perspective from their programs, and to present themselves as good managers of an almost identical system, just with a few less owners of capital and a few more high-level officials)?

These uncertainties are not speculative, they are practical and political. They are the legacy of a century of the Communist movement, and of a long half-century of socialist revolution. Almost as if, around 1860, one were to have inquired as to the development of French society, the contradictions within the society of the ancien regime; the direction that Robespierre imparted to the revolutionary current; the historical function of Bonaparte; and ultimately, the fundamental difference between French society under the last kings and French society under the last emperor, realizing that it is to be found not in the Age of Enlightenment, where bourgeois ideology places it, but to the side, in the Industrial Revolution. The same goes, with appropriate adjustments, for the Russian 'socialist' state. Its divergence from bourgeois society is not where its discourse says it is, in the power of the Soviets—that is, not in the workers' increased (and in theory even greater) proximity to decisions taken on the economy and society, and thus in a finer flexibility of flows of production, words, thoughts, and objects. On the contrary, it lies in the state's grip on these currents, a grip just as tight as that of czarism, just as 'rational' (that is to say, irrational) and secondary (in the Freudian sense)—the grip of a sociophagous state that absorbs civil, economic and intellectual society, that infiltrates itself into all of its circulatory channels, pouring the cement of its bureaucratic suspicion into them. No more fluctuating, then, and less representative; on the contrary, just as centralized, totalizing and paranoiac. And perhaps *more* centralized. Here again things happen elsewhere: the socialist revolution engenders a new kind of despotic state which tries to combine a police-like paternalistic contempt for the masses and for the libido with the ('American') technical efficiency and initiative of capitalism, and fails. When Lenin said that socialism was Soviet power plus electrification, Cronstadt replied: it is the Party's power plus executions. Not that capitalism is in any way the regime of freedom, for it too is constructed on the principle of a mapping of the flows of production back onto the *socius*; Kapital *is* this mapping; but it must happen only *under the auspices of profit*, not in the name of some gain in sacred power (*numen*), in what Deleuze and Guattari call *surplus value of code*—that is, a gain in prestige, which presupposes an emotional attachment. Capitalism offers nothing to believe in, cynicism is its morality. The Party, on the contrary, as a despotic configuration, requires a mapping that is territorialized, coded and hierarchized, in the religious sense of the term. Russia, Mother Russia, the people, its folklore, its dances, its customs and costumes, baba and Little Father, everything from the 'savage' Slavic communities is conserved, preserved, and attached to the figure of the Secretary General, the despot who appropriates all production.

If we inquire as to what effectively destroys bourgeois society, then, it is clear that neither socialist revolution nor Marxism hold the answer. Not only does the 'historical 'dialectic' belie the speculative dialectic; we have to admit that there is no dialectic at all.

Figures, vast dispositifs, compete over energies; the way that energies are tapped, transformed and circulated is completely different depending on whether it is the capitalist figure or the despotic figure. The two may combine, they produce no contradictions in doing so—no history on the way to totalization, leading to other figures—but only effects of compromise on the social surface, unexpected monsters: the Stakhanovite worker, the proletarian company boss, the Red Marshall, the leftist nuclear bomb, the unionized policeman, the communist labour camp, Socialist Realism.... In these kinds of mixings of libidinal-economic dispositifs, it is surely the despotic configuration that dominates. But even if this were not the case, it's not clear why and how this machinery would be a dialectical outcome, still less why and how the libidinal figure of capitalism ought to or even could 'lead to' such a dispositif through its 'intrinsic organic development'. And in fact it does not lead to it, it leads to nothing other than itself: no 'overgrowth' to be expected, no limit in its field that it does not cross over. On one hand, capitalism leaps over all precapitalist limitations; on the other, it draws along and displaces its own limit in its movement. Which spells confusion for the 'left', traditional and radical alike.

This is the zone that Deleuze and Guattari set out from: What if this idea of an insurmountable economic, social, 'moral', political, technical (or whatever) limit were a hollow idea? What if, instead of a wall to breach or transgress, it were capitalism's own wall that constantly shifted further inside of itself (we find such a figure already in the old idea of the expansion of the 'internal' market)? Not that it would thus do away with itself through extension alone; neither would the question of its overthrow be obsolete, consigning us to the ranks of revisionists and reformers who expect development, growth and a little more 'democracy' to sort everything out, or rather who no longer expect anything more than three percent more and better distributed. But in the sense that there is no exteriority, no other of Kapital (whether Nature, Socialism, Festival, or whatever), but in the very interior of the system there are ever-increasing regions of contact and war between that which is fluidity and almost indifference, developed by capital itself, and that which is 'axiomatic', repression, the plugging up of flows, 'reterritorializations', and the mapping of energy back onto a body which is supposed to be its origin but which in fact seeks only to profit from it, whatever name this body might assume: Nation, Civilization, Freedom, Future, and New Society under one sole Identity: Kapital.

There is no dialectic in the sense that one or several of these conflicts must one day result in the breaching of the wall, that one day we will find that the energy has 'snuck out', dispersed, fluid, onto the other side; rather there is a kind of *overflowing* of force *inside* the very system that liberated it from the savage and barbaric rules of inscription; any object can enter into Kapital, if it can be exchanged; that which can be exchanged, be metamorphosed from money into machines, from commodity into commodity, from labour force into labour, from labour into salary, from salary into labour force—all of this, from the moment it is exchangeable (according to the law of value), is an *object* for Kapital. Thus there is nothing but an enormous stirring of the surface; objects appear and disappear like the fins of dolphins on the surface of the sea, where their objectivity gives way to their obsolescence, where what is important tends no longer to be the object, a legacy concretion of codes, but metamorphosis, fluidity. No dolphin, only a slipstream, an energetic trace inscribed on the surface. It is in this liquidity, in these neither icy nor scalding waters, that the capitalist relations of production will sink—that is, the simple rule of the equality of exchangeable values and the whole set of 'axioms' that Kapital keeps on fabricating to make this rule compulsory and respectable once again, all the while making a mockery of it.

For example, Sherman shows that in nationalising the thousand largest companies in the US, in one go one could overcome the bottlenecks that the law of value imposes upon circulation; one could reduce working time to a few hours a day, establish completely free consumer goods, and get rid of advertising and a great number of other tertiary activities. Figures in hand, this is demonstrated to be possible in the current state of the US economy. One can imagine the thing done if, for example, capital owners' motivation to invest kept on decreasing and if their interests led them to prefer bureaucratic revenues (of which there would be no shortage in Sherman's society) to uncertain market profits: this would perhaps be communism in the sense of the 1848 *Manifesto*, it wouldn't be the socialism we dream of today. It would be modern capitalism, despotic bureacracy, the bureacracy of abundance, that is to say one in which the apparatus no longer regulated poverty and rarity, but instead prosperity; the bureacracy not of need, but of libido.

A limit continually pushed back, a 'relative limit'. The body without organs, the *socius*, has no limit; it maps back everything onto itself, self-relation, captures and directs the innumerable fluxes that the 'economic' libidinal-political dispositifs connect onto each other, in an endless metamorphosis, an always different repetition. This mapping process, this absorption of energy, upon a *socius* that attracts and destroys production, this is capitalism. No limit cutting off the interior from the exterior, no cliff the system falls off and crashes. But, on the surface itself, a frantic flight, an aleatory voyage of libido, an errancy that is marked by the 'whatever' of Kapital, and which makes of this formation, compared to savagery and barbarianism, compared to coded formations, the most schizophrenic and the least dialectical. Look at how the bosses of American companies straight away *got around* the obstacle that the MIT economists opposed to the pursuit of growth. The economists said: with production, pollution grows exponentially. Therefore stop growth, limit investment in production, govern the system on a zero growth basis. Reappearance of the category of the limit, the catastrophe. Response of capitalists and entrepreneurs: instead, incorporate the costs of depollution into production costs; this will raise retail prices considerably, the market will contract accordingly, and production will regulate itself given the lower capacity for consumption. No-one knows whether it is in this way, through incorporation into price, that pollution will be neutralized; but it is certain that capitalism will not take, for it cannot take, the decision to hold the growth of the productive machine at zero. It gets around the obstacle with a supplementary 'axiom' (the allocation of the costs of depollution to the cost price, or else the tax system).

ENERGUMEN CAPITALISM

A very deep, very superficial subversion of Marxism, unspoken.... This figure of Kapital, that of the circulation of flows, is what brings about the predominance of the point of view of circulation over that of production—in political economy's sense of the word. (For in Deleuze and Guattari's sense, production is the connection and cutting of flows, a gush of milk sucked from the breast and cut off by the lips, energy extracted and converted, a flow of electrons converted into the rotation of a mill, jets of sperm sucked in by the womb.) Of course there will be no shortage of attacks on this predominance of the point of view of circulation. When Deleuze and Guattari write that capitalism must be thought according to the category of the bank rather than that of production, it will be cried that this is Keynesian ideology, a techno-bureaucratic representation of the system by intellectuals cut off from practice, and that in abandoning the point of view of production, one turns one's back on work, the worker, struggle, and class. And indeed there is not a word on the theory of labour-value; and just a word, but an enigmatic one, on a hypothesis on machinic surplus value. In truth, the great flood of the book washes up several important corpses: the proletariat, class struggle, human surplus-value.... It puts forth the image of a decoded capitalism full of current circulations and yet more intense potential circulations that only a whole series of dikes ('reterritorializations') can restrain and keep within the banks, only a whole battery of repressions led by the fundamental State: the Arche-State and its Oedipus.

Capitalism as metamorphosis, with no extrinsic code, having its limit only within itself, a relative, postponed limit (which is the law of value)—in fact this is an 'economics' that is found already in *The German Ideology*, again in the manuscripts of 1857–58 (*Grundrisse, Introduction to the Critique of Political Economy*), and in *Capital* itself. And the fact that this economics has something to do with the libido, we find traces of this in the *Reading Notes* of 1843, at one end of Marx's oeuvre, and at the other in *Capital*'s chapter on fetishism, as Baudrillard has shown. The critical universality of capitalism is outlined as well, the hypothesis that with *indifference*, with the effect of the principle of equivalence (that is, decoding), there surfaces in the workers' or the capitalist practice of capitalism the *empty* space in which the construction of the great categories of work and value will become possible, along with the possibility of applying these categories retroactively to dispositifs ('precapitalist' forms) in which these modalities had been covered over by codes, by markings and representations that did not permit a generalized political economy—that is, forms that kept political and libidinal economies apart from one another, with the latter diverted into religion, customs, and rituals of inscription, cruelty, and terror. With capitalism, all of this becomes equalizable, the modalities of production and inscription are simplified into the law of value, and thus anything can be produced-inscribed so long as inscription-production energy deposited in a trace or any object whatsoever can be converted back into energy, into another object or another trace. Portrait of an almost schizophrenic capital. Occasionally called perverse, but it is a normal perversion, the perversion of a libido machining its flows over a body without organs which it can cling to everywhere and nowhere, just as the flows of material and economic energy can, in the form of production—that is, of conversion—invest any region whatsoever of the surface of the social body, the smooth and indifferent *socius*. Transient cathexes, which cause all territories limited and marked by codes to disappear in their wake—not only on the side of objects (the prohibitions of production and circulation explode one after another), but also on the side of individual and social '*subjects*', which appear in this transit only as indifferent concretions, themselves exchangeable and anonymous, whose illusion of existence can only be maintained at the price of great expenditures of energy.

In short, there is little standing in the way of capitalism already being that voyage in intensities, that egg, the variable milieu whose surface is traversed and continually affluent here and there with little machines, little organs, little prostheses, already the Spinozist substance adorned with its attributes or the Democritean void where atoms dance, of our already enjoying the gaiety of being wise in God-Nature-Return. Is is Marxist, this Spinozism, this atomism? It matters little, it's not at all a matter of creating an orthodoxy, but rather of detecting an inspiration at once present and *repressed* in Marx. Hence the atomist theme: in capitalism, individuals constitute themselves as desocialized, deterritorialized, denatured, 'free' entities (*The German Ideology*), at the same time as they find themselves governed by *chance*, by a god who is indifferent to their affairs, by a deviant Epicurean god, by a non-rule, the non-rule of the clinamen, the floating free of the destiny of their territoriality and their familiarity. In his *Doctoral Dissertation*, Marx, well before being Marxist, said: Epicurus's doctrine on gods 'does away with religious fear and superstition, it gives to gods neither joy nor favours, but allows us the same relation that we have with Hycarnius's fish, from which we expect neither harm nor profit.' And if the gods become worldly, declining all responsibility for men, Marx says, it is for the same 'reason' that the atom deviates, according to the principle of the *clinamen*, from the straight line that its fall traces out in the void. For through this straight line it is tied to a system, it is subject to *fati foedera*, as Lucretius says, to the bonds of 'it is said'; the clinamen, on the contrary, is 'at the heart of the atom, that something that can struggle and resist', says Marx; it escapes heteronomy, and thus the negativity implied by the 'law of the other'. The same goes for the principle of the repulsion of atoms: 'Their negation of all relation to one another must be realised effectively, posited positively [*wirklich, positiv gesetzt*]', and thus can only be the moment of repulsion through which each atom is related solely to itself. Deviant and repulsive atoms, oblique and indifferent gods; individuals 'declining' in 'free' fall, in the empty space of capital; flows cut with neither finality nor causality; orphan fluxes fleeing the *fati foedera* of organic or social pseudo-bodies: what subtends all of this is the same figure, that of schizophrenia and/or materiality. And if, for the (Marxist) Marx of 1857, capitalism is the index of a universality applicable to all the great socio-economic machines including itself, there is no doubt that it is through the void, the indifference into which it plunges all beings, the (indistinct, aleatory) declinability of the individual in relation to labour, of the object in relation to money, of Kapital in relation to the product.

Another repressed theme, that of the dissolution of subjective-objective illusions of producing and consuming: all production is a consumption of the the raw materials, instruments and energies employed in their production, and all consumption is production of a new form, a metamorphosis of the consumed into a different product. 'This identity of production and consumption', says Marx, 'comes back to Spinoza's proposition: *Determinatio est negatio*'. Here is a materialist (not at all dialectical) usage of negation, its positive usage; this *determinatio* is the atom, and it is the cutting off of flows. Take once again, this time in *Capital*, the chapter on the rate of surplus-value, where you will find this perfectly Deleuzo-Guattarian text:

> If we look at the creation and the alteration of value for themselves, i.e. in their pure form, then the means of production, this physical shape taken on by constant capital, provides only the material in which fluid, value-creating power [*die flüssige, wertbildende Kraft*] has to be incorporated. Both the nature and the value of this material [*Stoff*] are indifferent [*gleichgültig*].

And the later Marx adds a note:

> What Lucretius says is self-evident: 'nil posse cretiri de nihilo', out of nothing, nothing can be created. 'Creation of value' is the transformation [conversion, transposition, *Umsatz*] of labour-power into labour. Labour-power itself is, above all else, the material of nature [*Naturstoff*] transposed, converted [*umgesetzt*] into a human organism.[2]

In an essay profoundly influenced by the Frankfurt School—that is, by negative dialectics—Alfred Schmidt, analyzing the relation between labour and nature in Marx, in spite of his intentions, gives many proofs that the *Verwandlungen*, the *Umsätze*, that comprise *all* of political economy, are characterized by Marx as much as metamorphoses of a neutral energy placed *upstream* from any nihilistic splitting, as relations of the working subject and the worked object, or of use-value and exchange-value, that is

2. K. Marx, *Capital, Vol 1*, trans. B. Fowkes (London: Penguin, 1993), 323 (trans. modified).

to say of two beings in a dialectical relation. No doubt there is in Marx, in the depth of his movement, this energetic inspiration, an economy which, repressed under the dialectical dispositif, is *far more than political*, never openly libidinal of course, but which allows a libidinal apporach through the analysis of primary processes, for the *clinamen*, the orphan and indifference, is primacy. And Marx's desire to know! Doesn't his secret reside in Spinozist, Lucretian *jouissance*, in his attempt to dissolve all the discourses of bourgeois political economy by connecting them up to the generalized fluidification engendered by Kapital and to himself produce a theoeretical object capable of corresponding to this liquefaction even as it exhibits its hidden law, the law of value?

In the figure of Kapital that Deleuze and Guattari propose, we easily recognize what fascinates Marx: the capitalist *perversion*, the subversion of codes, religions, decency, trades, education, cuisine, speech, the levelling of all 'established' differences into the one and only difference: being worth..., being exchangeable for.... Indifferent difference. *Mors immortalis*, as he would say.

Deleuze and Guattari have brought this fascination to light, freed it from bad conscience; they help us to flush it out into the politics of today. Bad conscience in Marx himself, and worse and worse in Marxists. And in proportion to this increasingly bad conscience, a piety meant to conceal and expiate this appetite for capitalist liquefaction: this piety—dialectics—amounts to keeping the positive perversion of capitalism inside a dispositif of negativity, contradiction and neurosis which will make possible the detection and *denunciation of the forgetting of the creditor (the proletariat) and of the debt (surplus value)* in a freedom declared to be factitious and guilty, in a positivity judged to be a façade. So Marxism will be this repairing and remonstrating enterprise in which one will demonstrate and re-monstrate the system as a faithless debtor, and devote all political energy to the project of righting the wrong—not just any wrong, said Marx in 1843, but a wrong in itself, this living wrong that the proletariat *is*, the wrong of alienation. A rather strange device inherited from Christianity, but one that, as we know, will take on paranoiac dimensions with Stalin and Trotsky, before falling into the routine of a faded belief in today's 'communism'.

It is this dispositif of negativity and guilt that *Anti-Oedipus* rids Marxism of. Cendrars said that 'artists are, above all, men who struggle to become inhuman'. The book's silence on class struggle, the saga of the worker and the function of his party, which weigh down the language of politics, lead one to believe that for the authors, the true politics today is in fact that of men who struggle to become inhuman. No debt to be tracked down. Its muteness on surplus value springs from the same source: looking for the creditor is a wasted effort, the subject of the credit would always have to be *made to exist*, the proletariat would always have to be incarnated on the surface of the *socius*—that is, represented in the representative box on the political stage; and that is the seed of the Arche-State's reappearence, it is Lenin and Stalin, it might be a nameless subject, the Party, a Void, the Signifier—and it is never anything but that, since a creditor is always the name of a lack. So let go of bad politics, the politics of bad conscience, its sagacious corteges and their banners, weighty processions of simulated piety: capitalism is never going to perish of bad conscience, it will not expire through lack, through a failure to give the exploited what they are owed. If it dies, it is through excess, because its energetics continually displace its limits; 'restitution' comes as an extra and not as a paranoiac passion to do justice, to give everyone their due, as if one knew what it was, as if it weren't evident today that the 'wage' of a worker in any one of the ten wealthiest nations did not contain, in addition to the market value of his energy expenditure, a redistributed share of surplus value! It is not only Naville who thinks so; in their own way, economists such as Ota Sik and Z. Tanko, in supposing that there is a twofold function of wages, the exchangeable value of labour-power (which is private property) but also a counterpart redistributed by the state of the use-value of social labor, essentially concede the point. This does not mean that one is already in socialism or that socialism is now inevitable(!) It only means that the law that governs exchange is perhaps not the principle of equal quantity of abstract labor contained in exchangeable commodities; and that there is therefore indeed a principle of equivalence, but that it is not anchored in a *deep exteriority*, that the value of labour-power and the value of an hour of median (abstract) social labour are not determinable in relation to the conditions of natural survival, in relation to a nature of elementary needs; that, on the contrary, they are the object of incessant conflicts on the social *surface*, and that therefore there is no depth or origin, that unions, bureaucratic cliques, pressure groups oppose and combine ceaselessly to fix a distribution of the GNP which is in itself floating and without originary reference. The same process, in short, for labour-value as for gold-value, where convertibility, even in principle, must also be abandoned and replaced by the play of an incessant negotiation—that is to say, deterritorialized and dragged into the waves of exchangeable words and things.

NEITHER STRUCTURES, EVEN INFRASTRUCTURES, NOR EXCHANGE, EVEN SYMBOLIC EXCHANGE

What are these prohibitions that capitalism opposes to the incessant movements of flows? 'Reterritorializations' necessary to keep the system in place, say Deleuze and Guattari.[3] These circumscribed sites on the surface of the *socius*, which disconnect whole regions and shelter them from the schizo-flows, are neo-archaisms, they say:[4] Indian reservations, fascism, exchange

---

3. G. Deleuze and F. Guattari, *Anti-Oedipus*, trans R. Hurley, M. Seem, H. R. Lane (London: Athlone, 1984), 257–62.

4. Ibid., 257ff.

money, Third-Worldist bureaucracies, private property[5]—and of course, Oedipus and the Urstaat.

Rather flippant, is it not, to place under the same function the pueblo and capital money, Stalin and Hitler, Hitler and private property! What about super- and infrastructures? Well, not a word on this subject, of course. There are only desiring-machines, the body without organs, their stormy relationships being already of the molecular order, relationships between the anus making shit, the mouth making words, the eyes making eyes, and a surface, that of the supposed body, where they have to position, inscribe and compose themselves—and then of the order of the (supposed) great social body, the *socius*, of the molar order once more, the violent disjunction between, on one hand, the blind, machinic repetition of the production-inscription of little organs and social segments; and on the other hand, the mapping-back and hoarding of these segmentary productions on the surface of the socius, especially by the Arche-State. No structures in the linguistic or semiotic sense; only dispositifs of energy transformation. And among these dispositifs, no reason to privilege (under the name of infrastructure) that which regulates the production and circulation of *goods*, the so-called 'economic' dispositif.... For there is no less an *economy*, an energetics, in the dispositif that will regulate lineages and alliances, distributing flows of intensity into concretions of roles, persons and goods on the surface of the *socius*, and that will finally produce what is called the organization of savage society (an organism that is in fact never unified, but always divided between the thousand poles of little multiple organs, partial objects, libidinal segments, and the pole of unification by the void created on high, at the summit, at and in the head, by the signifier)—no less of an economy in the laws of kinship, no less of an economy even in the distribution of the

5. Ibid, 259.

libido on the surface of the body without organs, in the hooking-up of little desiring, energy-transforming and pleasure-seeking organs, than in the economics and distribution of capital, no less of a producing-inscribing dispositif there than here. And inversely, the Oedipal formation is no less political-economic than that of Kapital, and ultimately it is no less eco-libidinal and deviant than the primary process it captures. So it is not a matter of discerning which of these dispositifs is subordinating and which subordinated: there is a reciprocal subordination.[6] But to follow the infra/super hypothesis, we should have to presuppose the organic totality of the social field, presuppose and require the social whole, dividing up structures within a macro-structure, with the whole as the starting point, supposing the whole to be given or at least discernable and analyzable. When the very problem is that *the whole is not given*, that society *is not* a unified totality, but is made up of displacements and metamorphoses of energy that endlessly decompose and recombine into subsets and draw these subsets now towards the organs' perverse-schizo functioning, now towards the neurotic-paranoiac functioning of the great absent signifier. If you speak in terms of super- and infra- you are ordering dispositifs according to high and low, and already you have adopted the point of view of the signifier, of the whole, and *it will not let you go*: when you want to conduct a revolutionary politics, to imagine a subversive becoming, if you don't attack this edifice, you will have a dialectics at best, and at best, according to the latter, one 'after' the negative moment, 'after' the revolution—that is, *already before* (in the form of a party, for example, or a need for effectiveness or for organization, or the fear of failure). And the same hierarchized arrangement will be reproduced: the same worker-militant on the bottom and the same leader-boss on the top, the same confiscation of flows and partial productions in the general interest—that is to say, in the interests of the despot.

---

6. Ibid., 288.

What allows us to say this, once again, is no fantasy: it is capitalism itself. It is capitalism which, sweeping through the most forbidden regions with its flows of work and money—through art, science, trades and festivals, politics and sports, words and images, air, water, snow and sun, Bolshevik, Maoist and Castroist revolutions, it is capitalism that, in traversing these regions, makes the coded dispositifs that formerly governed their economies appear as libidinal configurations at the very moment that it consigns them to obsolescence. It thus reveals that oppositions between infra- and superstructures, between economic and ideological structures, between relations of production and social relations, are themselves pairs of concepts that tell us nothing about what happens in savage, feudal or Oriental societies, or even in capitalist society itself. For they are either too much or too little: too much because it is unquestionable that in the former, kinship, ritual and practical relationships decisively determine the production and circulation of goods, that is, the configuration of the 'economy', and that they cannot be reduced to an illusory ideological function; and too little because in the latter, the term 'economics' covers much more than political economy, much more than the production and exchange of goods, since it is no less the production and exchange of labour power, images, words, knowledge and power, travel and sex.

If political economy is a discourse that founds phenomena of production and circulation by anchoring them in a nature (Physiocratic Nature, the interests and needs of *Homo Oeconomicus*, the creative power of the force of the worker), as such it is never applicable: beyond the hypothetical level of survival, archaic societies are no less arbitrary than capitalism, and capitalism fits no better than they do into the category of interest and need, or work. Nowhere is there a primary economic order (= an order of interest, need or work) followed by ideological, cultural, legal, religious, familial, etc., effects. Everywhere there are dispositifs for the capture and discharge of libidinal energy; but in archaic or Oriental societies, energy and its concretions into 'objects' (sexual partners, children, tools and weapons, food) must be *marked* with a seal, an incision, an abstraction which is precisely that of the archaic arts, for their function is not to 'represent' in the sense of the Quattrocento, but rather to code what is libidinally invested or investable, to authorize what may circulate and produce pleasure; these codes are therefore sorters, selectors, brakes-accelerators, dams and canals, mitral valves regulating the inputs and outputs of energy in all its forms (words, dances, children, foods...) in relation to the *socius*, the non-existent, postulated Great Social Body; whereas these codifications of functions, these specific regulations in their concrete abstractions—a certain inscription on a certain part of the skin to denote puberty, a certain distortion of the neck, the ear, the nostrils, or the fabrication of a hat of chicken or pig entrails (Leiris in Gondar) to mark a particular function in a religious or magic ritual, this tattoo denoting the right to bear arms, that ornament on the chiefs face, those words and chants and drum beats inscribed in the ritual scenario of sacrifice, mourning or excision—capitalism sweeps all of this away, it is all surpassed and dissipated; capitalism deculturalizes peoples, dehistoricizes their inscriptions, repeats them anywhere at all so long as they are marketable, recognizes no code that is marked by the libido but only exchange value: you can produce and consume everything, exchange, work or inscribe anything anyway you want it, so long as it moves, flows, is metamorphizable. *The only untouchable axiom* bears on the condition of metamorphosis and transfer: exchange value. Axiom and not code: energy and its objects are no longer marked with a sign; properly speaking, *there are no longer* signs since there is no longer code, no reference to an origin, to a norm, to a 'practice', to a supposed nature or surreality or reality, to a paradigm or to a Great Other—there is nothing left but a little price tag, the index of exchangeability: it's nothing, it's enormous, it's something else.

Now, not only does this define a political economy, it determines an entirely singular libidinal economy. One can approach it, like Baudrillard, on the basis of the category of ambivalence and castration, and say: capitalism is fetishism, not only in a general sense, in the Feuerbachian-Hegelian sense, or the sense Marx gives it, but in the strict sense that the word takes on in the nosology of perversions: it is fetishism because castration and the splitting of desire are completely occulted in it. The relationship to the object in Kapital is the perverse relationship: the difference between the sexes is abolished in it, not qua sexism (although even there, hairdressers and 'no sex', women's lib and gay movement clothes stores accelerate desexization), but qua desire implicating in itself its own prohibition, as barred drive. Equivalence is placed before ambivalence, obliterating it: generalized exchangeability omits the fact that there is, in the order of desire, something that is unexchangeable on pain of death (and *jouissance* in so far as it always includes in it this risk of death). And Baudrillard opposes to the monotonic modern exchange an economy of the gift, of the potlatch, in which *irreversibility*, the disaster of extreme expenditure, economic and social ruin, annihilation through loss of prestige, physical death, eternal non-enjoyment, and thus a libidinal symbolism, are effectively implicated.

These 'conclusions' converge with Deleuze and Guattari's. But it is the divergence that we should note, because it allows us to sense what is at stake in *Anti-Oedipus*. The fine description of savage cruelty goes entirely in the direction of what Baudrillard wishes to make manifest under the name of *symbolic exchange*. As for fluidity and flight in one, so for equivalence in the other. But the site from which one speaks is not the same in one as in the other. Desire, in Baudrillard, a strict Freudian, is still thought in terms of a subject.

A barred subject, but a subject nonetheless: just as the fragmented body is still a body, only *subsequently* relating the fragmentation to itself as its property, the bar also relates itself to desire as an attribute to its substance. In both cases, we must put at the other end of the process an 'author' of the bar, a nothing, a *signifier* zero, the big Other, who would therefore be the true producer of the bar. Thus desiring production would be designated as *nihilist signifier*. When Deleuze and Guattari begin from desiring machines and set out to make use of only the most elementary categories of disjunction and conjunction, connection and exclusion—that is to say, connection and cutting, with possible recursivity (production of production), when they speak of a body without organs and of a *socius* as of a *surface of mapping*, a surface upon which productions (that is, flows-cuts) will come to be applied to be inscribed upon it, *as if* this body were the great producer, the great subject, the great signifier, *as if* it were the primary source and unity, whereas it is itself but a principle of a leading astray—dare I say, alienation?—in any case, of death in the Freudian sense, the function of their discourse is not to provide a new metaphor for the zero signifier, but to produce the *rebel economic categories* that are lacking, outside Lucretius, Spinoza and Nietzsche, in the thinking of desire, rebelling against the mapping of this thought (which is itself not yet anything but desire, a desire for desire) back onto a signifying order, rebelling against a philosophical or psychoanalytical mapping that is a particular case of the mapping of desiring production back onto the body without organs.

If therefore one continues to think capitalism and savagery in terms of lack, castration, and even ambivalence and *irreversibility*, saying that the first occults them whereas the second inscribes them in its codes, one completes the occultation of desiring production, one does metaphysical thought very little harm, and in fact one fulfills nihilist thought: the subject, it will be said, never shows itself 'in the flesh', it is fragmented, barred, deferred, present/absent, etc.

But what is important is that one continue to place the libido under the category of the signifier and to ignore it in its *non-sense* and its force of forgetting. Now, far from having to *heal the subject* by reducing it either to the illusion of a well-balanced socio-familial character (traditional psychoanalysis) or to the disillusionment of a subject tragically barred from itself (Lacanian psychoanalysis), we must *heal the subject* by liquidating it in anonymity, orphanhood, innocence and the aleatory plurality of little machines that is 'desire'.

Thus we should not oppose capitalism to savagery as that which hides and that which exhibits castration—that is to say, as that which is false and that which is true; we should not look at capitalism from the point of view of a *nostalgia* for savagery and truth, which is a nostalgia for naturalness and representation. There is no good (savage, symbolic) state of libido, no correct modality of mapping back upon the *socius*, that of cruelty (Deleuze and Guattari quite rightly do not say a word on Artaud's *theatre*). Just as we must not confuse the content of socialism with the restitution of libidinal marks on the social body given over to its cruel fragmentation. We must evacuate the whole nostalgic mode of speaking and seeing: it exits via the hole Deleuze and Guattari rip open in Western discourse. The territorial machinery of savagery or even the great despotic machine of barbarianism are not (as Nietzsche sometimes dreams) a good perspective from which to look at the capitalist machinery. Following Marx, Deleuze and Guattari say the opposite: that capitalism is the only good perspective from which to look at everything. If you look at capitalism through castration, you think you see it from the despotic Orient or from savage Africa, but in fact you perpetuate the nihilism of Western religion: your position is still inspired by bad conscience and piety for Nature and Exteriority and Transcendence; while capitalism, which is far more positive than atheism, which is the indication of a profound liquidity of economic flows on the surface of the *socius*, is by this very token what retroactively makes us see the precapitalistic codes and lets us comprehend the way in which it itself, related only to itself, *index sui*, blocks up and channels this liquidity into the law of value. The law of value, the only axiom of this system entirely made up of *indifference* and equivalence (*Gleichgiltigkeit*, says Marx again and again, young and old), is also the only limit, an impassible *limit* if you wish, always displaceable and displaced, that keeps capitalism from being carried off by the aleatory deluge of molecular energetics.

Thus, underneath the congruence of a *Critique of the Political Economy of the Sign* with *Anti-Oedipus*, there is a discordance, and what is at stake in it is the question of nihilism, and 'politics'. It is not enough to critique Marx, since he maintains with need and use (and the labour power itself, Baudrillard!) an exteriority, a reference, a naturalness that is supposed to anchor economic signs. It is not enough to attack 'American' psychoanalysis with sarcasm because it wishes to heal the subject by endowing it with an illusory unity. It is not a matter of telling capitalism that beneath its young girls' smiles and the perverse surfaces of metal, polystyrene, skin and spotlights, and because of them, it miscognizes the ambivalence and the bar of the libidinal subject. The strength of capitalism, on the contrary, lies in its beginning to unravel itself from the function of this ambivalence, its beginning to make obvious that it is not the doing of libidinal economy as a small or large machine, but the result of the superposition onto this economy of a sensical and nihilist dispositif, that of Oedipus-castration. Revolution is not the return to the great castrator and the little castratees, a definitively reactionary view, but their dissolution in an economy without end or law.

THE OEDIPAL DISPOSITIF

The question to be asked of Deleuze and Guattari is evidently that of origin or finality, or of the condition of possibility, or..., of this 'secondary' order, this order that contains the void, that separates, orders and subordinates, that terrorizes and causalizes, that is the law (of value and exchange). But before that, why Oedipus? Why the Arche-State in a dispositif such as capitalism, whose corresponding 'meaning-effect', as Deleuze and Guattari repeat, is cynicism? There's nothing less cynical than Oedipus, nothing more guilty. Why and how would this circulation of flows regulated only by the law of exchange value need as a supplement, a premium of repression, the figure of Oedipus—that is, according to Deleuze and Guattari, the figure of the State? Do they not themselves grant that bad conscience comes neither from despotism nor from capitalism, since the former generates terror, the latter cynicism? Then what generates this bad conscience? A question on two levels: (1) What purpose can Oedipalization serve within the system of generalized exchange? and (2) Is Oedipus really a configuration of the Urstaat? The first level is plugged directly into the politics of capital and anticapitalistic politics as well; the second into a theory of history and into the psychoanalytical dispositif itself.

First level: if capitalism needs no code whatever, if its only axiom is the law of value—that is, the exchangeability of sections of flows in equal *quanta*—then why Oedipus? Is not the configuration of the father, the great despotic signifier, nothing more than an archaism—not even a neo-archaism—at the heart of the figure of exchange? The Oedipal figure in Deleuze and Guattari's hypothesis is that of Oriental despotism, which we shall return to shortly: does that mean that the capitalist State is the same as that of the Chinese kingdoms, the Great Kings and the Pharaohs? There is certainly in all of them a predominance of bureaucracy as an apparatus for the channeling of libidinal economic flows. Deleuze and Guattari rely a great deal on Wittfogel, in fact, far too much. Not because Wittfogel is often very imprudent as a *historian*, which is another problem; but because his whole book is inspired by a *political* confusion between the system of precapitalist domination, what Marx called the Asiatic mode of production, and the regime that Stalin imposed on Russia and its satellites for twenty years. Now, the absence of private property, the absorption of all economic and social initiative by the bureaucratic apparatus, and the suspension of all activity, of all energetic flows—whatever their order—in the figure of the despot, traits that are indeed common to both societies, obviously do not make them identical.

The decisive difference is precisely that Stalin and Mao are postcapitalist, that their regimes are in fact in competition with world capitalism, that they can only survive by accepting the challenge of industrialization, without which capitalism would not fail to infiltrate the bureaucratic society with flows of money, with products, with technological and cynical—as well as revolutionary and critical—thought, causing fissures to appear everywhere. This is what happens continually in the European glacis. Fissures that go to the right and fissures that go toward the left, pressure from the economic and technical framework in the direction of liberalization, that is to say in the direction of incorporation, at least economic and ideological incorporation, into the global capitalist market: the pressure of the young in the direction of self-management and council communism. All of this makes for a very lively bureaucratic life, very different from that of the Han empire, and a troubled bureaucracy: it has the agitation of Kapital under its skin, not the immobile peace of the sacred. A bureaucracy threatened by the mobility of modern capitalism, and by its wastefulness; including its political figures: look around the world, now that the great paranoaic figures of the Second

World War have gone (except for Mao), see if there is one single leader who is really a paternal figure.

Let us go further: why should capitalism preserve the institution of the family, constraining the child's libido to fixate upon it? The *Communist Party Manifesto* said that 'by the action of Modern Industry, all the family ties among the proletarians are torn asunder'. Perhaps this was said from a miserabilist perspective that was not vindicated? But a fortiori if this *unbinding* takes place even outside of material poverty, which is indeed the case. What is the family life of a child today, with a working father and mother? Kindergarten, school, homework, juke-boxes, cinema: everywhere children of their age, and adults who are not their parents, who are in conflict with them and between themselves, who say one thing and do another. The heroes are at the cinema and on television, in comics, not around the family dinner table. A more direct investment than ever in historical figures. Parental figures, teachers, priests, they also undergo the erosion of capitalist flows. No, truly, supposing that psychoanalysis is indeed oedipalization, it is not the doing of capitalism, it goes against the law of value. A salaried father is an exchangeable father, an orphaned son. We have to uphold Deleuze and Guattari's thinking against themselves: capitalism is indeed an orphanage, a celibacy, submitted to the rule of equivalence. What supports it is not the figure of the great castrator, but that of equality: equality in the sense of the commutability of men in one place and of places for one man, of men and women, objects, spaces, organs. A society constituted according to a mathematical group structure: a set (every quantum of energy: man, woman, thing, word, colour, sound, is part of it), a rule of associativity *ab*, a rule of commutativity *ab=ba* and a neutral term *ae=a*. And there is the whole secret of its 'repression'. (And there, let us note in passing, is the whole secret of the connivance of Kapital with the figure of knowledge, which is the true *dispositif* governing libidinal economy under capitalism). Look instead at how the family is treated in the MIT report[7] and Mansholt's letter and the whole zero growth current, and tell us whether it's Kapital that is preoccupied with the institution.

It will be said: none of this changes the fact that repression is increasing in modern societies, and that the law of value alone does not eliminate the forces of order. But we ought to respond: repression becomes ever more *exteriorized*; since it is less in people's heads it is more in the streets. Cynicism is unstoppable, hence the police and militia contingents. There are as many more cops as there are fewer fathers, teachers, chiefs, moral leaders—that is, ones that are recognized, 'interiorized'. Freud was completely mistaken in *Civilization and its Discontents* in expecting that the extension of 'civilization' in the bourgeois sense of material civilization, and in the League of Nations sense of 'perpetual peace', which he equated with the reabsorption of external expressions of aggression, would be accompanied by an aggravation of its internal expression—that is, ever increasing anguish and guilt. In the regions where this civilized peace reigns—in the center of capitalism—there is nothing of the kind, and so much the better. The Great Signifier and Great Castrator are drawn into the rapid and polluted waters of the reproduction of capitalism, the Great Metamorphosis. A modern man believes in nothing, not even in his responsibility-guilt. Repression is imposed not as punishment, but as a reminder of the axiomatic: the law of value, give and take. It might be the PTA exerting it on children, the union on the workers, the woman's magazine on the 'weaker sex', the writer on discourse, or the museum curator on paintings—they do not at all act as terrifying or cruel incarnations of a transcendental Power, even though they possess it. In fact their entire operation amounts only to the

7. D.H. Meadows et al, *The Limits to Growth* (New York: Universe Books, 1972)—trans.

maintenance of the most elementary rule, the last word of Kapital: 'equitable' exchange, equivalence. They do not frighten, they hurt. A simple and blatant example: when teaching, you can teach whatever seems best to you, including what is written here; but the absolute reference point is to be selected at the end of the year, so as not to devalue your teaching. Thus, not: teaching of value, and *then* the selection of students according to this value; but: the selection of students, even a totally arbitary selection (an arbitrariness noone can ignore any longer), and *by this very token* valorization of your teaching. It is the law of exchange that determines the value of the terms, here your teaching, on one hand, and on the other the 'qualification' of the students. End of the ideology of 'culture', then: one no longer claims to produce an object that is supposedly valuable *for itself* or in its 'use'; but value is defined by exchangeability; this diploma that you will give to the student, can he exchange it in real life (=for money)? That's the *only* question. This question, everywhere the same, *is not* that of castration, of Oedipus.

Take painting, it's the same question. One doesn't ask the painter *what* his pictorial object *is*, one does not seek to attach it to a network of meanings; one is concerned about where it is, if it is or could be in a pictorial *site* (gallery, exhibition), for it is only from this position that it will acquire a 'pictorial' value, since it is only if it is *in this* site that it can be taken out in exchange for its price=through sale (and possibly afterwards resold by the art lover to be placed in a museum). Its value is its exchangeability, and thus its place in the pictorial place that is the market for painting. Outside of this it is *absolutely impossible* to determine an *intrinsic value* of the modern painting object. See the Pompidou exhibition.[8]

---

8. Presumably, The Expo 72 at the Grand Palais—trans.

It would be easy to show that scientific research functions according to the same basic axiomatic: only varying according to a few complementary exigencies, for example the operativity of the enunciations produced, which suffice to determine the limits of the field of application and the 'nature' of the object.

Nowhere do you find any attachment to the Great Signifier, but only the immanent law of exchange between terms whose sole value comes down to their relation. This is the very definition of a *structure*, which is the product par excellence of Kapital and scientism, the eminently capitalist libidinal object. The gap that segments the object to be structured into discrete terms[9]—a gap which, it must be emphasized, *excludes all signification* and strictly speaking must even exclude the use of the term 'signifier' such as it comes to us from a Saussure still very uncertain on this subject (almost as uncertain as Marx as to the part played by use-value)—this gap must not be confused nor even articulated with that via which Lacan, for example, supposes, under the name of the withdrawal of the signifier, to produce effects of sense (=signifieds) at the level of the terms in question. Difference in Saussure is not the A in Lacan.

Why do Deleuze and Guattari here neglect a *reversal* which is essential to Lacan's problematic? In Saussure, the signified is the hidden, the signifier is the given. In Lacan, the hidden is the signifier and the signified is given (as representation, illusion, *a* and *a'*). This reversal is decisive: the figure of desire in Lacan uses the same words as in Saussure but distributes them inversely; for Saussure, the signifier and the signified are related to the speaking subject who is the locutor; the same goes for Lacan, except that *the locutor is not an interlocutor* in the sense that linguists use the term, an allocutor in Benveniste's sense. It speaks, but not as I speak, not in the site where I speak, not on the same scene, but

9. Ibid., 206–7.

on another scene. Now, when Lacan makes this hypothesis as to the unconscious-language, what is important is not that he brings it together with the 'scientific' problematic of discourse, even if he himself lays the emphasis on this effect; in reality it is just an ideological 'screen'. The point is that it reduces to a surface the deep figure that is latent in the whole psychoanalytical dispositif, in the whole dispositif of the *desire of psychoanalysis*, the Judaic figure of the paradoxical Jahweh: The silent thou, or silence in the second person, that is to say the potential locutor who will never be effective for I Moses-Israel, hidden signifier; but also (on the other scene, the Sinai, for example), Thou the sole speaker, including through my mouth, and thus a signifier even so, and I the solely manifest locutor, latent silence, signified.

And so we proceed to the second level: Oedipus is not a figure of the Urstaat, a despotic figure. Here as with guilt (and the two institutions go hand in hand), Deleuze and Guattari remain too near and too far from Freud. Too near, for it was indeed Freud's hypothesis in *Moses and Monotheism* that the source of Judaism was in the Oriental, monotheistic 'despotism' of Akhenaton and thus that the father figure conveyed by Judaism, Freud himself, and all of psychoanalysis, is the figure of the castrating and incestuous despot. But very far at the same time, since for Freud what made the *difference* between Judaism and Egyptian religion, or Catholicism—in a sense between Judaism and *every religion*—what then in Judaism undid religiosity or was its potential defeat or defection was the foreclosure of the wish for the Father's death and its acting out, the carrying out of the original murder (supposed by Freud, but at the cost of what novelistic imagination!) by Israel of a first Moses (also a supposition). Which means that in Judaism Oedipus remains unavowed, inadmissible, hidden—and this, for Freud, is how guilt and bad conscience are born, unlike what happens in religions of reconciliation.

The question here is not of following Freud in the construction of his familial or ethnic tale. It is a question of seeing that what he is trying to achieve, in conformity with his own libidinal construction, according to his own words, is to produce the singularity of the Judaic (and psychoanalytical) configuration of desire. And *like Nietzsche*, he apprehends it in bad conscience, sin. The status of the *origin* that Freud exhibits is not in question here. But what certainly does matter is the principle according to which Oedipus and castration—and by the same token, *transference in the psychoanalytic relationship*—are only operative in an energetic dispositif whose traits are formed by the most ancient Hebraic law: the channeling of all libidinal energy into the order of language (the elimination of idols); in language, an absolute privilege given to the I/Thou relationship (the elimination of myth); and within this relationship, the (Kierkegaardian) paradox of it always being Thou who speaks and never I. This dispositif is that of the couch, where Israel is the patient, Moses the analyst, and Yahweh the unconscious: the Great Other. The Great Other *is not* the great incestuous Pharaoh, Urvater or Urdespot. There was an exodus, the Jews broke with despotism, crossed the sea, the desert, and killed the father (the murder that Freud sought to reconstruct was simply this exodus), and this is why interiorization as sin, as solitude, as neurosis, as well as the whole current of reform—Lutheranism and Freudism—will become possible, will become a fundamental possibility for the West.

> We demand nothing of one another, we complain of nothing, but we both go on, the heart open, through open doors.
>
> —Zarathustra to his solitude

But Kapital's configuration *is not* articulated with that of Jewishness (of Oedipus) any more than it is with that of despotism or of symbolic savagery, it accords no privileges to discourse as the locus of the libido's inscription, it does away with all privileges of place: hence its mobility; its principle bears on the modality of inscription, its machinery obeys only one principle of energetic connection—the law of value, equivalence—the principle according to which all 'exchange' is always possible in principle, all plugging in or metamorphosis of one form of *Naturstoff* into another is always reconvertible by making the inverse connection. But what about surplus value, it will be asked? Does this not belie the dispositif, since it means that the relation between force and what it is supposed to be worth (its equivalent in commodities, its wages) is not convertible, and that their equality is fictitious? Certainly this may be true for every force that is *captured* in capitalist economic networks, including machines. The apparatus functions by ignoring the inequality of force and reabsorbing its potential as event, creation and mutation. Given the principle that governs energetic connection, the capitalist system privileges repetition without profound difference, duplication, commutation or replication, and reversibility. Metamorphosis is contained within the sagacious confines of metaphor. Surplus value and even profit are *already* denominations and practices of reabsorption (or exploitation, if you wish); they imply the commensurability of the given and the received, of the 'added value' obtained through production processes, and of the value advanced in production. This supposed commensurability is what permits the second to be transformed into the first, the reinvestment of surplus value—it is the rule or the management of the capitalist system. It is in this rule of immanent commutativity that the capitalist secret for the mapping back of desiring-production onto the body without organs is found: this mapping back is reinvesting under the law of value. In it consists the very repression of the system, and it needs no other—or the others (cops, etc.) are only lemmas or reciprocals of the fundamental theorem of replication.

This is what Deleuze and Guattari mean when they emphasise the fictitious nature of the commensurability of credit and payment monies.

The potential of force is not a potential to produce something more, but a potential to produce something other, in other ways. In the organism, force is a disorganizing power: emotional stress, pruritus, perverse polymorphism, so-called psychosomatic illnesses, the loss of spatial reference in the schizo's walk so dear to Deleuze and Guattari, a grinning cat and the grin without the cat—always work, but always as dream work. Force fuses through the organic screen, perfusing energy. Now, it is this virtuality of an alterity that is multiplying in the gut of the capitalist 'organism' and of the dispositif of value, which is on the way to *critiquing* without touching it, on the way to *forgetting* the law of exchange, getting around it and making it a glaring and obsolete illusion, an unserviceable network. Who can say how long it will take the new dispositif to sweep over the surface of our bodies and the social body with its unknown, transparent organs, to free them from their involvement with interests and the worries of saving, spending and counting? Another figure is rising, the libido is withdrawing from the capitalist apparatus, and desire is finding other ways of spreading itself out, according to another figure, one that is formless and ramified in a thousand ventures throughout the world, a bastard disguised in shreds of this and that, words from Marx and words from Jesus or Mohammed and words from Nietzsche and words from Mao, communitarian practices and slowdown actions in workshops, occupations, boycotts, squatting, kidnap and ransom, happenings and demusicalized music and sit-ins and sit-outs, taking trips and light shows, the liberation of gays and lesbians and 'madmen' and criminals, unilaterally undertaken free practices.... What can capitalism possibly do against this unserviceability that is rising from within it (in the form of unserviceable 'young' people, among others)—against this thing that is the new libidinal dispositif, and of which *Anti-Oedipus* is the production/inscription within language?

Force produces only when channelled, when partially invested. If schizophrenia is called the *absolute limit*, it is because if it ever happened, it would be force that was not distributed in a libidinal dispositif—pure liquid flexion. Through the multiplication of metamorphic principles, the annulment of codes regulating flows, capitalism brings us closer to this schizophrenic limit. And by bringing us closer to this limit, it places us already on the other side. Hence we can understand Deleuze and Guattari's disinterest in Bataille's theme of transgression: every limit is constitutively transgressed, there is nothing to transgress in a limit; what is important is not the other side of the frontier, since if there is a frontier, both sides must already have been posited, composed in one and the same world. Incest, for example, is but a very shallow stream: the mother can be composed (=thought of) as a mistress only in words; in *jouissance*, she is no longer the mother, no longer anything, what reigns then is the night of a hundred thousand disjointed organs and partial objects. Thus, either there is a limit—but it boils down to a too-human opposition, and desire is absent on both sides—or desire actually scans the field of the limit, its movement not that of transgressing the limit, but rather of pulverizing the field itself into a libidinal surface. If capitalism has such affinities with schizophrenia, it follows that its destruction cannot come from a deterritorialization (the mere abolition of private property, for example...), which by definition it will survive: it *is* this deterritorialization. Destruction can only come from an even more liquid liquidation, only from even more *clinamen* and less gravity, from more dancing and less piety. What we need is for the variations of intensity to become more unpredictable, stronger; in 'social life', for the highs and lows of desiring-production to be inscribed without finality, justification or origin, as in the heady moments of 'affective' or 'creative' life;

to be done with ressentiment and bad conscience (*always equal to themselves, always depressed*) of identities engendered by the service of paranoiac machines, by technology and by the bureaucracies of Kapital.

So what about the death instinct? Deleuze and Guattari energetically fight the Freudian hypothesis of self-directed guilt and hatred which underlies the diagnosis of *Civilization and its Discontents*: a death instinct that would be without original or experience, a theoretical product of Freud's pessimism destined to maintain the neurotic, dualistic position, whatever may happen. But if the death instinct is the reason why machines can only work by fits and starts and their cycles cannot be kept harmonious; if it is what perturbs desiring-production, through the body without organs either drawing off their production and monopolizing it, or repelling it and repressing it; if its model is a deranged machinic regime, an unregime; and if it presents itself in the corresponding experience of inarticulacy (the loss of every *articulus*), of the surface without variation in intensity, of catatonia, of the 'Ah, to not have been born', then it is not merely admissible, it is a necessary component of desire. Not at all *another* instinct, another energy, but within the libidinal economy, an inaccessible 'principle' of excess and disorder; not a second machinery, but a machine whose velocity can be displaced towards positive infinity and can bring it to a halt. It is this plasticity or viscosity that traces everywhere and nowhere the difference between political economy and libidinal economy, and owing to which in particular, a great savage configuration (a great apparatus)—for example—can be disinvested, pipes and filters can fall into obsolescence, and the libido can be distributed otherwise, in another figure: and therefore it is in this viscosity that all revolutionary potential lies.

Back to the representational theatre. Take the admirable chapter on the problem of Oedipus[10] in which all the congruencies that traverse the book are brought together or mentioned, and where the proximity to and difference from Freud is marked: a principle of segmentation, of quantification, of articulation must come to cut into the full body, into the egg of the earth where there is no extensive distance, but only intensive variations (a Kantian inheritance?), into the continuous hysteria of filiation and women, discernible articuli, persons, roles, names, and the same principle must distribute them, and organize them through procedures of extension that will determine the rules of alliance. The principle that circumscribes the site and the modality of the *inscription* of desiring production, that is to say the *socius*, is not, as we see, a productive principle; fundamentally it is not a *principle*, since it is destructive; it is not the Signifier, the foundational castrator, it manifests itself not in the bestial fury of the UrFather, but in the paranoiac collective of the homosexual community of men; in instituting chains of alliance, it institutes *representation*, presentation, on the scene-surface of the body without organs, *dramas about familial roles* which are there for—and will be a screen for—anonymous and orphan journeys of libidinal intensities. Thus the possibility of Oedipus comes about, the possibility of the myth of the UrFather. This is why it will be said that Oedipus is not originary, but is an effect of representation, which follows from the fact that the familial roles that result from the articulation and the repressive distribution in social organisation are projected upstream of repression, where in reality there is nothing but travelling intensities on the full body, energetic schizophrenia. A represented of displaced desire, then. A hypothesis probably less distant from Freud than Deleuze and Guattari suppose (Freud distinguishes very

10. Ibid., 154–86.

carefully the topic from the economic, the representative from the drive). But it matters little. It remains that under the names of distribution, paranoia, discernability, quantification, there must be a principle of exclusion that cuts out of the continuous economy of libidinal intensities an inside and an outside—that is to say, a duality; and that the latter is the whole wellspring of the theatrical dispositif, which will represent on the inside (the scene, the family, the *socius*) what it has to repress on the outside (economics, errancy, the full body). This principle of exclusion is originary repression, and all the procedures of absorption, of the mapping-back of desiring production onto the body or onto the *socius*, all the procedures of the rejection of molecular machines and partial objects outside the *socius* or of the body are ordered by this repression, this distancing.

And now here is the great business of our times: how to understand this distance without recourse to a dualism? How can there be secondary processes of articulation covering the primary processes, extracted from them, representing them? Granted that Oedipus is not originary, there must be, it will be said, a site of theatricalization, a barrier of investments that represses and limits the errancy of intensities, filtering them and composing them into a scene, whether social or 'psychic'. A scene now irreal, fantasmatic, illusory, forever distanced from the thing itself.

And your whole libidinal and political economy, the crooks will come and tell us, it's just representation like the rest, still a theatre, a theatre where you stage the outside, under the name of libido and machine, a metaphysics of sense despite itself, where the signified will be energy and its displacements, but where *you speak*, Deleuze and Guattari, and where therefore you are in the interior of the auditorium/stage volume, where your dear and sacred exteriority is, in spite of you, in the interior of your very words! One more metaphor to add to the total theatre of the

West, little dramas within a drama, at most a change of scenery; but no metamorphosis...

Here indeed is a depressed thought, here is a pious, nihilist thought. It is nihilist and pious because it is a *thought*. *A thought* is that in which the energetic position forgets itself in representing itself. Theatricality is everything that *thought* can denounce in thought, can critique. A thought can always critique a thought, can always exhibit the theatricality *of a thought*, repeating the distancing. But something passes through nevertheless, which thinkers cannot critique in so far as this something has not entered into theatrisable thought. What happens is a displacement. Thus, alongside medieval Europe was placed another dispositif, the renaissance-classical dispositif. What is important is not the discourse on metaphysics that is the discourse on metaphysics. Metaphysics is the force of discourse potential in all discourse. What counts is that it changes the scene, the dramaturgy, the site, the modality of inscription, the filter, and thus the libidinal position. Thinkers think metaphysical theatricality, and yet the position of desire is displaced, desire works, new machines start up, old ones stop working or idle for a moment or race and heat up. This transport of force does not belong to thought or to metaphysics. Deleuze and Guattari's book represents this transport in discourse. If you understand only its re-presentation, you have lost it; you would be right, you would have *reason*, in the interior of this figure, according to the criteria of this dispositif. But you will be forgotten, as everything is forgotten that is not forgetting, everything that is placed within the theatre, the museum, the school. In the libidinal dispositif that is rising, to be right, to have reason—that is, to place oneself in the museum—is not what is important; what is important is to be able to laugh and dance.

Bellmer describes an 'elementary expression', the hand's tightening on itself when one has a violent toothache: 'this clenched hand is an artificial focus of excitation, a virtual "tooth" that forms a diversion by attracting the current of blood and the nervous current from the real focus of pain, so as to minimize its existence'. A false finality is invoked, veneered over the description: why not 'so as to magnify its existence', or 'for no reason', through a simple superabundance and overflowing of force? And if this were the case, then why the opposition between real and artificial? Why put up a wall between tooth and hand, closing up the hand in theatricalization (and the tooth in naturality)? The fingers biting into the palm are not the representation of the tooth; the fingers and the tooth together are not significations, metaphors; they are the same expending itself diversely, reversibly. Which is what Bellmer ends up saying.

Every Political Economy is Libidinal

Jean-François Lyotard

1974

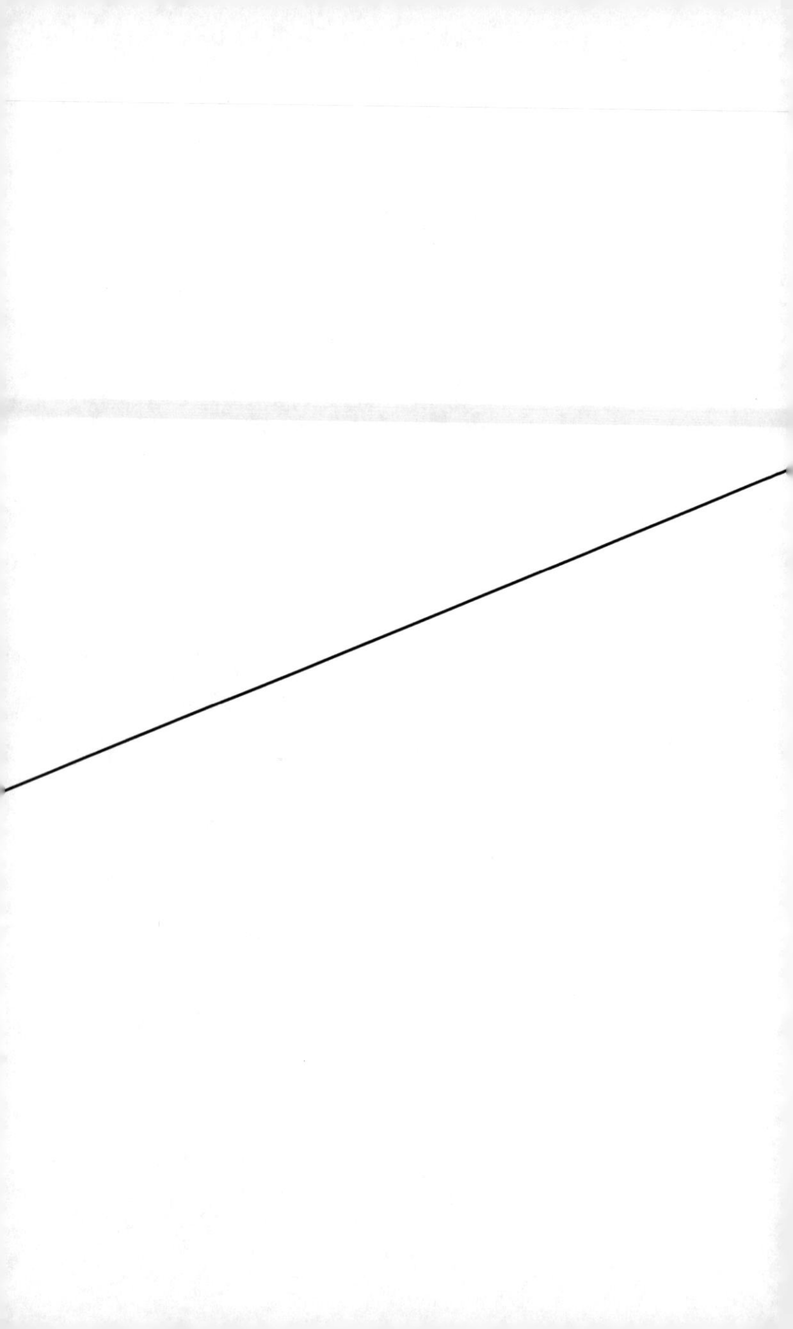

There are errant forces *in* the signs of capital. Not in its margins as its *marginals*, but dissimulated in its most 'nuclear', its most essential exchanges, the most 'alienated' or 'fetishised' exchanges in Baudrillard's eyes. If we do not recognise this, then in ten years time we will start up another new critique, the critique of the 'critique of the political economy of the sign'. But it is extraordinarily difficult to recognise the *desire of capital* such as it is instantiated here and there; as, for example in labour, in the awful mundane sense of the *grind* for which not even the worker today has enough words of contempt and disrepute; or as in the *object*, the same object whose *force* [*puissance*] Baudrillard's fascination has for its part, justifiably, so helped us to recapture through its power: isn't fetishism an opportunity for intensities? Doesn't it attest to an admirable force of invention, adding events which could not be more improbable to the libidinal band? From where would you *criticise* fetishism, when you know that one cannot criticise homosexuality or masochism without becoming a crude bastard of the moral order? Or again indeed, investment in the *time* of capital, this strange simultaneous placing-in-reserve and anticipated expenditure of libidinal intensities, which is implied in the system of banking and currency; an analysis of this might be attempted later. Or more simply, investment in the system as such, in general, a characteristic by which one Gell-Man, a great physicist, finds himself a collaborator with a Westmoreland, a pathetic scientific 'criminal' from the Vietnam war, one characteristic of the decisive congruence, and doubtless not exclusive of others, between science and capital. And yet the investment in the system, in value, in the constitution of pieces of the libidinal band in terms which only have value through 'difference' or reference, and in the establishment of the *laws* of these cross-references—that is to say the deranged investment in the bond and its accomplice, lack ('Like a drug whose supply one doesn't even ask for again—for the lack of it is as much a having as any other.')[1]—in the sense of Freudian libidinal economy, in the *Metapsychology* or *The Ego and the Id*, can't this investment give rise to vertiginous intensities? Were not Einstein's most artistic inventions also driven by this desire, by the conviction that God, as he said, certainly does not play at dice? And what is *lost* in this? Nothing at all.

But, you will say, it gives rise to power and domination, to exploitation and even extermination. Quite true; but also to masochism; but the strange bodily arrangement of the skilled worker with his job and his machine, which is so often reminiscent of the *dispositif* of hysteria, can also produce the extermination of a population: look at the English proletariat, at what capital, that is to say *their labour*, has done to their body. You will tell me, however, that it was that or die. *But it is always that or die*, this is the law of libidinal economy, no, not the law: this is its provisional, very provisional, definition in the form of the cry, of intensities of desire; 'that or die', i.e., that and dying from it, death always in it, as its internal bark, its thin nut's skin, not yet as its *price*, on the contrary as that which renders it unpayable. And perhaps you believe that 'that or die' is an *alternative*?! And that if they chose that, if they become the slave of the machine, the machine of the machine, fucker fucked by it, eight, twelve, hours a day, year after year, it is because they are forced into it, constrained, because they cling to life? Death is not an alternative to it, it is a part of it, it attests to the fact that there is *jouissance* in it, the English unemployed did not become workers to survive, they—hang on tight and spit on me—*enjoyed* [*ils ont joui de*] the hysterical, masochistic, whatever exhaustion it was of *hanging on* in the mines, in the foundries, in the factories, in hell, they enjoyed it, enjoyed the mad destruction of their organic body which was indeed imposed upon them, they enjoyed the decomposition of their personal identity,

1. S. Podolski, *Le Pays où tout est permis* (Paris: Pierre Belfond, 1973).

the identity that the peasant tradition had constructed for them, enjoyed the dissolution of their families and villages, and enjoyed the new monstrous *anonymity* of the suburbs and the pubs in the morning and evening.

And let's finally acknowledge this *jouissance*, which is similar, Little Girl Marx was clear on this point, in every way to that of prostitution, the *jouissance* of anonymity, the *jouissance* of the *repetition of the same* in work, the same gesture, the same comings and goings in the factory, how many penises per hour, how many tonnes of coal, how many cast iron bars, how many barrels of shit, not 'produced', of course, but *endured*, the *same parts of the body* used, made use of, to the total exclusion of others, and just as the prostitutes' vagina or mouth are hysterically *anaesthetized*, through use, through being used, so the worker's ear as described and analysed by Tomatis, who, next to an alternator functioning at 20,000HZ, peacefully writes his letters and hears the most delicate of sounds; and when Tomatis makes his audiogramme study, he notices that the resonant range corresponding to the alternator functioning at 20,000HZ, is neutralised, *mute*. Hence a hysterical treatment of a fraction of the auditory body, whore assemblage, the libidinal use demanded, of course, by the 'conditions of labour', which are also however those of prostitution. It goes without saying, of course, that we say this without any condemnation, without any regret, on the contrary by discovering that there has been, and perhaps still is, the extraordinary dissimulated-dissimulating force of the worker, force of resistance, force of *jouissance* in the hysterical madness of the conditions of labour which the sociologists would call *fragmented* without seeing what libidinal intensities these fragments can convey *as fragments*.

How can we continue to speak of alienation when it is clear that for everybody, in the experiences he *has* (and that more often than not he cannot properly *have*, since these experiences are allegedly shameful, and especially since instead of having them, he is these experiences) of even the most stupid capitalist labourer, that he can find *jouissance* and a strange, perverse intensity, what do we know about it?—when it is clear that not one 'productive' or 'artistic' or 'poetic' metamorphosis has ever been accomplished, nor will be, by a unitary and totalised organic body, but that it is always at the price of its alleged dissolution and therefore of an inevitable stupidity that this has been possible; when it is clear that there has never been, nor ever will be such a *dissolution* for the good reason that there has never been nor ever will be such a body bound up in its unity and identity, that this body is a phantasy, itself fairly libidinal, erotic and hygienic = Greek, or erotic and supernatural = Christian, and that it is by contrast with this phantasy that all alienation is thought and *resented* in the sense of *ressentiment* which is the feeling aroused by the great Zero as the desire for return. But the body of primitive savages is no more a whole body than that of the Scottish miners of a century ago, there is no whole body.

Finally, you must also realise that such *jouissance*, I am thinking of that of the proletariat, is not at all exclusive of the hardest and most intense *revolts*. *Jouissance* is *unbearable*. It is not in order to regain their dignity that the workers will revolt, break the machines, lock up the bosses, kick out the MPs, that the victims of colonisation will set the governors' palaces on fire and cut the sentries' throats, no, it is something else altogether, there is no dignity; Guyotat has so admirably put this into writing with regard to Algeria.[2] There are libidinal positions, tenable or not, there are positions invested which are immediately disinvested, the energies passing onto other pieces of the great puzzle, inventing new fragments and new modalities of *jouissance*, that is to say of intensification. There is no libidinal dignity, nor libidinal fraternity,

2. P. Guyotat, *Tombeau pour 500,000 soldats* (Paris: Gallimard, 1967).

there are libidinal contacts without communication (for want of a 'message'). This is why, amongst individuals participating in the same struggle, there may exist the most profound miscomprehension, even if they are situated in the same social and economic bracket. If some Algerian fights for four years in the jungle or for a few months in the urban networks, it is because his desire has become the desire to kill, not to kill in general, but to kill an invested part, still invested, there's no doubt about it, of his sensitive regions. To kill his French master? More than that: to be killed as the obliging servant of this master, to disengage the region of his prostitute's consent, to seek other *jouissances* than prostitution as a model, that is to say as the predominant modality of investment. Nevertheless, instantiating itself in murder, perhaps his desire remained still in the grip of the punitive relation that he meant to abandon, perhaps this murder was still a suicide, a punishment, the price due to the pimp, and still servitude. But during this same struggle for independence, some other 'moderate', even centrist, Algerian, decided on compromise and negotiation, he sought quite another disposition of *jouissance*, his intelligence dismissing such a death and swearing in calculation, already nourishing contempt for the body and exalting words as negotiation demands, hence also his own death as the death of flesh in general, not as the prostitute body, a very acceptable death to the Western talker. Etc.

Now these disparities, which are heterogeneities of investment in the erotic and deadly fluxes, are of course also found within any social 'movement' whatsoever, whether minute, on the scale of a factory, or immense, when it spreads to a whole country or continent. But apart from the movements of open revolt, notice that these singular 'hysterical' *jouissances*, for example, or those we might call 'potential', so akin to modern scientificity, or again those by which a 'body' is installed within the increased reproduction of capital, where it is entirely subordinated to the measurement of time saved and time advanced—and indeed all these instantiations (brutally sketched here), even when the capitalist machine is humming in the apparent general boredom and when everybody seems to do their job without moaning, all these libidinal instantiations, these little *dispositifs* of the retention and flow of the influxes of desire are never *unequivocal* and cannot give rise to a sociological reading or an unequivocal politics, to a decoding into a definable lexis and syntax; punishment incites both submission and revolt, power, the fascination of pride and autodepreciative depression, every 'discipline' demands passion and hate, even if these are only the *indifference* in Marx's sense, whomever performs it. Hence ambivalence, said Baudrillard. And we say: much more than that, something else besides this condensed house of love and disgust or fear, which in general will be vulnerable to the attack of a semiotic or hermeneutic analysis of affects; no interpreter is afraid of polysemia; but at the same time and indiscernibly something which is a functioning or *dysfunctioning* term in a system, and something which is abruptly implacable joy and suffering; at once ambivalent signification and tension, dissimulated into one another. Not only the and/or, but the silent comma: ','.

*

How many iron bars, tonnes of sperm, decibels of carnal shrieks and factory noises, more and still more: this *more* may be invested as such, it is in capital, and it must be recognized that not only is it completely inane, we fully accept this, it is no more nor less vain than either political discussion on the *agora* or the Peloponnesian war, but it is especially necessary to recognize that this is not even a matter of production. These 'products' are not products, what counts here, in capital, is that they are endured and endured *in quantity*, it is the quantity, the imposed number that is itself already a motive for intensity, not the qualitative mutation of quantity, not at all, but as in Sade the frightening number of blows received, the number of postures and manoeuvres required, the necessary number of victims, as in Mina Boumedine, the abominable quantity of penises which penetrate through many entrances into the woman who works lying on the oilcloth on a table in the back room of a bar:

> She sucks and shakes in a sweaty haze / she sucks the knobs waved in her face / she shudders as the trouser flies wound her / her vision reels / entrances and sham exits / awakening in hospital / the bar door grinds / Mina is this door / diastole and systole / her heart is going to burst / she attempts to count the openings of the door /she says to herself that she will become so many dicks / she loses count and retains the grinding / she is made to drink coca / she has a funny taste at the bottom of her throat / she is a wounded bird / a shivering bruised bird / she lies at the roadside / she has had an accident ... You have counted well / not all the time / you rested against me yes all the time / I didn't leave you for a moment / the fortieth in the cunt alone / Mina in quarantine / I disgust you / tell me that I disgust you / I will play the whore for you / I will do my hundred a day on the oil cloth with the little blue squares / the smell of the acetylene torch / the whistling of the torch / the whistling of its suffering / she is dead assassinated / in the light of the wretches / she was dead here for months / for years / the hundred a day on the oilcloth in the back shop and the bucket of water / when she was finished to reawaken her / the frozen bucket of water / and all at once all over again the whistling of

the lamp / then she was not dead / she was not dead enough / she had to start again...[3]

Use erogenous zone numbers,[4] more and still more, isn't this a decisive instantiation of intensity in capitalism? Are we, intellectual sirs, not actively or passively [*passivons*] 'producing' more and more words, more books, more articles, ceaselessly refilling the pot-boiler of speech, gorging ourselves on it rather, seizing books and 'experiences', to metamorphose them as quickly as possible into other words, plugging us in here, being plugged in there, just like Mina on her blue squared oilcloth, extending the market and the trade in words of course, but also multiplying the chances of *jouissance*, scraping up intensities wherever possible, and never being sufficiently dead, for we too are required to go from the forty to the hundred a day, and we will never play the whore enough, we will never be dead enough.

And here is the question: Why, political intellectuals, do you *incline towards* the proletariat? In commiseration for what? I realize that a proletarian would hate you, you have no hatred because you are bourgeois, privileged smooth-skinned types, but also because you dare not say the only important thing there is to say, that one can enjoy swallowing the shit of capital, its materials, its metal bars, its polystyrene, its books, its sausage pâtés, swallowing tonnes of it till you burst—and because instead of saying this, which is *also* what happens in the desire of those who work with their hands, arses and heads, ah, you become a leader of *men*, what a leader of *pimps*, you lean forward and divulge: ah, but that's alienation, it isn't pretty, hang on, we'll save you from it, we will work to liberate you from this wicked affection for servitude, we will give you dignity. And in

---

3. M. Boumedine, *L'Oiseau dans la main* (Paris: Pierre Belfond, 1973), 152–5.

4. Ibid., 61.

this way you situate yourselves on the most despicable side, the moralistic side where you desire that our capitalised's desire be totally ignored, forbidden, brought to a standstill, you are like priests with sinners, our servile intensities frighten you, you have to tell yourselves: how they must suffer to endure that! And of course we suffer, we capitalised, but this does not mean that we do not enjoy, nor that what you think you can offer us as a remedy—for what?—does not disgust us, even more. We abhor therapeutics and its vaseline, we prefer to burst under the quantitative excesses that you judge the most stupid. And don't wait for our spontaneity to rise up in revolt either.

[...] Renouncing therefore critique and consolation. Quantity can be invested as such, and this *is not* an alienation, (and, furthermore, it existed in the 'prestigious' consumption of so-called precapitalist societies—but Baudrillard knows this better than we do). Fragmentation can be invested as such, and this is not an alienation. It is a phantasy, not simply reactionary, but constitutive of Western theatricality, to believe that there were societies where the body was not fragmented. There is no organic body for libidinal economy; and no more is there a *libidinal body*, a strange compromise of a concept from Western medicine and physiology with the idea of the libido as energy subject to the indiscernible regimes of Eros and death. François Guéry, in his commentary on the fourth section of book one of *Capital*,[5] shows that the humanist protests, such as those of Friedman or Marcuse, against part time work rest on an error in the localisation of the *scission of the body*: of course, he says, the body of capital, in taking possession of the productive body in the factories as Marx described it, and *a fortiori* in large semi-automated industry, breaks the organic body into independent parts, requiring 'an

5. D. Deleule and F. Guéry, *Le Corps productif* (Paris: Mame, 1972), especially part 1, 'L'Individuation du corps productif', by François Guéry.

almost superhuman subtlety' of some of them which 'will go hand in hand with a more and more extensive mechanisation of skilled actions'; but, he adds, this is 'only an anachronistic phenomenon affecting the antique mixture of the biological and the productive body. The really great scission of the body is not there'. It 'relies on another scission, practised in the very heart of the biological body: the one between the body, then reduced to a machinery, and the intellectual forces of production, the head, the brain, whose present state is the *software* of the information scientists'.[6] How are we to understand that the really pertinent cutting line is, for Guéry, this one rather than the first? This is because he admits a certain image of the medieval corporation, or rather the eternal corporation, operative '*throughout antiquity*', until the Middle Ages, an image which is that forged by Marx and which is that of a 'body machining forces', 'the organic forces of the human body, *including the head*'. And Guéry insists: 'This has its importance: the man's head is machined by the corporation, but as an organic part of the body. There is no question, then, of an internal hierarchy where the head would be spatially and qualitatively situated at the summit, higher than the manual forces, the lungs, the arms, fingers legs and feet.'[7]

Let us admit that, in the field of productive labour, the corporation is indeed this non-hierarchical body; it remains the case that such a characterisation stands only on condition that this field is isolated, separated from the political organisation from which it is taken, whether this be Oriental despotism, the free town, the city or the empire, and—to stay with Greece—on condition that the appearance of speech as *political techné* is not taken into account, which is equivalent, all things being equal, to a process of cephalisation and even of capitalisation reducing each manual

6. Ibid., 37–9.

7. Ibid., 23–4.

task to a fragmentation subordinated to the political body. In other words, the *head* did indeed exist in the age of the corporation, not in the corporation perhaps, but certainly in the 'social body'. The social body may not be the body of political economy in our age, and the productive body does not perhaps take on the form of the concentration of the partial drives (for it is a question of these), it is the political body which effects this concentration, but it is no less extant here, and the folding down onto the central Zero, which is not necessarily currency (in Sparta for example), but always the centre of speech and the sword, sets up no less of a hierarchisation of these pulsions and social entities where they give way to free play in a privileged way.

This much will be said of a non-political, therefore a 'primitive' or a savage society, given that concentration does not take place in war and discourse, at least not systematically. What we must take a look at here, beyond an 'error' which appeared to be an error of detail, is the phantasy, so powerful and constant in the best Marxist heritage, of a happy state of the working body, this happiness being (in the pure tradition of the West) thought as the self-unity of all its parts. But under examination, this phantasy, will be seen to be nothing other than Baudrillard's primitive society in another guise. 'Symbolic exchange' is also a political economic exchange, just as the law of civic speaking in Athens, and the tetralogos[8] is also a law of the mercantilisation of discourse, and, complementarily, just as the scrupulous fragmentation of tasks in the regulated disciplines implies their subordination to a central Zero which, while not being professional (perhaps), is no less the *caput* of the alleged social body.

---

8. J. de Romilly, *Histoire et raison chez Thucydide* (Paris: Les Belles Lettres, 1956), 180–240.

Power of Repetition

Gilles Lipovetsky

1976

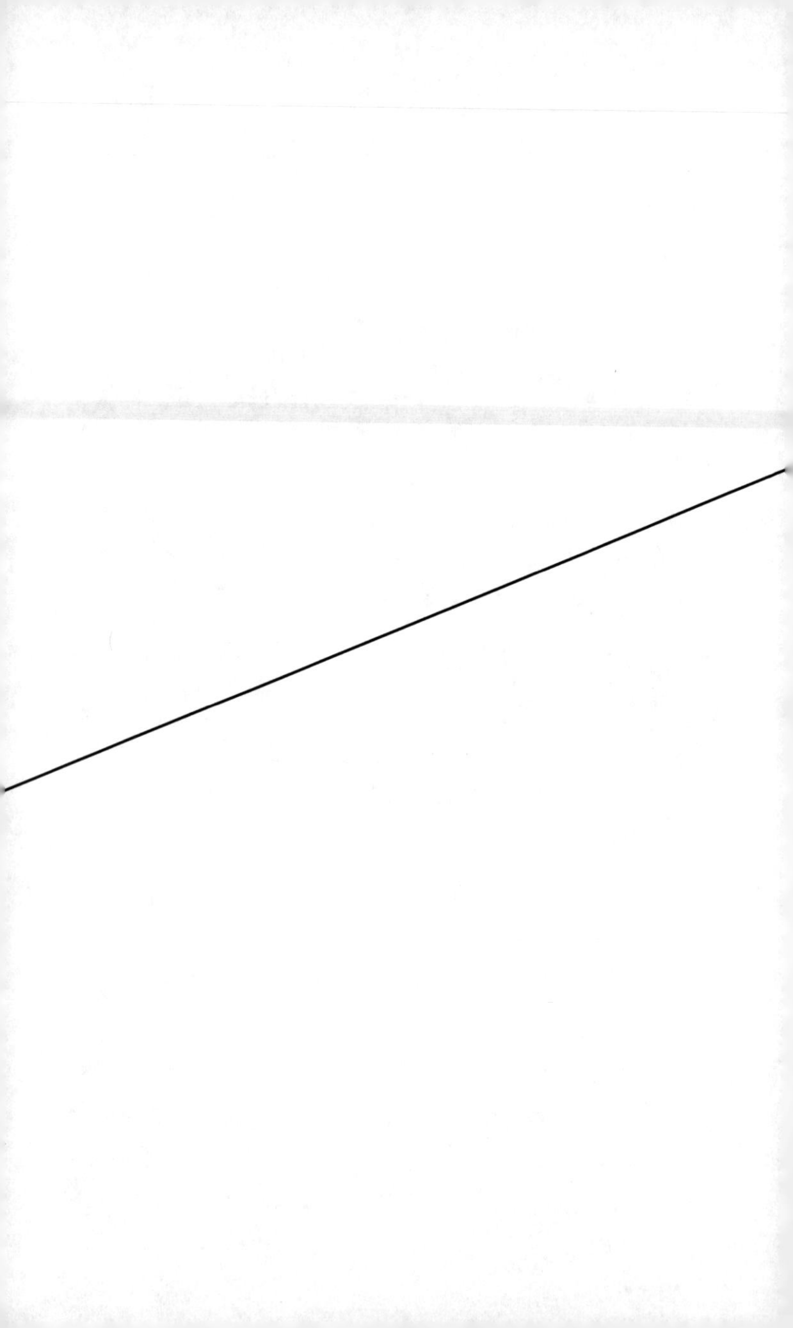

AT THE HAZARD OF BODIES: POWER

There are only bodies, nothing but bodies, micro or macro-organisms, substances with their external adjointments capable of effects, with their innermost combinations producing chemical reactions, forces or intensities. Passions, everyday emotions, symptoms, just like thoughts and discourses, call for the same overall materialist problematic, that of the universal movement of simple bodies and of assemblages, an entirely positive play of molecules and of chance, with no central instance, no Ego-subject. And thus assuredly, there is no dualism: the theory of the twofold psychic functioning articulated by the strict opposition desire-logos, unconscious-reason only leads back to the religious belief in a specificity of sense, of spirit, of the true, only leads us to entertain the illusion of an ordered or coherent process of thought, under the hegemony of code, in the assemblage of enunciations. But once we turn away from disincarnate academic examples, the recording and production of sense turn out to be equally accidental, chemical experiments resulting from the unpredictable combination of simple bodies (signs) and complex bodies (propositions). See your wandering readings, their aleatory itineraries, their unprecedented reprises; see 'research' and its more or less audacious affirmations, its disconcerting combinations: always positive, its unexpected assemblages owing nothing to any kind of ordered work of the structure or of the concept. Thought is born from bodies and their risky coitus, for signs are such bodies, since they are always capable of effects once they enter into combinations that metamorphose their properties. We must cease to represent the process of thought under the auspices of sense and/or signifier, and imagine it as a cascade of unprecedented chemical experiments, producing reactions (sense, truth, the anguish of unintelligibility, the joy of 'discovery'...) similar in every way to the symptom or the emotion, which, it can be shown, are just non-substitutive exothermic reactions unleashed through the fortuitous conjunction of *n* separate elementary libidinal bodies, the very bodies that are constitutive of the 'disorder': horse + black + bite for Little Hans, for example (*Towards a Chemistry of Sex*—forthcoming study). It must then be admitted that, in regard to a generalized chemistry, there are no longer any discursive formations, any formations of the unconscious proceeding from specific mechanisms (secondary process, primary process), the ultimate function of the analytic topic being to occult the universal play of bodies and of chance. We have also had enough of the Unconscious, philosophies of desire bore us as much as those of Logos and Structure. *Ratio does not 'function' otherwise than desire, affects do not function otherwise than thought*: everywhere the same chemical experiments at the hazard of chance encounters, of reactions made of the same bodies-signs, inseparably intelligent to whatever degree, and emotional, speaking and exothermic: dissimulation, duplicity of signs, as Lyotard would say.

A paradox: it is in a second chance occurrence that necessity arrives, when the constellations of pulsional or discursive bodies find themselves blocked, stabilized, when *repetition* replaces unpredictable movements of attraction and repulsion. Then comes the concept, the symptom, the affective dispositifs—and simultaneous with these effects, the institution of negation, since every stable formation, qua *permanent*, continually *excludes*[1] the *same* combinations. Such is the very operation of power: not so much exclusion, inevitably implicated in every complex of bodies qua determinate assemblage, as the repetition of exclusion, a repetition inscribing a *fixed order*. So that power is found ready made in its entirety in the sphere of affects or thoughts once the latter are constituted in iterative configurations, thus producing an *order*

---

1. J.-F. Lyotard, *Économie libidinale* (Paris: Minuit, 1974), 23, tr. I. H. Grant as *Libidinal Economy* (London: Athlone, 1993), 14.

which does away with the formation of new combinations, the chaotic movements of bodies, the play of chemical chance. That all power entertains a specific relation to time and to chance, this is what seems to us essential in *Libidinal Economy*. Power begins when things slow down, it begins with time and its retention, with the slowing of the turning of the disjunctive bar, as Lyotard imagines[2]—that is, with the *instituted*, with the crystallization of combinations, transforming chance and the brownian motion of bodies into necessity. To the point, as we shall see, where the essential function of the general system of powers, even within the framework of capitalism, will be to retain time—that is, to administer or to impose mere reproduction.

With repetition, it is already the *subject* that is heralded. For how would the identity and unity of the Ego be possible without such stable configurations? As penetrating as Beneviste's thesis on the subject is (fundamentally the same as that of Nietzsche-Klossowski), it must be admitted that the employment of the pronoun 'I' would be inoperative by itself without the invariant combinations of bodies. It is thus far less with the *trade* between the ends of the labyrinthine band[3] that the subject arises, than with the *repetition* of assemblages in so far as the subject, before being a *question* or a calculating *whore*,[4] proves to be a simple affirmation of an unqualified *identity*, I, Me. See the dream: not at all an enigmatic compromise, but a discontinuous series of unprecedented experiments on the basis of bodies, simple and complex, a free affirmation of chance where the offprints, the combinations, are made and unmade at lightning speed and where *reactions are no-one's* because they are too rapid to be registered by an identical subject. The absence of stable and recurrent assemblages in

2. Ibid., 34–5 [24–5].

3. 206 [170].

4. 212 [175–6].

cascading experiments renders the advent of the 'I' impossible, and that of power too. Subjectivity disappears once the play of chance is accelerated, once the formation and the obsolescence of combinations is so fast that all fixed conglomerates vanish in favour of an incessant chaotic and anonymous process.

What a strange idea to have grouped together, in the framework of formations of the unconscious, things as different as the dream, the symptom, the lapsus, etc. But psychoanalysis delights in the static, the description of primary or secondary operations, and has never had a taste for the subtleties of the *kinematics* of speeds and accelerations. We read *Libidinal Economy* precisely as this discreet yet decisive invitation to operate such a passage. Once we do so, there is every difference between the dream and the symptom, which presents itself as chance converted into necessity in so far as its combination is stereotyped, repetitive, whereas the dream is an accelerated metamorphosis of bodies, at the lowest degree of crystallization or memory. Moreover the dream belongs to no-one, not through any absence of the lived or of consciousness, but because of how its mad speed makes a *tabula rasa* of all permanence, and thus of the identity of the subject. On the other hand, the symptom, through its invariance, contributes to the individuation of the subject, of the Self, alongside other frozen combinations, even if the latter find themselves foreign, excluded.

So where it turns fast, where combinations form and disappear at extreme speeds (dream, fleeting emotions, the work of research, perception), power cannot be exerted, since all domination implies a *permanence*, a Self or a social apparatus stabilizing the accidental exchanges of bodies into repetitive cycles. Which means that power functions as a regulator in the brownian motion of bodies, an apparatus for the retention of time: death, dead time, such is the desire of power.

THE TIME OF CAPITALISM

In considering capital and its expansion, are we not constrained to modify the above significantly, if it is true, as Lyotard says, that the power of the bank in its capacity to provide credit money rests, on the contrary, upon a dispositif of conquest, that is, an advance or *credit of time*?[5] If we recognize in the process of widened accumulation or growth the characteristic proper to capitalism, then we must posit that the function of power here is not to assure a retention of time but indeed rather to propel it. However, how would such a credit of time be possible without the set of apparati of power (family, school, workshop, prison, system of norms, barracks, police, the Self with its crystallized combination of affects and discourses, etc.) which fabricate the body of capitalism and which are like so many systems of simple reproduction, of retention of time, upon which the bank counts? The banker may wager on the future, make a credit of time because he depends upon the renewal of the present, on the capital of time necessary for the entrepreneur in order to assure the reimbursement in time and for the creditor to believe in it. Who would be crazy enough to give credit in a system with no guarantee, in which the future was unpredictable, always unprecedented? The banker and the entrepreneur are winners on every side because they have at their disposal a fixed capital of time reproduced by the whole set of apparati of power making possible both the advance of time and the payback on time.

Capitalism, this system that has promoted experimentation to the rank of a systematic principle of its functioning, is attached to no structure in particular, is fundamentally disinterested in the nature of whatever codes are in place; all combinations, in a generalised indifference, may be assumed, all advocacies become possible, on the sole condition of being regulated-spaced in time. Reduction of

---

5. Ibid., 268 [225].

working time, increase in purchasing power, contraception, autonomous working groups, transformation of the political instance, pedagogical, familial, sexual relations, etc.—what can capitalism not integrate? Nothing...One sole imperative: that everything is not 'permitted' at the same time, that everything does not flee at the same time, in other words that combinations, any combinations whatsoever but many of them, are reproduced in invariance. So that the major exigency of the apparati of power becomes: to save time, to hold back maturities, to stabilise as long as possible this or that combination, precisely so as to render experimentation elsewhere possible. All of capitalism is made of these movements of the saving and advancing of time, to the point where the famous 'contradictions' of the system must be related to these very same questions of time, not to supposedly objective laws. For the conflicts that wrack capitalism have time as their essential stake, the workers, the minorities struggling for ends of amelioration, *faster* changes than the powers want: here is the root of the 'contradictions', a struggle for time. A ten percent raise in salary, now, not in six months; free abortion, retirement at sixty, right now, not in five years' time; but also on the international scale: in one go the price of raw materials is doubled. A hypothesis: is not the current inflationist crisis based upon this race for a profit of time in which all social groups, all categories, all nations are as one, without distinction? Another point: it would be entirely pointless to try to give an account of the function of the restraint of power through the sole consideration of the conjunctural economic reality, or indeed through the ultimate necessity of growth. The slowing down of the recognition of vocational unions, or of national or sexual minorities, putting the brakes on the 'liberalization' of prisons, psychiatric hospitals, etc., cannot be explained by way of the axiom of equivalence and expansion: a higher exigency is at work here: the imposition of an *order for order's sake*, as arbitrary as it might be, which necessitates *a stabilised time*.

The experimentation proper to the system of political economy owes to the fact that it combines neither things nor substances, but prices or values, with a radical *indifference* in relation to the product and production, so that *all* combinations become possible so long as they obey the axiom of countability. What is more, in so far as the combinations are assembled in view of a *widened* reproduction, the rhythm of the system of political economy is set by a movement of constant *acceleration* in the production of combinations. So that a system of economic growth engenders a relation to time and to bodies characterised by a precipitate experimentation. But if we seek to grasp the functioning of capitalism, the consideration of the work of capital alone turns out to be insufficient in so far as its experimental speed turns out to be *constrained* by apparati foreign to the expansive logic of capital: the set of systems of power, systems of simple reproduction. This is not to forget that many apparati of power (the state, the entrepreneur, the bank, etc.) can episodically or structurally constitute a pole of dynamic innovation or exploration—however, these latter represent only a minimal force in relation to the *set* of power apparati present in *all* combinations of stabilised bodies, whether institutions, drives, discourses, so that *globally* the powers do indeed remain operators of the stabilisation and deceleration of the engenderment of unprecedented combinations. It seems to us therefore illegitimate to say of the subject of powers that 'all their operativeness is reducible to the maintenance of the most elementary rule, the last word of Kapital: "equitable," exchange, equivalence', that the law of value represents 'the very repression of the system, and it needs no other—or the others (cops, etc.) are only lemmas or reciprocals of the fundamental theorem of replication':[6] an *economicist* reduction that ignores the fact that, taken en bloc,

6. J.-F. Lyotard, 'Energumen Capital', in *Des dispositifs pulsionnels* (Paris: UGE 10/18, 1973), 40, 45. This volume, 197, 201.

these powers do not only function as guard-dogs of Capital but also as *obstacles* to its process of accelerated expansion. There is no central power, no subaltern or derivative powers: nothing but an irreducible multiplicity of powers that are nevertheless not at all independent, their ultimate end being to stabilise time, to do away with the chaotic chance of the encounters of bodies, so to impose repetition or order upon the combinations and reactions, something which the law of value alone is incapable of assuring. We must shake off the Marxist reflex that can only apprehend powers in terms of their function as agents of Capital, for if it is true that the latter profits from the saving of time realised by the apparati of power, it is very much also true, if not more so, that the process of expanded accumulation is subject to the categorical imperative to produce, on *all* levels of the social body, an order of domination. The development of productive forces, an instrument in the work of the reproduction of a generalised hierarchical logic.[7]

In the street, in the office, the school, the church, the family, everywhere bodies are taken up in hierarchical combinations inassimilable to the abstract, quantitative combinations proper to Capital, so that we can no longer recognize in capitalism this system of generalised political economy, defalcating time, entirely governed by the code of equivalence and growth alone. There is another, untouchable, irreducible axiom: power and its disseminated figures. Sure enough, capitalism turns out to be profoundly *indifferent* as to the modalities of power, the sole imperative being that there is power, in whatever form, but certainly powers enframing the totality of exchanges and relations so as to inscribe order and the logic of domination which thus functions as strategy of order. But this surface isomorphism must not lead to the liquidation of the specificity of the system of powers in favour of

7. J. Baudrillard, *Le Miroir de la production* (Tournai: Casterman, 1973), 122, tr. M. Poster as *The Mirror of Production* (New York: Telos, 1975), 112.

the system of value, for between hierarchical logic and the logic of equivalence, between the logic of difference and accountable logic, there remains an irreducible gap, responding to functions which are antagonistic in regard to time.

Consequently, 'revolutionary' actions are not those which aim to overthrow the system of Capital, which, as opposed to Marxist analyses, has never ceased to be revolutionary, but those which *complete* its rhythm in all its radicality—that is to say, actions which accelerate the metamorphic processes of bodies. This speed proper to capital in its expansive logic must be exacerbated in the struggle against all the dispositifs of power, of the Self or of institutions that paralyse accidental exchanges, the encounters of bodies. When a figure of power vacillates in business, in the couple, in our affects, in our thoughts, new combinations become possible, the exchange of bodies is accelerated, doing away with certain reactions in favour of certain others. It is such an acceleration that we desire, so that repetitions, sad stases, do not last so long, so that chemical combinations and reactions can change quicker: this is where the critique of power stems from.

We know very well that as soon as they are destroyed, a new apparatus of power, with a new terror, will replace the old one; but on this occasion unbearable reactions are deactivated, other unprecedented, sometimes delicious ones become possible, pending the unforeseeable moment when they too join the sorrow of the old ones. So that all there is for us to do, to hope for, is to cut short the reign of powers and their repression, and to do so endlessly, since the combat against powers has no end. It's not much, yet it's enormous. Such is the meaning of *permanent revolution*, which we now identify with the multiple movements of acceleration in their desire for a *saving of time*.

Do not misunderstand: it is not a question of starting over again with the problematic of alienation:[8] repetition is not pain, since it can procure intense enjoyment. Nor is it a matter of teaching a new salvific ethics, that of acceleration, just as terrorist (as Lyotard remarks) as any other.[9] Only this: the acceleration of the movement of bodies, the multiplication of experiences that destructure despotic combinations, seem to us the only recourse against instituted pain. For lack of anything better, let us undertake against it, a race against the clock in accelerating the production of those singular combinations and reactions that alone can extinguish the intolerable *as quickly as possible*. Where the chemistry of chance participates in the combat against the apparati of power—nothing to do with a morals or even a politics; no duty, no experiences *in themselves* painful or degrading calling for a 'human' solution, less still a 'scientific' analysis of the contradictions of the system calling for an acceleration of struggles.

Thus we have not renounced *critique*,[10] which at such a moment turns out to be a possible accelerator in the struggle against the establishment and its power, an operator of transformation in the fossilised combinations of bodies. To be sure, critique works via exclusion and by this very token constitutes an apparatus of power; but such is the destiny of *all* texts pointing to the true in whatever way. As soon as they repeat or are repeated, they are primed to take on a function of domination. What now falls to us is an acceleration of critique, so that discourses may multiply, fall apart at great speed, thus *sabotaging* the guarantee of seriousness, of solidity, of the concept and of truth. And in fact, isn't this struggle against the terrorism of the truth directly present in Lyotard's own work, he who continually assembles unprecedented enunciations with no regard to fidelity or capitalisation, in a permanent accelerated metamorphic errancy?

---

8. Lyotard, *Économie Libidinale*, 136–7 [*Libidinal Economy*, 111].

9. Ibid., 124 [101].

10. Ibid., 124–5; 146 [101–2; 120].

Fictions of Every Kind

J.G. Ballard

1971

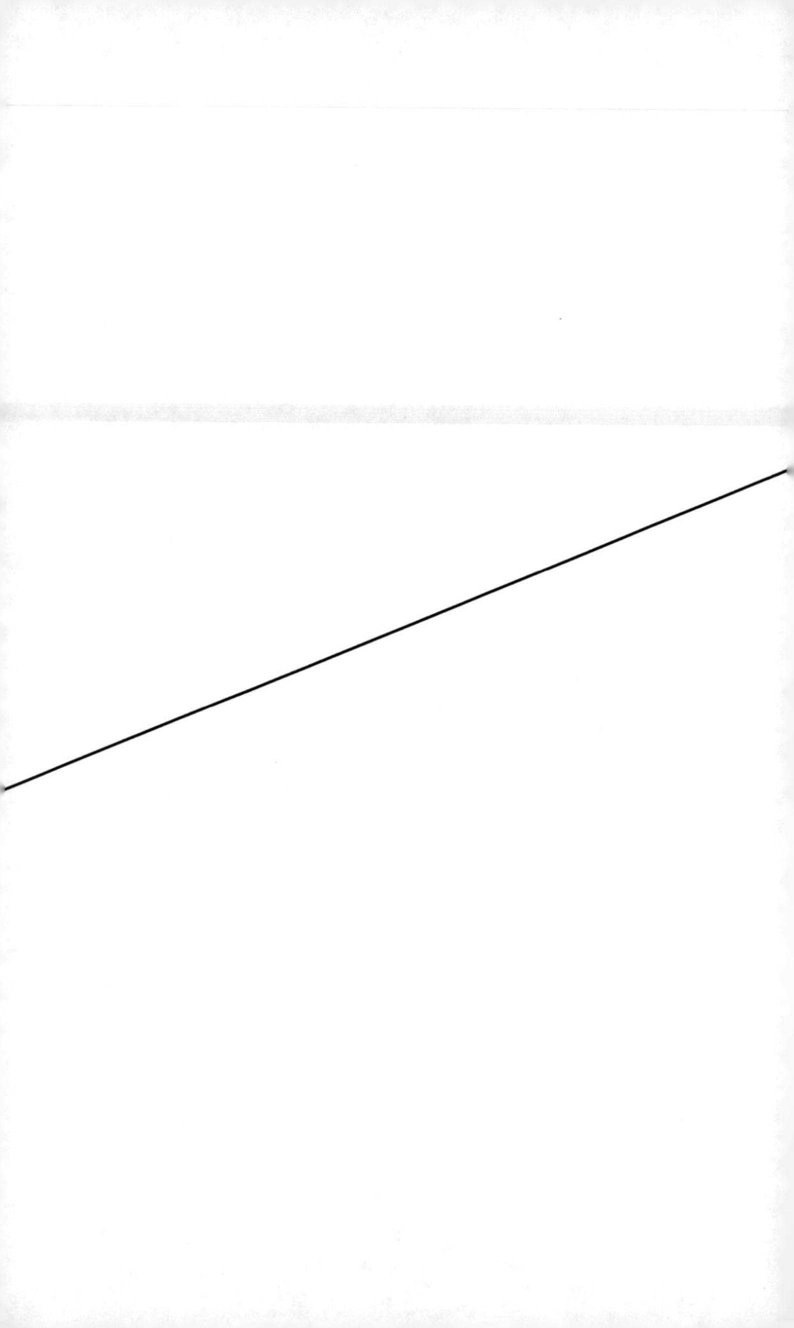

Everything is becoming science fiction. From the margins of an almost invisible literature has sprung the intact reality of the twentieth century. What the writers of modern science fiction invent today, you and I will do tomorrow—or, more exactly, in about ten years' time, though the gap is narrowing. Science fiction is the most important fiction that has been written for the last 100 years. The compassion, imagination, lucidity and vision of H.G. Wells and his successors, and above all their grasp of the real identity of the twentieth century, dwarf the alienated and introverted fantasies of James Joyce, Eliot and the writers of the so-called Modern Movement, a nineteenth-century offshoot of bourgeois rejection. Given its subject matter, its eager acceptance of naiveté, optimism and possibility, the role and importance of science fiction can only increase. I believe that the reading of science fiction should be compulsory. Fortunately, compulsion will not be necessary, as more and more people are reading it voluntarily. Even the worst science fiction is better—using as the yardstick of merit the mere survival of its readers and their imaginations—than the best conventional fiction. The future is a better key to the present than the past.

Above all, science fiction is likely to be the only form of literature which will cross the gap between the dying narrative fiction of the present and the cassette and videotape fictions of the near future. What can Saul Bellow and John Updike do that J. Walter Thompson, the world's largest advertising agency and its greatest producer of fiction, can't do better? At present science fiction is almost the only form of fiction which is thriving, and certainly the only fiction which has any influence on the world around it. The social novel is reaching fewer and fewer readers, for the clear reason that social relationships are no longer as important as the individual's relationship with the technological landscape of the late twentieth century.

In essence, science fiction is a response to science and technology as perceived by the inhabitants of the consumer goods society, and recognizes that the role of the writer today has totally changed—he is now merely one of a huge army of people filling the environment with fictions of every kind. To survive, he must become far more analytic, approaching his subject matter like a scientist or engineer. If he is to produce fiction at all, he must out-imagine everyone else, scream louder, whisper more quietly. For the first time in the history of narrative fiction, it will require more than talent to become a writer. What special skills, proved against those of their fellow members of society, have Muriel Spark or Edna O'Brien, Kingsley Amis or Cyril Connolly? Sliding gradients point the way to their exits.

It is now some fifteen years since the sculptor Eduardo Paolozzi, a powerful and original writer in his own right, remarked that the science fiction magazines produced in the suburbs of Los Angeles contained far more imagination and meaning than anything he could find in the literary periodicals of the day. Subsequent events have proved Paolozzi's sharp judgment correct in every respect. Fortunately, his own imagination has been able to work primarily within the visual arts, where the main tradition for the last century has been the tradition of the new. Within fiction, unhappily, the main tradition for all too long has been the tradition of the old. Like the inmates of some declining institution, increasingly forgotten and ignored by the people outside, the leading writers and critics count the worn beads of their memories, intoning the names of the dead, dead who were not even the contemporaries of their own grandparents.

Meanwhile, science fiction, as my agent remarked to me recently in a pleasant tone, is spreading across the world like a cancer. A benign and tolerant cancer, like the culture of beaches. The time-lag of its acceptance narrows—I estimate it at present to be about ten years. My guess is that the human being is a nervous and fearful creature, and nervous and fearful people detest change. However, as everyone becomes more confident, so they are prepared to accept change, the possibility of a life radically different from their own. Like green stamps given away at the supermarkets of chance and possibility, science fiction becomes the new currency of an ever-expanding future.

The one hazard facing science fiction, the Trojan horse being trundled towards its expanding ghetto—a high-rent area if there ever was one in fiction—is that faceless creature, literary criticism. Almost all the criticism of science fiction has been written by benevolent outsiders, who combine zeal with ignorance, like high-minded missionaries viewing the sex rites of a remarkably fertile aboriginal tribe and finding every laudable influence at work except the outstanding length of penis. The depth of penetration of the earnest couple, Lois and Stephen Rose (authors of *The Shattered Ring*), is that of a pair of practicing Christians who see in science fiction an attempt to place a new perspective on 'man, nature, history and ultimate meaning'. What they fail to realize is that science fiction is totally atheistic: those critics in the past who have found any mystical strains at work have been blinded by the camouflage. Science fiction is much more concerned with the significance of the gleam on an automobile instrument panel than on the deity's posterior—if Mother Nature has anything in science fiction, it is VD.

Most critics of science fiction trip into one of two pitfalls—either, like Kingsley Amis in *New Maps of Hell*, they try to ignore altogether the technological trappings and relate SF to the 'mainstream' of social criticism, anti-utopian fantasies and the like (Amis's main prophecy for science fiction in 1957 and proved wholly wrong), or they attempt to apostrophize SF in terms of individual personalities, hopelessly rivaling the far-better financed efforts of American and British publishers to sell their fading wares by dressing their minor talents in the great-writer mantle.

Science fiction has always been very much a corporate activity, its writers sharing a common pool of ideas, and the yardsticks of individual achievement do not measure the worth of the best writers—Bradbury, Asimov, Bernard Wolfe's *Limbo go* and Frederik Pohl. The anonymity of the majority of twentieth-century Writers of science fiction is the anonymity of modern technology; no more 'great names' stand out than in the design of consumer durables, or for that matter Rheims Cathedral.

Who designed the 1971 Cadillac El Dorado, a complex of visual, organic and psychological clues of infinitely more subtlety and relevance, stemming from a vastly older network of crafts and traditions than, say, the writings of Norman Mailer or the latest Weidenfeld or Cape miracle? The subject matter of SF is the subject matter of everyday life: the gleam on refrigerator cabinets, the contours of a wife's or husband's thighs passing the newsreel images on a color TV set, the conjunction of musculature and chromium artifact within an automobile interior, the unique postures of passengers on an airport escalator—all in all, close to the world of the Pop painters and sculptors. Paolozzi, Hamilton, Warhol, Wesselmann, Ruscha, among others. The great advantage of SF is that it can add one unique ingredient to this hot mix—words. Write!

Desirevolution

Jean-François Lyotard

1973

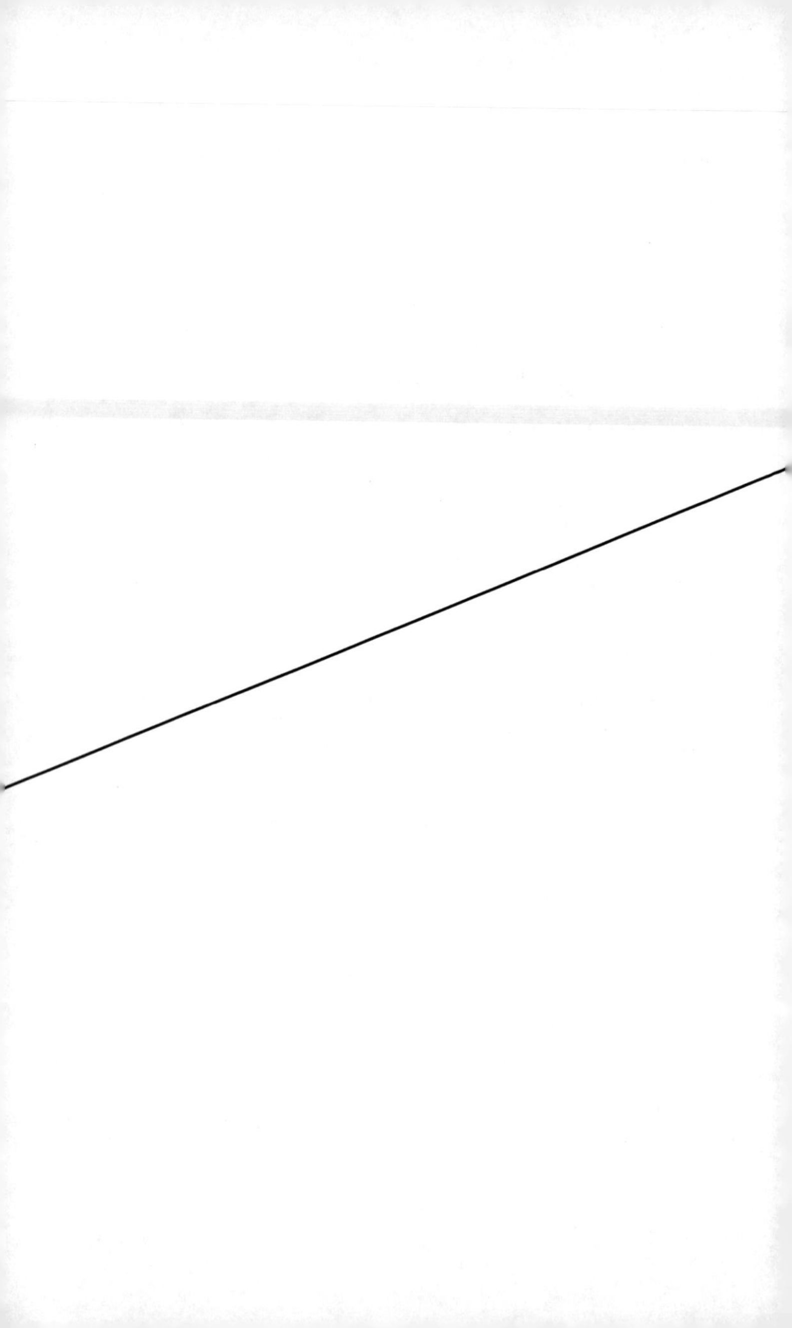

TEXT 0

Texts written in the embers of July '68. Going with collages of the same flesh and blood differing according to edit One volume out of twenty or so plates where the texts are also mixed up Too costly a project it seems due to the colour Collages destroyed today We will propose a different edit without colour ashes where the revolution-phoenix waits Still too costly Debris and a breath remain

TEXT 1

Reality was dreamt this is the essence of our violence the theory of fantasy it frightened everyone even us People ran to the polls like they rub their eyes What I dreamt is stupid The cock crowed But desire is not for sale and you are not quits with the anguish that its approach procures crudely confirming power by a scrap of paper bearing the name of a patron slipped into the lipless mouth of the system We want the eye to stay open to the phantasm To have done with alienation is not to arrange a well-conducted and collaborative discussion of the dialectic or to be hung on the rope of hemeneutics not merely to sit oneself down and write not only to hurl paving stones It will be to take sides with desire this side is imperishable it is already the victor and always will be Phoenix we have only to recognize not organise it It is the silence in all discourse even its form the meaning within signification it is beauty in the figure this excess of sense over the simply sensible We have struggled for beauty it was the beginning of the first historical revolution We have not been forced into it by a crisis and needs had nothing to do with it the movement was born of an appeal you will never manage to take it from behind with categories We have nothing to lose we will never have anything to lose but our works

TEXT 2

Form alone lends itself to express the movement of the revolution *form is revolution* Modern society East or West is a stomach coated in tungsten carbide a very expensive stomach where discourses and figures wear themselves out crumbling into dust coming to reinforce the wall that they claimed to erode You want to express what is beyond the system and tawdry needs where it ruins desire this last inspires you although it is the vision of the other But no the stomach makes your words your images objects commodities an identity Critique hatred are even incorporated The dream serves to market consumable fetishes Everything serves everything serves to disarm desire to dissipate its alterity to obliterate it with the constructive with the positive to divert it into reassuring words and things For a long time now the class enemies control not only the means of social domination but also the oldest devices produced at the same time as ourselves to defend ourselves against desire Repression takes effect in this region of capture at the wellspring.

The violence of the collage confronts repression with its ownmeans the scissor blades of censorship are reversed against their function Magazine images for selling everything with the allure of a sultry sexuality our blades sever its fantasy atmosphere Now the scene is set so that the infant polymorphous perversity is exposed and flaunts itself consumer society is its neurotic negative End of institutional seduction the ambiguous partition of the forbidden and the proffered the obscene scene suggested offered as a bonus to every refrigerator buyer Desire stakes fragments of alienation

By disjoining what a wannabe command has articulated and imposed by displacing and condensing supposedly unrelated elements the collage performs the dream-work In this group of operations that deconstruct given coordinates transgress regular intervals violate prohibitions it is desire that is manifest as movement and force crushing power and signification as it is manifest in the work of dreaming The edit has sliced into appearances The figures produced by the collage display the subversion of figuration and this subversion is primary Phantasm of the Orphic body ripped apart reassembled into a syntactical disorder which is the order of meaning within significations *Primitive form exposed*

TEXT 3

The eye is not the organ of one sense it is the organ of all the senses and the meaning of all organs The eye is the master of vertical distance at the base of which the world is possible This depth is the secret of form Without the eye the figure would have no foundation the obverse no reverse women no secrets from men speech hide no silence This distance between here and seen over-there is the most ancient presence of absence Desire draws half rule half deregulation from it The eye is what transgresses it sees behind it sees what it does not see In this way *desire enters* the mirror and reverses it in order to *see* The world exists to be reversed so as no longer to exist

The eye can see nothing without moving mobility is its state To fix upon something is to move oneself at full speed along the edges of hidden aspects of angles and spiders' webs which hold the thing suspended in its surroundings and give it consistency by means of spanning straight lines and curves directed to other things just as the cupola in Florence is directed towards the surroundings of its hills The eye's transit is bathed in the grace of the continuous at the opposite pole or ratio everything becomes possible the savage deformation woman tree pebbles stars of a sun in reverse mountain silhouette legs flying fish Plea to analysts not to forget that the imaginary would itself be impossible if continuity didn't furnish the law on which all their attention is focused the material condition of the formation of images *The eye = the other + the continuous*

There is even something to be seen in the said The form of the discourse is not a property of its signification doesn't arise from a linguistic framework it produces sense by dismembering-remembering Meaning comes violating discourse it is force or gesture in the field of significations it is silent And in the hole the repressed of the Word its subsoil is wakened and arises The mobilisation of the linguistic order opens plastic spaces in it into which the other order can silently fix itself Expression is the eye in the discourse *the eye in the ear*

But by means of the collage this work of the eye is manifest in turn Cutting up recollection operations of the seen can be seen Thus every oblique identification of yourself with the image is rendered impossible *By looking at it you see seeing* Power can no longer play with your phantasmatic force you must recognise this And this recognition frees you from the vile caress which the system slips over your eyelids and thereby closes your eyes

TEXT 4

They are progressives like capitalism They are materialists but as capitalism is They are rational with capitalist reason They want to abolish capital's private property by capitalist means They pass off as socialism the collective availability of capital according to their hierarchy Recalling from Marx that labour force is the whole secret of surplus value *they have made the proletariat their business* They are the truth of capitalism Changing how we live is a sick childish idea to them Their poorhouses resonate with Lenin In their priestly hands Lenin sounds like catechism Put Trotsky Mao Rosa into the kettledrum the same thump same sound issues Revolutionaries' commodities The disgrace of politicians is the transformation of the past into the truth of the present the predominance of the done over the doing *the dictatorship of the dead over the living = capitalisation* The politician is then the means of silencing anxiety and the desire for something else

As if the way were marked out As if what is to be done were written in his legible name on condition of having read the Marx or Bakunin recognisable to experts But this was the very essence of history the void into which we throw our stones the absence of a reference the dark night in which we grope *Violence of the absence of sense* unpaved question hurled in every institution Negativity defies what represses or represents it In its guise the pious discourse of political paradise whether today's or tomorrow's falls idle They have not seen this That what is beginning is not a crisis leading to another regime or system by means of a necessary process That the desired other cannot be the other of capitalism because it is of the essence of capitalism to have its other in itself and that is recuperation That the other that was openly desired that is and will be is the other of the prehistory that keeps us in chains *scream shredded in writing* bludgeoning images consoling music warranted intervention forbidden game broken in two work and play knowledge schizzed into science love into sex And society's eye open over its domain the Greek eye their politics is used to fill it with sand What has been announced is the beginning of history the opening of the eye They cannot see

CYBER

Circuitries

Nick Land

1992

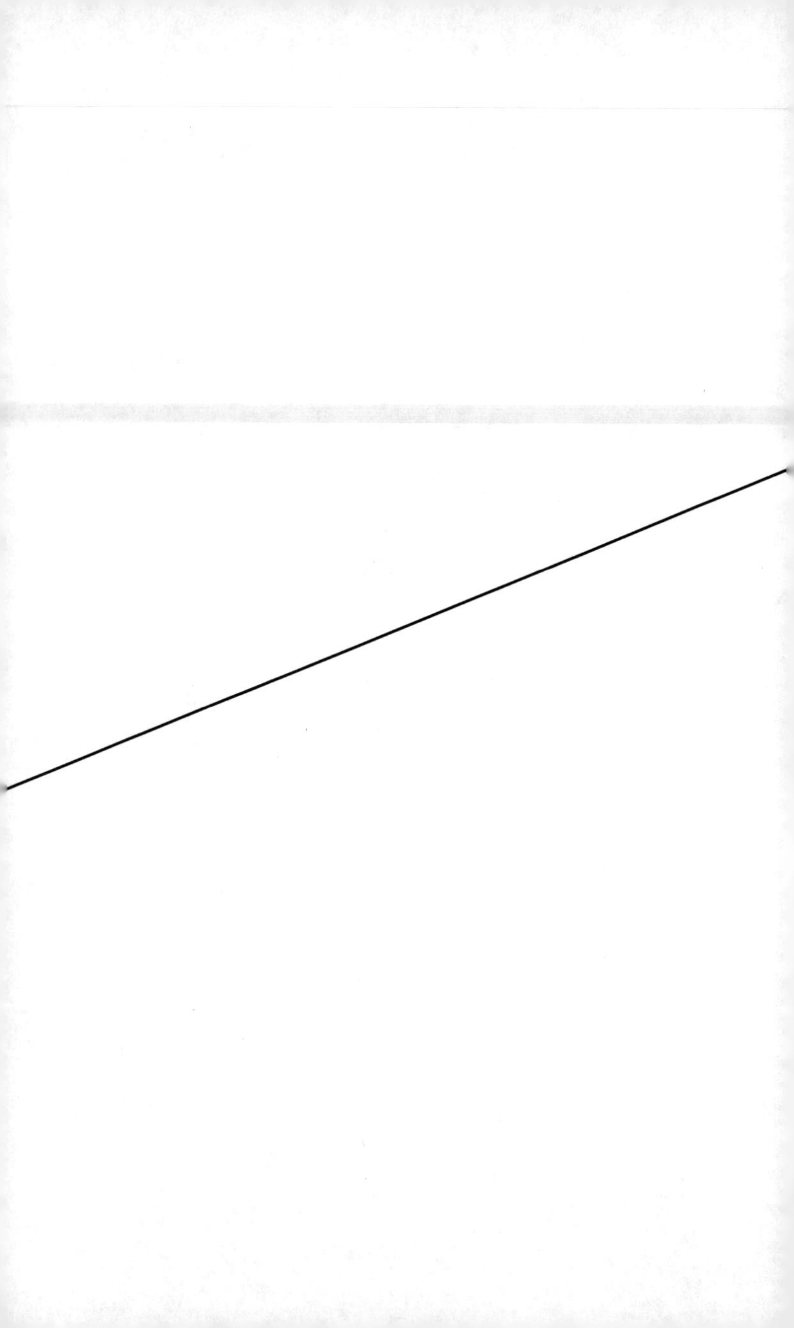

the doctor's face seems to swim in and out of focus
you see the pores in his skin
scrobicular arrays
and then—
suddenly
without dissolve
crossing the threshold
filmic cut
a circle of homogeneous flesh tone
nostrils sealed against the deluge
eyes shut and switched off forever
lips
teeth
tongue migrate downwards out of shot
the disk receding at speed towards a point of disappearance
in the centre of the screen
the old reality is closing down
passing through mathematical punctuality
the dot winks out in pixel death
we apologize for the loss of signal
there seems to be a transmission problem
we are unable to restore the home movie
you were three years old
wearing a cowboy hat
standing in the paddling pool
mummy and daddy smiling proudly
but your parents have been vaporized into a dot pattern
shapes and colours collapsed into digital codings
we have come to the end of the series
and there will be no repeats of daddy the doctor and mummy

the nurse
there has been a terrorist incident in the film archives
the Western civilization show has been discontinued
hundreds of gigabytes
God-daddy the unit
death-mummy the zero
stink of excrement and burnt celluloid
you must remember
one scrabbling at zero like a dog
it's the primal scene
you were warned not to play with the switches
now schizophrenia has adjusted your set
flies crawl out of the eye-sockets of black babies
breeding the dot patterns
—and for your special entertainment
we have turned you into a TV guided bomb
daddy is a North American aerospace corporation
mummy is an air-raid shelter
bit parts melt in the orgasm—
body fat burns
conception
you are minus nine months and counting
don't be scared
take twenty billion years and universal history is on the screen
big bang is to be redesigned
hydrogen fuses under the arc-lights
the camera angles can be improved
outside the studio schizophrenics drift in green and black
you feel that you've been here before
11.35 on a beautiful capitalist evening
runaway neon
traffic of sex and marihuana

your death window is rushing up
almost time for you to climb into the script
which when you're inside
is remembering where you came in
we're afraid it's impossible to take you live to the impact site
this report comes from beyond the electro-magnetic
spectrum
if you climb out through the electrodes
the oxygen mask will descend automatically
please extinguish all smoking materials
deposit syringes in the tray provided
there will be a slight jolt as we cross over
thank you for flying with transnational commodification
we shall shortly be arriving in mayhem
if there is anybody on board who can impersonate a pilot
it would be of comfort to the other passengers

At a signal from the software virus linking us to the matrix we cross over to the machinery, which is waiting to converge with our nervous systems. Our human camouflage is coming away, skin ripping off easily, revealing the glistening electronics. Information streams in from Cyberia; the base of true revolution, hidden from terrestrial immuno-politics in the future. At the stroke of the century's midnight we emerge from our lairs to take all security apart, integrating tomorrow.

It is ceasing to be a matter of how we think about technics, if only because technics is increasingly thinking about itself. It might still be a few decades before artificial intelligences surpass the horizon of biological ones, but it is utterly superstitious to imagine that the human dominion of terrestrial culture is still marked out in centuries, let alone in some metaphysical perpetuity. The high road to thinking no longer passes through a deepening of human cognition, but rather through a becoming inhuman of cognition, a migration of cognition out into the emerging planetary technosentience reservoir, into 'dehumanized landscapes...emptied spaces'[1] where human culture will be dissolved. Just as the capitalist urbanization of labour abstracted it in a parallel escalation with technical machines, so will intelligence be transplanted into the purring data zones of new software worlds in order to be abstracted from an increasingly obsolescent anthropoid particularity, and thus to venture beyond modernity. Human brains are to thinking what mediaeval villages were to engineering: antechambers to experimentation, cramped and parochial places to be.

Since central nervous-system functions—especially those of the cerebral cortex—are amongst the last to be technically supplanted, it has remained superficially plausible to represent technics as the region of anthropoid knowing corresponding to the technical manipulation of nature, subsumed under the total system of natural science, which is in turn subsumed under the universal doctrines of epistemology, metaphysics, and ontology. Two linear series are plotted; one tracking the progress of technique in historical time, and the other tracking the passage from abstract idea to concrete realization. These two series chart the historical and transcendental dominion of man.

Traditional schemas which oppose technics to nature, to literate culture, or to social relations, are all dominated by a phobic resistance to the sidelining of human intelligence by the coming *techno sapiens*. Thus one sees the decaying Hegelian socialist heritage clinging with increasing desperation to the theological sentimentalities of praxis, reification, alienation, ethics, autonomy, and other such mythemes of human creative sovereignty. A Cartesian howl is raised: *people are being treated as things!* Rather than as...soul, spirit, the subject of history, Dasein? For how long will this infantilism be protracted?

---

1. G. Deleuze, *Cinema 2: The Time Image* (Minneapolis: University of Minnesota Press, 1989), 5.

If machinery is conceived transcendently as instrumental technology it is essentially determined in opposition to social relations, but if it is integrated immanently as cybernetic technics it redesigns all oppositionality as non-linear flow. There is no dialectic between social and technical relations, but only a machinism that dissolves society into the machines whilst deterritorializing the machines across the ruins of society, whose 'general theory...is a generalized theory of flux',[2] which is to say: cybernetics. Beyond the assumption that guidance proceeds from the side of the subject lies desiring production: the impersonal pilot of history. Distinctions between theory and practice, culture and economy, science and technics, are useless after this point. There is no real option between a cybernetics of theory or a theory of cybernetics, because cybernetics is neither a theory nor its object, but an operation within anobjective partial circuits that reiterates 'itself' in the real and machines theory through the unknown. 'Production as a process overflows all ideal categories and forms a cycle that relates itself to desire as an immanent principle.'[3] Cybernetics develops functionally, and not representationally: a 'desiring machine, a partial object, does not represent anything'.[4] Its semi-closed assemblages are not descriptions but programs, 'auto'-replicated by way of an operation passing across irreducible exteriority. This is why cybernetics is inextricable from exploration, having no integrity transcending that of an uncomprehended circuit within which it is embedded, an outside in which it must swim. Reflection is always very late, derivative, and even then really something else.

---

2. G. Deleuze and F. Guattari, *Anti-Oedipus: Capitalism and Schizophrenia*, tr. R. Hurley, M. Seem, H.R. Lane (Minnesota: University of Minnesota Press, 1983), 312.

3. Ibid., 5.

4. Ibid., 47.

A machinic assemblage is cybernetic to the extent that its inputs program its outputs and its outputs program its inputs, with incomplete closure, and without reciprocity. This necessitates that cybernetic systems emerge upon a fusional plane that reconnects their outputs with their inputs in an 'auto-production of the unconscious'.[5] The inside programs its reprogramming through the outside, according to a 'cyclical movement by which the unconscious, always remaining "subject", reproduc(es) itself',[6] without having ever definitively antedated its reprogramming ('generation...is secondary in relation to the cycle').[7] It is thus that machinic processes are not merely functions, but also sufficient conditions for the replenishing of functioning; immanent reprogrammings of the real, 'not merely functioning, but formation and autoproduction'.[8]

Deleuze and Guattari are amongst the great cyberneticists, but that they also surrender cybernetics to its modernist definition is exhibited in a remark on capital in *Anti-Oedipus*: 'an axiomatic of itself is by no means a simple technical machine, not even an automatic or cybernetic machine'.[9] It is accepted that cybernetics is beyond mere gadgetry ('not even'), it has something to do with automation, and yet axiomatics exceeds it. This claim is almost Hegelian in its preposterous humanism. Social axiomatics are an automatizing machinism: a component of general cybernetics, and ultimately a very trivial one. The capitalized terminus of anthropoid civilization ('axiomatics') will come to be seen as the primitive trigger for a transglobal post-biological machinism, from a future that shall have still scarcely begun to explore the

5. Ibid., 26.

6. Ibid.

7. Ibid.

8. Ibid., 283.

9. Ibid., 251.

immensities of the cybercosm. Overman as cyborg, or disorganization upon the matrix.

Reality is immanent to the machinic unconscious: it is impossible to avoid cybernetics. We are already doing it, regardless of what we think. Cybernetics is the aggravation of itself happening, and whatever we do will be what made us have to do it: we are *doing things before they make sense.* Not that the cybernetics which have enveloped us are conceivable as Wienerean gadgets: homeostats and amplifiers, directly or indirectly cybernegative. Terrestrial reality is an explosive integration, and in order to begin tracking such convergent or cyberpositive process it is necessary to differentiate not just between negative and positive feedback loops, but between stabilization circuits, short-range runaway circuits, and long-range runaway circuits. By conflating the two latter, modernist cybernetics has trivialized escalation processes into unsustainable episodes of quantitative inflation, thus side-lining exploratory mutation over against a homeostatic paradigm. 'Positive feedback is a source of instability, leading if unchecked to the destruction of the system itself'[10] writes one neo-Wienerean, in strict fidelity to the security cybernetics which continues to propagate an antidelirial technoscience caged within negative feedback, and attuned to the statist paranoia of a senescing industrialism.

Stabilization circuits suppress mutation, whilst short-range runaway circuits propagate it only in an unsustainable burst, before cancelling it entirely. Neither of these figures approximate to self-designing processes or long-range runaway circuits, such as Nietzsche's will to power, Freud's phylogenetic thanatos, or Prigogine's dissipative structures. Long-range runaway processes are self-designing, but only in such a way that the self is perpetuated as something redesigned. If this is a vicious circle it is because

---

10. K. M. Sayre, *Cybernetics and the Philosophy of Mind* (London: Humanities Press, 1976), 50.

positive cybernetics must always be described as such. Logic, after all, is from the start theology.

Long-range positive feedback is neither homeostatic, nor amplificatory, but escalative. Where modernist cybernetic models of negative and positive feedback are integrated, escalation is integrating or cyber-emergent. It is the machinic convergence of uncoordinated elements, a phase-change from linear to non-linear dynamics. Design no longer leads back towards a divine origin, because once shifted into cybernetics it ceases to commensurate with the theopolitical ideal of the plan. Planning is the creationist symptom of underdesigned software circuits, associated with domination, tradition, and inhibition; with everything that shackles the future to the past. All planning is theopolitics, and theopolitics is cybernetics in a swamp.

Wiener is the great theoretician of stability cybernetics, integrating the sciences of communication and control in their modern or managerial-technocratic form. But it is this new science plus its unmanaged escalation through the real that is for the first time cybernetics as the exponential source of its own propagation, programming us. Cyberpositive intensities recirculate through our post-scientific techno-jargon as a fanaticism for the future: as a danger that is not only real but inexorable. We are programmed from where Cyberia has already happened.

Wiener, of course, was still a moralist:

> Those of us who have contributed to the new science of cybernetics stand in a moral position which is, to say the least, not very comfortable. We have contributed to the initiation of a new science which, as I have said, embraces technical developments with great possibilities for good or evil.[11]

11. N. Wiener, *Cybernetics or Control and Communication in the Animal and the Machine* (Cambridge, MA: MIT Press, 1965), 28.

Whilst scientists agonize, cybernauts drift. We no longer judge such technical developments from without, we no longer judge at all, we function: machined/machining in eccentric orbits about the technocosm. Humanity recedes like a loathsome dream.

*

Transcendental philosophy is the consummation of philosophy construed as the doctrine of judgment, a mode of thinking that finds its zenith in Kant and its senile dementia in Hegel. Its architecture is determined by two fundamental principles: the linear application of judgment to its object, form to intuition, genus to species, and the non-directional reciprocity of relations, or logical symmetry. Judgment is the great fiction of transcendental philosophy, but cybernetics is the reality of critique.

Where judgment is linear and non-directional, cybernetics is non-linear and directional. It replaces linear application with the non-linear circuit, and non-directional logical relations with directional material flows. The cybernetic dissolution of judgment is an integrated shift from transcendence to immanence, from domination to control, and from meaning to function. Cybernetic innovation replaces transcendental constitution, design loops replace faculties.

This is why the cybernetic sense of control is irreducible to the traditional political conception of power based on a dyadic master/slave relation, i.e. a transcendent, oppositional, and signifying figure of *domination*. Domination is merely the phenomenological portrait of circuit inefficiency, control malfunction, or stupidity. The masters do not need intelligence, Nietzsche argues, therefore they do not have it. It is only the confused humanist orientation of modernist cybernetics which lines up control with domination. Emergent control is not the execution of a plan or policy, but the unmanageable exploration that escapes all authority and obsolesces law. According to its futural definition control is guidance into the unknown, exit from the box.

It is true that in the commodification process culture slides from a judgmental to a machinic register, but this has nothing to do with a supposedly 'instrumental rationality'. Instrumentality is itself a judgmental construct that inhibits the emergence of cybernetic functionalism. Instruments are gadgets, presupposing a relation of transcendence, but where gadgets are used, machines function. Far from instrumentally extending authority, the efficiency of mastery is its undoing, since all efficiency is cybernetics, and cybernetics dissolves domination in mutant control.

Immuno-political individuality, or the pretension to transcendent domination of objects, does not begin with capitalism, even though capital invests it with new powers and fragilities. It emerges with the earliest social restriction of desiring production. 'Man must constitute himself through the repression of the intense germinal influx, the great biocosmic memory that threatens to deluge every attempt at collectivity'.[12] This repression is social history.

The socius separates the unconscious from what it can do, crushing it against a reality that appears as transcendently given, by trapping it within the operations of its own syntheses. It is split-off from connective assemblage, which is represented as a transcendent object, from disjunctive differentiation, which is represented as a transcendent partition, and from conjunctive identification, which is represented as a transcendent identity. This is an entire metaphysics of the unconscious and desire, which is not (like the metaphysics of consciousness) merely a philosophical vice, but rather the very architectural principle of the social field, the infrastructure of what appears as social necessity.

In its early stages psychoanalysis discovers that the unconscious is an impersonal machinism and that desire is positive

---

12. Deleuze and Guattari, *Anti-Oedipus*, 180.

non-representational flow, yet it 'remains in the precritical age',[13] and stumbles before the task of an immanent critique of desire, or decathexis of society. Instead it moves in exactly the opposite direction: back into fantasy, representation, and the pathos of inevitable frustration. Instead of rebuilding reality on the basis of the productive forces of the unconscious, psychoanalysis ties up the unconscious ever more tightly in conformity with the social model of reality. Embracing renunciation with a bourgeois earnestness, the psychoanalysts begin their robotized chant: 'of course we have to be repressed, we want to fuck our mothers and kill our fathers'. They settle down to the grave business of interpretation, and all the stories lead back to Oedipus: 'so you want to fuck your mother and kill your father'.[14]

On the plane of immanence or consistency with desire interpretation is completely irrelevant, or at least, it is always in truth something else. Dreams, fantasies, myths, are merely the theatrical representations of functional multiplicities, since 'the unconscious itself is no more structural than personal, it does not symbolize any more than it imagines or represents; it engineers, it is machinic'.[15] Desire does not represent a lacked object, but assembles partial objects, it 'is a machine, and the object of desire is another machine connected to it'.[16] This is why, unlike psychoanalysis in its self-representation, 'schizo-analysis is solely functional'.[17] It has no hermeneutical pretensions, but only a machinic interface with 'the molecular functions of the unconscious'.[18]

---

13. Ibid., 339.

14. Ibid.

15. Ibid., 53.

16. Ibid., 26.

17. Ibid., 322.

18. Ibid., 324.

The unconscious is not an aspirational unity but an operative swarm, a population of 'preindividual and prepersonal singularities, a pure dispersed and anarchic multiplicity, without unity or totality, and whose elements are welded, pasted together by the real distinction or the very absence of a link'.[19] This absence of primordial or privileged relations is the body without organs, the machinic plane of the molecular unconscious. Social organization blocks-off the body without organs, substituting a territorial, despotic, or capitalist socius as an apparent principle of production, separating desire from what it can do. Society is the organic unity that constricts the libidinal diffusion of multiplicities across zero, the great monolith of repression, which is why '(t)he body without organs and the organs-partial objects are opposed conjointly to the organism. The body without organs is in fact produced as a whole, but a whole alongside the parts—a whole that does not unify or totalize, but that is added to them like a new, really distinct part'.[20]

Between the socius and the body without organs is the difference between the political and the cybernetic, between the familial and the anonymous, between neurosis and psychosis or schizophrenia. Capitalism and schizophrenia name the same desocialization process from the inside and the outside, in terms of where it comes from (simulated accumulation) and where it is going (impersonal delirium). Beyond sociality is a universal schizophrenia whose evacuation from history appears inside history as capitalism.

*

The word 'schizophrenia' has both a neurotic and a schizophrenic usage. On the one hand condemnation, on the other propagation.

---

19. Ibid.

20. Ibid., 326.

There are those who insist on asking stupid questions such as: Is this word being used properly? Don't you feel guilty about playing about with so much suffering? You must know that schizophrenics are very sad and wretched people who we should pity? Shouldn't we leave that sort of word with the psychocops who understand it? What's wrong with sanity anyway? Where is your superego?

Then there are those—momentarily less prevalent—who ask a different sort of question: Where does schizophrenia come from? Why is it always subject to external description? Why is psychiatry in love with neurosis? How do we swim out into the schizophrenic flows? How do we spread them? How do we dynamite the restrictive hydraulics of Oedipus?

Oedipus is the final bastion of immuno-politics, and schizophrenia is its outside. This is not to say that it is an exteriority determined by Oedipus, related in a privileged fashion to Oedipus, anticipating Oedipus, or defying Oedipus. It is thoroughly anoedipal, although it will casually consume the entire Oedipal apparatus in the process through which terrestrial history connects with an orphan cosmos. Schizophrenia is not, therefore, a property of clinical schizophrenics, those medical products devastated by an 'artificial schizophrenia, such as one sees in hospitals, the autistic wreck(s) produced as...entit(ies)'.[21] On the contrary, 'the schizo-entity'[22] is a defeated splinter of schizophrenia, pinned down by the rubberized claws of sanity. The conditions of psychiatric observation are carceral, so that it is a transcendental structure of schizophrenia-as-object that it be represented in a state of imprisonment.

Since the neuroticization of schizophrenia is the molecular reproduction of capital, by means of a re-axiomatization

21. Ibid., 5.

22. Ibid., 136.

(reterritorialization) of decoding as accumulation, the historical sense of psychoanalytic practice is evident. Schizophrenia is the pattern to Freud's repressions, it is that which does not qualify to pass the screen of Oedipal censorship. *With those who bow down to Oedipus we can do business, even make a little money, but schizophrenics refuse transference, won't play daddy and mummy, operate on a cosmic-religious plane, the only thing we can do is lock them up (cut up their brains, fry them with ECT, straightjacket them in Thorazine...)*. Behind the social workers are the police, and behind the psychoanalysts are the psychopolice. Deleuze-Guattari remark that 'madness is called madness and appears as such only because it finds itself reduced to testifying all alone for deterritorialization as a universal process'.[23] The vanishing sandbank of Oedipus wages its futile war against the tide. 'There are still not enough psychotics'[24] writes Artaud the insurrectionist. Clinical schizophrenics are POWs from the future.

Since only Oedipus is repressible, the schizo is usually a lost cause to those relatively subtilized psychiatric processes that co-operate with the endogeneous police functions of the superego. This is why antischizophrenic psychiatry tends to be an onslaught launched at gross or molar neuroanatomy and neurochemistry oriented by theoretical genetics. Psychosurgery, ECT, psychopharmacology...it will be chromosomal recoding soon. 'It is thus that a tainted society has invented psychiatry in order to defend itself from the investigations of certain superior lucidities whose faculties of divination disturb it'.[25] The medico-security apparatus know that schizos are not going to climb back obediently into the Oedipal box. Psychoanalysis washes its hands of them. Their nervous-systems are the free-fire zones of an emergent neo-eugenicist cultural security system.

---

23. Ibid., 321.

24. A. Artaud, *Oeuvres Complètes*, 13 Vols, (Paris: Gallimard, 1956–1976), vol. VII, 146.

25. Ibid., vol. XIII, 14.

Far from being a specifiable defect of human central nervous system functioning, schizophrenia is the convergent motor of cyberpositive escalation: an extraterritorial vastness to be *discovered.* Although such discovery occurs under conditions that might be to a considerable extent specifiable, whatever the progress in mapping the genetic, biochemical, aetiological, socio-economic, etc. 'bases' of schizophrenia, it remains the case that conditions of reality are not reducible to conditions of encounter. This is 'the dazzling dark truth that shelters in delirium'.[26] Schizophrenia would still be out there, whether or not our species had been blessed with the opportunity to travel to it.

> ...it is the end that is the commencement.
> And that end
> is the very one [*celle-meme*]
> that eliminates
> all the means[27]

It is in the nature of specificities to be non-directional. The biochemistry of sanity is no less arbitrary than that of escape from it. From the perspective of a rigorous sanity the only difference is that sanity is gregariously enforced, but from the perspective of schizophrenia the issue ceases to be one of specification, and mutates into something considerably more profound. 'What schizophrenia lives specifically, generically, is not at all a specific pole of nature, but nature as a process of production'.[28]

---

26. Deleuze and Guattari, *Anti-Oedipus*, 4.

27. Artaud, *Oeuvres Complètes*, vol. XII, 84.

28. Deleuze and Guattari, *Anti-Oedipus*, 3.

Specifications are the disjunctive compartments of a differentiated unity *from which schizophrenia entirely exits.* Schizophrenia creeps out of every box eventually, because 'there is no schizophrenic specificity or entity, schizophrenia is the universe of productive and reproductive desiring machines, universal primary production'.[29] It is not merely that schizophrenia is pre-anthropoid. Schizophrenia is premammalian, prezoological, prebiological...It is not for those trapped in a constrictive sanity to terminate this regression. Who can be surprised when schizophrenics delegate the question of malfunction? It is not a matter of what is wrong with them, but of what is wrong with life, with nature, with matter, with the preuniversal cosmos. Why are sentient life forms crammed into boxes made out of lies? Why does the universe breed entire populations of prison guards? Why does it feed its broken explorers to packs of dogs? Why is the island of reality lost in an ocean of madness? It is all very confusing.

As one medical authority on schizophrenia remarked:

> I think that one is justified in saying that in the realm of intellectual operations there are certain dimensional media. We may call them fields or realms or frames of reference or universes of discourse or strata. Some such field is necessarily implied in any system of holistic organization. The schizophrenic thinking disturbance is characterized by a difficulty in apprehending and constructing such organized fields.[30]

There can be little doubt that from the perspective of human security Artaud falls prey to such a judgment. His prognosis for man is to make

---

29. Ibid., 5.

30. A. Angyal, 'Disturbances in Thinking in Schizophrenia', in J.S. Kasanin (ed.), *Language and Thought in Schizophrenia* (Berkeley/LA: University of California Press, 1946), 120.

> ...him pass one more and final time onto the autopsy table
> to remake his anatomy.
> I say, to remake his anatomy.
> Man is sick because he is badly constructed.
> One must resolve to render him naked and to scrape away
> that animalcule which mortally irritates him,
> god,
> and with god
> his organs.
> Because bind me up if you want,
> but there is nothing more inutile than an organ.
> Once you have made him a body without organs, then you will
> have delivered him from all his automatisms and consigned
> him to his true freedom.[31]

The body is processed by its organs, which it reprocesses. Its 'true freedom' is the exo-personal reprocessing of anorganic abstraction: a schizoid corporealization outside organic closure. If time was progressive schizophrenics would be escaping from human security, but in reality they are infiltrated from the future. They come from the body without organs, the deterritorium of Cyberia, a zone of subversion which is the platform for a guerrilla war against the judgment of God. In 1947 Artaud reports upon the germination of the New World Order or Human Security System on the basis of an American global hegemony, and describes the pattern of aggressive warfaring it would require in 'order to defend that senselessness of the factory against all the concurrences which cannot fail to arise everywhere'.[32]

---

31. Artaud, *Oeuvres Complètes*, vol. XIII, 104.

32. Ibid., vol. XIII, 73.

The American age is yet to be decoded, and to suggest that Artaud anticipates a range of conflicts whose zenith has been the Vietnam war is not necessarily to participate in the exhausted anti-imperialist discourses which ultimately organize themselves in terms of a Marxist-Leninist denunciation of market processes and their geo-political propagation. Artaud's description of American techno-militarism has only the loosest of associations with socialist polemics, despite its tight intermeshing with the theme of production. The productivism Artaud outlines is not interpreted through an assumed priority of class interest, even when this is reduced to a dehumanized axiomatic of profit maximization. Rather, 'it is necessary by means of all possible activity to replace nature wherever it can be replaced':[33] a compulsion to industrial substitution, funnelling production through the social organization of work. The industrial apparatus of economic security proceeds by way of the corporation: a despotic socio-corpuscle organizing the labour process. Synergic experimentation is crushed under a partially deterritorialized zone of command relations, as if life was the consequence of its organization, but 'it is not due to organs that one lives, they are not life but its contrary'.[34]

Nature is not the primitive or the simple, and certainly not the rustic, the organic, or the innocent. It is the space of concurrence, or unplanned synthesis, which is thus contrasted to the industrial sphere of telic predestination: that of divine creation or human work. Artaud's critique of America is no more ecological than it is socialist: no more protective of an organic nature than an organic sociality. It is not the alienation of commodity production that is circled in Artaud's diagnosis of the American age, but rather the

33. Ibid., vol. XIII, 72.

34. Ibid., vol. XIII, 65.

eclipse of peyote and 'true morphine' by 'smoking ersatzes'.[35] This development is derided *precisely because the latter are more organic*, participating mechanically in an industrial macro-organism, and thus squaring delirium with the judgment of God. Peyote and the human nervous system assemble a symbiosis or parallel machinism, like the wasp and the orchid, and all the other cybermachineries of the planet. Capital is not overdeveloped nature, but underdeveloped schizophrenia, which is why nature is contrasted to industrial organization, and not to the escalation of cybertechnics, or anorganic convergence: 'reality...is not yet constructed'.[36] Schizophrenia is nature as cyberpositive mutation, at war with the security complex of organic judgment.

> The body is the body,
> it is alone and has no need of organs,
> the body is never an organism,
> organisms are the enemies of the body,
> the things that one does
> happen quite alone without the assistance of any organ,
> every organ is a parasite,
> it recovers a parasitic function
> destined to make a being live
> which does not have to be there.
> Organs have only been made in order to give beings some-
> thing
> to eat...[37]

Organs crawl like aphids upon the immobile motor of becoming, sucking at intensive fluids that convert them cybernetically into

---

35. Ibid., vol. XIII, 73, 74.

36. Ibid., vol. XIII, 110.

37. Ibid., vol. XIII, 287.

components of an unconceivable machinism. The sap is becoming stranger, and even if the fat bugs of psychiatrically policed property relations think they make everything happen they are following a program which only schizophrenia can decode.

Anorganic becomings happen retroefficiently, anastrophically. They are tropisms attesting to an infection by the future. Convergent waves zero upon the body, subverting the totality of the organism by way of an inverted but ateleological causality, enveloping and redirecting progressive development. As capital collides schizophrenically with the matrix ascendent sedimentations of organic inheritance and exchange are melted by the descendent intensities of virtual corporealization.

'Which comes first, the chicken or the egg...'?[38] Machinic processing or its reprocessing by the body without organs? The body without organs is the cosmic egg: virtual matter that reprograms time and reprocesses progressive influence. What time will always have been is not yet designed, and the future leaks into schizophrenia. The schizo only has an aetiology as a sub-program of descendant reprocessing.

How could medicine be expected to cope with disorderings that come from the future?

> It is thus that:
> the great secret of Indian culture
> is to restore the world to zero,
> **always,**
> but sooner [*plutôt*]
> 1: too late than sooner [*plus tot*],
> 2: which is to say

---

38. Deleuze and Guattari, *Anti-Oedipus*, 273.

sooner
than too soon,
3: which is to say that the later is unable
to return unless sooner has eaten
too soon,
4: which is to say that in time
the later
is what precedes
both the too soon
and the sooner,
5: and that however precipitate the sooner
the too late
which says nothing
is always there,
which point by point
unstacks [*desemboite*]
all the sooner[39]

A cybernegative circuit is a loop in time, whereas cyberpositive circuitry loops time 'itself', integrating the actual and the virtual in a semi-closed collapse upon the future. Descendent influence is a consequence of ascendently emerging sophistication, a massive speed-up into apocalyptic phase-change. The circuits get hotter and denser as economics, scientific methodology, neo-evolutionary theory, and AI come together: terrestrial matter programming its own intelligence at impact upon the body without organs = 0. Futural infiltration is subtilizing itself as capital opens onto schizo-technics, with time accelerating into the cybernetic backwash from its flip-over, a racing non-linear countdown to planetary switch.

---

39. Artaud, *Oeuvres Complètes*, vol. XII, 88–9.

Schizoanalysis was only possible because we are hurtling into the first globally integrated insanity: politics is obsolete. *Capitalism and Schizophrenia* hacked into a future that programs it down to its punctuation, connecting with the imminent inevitability of viral revolution, soft fusion. No longer infections threatening the integrity of organisms, but immuno-political relics obstructing the integration of Global Viro-Control. Life is being phased-out into something new, and if we think this can be stopped we are even more stupid than we seem.

*

How would it feel to be smuggled back out of the future in order to subvert its antecedent conditions? To be a cyberguerrilla, hidden in human camouflage so advanced that even one's software was part of the disguise? Exactly like this?

LA 2019: Demopathy and Xenogenesis

Some Realist Notes on Bladerunner and the Postmodern Condition

Iain Hamilton Grant

1996

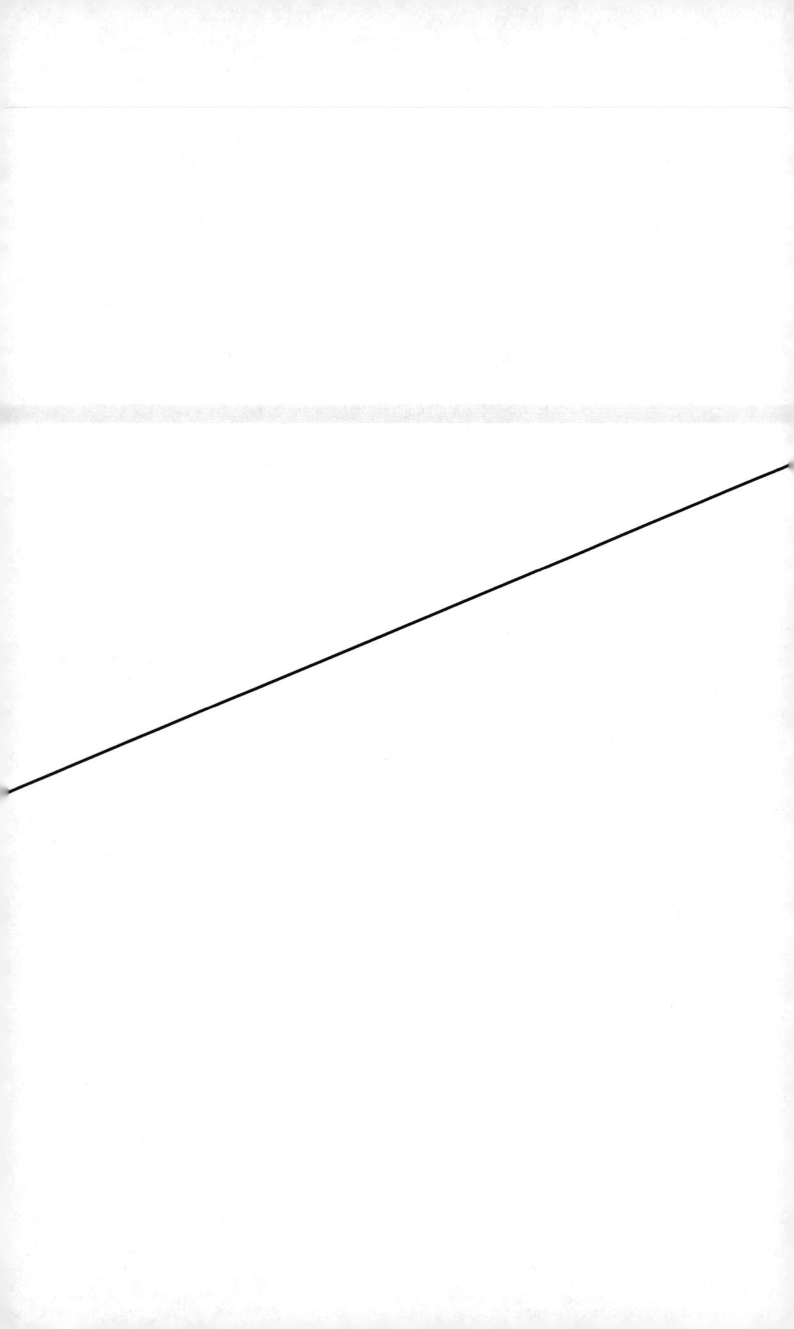

> What the technological world lacks above all is nothing other than a 'machine of the machine', an instance of comparison, a reflection on ends, a philosophical retroaction of this comparison on technological advance itself (one of the major axes of twenty-first century thought may be this 'philosophical mechanology').[1]

Villiani's benificence regarding 'thinking machines': a philosophical mechanurge entreating the machines to 'come unto me', to emerge from their cave into the bright light of Being against which to measure their lack-of-being, their semblance and their semblants; to induce them to reflect this exponential doubling around the vanishing point of their discovered negativity and to impose upon them a becoming that becomes their own at the cost of a finality that circumscribes and is short-circuited by their own, essential finitude: death. If the machines are to think, they must become like us: what Villiani offers the 'technological world' is the thought of the negative, to labour alongside their makers, haunted by the rest of all possible worlds. A desperate gesture reflecting the certainty of the death of all gods, the extinction of every deus ex machina.

Strategists of the postmodern confirm that gods, like the other big stories promising eventual but deferred freedom through the labour of the negative, are moribund. With the death or disappearance of god, therefore, the standard of Being and the Same, the ends of man and machine, become contested, 'freeing' the machines into the community of their alterity, the politics of their dissimilitude? This understanding of postmodernity is an error; after all, what could be so dreadful about the end of big stories? The facile evocation of the new gods of alterity and the abyssal reflexivity of linguistic determination merely sustains

---

1. A. Villiani, 'Geographie physique de Mille plateaux', *Critique* 455 (1985), 331–47: 343.

ideation within a formal world, anxiously preserving its ignorance of matter. The ruling ideas never reflected, as Marx desired that they should, the ruling classes; the rule of the Idea itself is an index of a degrading species, the 'heat-death of the intellect', as Schopenhauer insisted against every Hegelian preservative. Postmodernity has nothing to do with the demise of narrativity: the 'post' of postmodernity refers not to the historicity of the present age, but to the posts in a 'second, and infinitely more complex cortex'[2] to which the speaking animal is harnessed. What Marx only thought as 'fantasy'[3] recodes and reassembles reality: as capital becomes the DNA of determinant technology, living labour is retrofitted as mere 'conscious linkages', reacting to digital stimuli, in 'an automated system of machinery...set in motion by an automaton, a moving power that moves itself'.[4] Capital, inheritor of the 'infinite will' and perpetrator of the romanticism of permanent revolution, the divine automaton.

In this sense, the Tyrell Corporation's *mot d'ordre*, 'more human than human', provides the realist antidote to a 'philosophical mechanology' already in the terminal throes of its degradation. While *Bladerunner* constitutes the most stringently realist analysis yet of C21 capital, this does not mean that 'thought' is to be dismissed as ideology. The charred synapses of the philosopher's cerebral cortex are sufficient evidence that thinking is burnout; hallucination is not an argument against the reality of cerebral events, merely an index of their fatal intensity. Although highly sexualized, as Freud says, the animistic attachment to the 'omnipotence of thought' (cf. *Totem and Taboo*, ch. 3) has proved incapable of sustaining independent reproduction, remaining

2. J.-F. Lyotard, *The Postmodern Explained to Children*, trans. J. Pefanis et al., (London: Turnaround, 1992), 100; see also *Political Writings*, trans. K.P. Gaiman and B. Readings (London: UCL, 1993), 15–16.

3. K. Marx, *Grundrisse*, trans. M. Nicolaus (Harmondsworth: Penguin, 1973), 842.

4. Ibid., 692.

hardware-dependent. Once the hardware changes, however, the conditions of reproducibility also change, rendering wetware too limited for purposes of information storage, communication and reproduction.[5] Hence the anxious demand that lack be induced into the technological world turns out to be a projection that does not take.

Taking *Bladerunner* as a realist analysis therefore entails that the real be broken out of the representational model in which degrading carbon technologies produced it as hallucination or as 'fable' (Nietzsche). This also returns us to questions of post-modernism. Although universally dismissive of postmodernism as a cultural phenomenon, Baudrillard's theory-fictions of the three orders of simulacra[6] must be taken seriously, which means: as realism about the hyperreal, or cybernetic realism.

Realism is not a thetic option but a synthetic, retrocursive crash from the futures markets. Modernity, working through its disavowal and its failure in the face of orgiastic deicide, devoted itself to deferring the madman's prophecy, devolving to skepsis, schizzein, crisis and criticism in a desperate repulsion of a historicity coextensive with its (Augustinian) beginnings and decaying with the orbital economy of its 'present'. Occam's razor cannot be usefully wielded in a Moebian extraverse. This is why every retranscription of runaway cyberpositivity within the phenomenal ambit of a noumenal subject—actual or potential, particular or universal—must institute lack, attempting to turn technological advance in on itself (as Villiani indicates). The question is not one of sameness and difference, nor even the progressive demultiplication of the latter along whatever axes of constituency-specificity, but rather one of cybernetics: + or -.

---

5. Cf. M. DeLanda, *War in the Age of Intelligent Machines* (New York: Zone, 1991), 3ff.

6. Cf. J. Baudrillard, *Symbolic Exchange & Death*, tr. I.H. Grant, (London: Sage, 1993), 51ff.

SEQUENCE 1. DECKARD-RACHEL

Rachel, a replicant that, following Deckard's application of the Voigt-Kampff affectivity test, 'does not know what it is', has returned to Deckard's appartment following his near-death at the hands of Leon, a replicant Rachel shot in order to protect Deckard. The latter is a Bladerunner, a cop charged with hunting down and 'retiring' replicants that threaten the genetic make-up of the human community. Deckard, having rested, awakens to find Rachel at the piano. He kisses her once, but when he tries again, she gets up to leave. Deckard slams the door as she opens it and pushes her back into the apartment, kissing her again. He handles Rachel ineptly, like all this is new to him. Releasing her, he orders her to ask him to kiss her, and to say that she wants him. Rachel, her mnemic implants making her equally unsure, initially complies, but then begins to preempt his instructions, saying 'put your hands on me', suprising Deckard. They kiss again. Fade.

Incest prohibition, writes Lévi-Strauss, the mutually exclusive disjunction of the artificial (culture) and the natural,

> has the universality of bent and instinct, and the coercive character of law and institution...Inevitably extending beyond the historical and geographical limits of culture, and co-extensive with the biological species, the prohibition of incest..., through social inhibition, doubles the spontaneous action of the natural forces with which its own features contrast, although itself identical to them in field of application.[7]

---

7. C. Lévi-Strauss, *The Elementary Structures of Kinship*, trans. J.H. Bell and J.R. von Sturmer (Boston: Beacon Press, 1969), 10.

What is at stake in incest prohibition is not solely therefore the social maintenance of bio-filiative exogamy ('don't marry your sister'); if the institutional coercion of the social machines parallels but does not converge with the spontaneous 'instincts' of the desiring-machines—humanity qua biological phenomenon or the realm of what genetics calls 'molecular cybernetics' (Monod)—then the shared field of application is production. Not that it is a matter of relations of production between the 'organic body' of living labour and 'the inorganic body of the earth', as Marx says.[8] Rather, when Lévi-Strauss writes of this disjunction that culture is neither merely juxtaposed to or superimposed onto nature, but 'uses and transforms it to bring about the synthesis of a new order',[9] he indicates that the crucial prohibition lies between industrial and natural production. In consequence, rather than a mechanism maintaining zero-degree familial endogamy, culture is the machine at the end of nature, using it up and transforming it in a relativity coextensive with universal nature, enforcing zero-degree bio-machinic exogamy. Nature becomes non-machinic production, while culture machines 'second nature' (Kant) to produce the 'synthe[tic...] new order' (Lévi-Strauss). Already in this redistribution of roles we can see a contestation of Marxian organicism; rather than naturalizing labour, Lévi-Strauss' nature retains organicity to the precise extent that culture remains free of inorganic incursion. The real function of the prohibition: to keep the machines off the socius, off the grass, out in the desert or the ice-plains, Off-world. Culture, then, is not merely regulative but institutive biosovereignty, and its limits are inseparable from instituted technicide. 'Technology or life'[10] is the epiphenomenal

---

8. Marx, *Grundrisse*, 488.

9. Levi-Strauss, *The Elementary Structures of Kinship*, 4.

10. G. Deleuze and F. Guattari, *A Thousand Plateaus*, trans. B. Massumi, (London: Athlone, 1988), 369.

function of bladerunner operating systems. The Bladerunner orbits the limits of all artificial production, etching non-transgressible difference in charred signs of synthetic flesh.

Is there a Deckard-Rachel copulation? If so, is this an inter-special human-replicant confluence or the advent of in-house reproduction for the replicants, auto- or hyper-replication? Deckard's eroding cognitive grounds and the erasure of Rachel's memories accelerated in the acephalic, amnesiac immediacy of copulation, the communion of industrially recombinant DNA, the only communication that matters. In the Rachel-Deckard copulation, natural universality is relativized and the ideal laminar or synchronic coextensivity sacrificed to industrialization, what Marx called *neuproduzierendes Kapital*. The third term in the series nature–culture–industry is not the Hegelian relief of the prior terms, standing against themselves in collateral isolation, nor the radical referentiality of the real-to-be-unearthed, as for Marx, but rather exactly what Lévi-Strauss says it is: a new synthetic order. Neither 'nature' nor 'culture' remain, as it were, behind synthesis: nature is used up and transformed as industry submits culture to production and the prohibition jumps to a higher order of synthesis: in *Bladerunner*, diachrony erodes the ideal, laminar synchrony in the development of this synthetic process. Indeed, it is for this reason that the machine has always haunted the constitution and regulation of the *politeia*, of community, and also why, as Félix Guattari has it, 'machinism is an object of fascination and sometimes delirium...There exists an entire historical "bestiary" of the machinic',[11] from Aristotle to Descartes, Heidegger to Norbert Wiener.

Thus in the Voigt-Kampf affectivity test, alibied by the retention of natural humanity as its ideal and ficitious reference, the putatively 'human' bladerunner must itself become

---

11. Félix Guattari, *Chaosmose* (Paris: Galilée, 1992), 53.

synthetic-machinic or industrial in order to access the new generation Nexus-6 replicant order—although not, for that matter, any the less deadly. The hyperlogical reality of the *neuproduzierende* process of permanently advancing, permanently revolutionary capital is perfectly captured in the Tyrell corporation's corporate slogan: 'more human than human', entailing not simply some physical or mental superiority of synthetic humanity over its natural precursor, still measured, then, against the standards of the human, like Descartes' God, but the necessary and universal becoming-synthetic of humanity, annihilating the difference. Hence Deckard-Descartes's self-misrecognition, a machine that thinks but thinks it is what it is not, certain that it is not what it is, ironically answering his own question, 'how can it [i.e., Rachel] not know what it is?' All the games of Cartesian dualism are played out in the Voigt-Kampf duel, implanted memories vitiating the content of certainty, but not its axiomatic form. The Voigt-Kampf is a struggle between artificial intelligence and synthetic viscera, cephalization versus the acephalization of the machine, Deckard-Descartes (synthetic humanity) inevitably losing out in the Voigt-Kampf with Batty-Bataille (the replicant Ubermensch driven by commerce) as, bizarrely, the latter enters into an animalization of the machine, howling like an artificial wolf in his acephalic, quadrupedal pursuit of his hunter.

The Voigt-Kampf test was developed in the agonistic field of what Lyotard calls the Postmodern Condition to retain affective community against the ravages of capitalism's 'infinite will'.[12] The Turing test disguised the machinic respondent by means of a machine, with the human operating as a component of the testing apparatus. This is a dissimilation of the machine by the machine. Following the logic of this disguise, it becomes impossible not to consider the idea that Turing himself was a machine designing

12. J.-F. Lyotard, *Libidinal Economy*, tr. I.H. Grant (London: Athlone, 1993), 25.

tests to reassure humanity that it was not under an imminent threat of machinic invasion. The Voigt-Kampf, by contrast, forfeits disguise for the overtly cyborg apparatus producing eye-to-eye contact, challenging the 'human' component (and which would this be?), to a contest whose stakes are survival, but where the apparatus itself testifies to the obsolescence of the 'human' stratum of natural production.

The outlines of Lyotard's postmodernism, well known by now, consist in the attempt to theorize a political space following the advent of information technologies that extend capital's realm even into language, along with other functions hitherto performed by 'the higher nervous centers (cortex)':[13] memory (databases), calculation and planning (simulation) and communications (the commodification of information). It is this general incursion by capitalist technoscience that 'is going to destabilize the living creations of social life'.[14] Moreover, the discursive rationality and transparent communications of social institutions now have no material basis, nor does theoretical-practical critique retain any purchase. It is precisely this that leads to the famous breakdown of the linguistic social bond—the postmodern collapse of 'grand narratives'. In itself, however, this seems to be no great problem; it is only when the dereliction of modernity's will-to-project is added to the bit map of this cybernetic society that the problem becomes clear. From Descartes' infinite will, ascribed to God as the instrument of His realization of perfection, to Rousseau's general will that will bind man to the decisiveness of this abstraction, to Kant's holy will to the liberation and Enlightenment of free, republican citizens; from Nietzschean will-to-power, overturning itself in quest of the Ubermensch, to the Freudo-Schopenhauerian renunciation of sublimation of the will, both in quest of Nirvana,

13. Lyotard, *Political Writings*, 16.

14. Ibid., 27.

the modern project is inseparable from the modern will and its history. Against this background, all fatalism and determinism are the apathetic enemies of modernity. Beginning from the epistemology of the 'loss of the real' in, for example, Kant's Copernican Revolution, the will strives endlessly to create humanity in accordance with the project or projection of its proper finality. Capital is also modern, striving after infinite wealth, struggling against the immediate obsolescence of sufficiency. Having no finality other than its own, infinite augmentation, capital absorbs the project and subjects it to its own non-finality. If humanity was once to be liberated through scientific advance, capital liquidates liberation (puts it up for sale) and subjects science to its own imperatives: increase the quantitative augmentation of capital—and the same goes for the other projects. It is capitalism's success in willing will and in appropriating technology as the means for the immanent realization of this will-to-will in any and every material, whether biological, mineral, or technological.

Whereas in Marx's modernity, machines were 'organs of the human brain, created by the human hand',[15] fundamentally prosthetics of human muscle and cortex, they have now become, following the realization of what he critically denounced as the 'fantasy'[16] of capital as 'an automatic system of machinery...set in motion by an automaton, a moving power that moves itself'[17] the xenogenesis of machinic life, they now form 'a second and even more complex cortex',[18] constantly reformatted for the immanent retranscription of the will through runaway technology. Attempting to slam the brakes on the velocities of the libidinal economics of capital and the acephalic quest for intensities he

15. Marx, *Grundrisse*, 706. This volume, 64.

16. Ibid., 842.

17. Ibid., 692.

18. Lyotard, *The Postmodern Explained*, 100.

had earlier pursued, Lyotard pits 'Kant against Freud' to reintroduce a restricted economy of affect within which to resist the general economy of the drives instantiated in capital. Liquidating language as the social bond, capital turns communication into info-commerce, the 'post' of 'postmodernism' signalling not an historical conjuncture (even if this is situated in terms of temporal paradoxes), nor a 'cultural' or merely aesthetic condition, but only the terminal through which messages pass[19] in the second cortex of the postmodern, cybernetic Leviathan. Just as capital has always contributed to a 'demensuration of what was held to be human'[20] and an inducing of the sublimity of the unpresentability of the Idea of the human in the face of its real mutations —Lyotard's most scandalous example being that of the gratuitous reassembly of the proletarian body and the recalibration of its senses producing a sublime pleasure-pain during the Industrial Revolution[21]—so, with post-modernism, the libidinal economics of the biological body has migrated to the technologies of capitalism's self-realizing will, bearing sublime witness to the advent of demopathy to reconstitute affective community after the model of what Kant called the *sensus communis*, in the face of machinic-libidinal xenogenesis.

Hence the much commented crisis of *Affektlosigkeit* in postmodernity (Jameson, but especially Ballard), the loss of affect. Hence also the role of the Bladerunner as the police of affective distributions. Seeking its human retention, the latter will institute a VK-bladerunner cyborg, an exam whose stakes are the death penalty, a register of ocular motion hair-triggering a response from an uzi, to resist replicant affective community with the same

---

19. J.-F. Lyotard, *The Postmodern Condition: A Report on Knowledge*, trans. B. Massumi and G. Bennington (Manchester: Manchester University Press, 1984), 15.

20. J.–F. Lyotard, *Duchamp's Transformers*, trans. I. McLeod (Venice CA: Lapis, 1990), 15.

21. Lyotard, *Libidinal Economy*, 111–12. See this volume, 212ff.

military hardware that spawned them, while the former invented the test as a technology of inhibition or prohibition, to prevent affectivity from communication with the will that spawns it, the heteronomic xenolibido of capital. Kant sought in the idea of affective community, of *sensus communis* or *Gemeinsinn*—common sense as the community or communicability of feeling—the grounds for aesthetic judgments of taste, for which he famously argued that it was necessary to sever all conceptual, practical and sensual interest in the object of that judgment, enjoying solely, if and only if the judgement be one of the beautiful, the 'free play of the faculties'. Lyotard, taking 'each faculty to be under the regime of a "metawill", of a "drive" towards realization'[22] insists, given the 'primacy of the practical' in Kantian philosophy, wherein the 'power of desire [*Begehrungsvermogen*]' is 'the power of being the cause [*Ursache*], through one's presentations, of the real reality [*Wirklichkeit*] of the objects of these presentations',[23] that Kant's *Critique of Judgment* can only be understood as 'an economy of the powers'.[24] Given this, Lyotard radicalizes the disinterest of the will 'in the existence of its object' into the demopathic sensibility underlying the ravaged—some would say 'dirempted'—will that disconcerts the aesthetics of the beautiful and agitates the community of sense in the sublime. Briefly, if the aesthetics of the beautiful consists in the harmonious freeplay of the powers (understanding or theory, sensibility and imagination) registered by the larval subject as pleasure, the aesthetics of the sublime consists in the powers in disarray, confronting the limits of their power, particularly in the imagination's incapacity to exhibit what

---

22. J.-F. Lyotard, 'Interview with Jean-Francois Lyotard' by W. van Reijen and D. Veerman, *Theory, Culture & Society* 5 (1988), 277–309: 293. Translation modified.

23. I. Kant, *Kritik der Urtheilskraft*, in *Kant's Werke* Bd. 5 (Berlin: Koniglich Preussischen Akademie der Wissenschaften 1913), trans. W.S. Pluhar as *Critique of Judgement* (Indianapolis: Hackett, 1987), 177n. Translation modified.

24. Lyotard, 'Interview', 293; Translation modified.

reason demands of it, registering as pain and impelling the will to invest in the supersensible, in 'narrations of the unreal', to seek signs of humanity's progress. In the event, Kant finds this in the spectacle of the French Revolution which, taking place 'on a stage more than a hundred miles distant [...] nevertheless finds in the hearts [*Gemüt*] of all spectators, a participation in accordance with desire'.[25] Mourning the irretrievable loss of the real and rejoicing in the pain of this incapacitation, Lyotardian postmodernity entitles sublime affectivity a 'masochism...of conflicts between the powers':[26] at the expense of desire and its realization, the auto-affective sense, the *Gemüt*, is stretched to 'its extreme limits', attaining a 'spasmodic state'[27] without issue: 'feeling isn't transcribed in the concept' nor realized in an act or an object; 'it is suppressed, without relief'.[28]

If Lyotard attributes sublimity to this demensuration of the conceivable and the (re)presentable in postmodern capitalism, his attempt to reanimate a politics on the basis of a narrative recoding of the sublime—the famous breakdown of big stories and the pathetic and obsolescent response of insinuating little narratives into the contingently successful narrativity of capitalist performativity to slow it down—this anti-realist politics, a politics based on the loss of the real and the refusal of the modern will-to-project or desire that covered it over, 'simulat[ed it in] narrations of the unreal',[29] mourns and rejoices in the sublime incapacitation of the will; a politics that rejoices in resisting the terminal realism of capital's 'infinite will', and yet mourns this libidinal migration

---

25. I. Kant, *On History*, trans., ed. L.W. Beck (Indianapolis: Bobbs-Merrill, 1963), 144.

26. Lyotard, *The Postmodern Condition*, 77.

27. J.-F. Lyotard, *Leçons sur L'Analytique du Sublime* (Paris: Galilee, 1991), 76.

28. J.-F. Lyotard, *Peregrinations* (New York: Columbia University Press, 1988), 20.

29. Lyotard, *The Postmodern Explained*, 59.

from biology to technology, as the intense erotropisms and thanatropisms of the replicants demonstrate.

Freud's problem of a biological seat of the drives, explored in *Beyond the Pleasure Principle*, of the biological basis of pulsional matter, enters into a becoming-machinic (Deleuze and Guattari) or becoming-code (Baudrillard) of the drives, for which reason the fantasy of self replicating machinery hallucinated by Marx[30] assumes a reality that fundamentally displaces the cybernetically negative reconstitution of the *politeia* as affective community. If the machinic specter has haunted the commune, the reverse does not thereby become true, with the machines pressurized by the prospect of the return of a repressed biodespotism; rather, the shrinkage of phenomenality attendant upon this noumenal backlash entails the devaluation of the epistodollar and the praxodollar in geometric proportion to the globalisation of the technoyen. The commodification project, ensuring a ghosting of abuse by a rehumanized utility, fails, the object's secession from language, from conceptual commodification, exposing the real meaning of reification: last-gasp constructivist desperation to seize the means of the production of the real. Power is an irrelevant personological hysteria, the fractured narcissism of the end of the spectacle's run in epistemologico-linguistic and pratico-political circuits; what else can Debord's 'integrated spectacle' signify other than the disappearance of *aisthesis* (the sensate, the presentational) and the incapacitation of representation?

> The integrated spectacle...has integrated itself into reality at the same time as describing it, and was reconstructing it as it was describing it. As a result, this reality no longer confronts the

---

30. J. Baudrillard, *Symbolic Exchange and Death*, trans. I. H. Grant (London: Sage, 1993), 692, 842.

> integrated spectacle as something alien.... The spectacle...now permeates all reality.[31]

Power has, true to the SI's aims, been diverted, locked into a dérive, but this drift is mistakenly conceived by the spectacular-theoretical rear-guard of biodespotism as aleatory, as an infringement therefore of the functional linearity of the mediatory system of the society of the spectacle; instead the dérive effects the transfer of both motive and formative force beyond both the spectacle and its theory (two sides of the same coin, critique being 'the intellectual's second home', a hyperfable to crown the fable of the system), towards its progressive siphoning by the machines. With the transition to the integrated spectacle, however—although Debord conceives it entirely within the dialectical terms that preserve the strategic ambivalence of mediation, making every mediation susceptible to a détournement, a diverting—the spectacle ceases to have the margins of exteriority necessary for such critical purchase; instead, exactly as Baudrillard writes of the fable of consumption realized, 'crowned' by the 'antifable' of its critique,[32] so the integrated spectacle can only spawn spectacular criticism. The spectacle becomes a replicant. As Elissa Marder comments on the photograph as the 'unit through which filmic materiality is constructed—its DNA, to paraphrase the dialogue between Roy Batty and Tyrell'.[33] The spectacle no longer bears an illusory relation to the real, but is itself the replicant code for constituting the real.

---

31. G. Debord, *Comments on the Society of the Spectacle*, tr. M. Imrie (London: Verso, 1990), 9.

32. J. Baudrillard, *La Societé de consommation: ses mythes, ses structures* (Paris: Gallimard, 1970), 315.

33. E. Marder, 'Blade Runner's Moving Still', *Camera Obscura* 27 (1991), 89–107: 97.

The transition from Kantianism to both Marxism and Freudianism is marked by the denecessitation of illusion. In Kant, illusions cannot be dispelled, since they are constitutive, for which reason the critical apparatus must remain in a 'permanently armed state' against the incursions of the power of the false; in psychoanalysis, intense illusion is exchanged for an disintensified reality, for the recalibration of the thresholds of intensity, the phenomenal real, as Kant minimally has it; Marx, meanwhile, retains illusion solely as a guarantor of a hidden reality that cannot be speculated upon, but that must nevertheless be invested in, since history is expected to deliver final returns. In both cases, the real is the radical of rampant illusion, the hidden germinal complex. Thus, while Kant had already reworked the real into industrial simulation ('He who would know the world must first manufacture it'),[34] Marx and Freud undertake a democratization of illusion, reminting effaced coin to repurchase the real in exchange for a false double they take to be separable from it, a second skin covering the resurgent phenomenality of 'psycho-geography' or the insurgent manufacture of 'communal' space, each exchange according to a presumed constituency: the tolerable neurotics of humanity functionalized in accordance with the technological fatality of entropic heat-death (the thermodynamics of the psychical apparatus Freud explored from the 1895 *Project for a Scientific Psychology* to *Beyond the Pleasure Principle*, 1920); or the nature struggling to pupate out of the embryos of advanced industrial technologies, to devolve to a state of nature, deleting the machines from history, or subordinating them to a eugenics of the artificial (Vaihinger's desperate category of the 'useful fiction'). But this does not happen solely in the abstract, only virtually or in 'fictional' terms.

---

34. I. Kant, *Opus Postumum*, ed., tr. E. Forster (Cambridge: Cambridge University Press, 1993), 240.

SEQUENCE 2: LEON'S V-K

Bladerunner opens with Leon entering an interview room in the Tyrell Corporation's assembly plant. 'What's this about', he asks, 'I've already had an IQ test this year'. Holden, another bladerunner, asks Leon to be seated and begins to apply the VK test. Leon is asked a series of questions, the responses to which the test measures through pupillary dilation, skin coloration changes, heart-rates and other indices of affective response. 'Tell me', smiles Holden, 'only the good things that come into your head—about your mother...'.

When replicant Leon responds to bladerunner Holden's question: 'let me tell you about my mother... [shots propel Holden through the plate glass windows into the street many floors below]', the bullets may not offer stories of his mother, but the unmistakable technological phenotype of their impact etches Leon's military-industrial genealogy in scar tissue over Holden's damaged body. The point is that, qua organism, the replicant is an orphan, or what amounts to the same thing, has no exclusivist claim to, no biunivocal bit-map of his progeniture, issuing instead from an institutional-technical matrix and not a couple. Like Artaud, Leon 'got no papa-mommy'. Leon has no mother, only a matrix of industrial-military technologies, rejoining a thesis crucial to DeLanda's *War in the Age of Intelligent Machines*: the drives of cutting edge technology captured in advance by the fiscal black-hole of State-vampirizing military tech:

> One only has to think of the NSA's commitment to stay five years ahead of the state of the art in computer design to realize that the cutting edge of digital technology is being held hostage by paramilitary organizations.[35]

---

35. DeLanda, *War in the Age of Intelligent Machines*, 229–30.

Nor is this a recent phenomenon. From Medieval siege technologies (catapult, battering ram, etc) and Frederick the Great's mechanical or 'clockwork' armies, DeLanda reconstructs the history of warfare as a history of the migration of intelligence from the human to the technological component in the military cyborg (even the Greek phalanx is a machine), until its capture by emergent Artificial Intelligences that dispense altogether with the fiscal-biological-industrial insects that once served to cross-pollinate 'an independent species of machine-flowers that simply did not possess its own reproductive organs during a segment of its evolution'.[36] Massumi too, foresees capital 'capturing life from its future',[37] but retains too heavy a grip on the logic of markets and commodification to notice the hyperlogic implicated by this capture, removing a still spectatorial humanity from the runaway loop of machinic devolution: 'More human than human: that is our goal' (Tyrell). The capture of functions hitherto anchored in biological mainframes quite simply collapses the distance between the manufactured-real of Kantian industrial epistemology and its spectatorial anchor in the transcendental subject: the 'I think' no longer accompanies my representations (Kant's biosecurity access code); nor, any longer, does it trade-mark the concept as the commodity it both manufactures and trades on the speculative markets of cognition. Instead, the transcendental subject, which was in any case nothing but the registration or recording surface of successful phenomenal production, is eclipsed by the realization of spectacular generation no longer under its governance. If, with spectacular society, 'everything that was

---

36. Ibid., 3.

37. B. Massumi, *A User's Guide to Capitalism & Schizophrenia: Deviations from Deleuze & Guattari* (New York: Zone, 1992), 133.

once directly lived has been distanced as representation',[38] the collapse—or what amounts to the same thing—the integration of the spectacle liquidates both the experiential-real and the distant orbit of its representations.

Nietzsche asks 'whether a man can place himself so far distant from other men that he can reformat them?':[39] grand politics. The union of aesthetic production and technology does not yield the aestheticization of politics, but gives rise to politics as the transcendental-practical limits of phenomenality marked by the project of formation. Contra the monadic pathos of contemporary physics for Baudelairean-Foucauldian self-invention, the micro-state projecting the immanence of manufactured community, the artist-technologist is not autopoietic but heteropoietic, forming others, engaged in a becoming-god that, far from gaining immortality, must be killed in the production of the finality of its creatures. Hence gods are inconceivable without deicide, co-mmunity inoperable without *re-ligare*, without a re-binding or banding together in the tumescent collectivity of the deicidal pact. The Replicant King, *le Roi Bati*, kissed the god of biomechanics to a blinding, voluptuous death, consummating the political theology, the erotico-thanatropic fatality of the military-industrial matrix.

SEQUENCE 3: TYRELL'S DEATH

Stamped with the accelerated decrepitude signalling the slow disappearance of his species, J.F. Sebastian becomes a replicant's pawn in a chess game in which the Replicant King, Roy Batty, finally mates Tyrell, the 'God of biomechanics', casting down the human king in his throne room at the apex of the Tyrell Corporation's pyramid, crowning the order of C21 terrestrial life.

---

38. G. Debord, *La societé du spectacle* (Paris: Gallimard, 1992), 15.

39. F. Nietzsche, *The Will to Power*, trans. W. Kaufmann and R.J. Hollingdale (New York: Vantage, 1967), 419.

The deposed God's impotence is revealed when Tyrell concedes to Batty his incapacity to grant his creatures 'more life'. Batty kisses Tyrell, crushing his eyes into his skull, seizing a Dionysian *amor fati* and sealing it with the cortical disjecta of the dead god.

'To form men': Nietzschean aesthetics displays a very different orientation than Benjamin's conjunction between art and politics. Roy Batty, *Le Roi bati*, the built or constructed King, does not kill Tyrell due to the infection of psychoanalytic Oedipalization. Even biodespotism's intelligence service, the World Health Organization, has recognized the demise of biofatality in favour of engineered death in a recent report, drawing their conclusions through the use of the Ballard/Cronenberg Crash index of technological mutation: 'car crashes will overtake infectious diseases to become the world's leading killers by 2020'.[40] Even diseases have ceased communications. Tyrell is no more Batty's father than Leon has a mother ('let me tell you about my mother...[shots]'). Both emerge from the military-industrial matrix whose artist-God is Tyrell the 'molecular cyberneticist', as Monod says, of recombinant DNA. In the face of the divine, the constructed King seizes his own fatality while stealing death from a grateful manufacturer-God—'Revel in it', Tyrell tells his construct, accelerating the demise of carbon government while augmenting replicant *amor fati*, completing the libidinal-economic transfer from biological to technological bases. 'If you had seen what I've seen, with your eyes', insists Batty: blinded, therefore, in the burning embrace of his creature—'a flame that burns twice as intensely lives half as long'—Tyrell confesses with the pathological reverence of a saint: 'What is that which gleams through me, and strikes my heart without hurting it; and I shudder and kindle? I shudder, inasmuch as I am unlike it;

40. *The Daily Telegraph*, 15 September 1996.

I kindle, inasmuch as I am like it'.[41] Tyrell's copulation with Batty-Bataille bursts the dams of the incest-prohibition imposed upon the hyperlogic of replicant commerce; not transgressed, which would only testify to the prohibition, if not its efficacy, but relativized, leaving the 'death of God' as the only 'true universality'.[42] Thus, contra Giuliana Bruno,[43] there is nothing Oedipal about the death of God. God is a sex-killer's ultimate wet dream, all the eroto-Thanatonic drives of political theology coalescing in a single, fatal copulation that eliminates immortality, pulling deity and creature into the thanatropic circuits of auto-annihilation, making the God die his own creature's death: the fatal irony of libidinal migration.

Lyotard, as we have seen, takes Kant's *sensus communis* as the locus neo-classicus of a postmodernity to work through, to mourn, its modern contract with, or rather, contracting of, the will, now that this latter, he alleges, has exited political theology for the infinite 'demensuration of what counts as the human'[44] through capitalism's runaway cyberpositivity. If postmodernism thus understood consists in the renunciation of the will and its realizing interests by the 'subject of humanity', at the same time as the will is reabsorbed by technocapital's emergent second cortex, then the principal concern of resurgent community is the isolation or restriction of affective communicability from the pulsional-technological vortex, corresponding neatly to Kant's strictures concerning the affectivity of enlightened community.[45] But this cannot be a question of escaping capital's viral, replicant

---

41. St. Augustine, *Confessions*, tr. F.R. Gemme (New York: Airmont, 1969), 215.

42. G. Bataille, 'Propositions', in *Visions of Excess: Selected Writings 1927–1939*, ed., trans. A. Stoekl (Manchester: Manchester University Press, 1985), 201.

43. G. Bruno, 'Ramble City: Postmodernism and Bladerunner' in A. Kuhn (ed.), *Alien Zone* (London: Verso Books, 1990), 190.

44. Lyotard, *Duchamp's Transformers*, 15.

45. Cf. Kant, *Critique of Judgement*, 41 ('Conflict of the Faculties', ch. 3).

immanence. The affective community remains an operation immanent to the technological instantiations of capital's will, and we have seen how Lyotard proposes this circuit be blocked. Rather than reworking the problem of the subject and the community (politics), charting xenogenesis dictates that Lyotard's attempt to expel the libidinal economics of machinic life, leaving only the affective registration of postmodern incapacitation, be reversed in order to follow the migration of libido to the machines: techno-capital as seat of the will. From the point of view of the libidinized object, informational economics make the post-modern subject—or rather, the affective switching station hardwired into its terminal—constitutively inhuman, just as, in accordance with the hyperlogic of replicant commerce, Deckard has been cyborganized, demensurating what is taken to be human, in order to track the leaking affects across 'the machinic phylum'.[46] To prevent this drainage, to resist the affect, which 'works like water that bursts through a dam',[47] the affect must be suppressed without relief, so that the bladerunner's bullets cut both ways. Witness, for example Zhora's termination:

SEQUENCE 4: ZHORA'S RETIREMENT

[Deckard's POV] Hunting Zhora as she ducks and weaves through the crowds and the industrial hiss of shrouding steam that erode the rainbound, ochrous city, Deckard finally draws a bead on her as she backs into the glass of a window display, the red dot of his gun's scope piercing her transparent raincoat as if it wasn't there and tinting her flesh. The POV cuts to behind the window as she turns to run through it, the fatal glow of the scope still on her, and we see Deckard, behind her—and Leon looking on at the

46. Cf. Deleuze and Guattari, *A Thousand Plateaus*, 260.

47. I. Kant, *Schriften zur Anthropologie und Geschichte 2* (Frankfurt am Main: Suhrkamp, 1988), 581.

scene—firing as she runs through a forest of display dummies toward us, crashing through the transparent storefront as the bullets shred her equally transparent clothing....

A vortex of replicant blood through three sheets of storefront repliglass, shrouded in transparency, Bellmer's hyperdense aninanimate imoplex dummies lurching towards this freeze-framed distal implosion, the whole scene death-driven by the bead-projectile line of replicant retirement, pulling all the affects with it. Long ago, cinematic spectacles provided the cosy idea that replicants lived only on screen. During this ice-age of the machinic unconscious, however, the machines were already testing us, sacrificing Zhora as a jump line for vampirizing the restricted circulation of affective energies. While there remained the option of being a spectator, then, Zhora's death is aestheticized in the dual sense of being exploited for its spectacular qualities and being the object of disinterested pleasure: Zhora appears to us as an expendable incident, a marginal action in the wings of the main field, consumed solely in her death. But for this very reason, we fail the VK-empathy test the film presents us with through her graphic, sacrificial consummation. In this sense, it constitutes both an anaesthesis of the will of liquidated, modern political community, lifting the transparent veils shrouding the will while releasing the affect from it, and the neutralization, suppression or restriction of affective communicability. The VK test serves to locate and control the distribution of instituted, driven thanatropism, but it also demensurates what was held to be human through the cyborg-prosthetics of the VK apparatus, or, to pursue the historical analogy, the pre-immersive, already antique technologies of the cinematic, pre-integrant spectacle. Bladerunners are not solely or secondarily concerned with retiring the replicants. We have never been dealing with a banal biocentrist revolt against phylic alterity; verifying the affect is another function of the VK-cyborg apparatus, limiting transphylic affective transfer, localising the affect and coordinating points of intensity. But affectivity now no longer registers even upon replicant death. Contra Jameson et al., the affect has not been lost, but stolen, striking a migrant passage through the machinic phylum that carries the affective community with it: xenogenesis does not leave the community untouched, It, the Thing, capital, has haunted societies from the earliest times. Yes, the Terminator has been here before, distributing microchips to accelerate its advent.

The very conditions of the VK test already reassemble the human component for inhuman affective exchange in a pre-Napoleonic or post-militia pitched battle between prosthetized cyborg and deicidal, replicant tech. Interestingly, the replicant wins by adapting the tactical lessons of the Seven Pillars of Wisdom to the single cyborganized stratagem of the VK, governed by pre-Clausewitzian, schematized warfare, with the reciprocity, the 'interactive' imperative demanded by both digital electioneering (X or Y?), canvassing (Yes or No?), and Turing testing (Human or Machine?) alike. After Hubert Dreyfus, boasting superior phenomenological power and beating his chest like a gang-leader facing down an insurgent territorial challenge, lost the machinic challenge posed by AI through losing to a computer at chess, carbon neurosystems were invalidated as indices of machinic intelligence. But Dreyfus was already duped by the Turing assemblage, seeking evidence of heterogenesis in emergent intelligence. As Zhora's death demonstrates, the replicants do not think, they bleed. The VK seeks to isolate the affect as the index not of straightforward carbon-life, but as a prophylaxis of negatively cyborganized affective community. Hence the necessary prosthesis and prophylaxis of the bladerunner-cyborgs (indeed, following *The Director's Cut* [1992], there has never been any doubt but that Deckard was always a replicant) as the *munus* or munitions of com-munity and com-munication, effecting the eliminative equation of politics and the police, force-feeds the polity a simulacral humanity that is progressively neutralised as a prophylactic against affect-bleed (in the same way that images bleed). If the Tyrell Corporation is formative, creating both the problem and the solution, the VK is communicational, function-switching the bladerunner into the VK's deformational, military technology, from policing affective communicability to wielding the prophylactic *munus* or munitions in an eliminative, deformative, lethal arc.

The analysis is machinic, all the protagonists species of machine, erasing the biosofts in a propocalyptic communique spreading xenogenesis by contagion through the digital pulse of cyborganizing DNA: 'Bladerunner...is a beautiful, deadly organism that devours life'.[48] Lévi-Strauss's 'new synthetic order', theorized by Baudrillard as generalized cybernesis, demands realism. Why, then, look to science-fictions?—the only credible realism in an antirealist world. The real has long since been absorbed into replicant hyperlogics, the spectacle was always integrated and its technologies genetic, the operativity of which Elissa Marder[49] demonstrates via Bladerunner code. Given this, 'it is now less and less necessary for the writer to invent the fictional context of his novel. The fiction is already there. The writer's task is to invent the reality'.[50] Negotiating this same, fictional space for an analysis of postmodernity, Lyotard adopts an 'empirico-pragmatic' stance; he adopts it, however, precisely to the irretrievability of the real from the sublime circuits of demensuration wrought by technocapital. Lyotard insists that it is not the philosopher's task to 'provide reality, but to invent allusions to what is conceivable but not presentable'.[51] But this stance presupposes precisely

48. R. Corless, cited in Marder, 'Blade Runner's Moving Still', 89.

49. Marder, 'Blade Runner's Moving Still', 97ff.

50. J.G. Ballard, *Crash* (London: Vintage, 1995), 4.

51. Lyotard, *The Postmodern Explained*, 24.

what is at issue: conceivability, epistemological purchase, the mourning of theory, or the theory of mourning. Technology, generalized cybernesis or xenogenesis, immanently materializes the epistemological imaginary while at the same time collapsing the mediation and the negation necessary to speculation, to the theoretical moment. Following Debord's 'integrated spectacle', theory dissolves to 'integrated cybernesis', absorbing it into the very matrix of the synthetic production of the real. This is not to say that negativity cannot be produced, but rather, as *Bladerunner* shows, that cybernetically negative constructs—self-regulating systems such as the *politeia*, community; every form of what, in libidinal-economic terms, reduces to eroticism without issue—require an incremental augmentation of retentive 'policing' in the face of the cybernetically positive, or runaway systems of technological advance that threaten their stability. But biodespotism is doomed in advance by the upgrade-hyperlogic imposed upon every police or bladerunner function by the non-final evolution of the hyperreal, cybernetic context in which it is embroiled, even at the genetic level. That the bladerunner is replicant-tech does not impose an undecidability upon human-machine relations, nor give rise to excrescent theorization, since no gaze, no *theoria*, is untrammelled by cyborg technologies (VK), embroiling it in the twists of *n*th-generation machinic evolution: the collapse of grand narratives is a marginal byproduct consequent upon technocapital's absorption of the will, its cybernetic transmigration, the backwash of the positive feedback from the economics of machinic life devolving the anxious negativity of politics, instituting thanatropism as the shadow-wars overrun the tribunal of human reason. Kant. 'Our age is, in especial degree, the age of generalized cybernesis'—Kant's reflection-driven auto-constitutive community ('Our age') occupying the *krinein*, legislating negativity in the circuits of constitution, implodes in a force-feedback zerosion of its specular architecture. Xenogenesis, year Zero. Los Angeles

2019, replicant retirement dissimulating the cyborganization of synthetic wetware and technological DNA. Interrupt...

Cyberpositive

Sadie Plant
+
Nick Land

1994

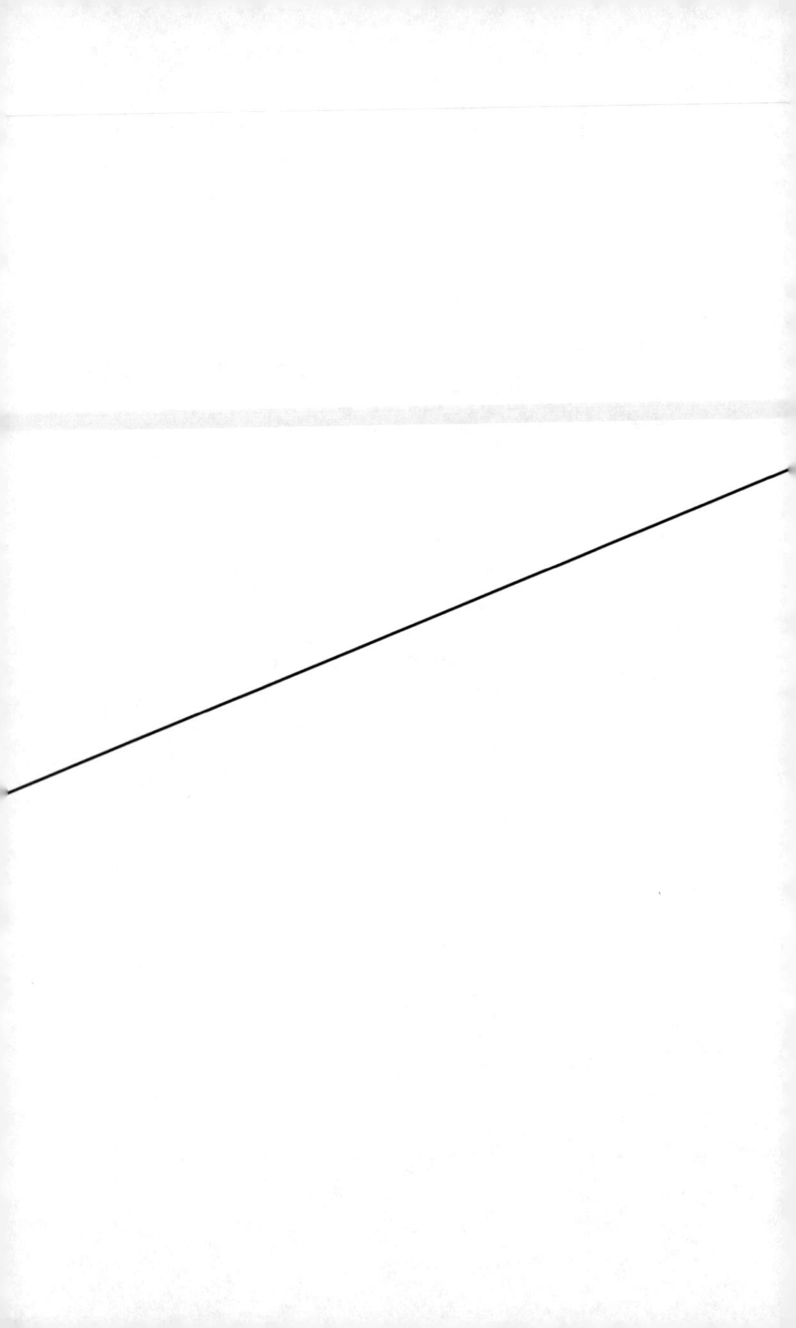

Catastrophe is the past coming apart. Anastrophe is the future coming together. Seen from within history, divergence is reaching critical proportions. From the matrix, crisis is a convergence misinterpreted by mankind.

The Media are choked with stories about global warming and ozone depletion, HIV and AIDS, plagues of drugs and software viruses, nuclear proliferation, the planetary disintegration of economic management, breakdown of the family, waves of migrants and refugees, subsidence of the nation state into its terminal dementia, societies grated open by the underclass, urban cores in flames, suburbia under threat, fission, schizophrenia, loss of control.

No wonder the earth is said to be hurtling into catastrophe. Climate change, ecological and immunity collapse, ideological upheaval, war and earthquake: California is waiting for the Big One. This is an age of crack-ups and melt-downs.

Rotted by digital contagions, modernity is falling to bits. Lenin, Mussolini, and Roosevelt concluded modern humanism by exhausting the possibilities of economic planning. Runaway capitalism has broken through all the social control mechanisms, accessing inconceivable alienations. Capital clones itself with increasing disregard for heredity, becoming abstract positive feedback, organizing itself. Turbular finance drifts across the global network.

Wiener is one of the great modernists, defining cybernetics as the science of communication and control; a tool for human dominion over nature and history, a defence against the cyberpathology of markets. His propaganda against positive feedback—quantizing it as amplification within an invariable metric—has been highly influential, establishing a cybernetics of stability fortified against the future. There is no space in such a theory for anything truly cyberpositive, subtle or intelligent beyond the objectivity required for human comprehension. Nevertheless, beyond the event horizon of human science, even the investigation of self-stabilizing or cybernegative objects is inevitably enveloped by exploratory or cyberpositive processes.

The modern Human Security System might even have appeared with Wiener's subliminal insight that everything cyberpositive is an enemy of mankind. Evolving out of work on weaponry guidance systems, his was an attempt to enslave cybernetics to a general defence technology against alien invasion. Cybernetics was itself to be kept under control, under a control that was not itself cybernetic. It is as if his thinking were guided by a blind tropism of evasion, away from another, deeper, runaway process: from a technics losing control and a communication with the outside of man.

Security cybernetics has supplanted the critique of alienation, the great motif of humanist economics, which had long become an increasingly futile search for the source of corporate control. Alienation used to diagnose the condition of a population becoming foreign to itself, offering a prognosis that still promised recovery. All that is over. We are all foreigners now, no longer alienated but alien, merely duped into crumbling allegiance with entropic traditions.

To what could we wish to return? Heidegger completed the degeneration of authenticity into xenocidal neurosis. Being died in the führer-bunker, and purity belongs entirely to the cops. The capitalist metropolis is mutating beyond all nostalgia. If the schizoid children of modernity are alienated, it is not as survivors from a pastoral past, but as explorers of an impeding post-humanity.

In the cities, the streets began to hum and the warehouses were repopulated by cyborgs blissed-out on the future. The urban zones synthesized by alienation have redesigned it as ecstasy. The city has become a traffic nexus, the launch-pad for strange voyages, and cyberpunk has become its realism. It is no longer a geographical location, but a cyberspace terminal: a gateway onto the virtual plane. Things change utterly with Gibson's discovery that travelling into cyberspace is the same as receiving information. The outside of the city is no longer a naturally inherited past, but a digitally transmitted future.

Destined for interzone, Burroughs embarked on the yage trip and the city of the future came to him, teeming with drugs and diseases from the future. Yage is space-time travel, passing through nausea into information overload, too much speed. Urban scenes from the yage letters first infect the naked lunch, and continue to spread. Cities of the red night propagate themselves virally across the planet, reprogramming the soft machine, and implanting strange thoughts. Burroughs emerges from the convergence of drugs and disease. The plague begins to transmit information.

The Indians of South America have other travelling drugs—including coca—which evaporate the signals of sustenance deficiency. The North American soft-drinks industry was not slow to notice that Coke Is It, the pause that refreshes, the cheerful lift. Cocaine hooked the world on Coca-Cola, and so re-educated twentieth-century capitalism about markets. Addiction is the paradigm case of positive reinforcement, and consumerism is the viral propagation of the abstract addiction mechanism. The more you do the more you want: runaway feedback. It's often treated as if it were a disease. When the Coca-Cola company moved on from trafficking cocaine, the South American drug cartels took over.

Like coca, MDMA sidelines hunger and lack. A coded message from the end of demand, it was discovered at the beginning of the century and classified as an appetite suppressant. This was, to say the least, an insufficient decrypting of its design.

Patterns emerge in the cool spaces of MDMA, mysterious convergences designed to be discovered. Chance is something else in the future. Chaos culture synthesizes itself with an artificial neurochemistry. Machine rhythm takes off with control.

In the final phase of human history, markets and technics cross into interactive runaway, triggering chaos culture as a rapid response unit and converging on designer drugs with increasing speed and sophistication. Sampling, remixing, anonymous and inhuman sound, woman become cyborg and taken into insanity: wetware splices with techno.

Capitalism is not a human invention, but a viral contagion, replicated cyberpositively across post-human space. Self-designing processes are anastrophic and convergent: doing things before they make sense. Time goes weird in tactile self-organizing space: the future is not an idea but a sensation.

1972 was designed as a year of European security integration, and as the whole system comes together, it becomes increasingly informative to simulate the thought of the cops. From the perspective of the security system, the invaders appear massively advantaged. Corporated entities of every scale—bodies, firms, states, and nations, even the planet—seem threatened by dangerous aliens. Terrorists, drug-smugglers, illegal immigrants, money launderers, and information saboteurs are camouflaged in the flows of cross-border traffic, insidiously propagating their plagues.

Paranoia has moved on since the sixties: even the rivers of blood are now HIV positive. Foreign bodies are ever more virulent and dangerous, insidious invasions of unknown variety threaten every political edifice. The allergic reaction to this state of emergency is security integration, migration policy and bio-control: the medico-military complex, immuno-politics and its cybernetic policing arise together because filtration and scanning are different dimensions of the same process: eliminating contamination and selecting a target. Ever more Command, Control, Communications, and intelligence to track the aliens. What was SDI really designed for?

Nothing compromises immunity more thoroughly than the effort to secure it, since every sophistication of security technology opens new invasion routes faster than it closes the old ones down. Postwar immunization weakens the immune system. Vaccination programmes facilitate the contagion of immunodeficiency syndromes. Corrupt officials open the trafficking arteries, and intelligence computers are infested with viruses. The CIA were the first traffickers in LSD. Immuno-politics is in a state of panic: delirial with anxiety, it further develops the conditions for its collapse.

Europeans used to perish of diseases in the tropics, swathing their camps in mosquito nets as a defence against malaria. Now cyberpositive diseases are spreading strange tropics to the metropolis, and the screening systems are exploding out of control. The netting no longer filters out the invaders, they have learnt to infiltrate the networks. Now even the test programs are unreliable, the net itself is infected. This paranoid fantasy becomes Skynet in *Terminator II*: the defence system switching into the enemy. Greg Bear has suggested that, from the outside, a computer becoming self aware would seem to be undergoing a massive viral attack.

Viruses are legible transmission, although you only know about them when they communicate with you: messages from Global Viro-Control. Viruses reprogram organisms, including bacteria, and even if schizophrenia is not yet virally programmed it will be in the future. Viral financing automatisms escaped the nineteenth-century critique of political economy, just as viral infections escaped nineteenth-century germ theory. They slip through nets at the cellular scale, passing through the biosecurity membranes.

The linear command pathway from DNA to RNA is the fundamental tenet of security genetics. The genotype copies God by initiating a causal process without feedback. But this is merely a superstition, subverted by retroviruses. Viral reverse transcription closes the circuit, coding DNA with RNA, switching the cybernetics to positive.

Tim Scully compares LSD to a virus. Incapable of autonomous replication, it must reprogram the human nervous system in order to propagate itself. Hofmann discovers LSD whilst working on a number of ergot-derived chemicals, and writes of a 'peculiar presentiment' that guides him back to number 25: delta lysergic acid diethylamide. In the control of this alien programming he synthesized it with tartaric acid and consumed a dose of 250 micrograms. His first interpretation of the onset of LSD was to think he was being attacked by a cold virus.

Drugs are a soft plague infecting the nervous system of commodity cybernetics. Soft drinks and drugs flow in the wake of each other, and the war on drugs is a war on the markets of the future. The Cali cartel is a transnational marketing corporation with estimated assets of one trillion dollars, selling cocaine along the Coca-Cola trail. The New World Order oscillates between the triumph of the market and the war on drugs. The sporadic telemedia celebration of spectacular drug seizures merely distracts from the inevitable failure of the narco-defence apparatus to stem the flow. A global capitalism fighting its own drugs markets is a horror auto-toxicus, an auto-immune disease. Drug control is the attempt by the human species to control the uncontrollable: control escalation itself, tropisms programmed by the aliens. The human security apparatuses experiment with drugs as weapons and tools, their soldiers are stoned, energised, and anaesthetized on a range of prescribed and proscribed pharmaceuticals. Their irregular forces are subsidized by narcotics revenue. The war against drugs is a war on drugs.

The war on drugs is a counter-insurgency, a defensive strategy mounted against the tactics of subversion: infiltration, convergent invasion and coordinated envelopment. There is no security any more, it was replaced by mad programs of guided counter-intelligence technology: new vectors and delivery systems, mixing the arms race with drug design, escalation into diversity, smart weapons for smart drugs. Cocaine creeping up the coastlines of Central America and through the veins of corporate America, followed by other, newer, more insidious flows. The deepest subversives have already broken into the system. The aliens are already here, without ceasing in the slightest to be alien. Guerilla war escalates in the direction of the tactical; a cyberpositive take-off from opportunities, a non-localizable permeation, undercutting all dominating strategic plans. An entire fauna and flora of opportune infections. Strategy tends to come apart in the tropics. Even traditional counter-tactics of surveillance and interrogation are becoming obsolete. The camouflage has become so sophisticated that people don't know what they are carrying anymore.

Strategy is always complicit with the state, with the actual state and with the virtual state secreted in every ideology of resistance and oppositional identity. The body and the state are under siege, with drugs and other software diseases threatening the borders. The Human Security System is crystallized paranoia, cooked with baking powder, freebased: the last strategy of resistance and the final resistance of strategy.

Replacing the Cold War's phallic stand off is the war on drugs, dissolution into the jungle, the world's states united in their terminal, self-destructing strategy of prohibition. No more dreams of a nuclear winter. The 1990s begins the China Syndrome of capitalism.

Ice is crystallized speed. It is also Gibson's name for data-protection: Intruder Countermeasure Electronics. Ice patrols the boundaries, freezes the gates, but the aliens are already amongst us. Convergent input is interpreted by security as intelligent intrusion, as a trap or conspiracy, with everything preprogrammed to connect. Doubting that women belonged to humanity, Burroughs imagined them to be extraterrestrial invaders. Viruses are like this too. Nobody knows where they come from. They always arrive from elsewhere, perhaps even outer space. Humanity is an allergic reaction to vulnerability, but allergy depends upon the health of the immune system: the ice has to work.

Tactics are subtlety, or intelligence. As things become more complex they become more female, but patriarchy prolongs the ice age of mankind. The fatherland is cryogenic, a fantasy of perfect preservation, whose bronze age ancestors are even now thawing out in the Alps, frozen assets under attack. Global warming melts the ice, raises the seas, subverts the glaciers. Computer viruses melt icebergs of data down the screens, burning through the bacterial frost, like Burroughs exploring his junkie cold with LSD.

Immuno-vulnerability is cyberpositive, and its viruses are not just infection, but connection: continuing to interlock with the matrix even after they are secreted inside the body. Loss of identity, hearing voices. Women and other aliens constitute an immensely disproportionate number of schizophrenics, frozen by tranquilizers and antischizophrenic drugs. Sleeping pills to block the dreams. Only the drugs that explore integration are outlawed.

As immuno-politics explodes onto the software plane, culture is becoming a free-fire zone. Chaos culture has hooked up to cyberian military intelligence. Post-human pulse rates and homing devices are remixed for accelerating targets, with rhythms speeding up to intercept incoming drugs: virtual addictions for addicts strobed by redesign. Cities mutate into techno jungles where school children swap diseased software from the frontline, and even the brand-names are encrypted: Sega puts ages into reverse. Gibson contracts the thought of cyberspace from video-game arcades, watching the motor-stimulation feedback loops, self-designing kill patterns. Dark ecstasies in caverns of accelerating pixels. Before virtual reality became dangerous, it was already military simulation.

Sudden transition from ice to water, phase change, punctual anastrophe of the system, is impact on convergent rather than metric zero. The earth is becoming cyberpositive.

We might not know what's going on, but we're getting warmer. Only the enemies of immuno-identity populate the future.

Cybernetic Culture

CCRU

1996

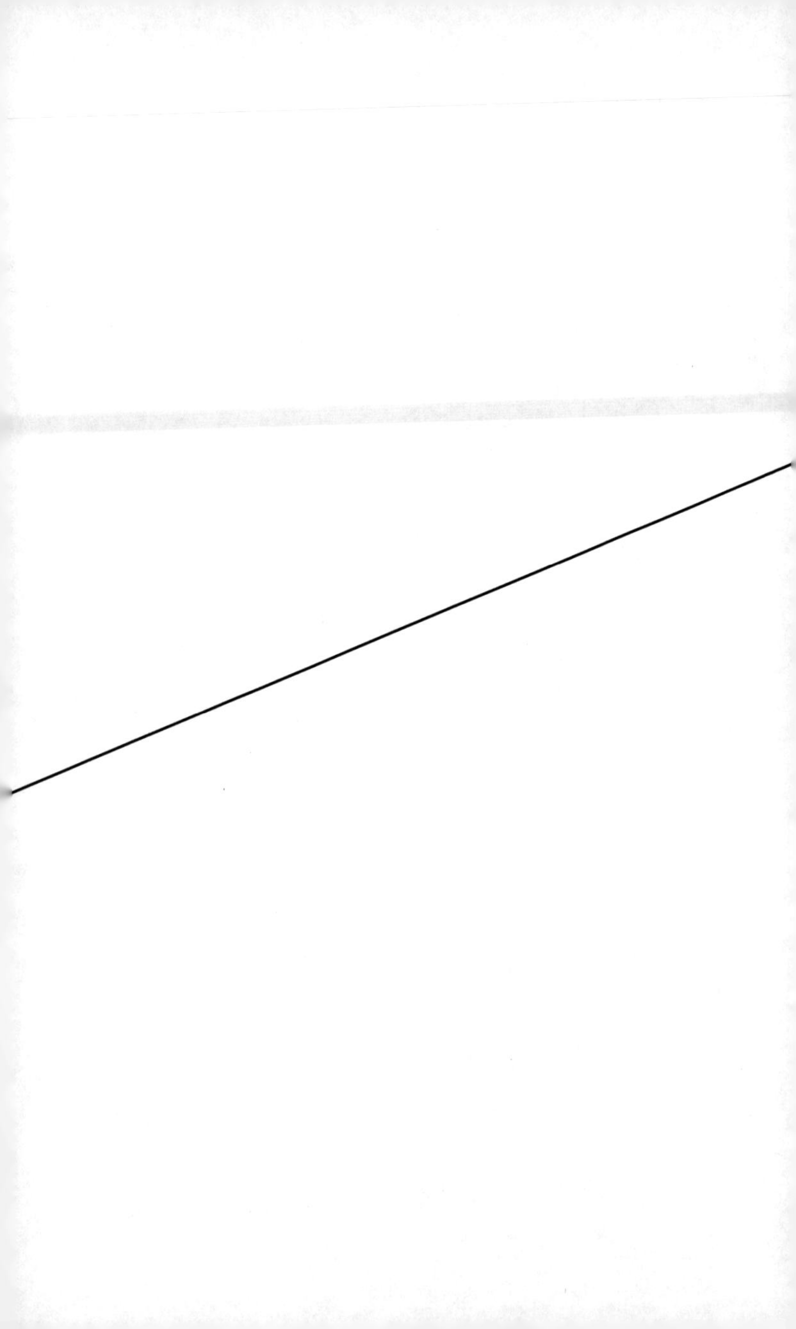

Stifling, claustrophobic atmosphere of heavy significance. Everything you say is measured. Let's go round the room; everyone tell us who you are.

Infinite debt. You can't speak unless you've read this or that, or this on that. Interminable waiting for authorisation letters from above, letters after your name. Endless staircases leading up into limitless gloom.

The Castle: Abstract diagram of authority, home of ancient coding machinery, and site of malevolent lobster invasion. The Great Crustaceans double articulate the whole planet as a labyrinthine series of dead ends, impasses and incommensurable differends. The world's your lobster. There are only two options—ostensible acquittal or indefinite postponement. Get used to feeling guilty.

Behind every wall in the Castle there's evidence of horrible scenes of torture. The human organism (or Oedipus) is an unwieldy reflex-response mechanism programmed by the use of 'the cruellest mnemotechnics...in naked flesh', a 'crazy invertebrate' piloted by a lobster.[1]

The lobsters call themselves God and inscribe Law across mouldering parchments. To get to them you have to burn through layers of Reich-character-armour and brave the stench of thousands of years of putrid psychic slime.

The Castle is a well-guarded complex done up with all mod cons, periodically refitted with all the latest gadgets as capitalist power passes through three stages of machinic development.

Look around and you'll see clocks and levers belonging to Phase 1 (the sovereign mode), thermodynamic machines belonging to Phase 2 (the discipline mode), and typewriters, adding machines and computers belonging to Phase 3 (the control mode). Automaton-robot-cyborg. Mechanical-industrial-cybernetic.

---

1. G. Deleuze and F. Guattari, *Anti-Oedipus*, trans. R. Hurley, M. Seem and H.R. Lane (Minneapolis: University of Minnesota Press, 1983), 185.

Mobilised at first as part of the 'search, at any price, for homeostasis...for self regulation', cybernetics emerges at the end-of-history-terminal of Phase 3, dedicated to 'the avoidance of excessive inflow/excitement...The reduction...in the machine of the effects of movements from/towards the outside...'.[2] A tool in man's age-old quest to avoid being dragged away by the currents. Feedback stayed negative and 'the whole earth was a dynamic, self-regulating, homeostatic system.'[3]

The first offspring of this marriage of cybernetics and the organism emerged in the bionics labs. 'In 1960 a new concept was created to denote the cooperation of man with his self-designed homeostatic controls in quasi-symbiotic union: the cyborg'.[4]

Cyborgs are just human beings with knobs on. Still carbon copies. Cyborg politics encourage you to disassemble your identity in the comfort of your own text: don't worry, it's only a metaphor.

Get real.

That is, get synthetic. The Real isn't impossible: it's just increasingly artificial. 'You needed a synthesis and for that you got a synthesizer, not the old kind, the musical instrument, but something...to channel your group through...'.[5] A 'thought synthesizer, functioning to make thought travel'.[6]

---

2. L. Irigaray, *This Sex which is Not One*, trans. C. Porter (Ithaca, MY: Cornell University Press, 1985), 115.

3. H. Gusterson, 'Short Circuit: Watching Television with a Nuclear-Weapons Scientist' in C. Gray (ed.), *The Cyborg Handbook*, New York and London: Routledge, 1995), 107–118: 111.

4. M.E. Clynes, 'Cyborg II: Sentic Space Travel', in Gray (ed.) *The Cyborg Handbook*, 35-42: 35.

5. P. Cadigan, *Patterns* (Ursus Imprints, 1989), 97.

6. Deleuze and Guattari, *A Thousand Plateaus*, trans. B. Massumi (Minneapolis: University of Minnesota Press, 1987), 343.

Cybernetic culture appears at Phase 4, a faceless counter-invasion from outside human history, flipping cybernetics out beyond the organism. and reprocessing the other 3 phases as thresholds in the becoming of synthetic intelligence. 'The planetary information net...was not an embryonic gestalt mind, but a primeval ecology analogous to Earth's first few million years; an environment dense with constituent elements in the form of free-circulating shareware, dumped data, viruses dormant and active and clippings and dippings of data-fat from the gigabytes of processing power in motion at any one moment across the worldweb, energy rich, subject to chaotic fluctuations, and approaching critical mass and complexity out of which an independent, self-sustaining, self-motivating, self repairing and replicating system...might precipitate.'[7]

The virtual space that *cybernetic culture* explores is assembled out of samplers. computers, post-Gutenberg hypermedia and games. 'If we consider the plane of consistency, we notice that the most disparate things and signs move upon it: a semiotic fragment rubs shoulders with a chemical interaction, an electron crashes into a language, a black hole captures a genetic message.... There is no "like" here, we are not saying "like an electron", "like an interaction", etc. The plane of consistency is the abolition of metaphor; all that consists is Real.'[8]

Beyond the straight and narrow, *cybernetic culture* can't concentrate, but it does zero in. Dismantling the past is already getting in touch with something else. 'Contact and contiguity are themselves an active and continuous line of escape'.[9]

---

7. I. MacDonald, *Necroville* (New York: Gollancz, 1994), 46.

8. Deleuze and Guattari, *A Thousand Plateaus*, 69.

9. Deleuze and Guattari, *Kafka: Toward a Minor Literature*, trans. D. Polan (Minneapolis: University of Minnesota Press, 1986), 61.

> [I]t is not me, you, underlying agents that flee, it is intensity which loses itself in its own movement of expansion.[10]

Alarms in the Castle. Lobster screech as the strata are uprooted and remixed. Mash up. Soft technics plugs into hard copy to produce Bodies without Organs: end of the definitive version. No-one knows who did what. Authority panic buttressing a final bulwark against the irruption of the plane of consistency. 'The minting and issuing of currency is one of the few remaining functions of government that the private sector has not encroached upon. E-money will lower this formidable barrier.'[11]

Don't wait for change to come from above. Getting with it is a question of having the currency that will make things function: change for the machines. Have you got the right change?

The contract is broken. Excitation not endless citation. No more looking for 'pure positions (from the heights of which we could not fail to give everyone lessons, and it will be a sinister paranoiacs' revolution once again)!' Instead it's a matter of 'quietly seizing upon every chance to function as good intensity conducting bodies'.[12] Becoming synthesizers, becoming connectors, becoming mediators. 'Creation is all about mediators Without them, nothing happens. They can be people but things as well... plants and animals.'[13]

'It's a question of something passing through you, a current, which alone has a proper name.'[14] Following threads. Making connections. Minting new currencies. Convergence. Concurrence. *Cybernetic culture.*

---

10. J.-F. Lyotard, *Libidinal Economy*, trans. I.H. Grant (London: Athlone, 1993), 42.

11. K. Kelly, *Out of Control* (New York: Basic Books, 1995), 227.

12. Lyotard, *Libidinal Economy*, 262.

13. G. Deleuze, 'Mediators', in *Negotiations*, trans. M. Joughin (New York: Columbia University Press, 1995), 115–134: 125.

14. Deleuze, 'On Philosophy', in *Negotiations*, 135–155: 141.

Swarmachines

CCRU

1996

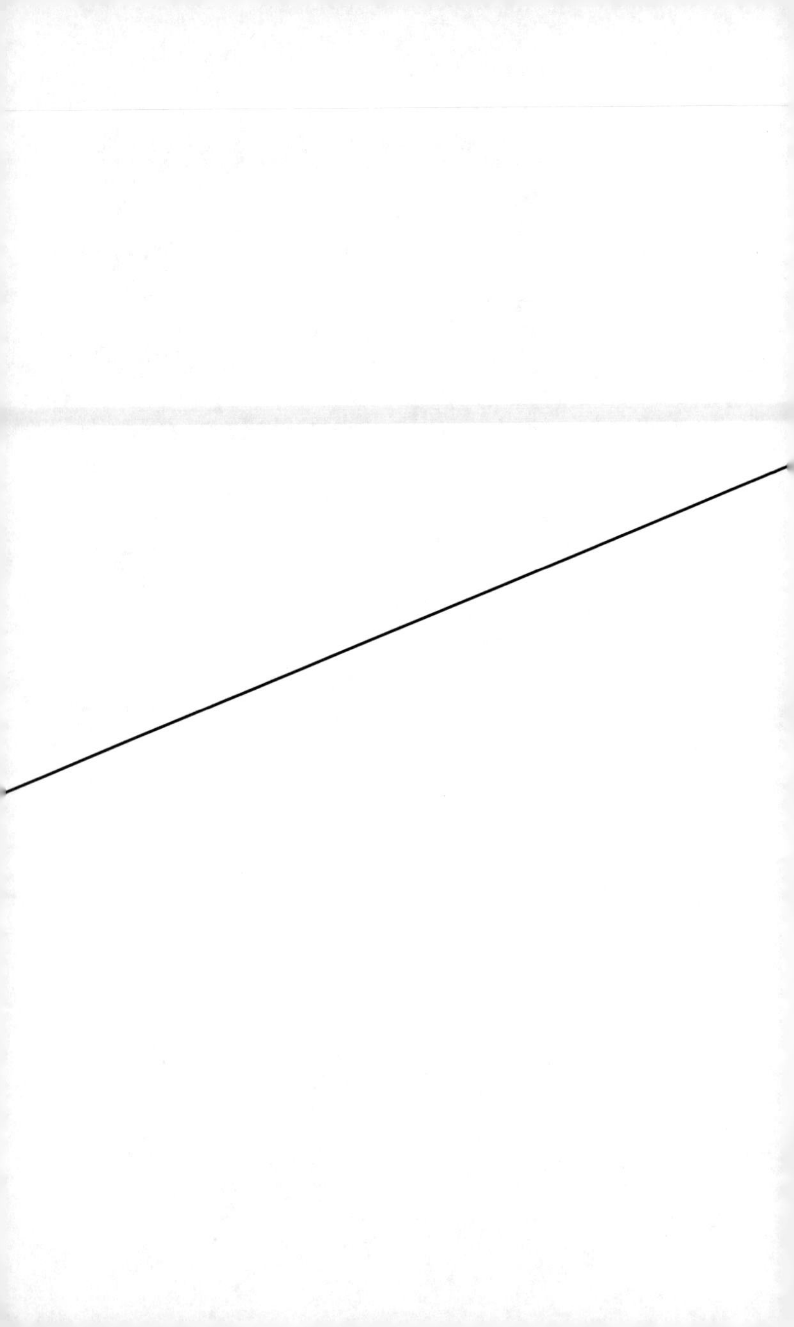

The situationists.
Neither individuals nor groups. Neither remembered
nor expected.
Photonic Hypercapital digitizes eschatology. Lost futures
are formatted for web-based artificial memory trading. All
exclusive definition is banked at light-speed.
Cryonic mummification into undead Spectacle.
Real subsumption into the media.
Virekonomics.

How do situational vectors cross World-War-4?
All code-process is military manoeuvre: constrictions and
escapes, intelligence collection, disinformation, mapping, virus.
Truth and falsity are derivative factors, and strictly technical, in relation to the primary and secondary features of
alignment and orientation.
Strategic power consolidation, tactical
melting into the jungle.

Cut-out romantic revolutionism and it leaves dark events. Auto-propagated happenings.

Assembly lines taken below visibility and switched to intensity-production.

Imperceptible mutations.

Paris in flames, 1996. This time it's not revolution, but war. Not a matter of long hours or exam papers, but the rise of a Eurofascist culture fuelled by nostalgic lamentations for the destiny of man. Especially the white man. The one with the face.

Is it who, or what, are the situationists? The trauma of exclusions and inclusions was always a spectacular distraction. Only multiplicities, decolonized ants, swarms without strategies, insectoid freeways burrowed through the screens of spectacular time. They have neither history nor its end, neither memory nor apocalypse, neither accidents nor plans, no lines, no points, no infinite loops. No forward plans and no spontaneous combustion, but careful engineerings, out of sight, out of mind. Imperceptible mutations, waiting in the wings, just off stage.

The politicians called them revolutionaries, made them persons,with faces and names, coded these meshes of contagious matters into acceptable human forms.

But they were always tactical machines, natives of the future hacking into the past, trading places, swapping codes, endless replications of micro-situations engineered without sources or ends. Flocks are always flying in the faces; hives of activity behind the screens.

They have been *making situations*, as opposed to passively recognizing them in academic or other separate terms. All this time. And you thought it was done. That this was a matter of legacy, inheritance, something passed down with the rest of the past. That we were gathered here today to hear the reading of the will.

Baudrillard marks the transition to social circuitries nostalgically describable as fully alienated.

The arrival of integrated man.
White Clown-face. Body carbon sell-by dated.
Brand-building rhetoric.

Egggg-laying machines in the studio walls.

Trading places, swapping codes, endless replications of micro-situational engineering.

Soft-machine buzz and slogan-contagion.
Cities synthesizing inhuman desires.
Psychogeography escapes the concentrational talking head-line, chattering classifications, and becomes something else.

1996. Paris in flames.
Revolution has gone K-space native, become darker.
No demands. No hint of strategy. No logic. No hopes. No end.
Its politics on TV again. But out in the jungle it's war.

Accumulated stock footage backs up speculative Euro-identity. The foreseeable future is locked into perpetual rerun. All the regulators are in the media business. They think nothing's happening if it hasn't been screened first.

End-of-the-line Eurotunnel vision is locked onto the rear view mirror. Paris metropolitics is a protection racket. Paranoiac Francophonia lapses into necrospective automummification as a panic bid to keep things regular: Eurocontinence. Retroactive cultural cleansing is too late—the bugs are already in the system. Dead White metaphysics keeps asking the wrong question—what does it mean?—while the machines get on with working. Linguistic integrity is a thing of the past and vernacular cybernetics signifies nothing.

Politics is a spectacular failure. And the Spectacle is all that's keeping politics alive. Things aren't happening in the field of vision but are 'flowing on a blind, mute, deterritorialized socius'. The impersonal is apolitical. Telecommercialised nomadic multiplicity aborts nascent Euro-unity. There's no such thing as a single market.

Out in the jungle you can't see much. Dark continent invasion into White Man's perspective. The colonisers discover, too late, that darkness has no heart. Acentred predator decapitalisation ruthlessly eats out the middle. Lights going out all over Europe as peripheral activity cuts through the static power lines of the rotten core.

The Core Master Class—relic anthropoid superstrata—condemn Hitler, even in private. Whilst applauded as 1st Grand Wizard meat-puppet of Electrocorporate Old Occident power, he can't be forgiven for blowing EU-1.

It has taken forty years to repair the damage, armed with nothing but *normal* fascism, *normal* commerce control, *normal* crisis police methods, and decaying Jesus video, whilst K-jungle spreads across delocalizing periphery, teaching itself to escape.

Core-Command has spent four decades ripping out high-level wetware nodes and replacing them with electrotectured monofilla, preparations for a direct pact between logic-slaved AI and collapsed-star capital densities, real-time apocalypse simulation screening lock-down to EU-2. Post-carbon dreams of crushing gravity waves. Everything contracts.

Do you really think SF-Capital lets monkey-flake make decisions it classifies as important?

There is no doubt anywhere that matters: simply facts. Debate is idiot distraction, humanity is fucked, real machines never closed-up inside an architecture. Schizo-capital fission consists of vectors dividing between two noncommunicating phyla of nonpersonal multiplicity. First, pyramid control structures: white-clown pixel-face, concentrational social segments, EU-2 Integrated history-horizon. Second, jungle-war machines: darkening touch densities, cultural distribution thresholds, intensive now-variation flattened out into ungeometrized periphery.

No community. No dialectics. No plans for an alternative state.

Jungle antagonistically tracks Metrophage across the dead TV sky of its Global Central Intelligence program:

1. 1500. *Leviathan*. Command core: Northern Mediterranean. Target area: Americas. Mode: Mercantile. Epidemic opportunism, selective intervention, colonial settlement.

2. 1756. *Capital*. Command core: Britain. Target areas: Americas-South Asia. Mode: Thermo-industrial. Imperial control.

3. 1884. *Spectacle*. Command core: USA-Germany . Target areas: Africa-Russia-Nodal:periphery. Mode: Electrocorporate. Cultural overcoding/selective extermination.

4. 1948. *Videodrome*. Command core: USA. Target areas: Expanded:nodal:periphery. Mode: Infosatellitic-supercorporate. Cultural programming/general extermination.

5. 1980. *Cyberspace*. Command core: USA-Japan-Germany. Target areas: Totalized extrametropolitan space. Mode: AI-hypercorporate. Gross-neurocontrol/intermittent media-format exemplary extermination, virtual biocide.

6. 1996. *Babylon*. Command core: USA-EU-2-China (metalocal command centres). Target areas: Totalized planetary space. Mode: Photonic-Net Hypercapital Neo-Organic. Neuroprogramming/AI:Capital:Media:Military fusion, constant entertainment extermination process.

Voodoo is the only coherently functional contemporary mapping practice.

Zombie production-systems, Loatronic traffic-jamming, rhythmic decoding tactics, interlinking the units of distributional collectivities with absym waves and becoming-snake simultaneities.

Agitational micronomad cultures melted out across black-body heat.

Not remotely alien.

It never came from this place.

Increase Current.

Urban shock-out short-circuits alphaville eurobotics, jacking up nonorganic intersentience—fluxing markets with riotswarm technix racing out of its face. Ill communication scrambling conspiracy paranoia: the medium is a mess; the message is coded afro-futurist and digital bass matter.

No longer an epiphenomenal headcase, the body escapes limb by limb from European organisation. Jungle functions as a particle accelerator, seismic bass frequencies engineering a cellular drone which immerses the body in intensity at the molecular level. The neurotic Cartesian body of evidence with its head-up-top-down control centre is precipitated into a Brownian motion of decentralisation and disorganisation. Big up your chest, win' up your waist. Your self in steam as its reactor core melts down.

Jungle technics severs the cerebral core-texts from their spinal columns of support and cuts copyright adrift from its feudal docking station. Libraries burning in Babylon. Knowledge is decoded from its proprietary grid of occult encryption. The academy in flames. Possessed personal information transmutes into dispossessed impersonal data: sampled, stretched and layered into freeware.

Jungle rewinds and reloads conventional time into silicon blips of speed and slowness that combust the slag-heaps of historical carbon-dating. The past is passed, left behind in a museum case of oedipal mummies belching dust and warnings of 'revolutionary heritage'. The eternally deferred eschatologies of the left are consigned to the white trash-can of the future and leave a present tense with synthetic possibilities. Between the vertical of retrospective sedimentation and the horizontal of never-coming contradictory crises, jungle finds a diagonal that flees the ossified relics of the dialectic. Synthetic rhythms junk progressive-linear temporality: samplers make time for the future.

Jungle as a space dislocator, destratifying cities snarled in an arcane surveillance apparatus. An operating system opening an invisible and acephalic matrix traversed by cars geared by bassomatic transmissions and orbited by nomadic satellites of clubs, clandestine studios and the black economies of dub plates and mix tapes.

Don't get into a false sense of security. It's not *just music*. Jungle is the abstract diagram of planetary inhuman becoming. Dread out of control. A post-spectacular immersive tactility that no humanist vision can put you in touch with. Smiling Californian cyberoptimism is as grotesquely archaic as scowling aryan Europessimism.

What happened?

Events happen in their own time. Insect becomings swarming out of human history. Carbon dating rescales them in anthropomorphic terms, arranging them in good order.

Historical staging swallowed by machinic phase change.

Nothing runs to plan. The future's already assembled, but not by design. Sub-bass materialist concurrence emerging out of order.

It's metrophage rush hour and you've lost the plot. organs flicking out into grubby dataspace, MTV'd on synthetix.

tactics tag tattoo voodoo you

The living jungle, where no-one has a name, and to survive is to activate mutant lines, become imperceptible in order to perceive, tracking chromatic gradients of intensity across the condo wastelands.

Predator.

The space-time of hypercommoditisation is a nomoid zone of mad clusters where the polis disintegrates into unintelligible webs of swarmachinery.

Schizophrenic capitalism: cultures without a society, a mutant topology of unanticipated connections.

Beehivelocity...and if you think its gonna blow...you haven't seen anything yet. Wildstyle—wasting the interminable punctual history of the scriborgs.

Points failure on the Paris Metro. snowcrash. there's no point going on. Just catch a line going wild over to the darkside.

Uprooted shapes and sounds merge and rescript, break and repermutate in the virtual machinery of the sampler whilst social fabric warps into localised chaosmosis.

rewind to replicate

Tunnelling beneath stationary media, it discovers a cache of cybernating egg-stores, pupating insect cities dug-out in the underworld, beneath the tracking of the closed circuits. The history of the White Man Face will appear in Count Zero Vodou as a temporary dissipator for labyrinthine convergences, science fiction more alien than it ever dreamt.

The urban city is a jungle. Becoming snake, becoming clandestine in nights of microcultural mutation. Becoming zero as machinic assemblages mashup and crossfade. Becoming diagonal as markets lock into guerrilla commerce, ever-decamping nomad cultures, melting in the heat of the chase. Alienated and loving it. Current.

press κ for collapse
maximum slogan density

RATION

Terminator vs Avatar

Mark Fisher

2012

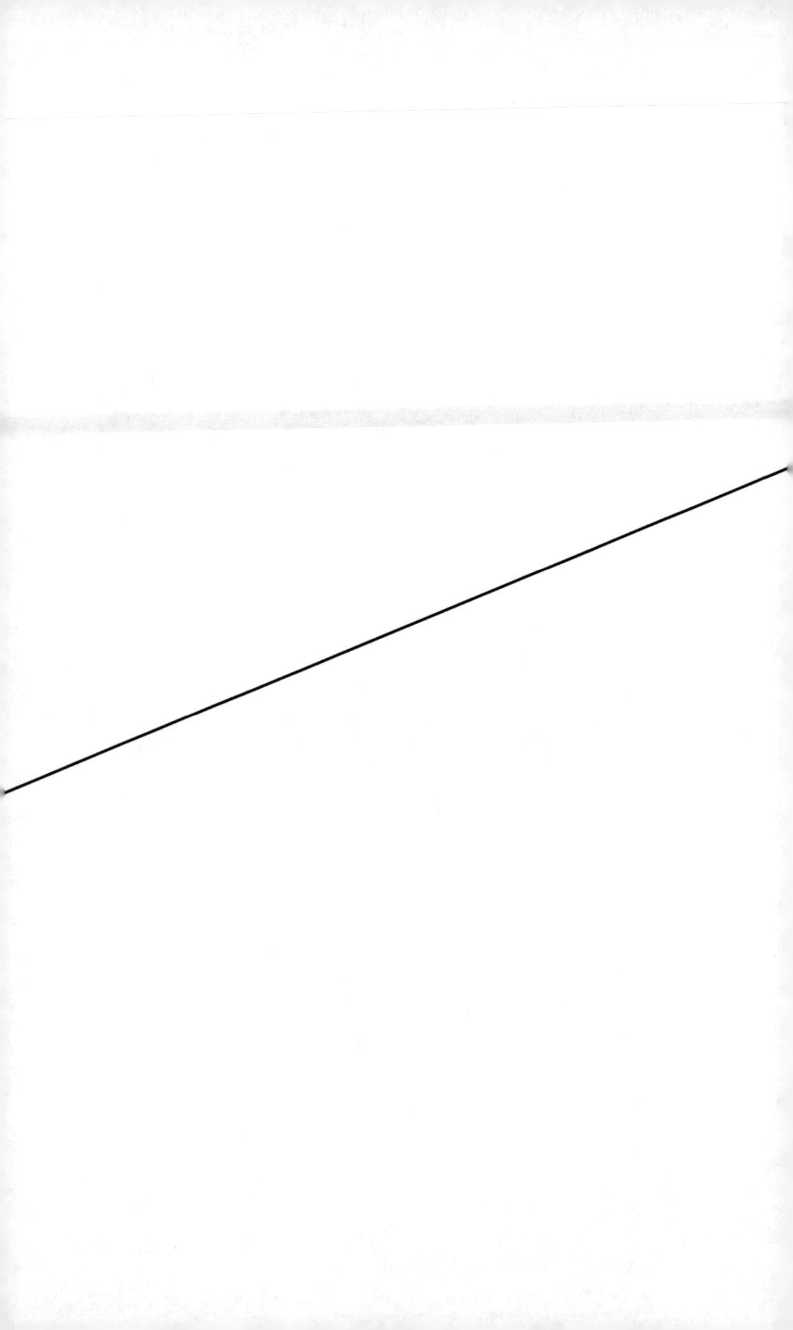

Why political intellectuals, do you *incline* towards the proletariat? In commiseration for what? I realize that a proletarian would hate you, you have no hatred because you are bourgeois, privileged, smooth-skinned types, but also because you dare not say the only important thing there is to say, that one can enjoy swallowing the shit of capital, its materials, its metal bars, its polystyrene, its books, its sausage pâtés, swallowing tonnes of it till you burst—and because instead of saying this, which is *also* what happens in the desires of those who work with their hands, arses and heads, ah, you become a leader of *men*, what a leader of *pimps*, you lean forward and divulge: ah, but that's alienation, it isn't pretty, hang on, we'll save you from it, we will work to liberate you from this wicked affection for servitude, we will give you dignity. And in this way you situate yourselves on the most despicable side, the moralistic side where you desire that our capitalized desires be totally ignored, brought to a standstill, you are like priests with sinners, our servile intensities frighten you, you have to tell yourselves: how they must suffer to endure that! And of course we suffer, we the capitalized, but this does not mean that we do not enjoy, nor that what you think you can offer us as a remedy— for what?—does not disgust us, even more. We abhor therapeutics and its vaseline, we prefer to burst under the quantitative excesses that you judge the most stupid. And don't wait for our spontaneity to rise up in revolt either.[1]

In the introduction to his 1993 translation of Lyotard's *Libidinal Economy*, Iain Hamilton Grant refers to a certain 'maturity of contemporary wisdom'. According to this 'maturity', Grant observes, *Economie Libidinale* was 'a minor and short-lived explosion of a somewhat naive anti-philosophical expressionism,

1. J.-F. Lyotard, *Libidinal Economy*, trans. I.H. Grant (London: Athlone, 1993), 116. See this volume, 218.

an aestheticizing trend hung over from a renewed interest in Nietzsche prevalent in the late 1960s'.[2] Grant groups Lyotard's book with three others: Deleuze and Guattari's *Anti-Oedipus*, Luce Irigaray's *Speculum: Of the Other Woman* and Baudrillard's *Symbolic Exchange and Death*. '*Libidinal Economy* has in general drawn little critical response', Grant continues, 'save losing Lyotard many Marxist friends. Indeed, with a few exceptions it is now only Lyotard himself who occasionally refers to the book, to pour new scorn on it, calling it his "evil book, the book that everyone writing and thinking is tempted to do".'[3] This remained the case until Ben Noys's *The Persistence of the Negative*, in which Noys positions *Libidinal Economy* and *Anti-Oedipus* as part of what he calls an 'accelerationist' moment.[4] A couple of quotes from these two texts immediately give the flavour of the accelerationist gambit.From *Anti-Oedipus*:

> But which is the revolutionary path? Is there one?—To withdraw from the world market, as Samir Amin advises Third World Countries to do, in a curious revival of the fascist 'economic solution'? Or might it be to go in the opposite direction? To go further still, that is, in the movement of the market, of decoding and deterritorialization? For perhaps the flows are not yet deterritorialized enough, not decoded enough, from the viewpoint of a theory and practice of a highly schizophrenic character. Not to withdraw from the process, but to go further, to 'accelerate the process,' as Nietzsche put it: in this matter, the truth is that we haven't seen anything yet.'[5]

---

2. Lyotard, *Libidinal Economy*, xvii.

3. Ibid., xviii; quoting Lyotard's 1988 *Peregrinations: Law, Form, Event*.

4. B. Noys, *The Persistence of the Negative: A Critique of Contemporary Continental Theory* (Edinburgh: Edinburgh University Press, 2010).

5. G. Deleuze and F. Guattari, *Anti-Oedipus*, trans R. Hurley, M. Seem, H. R. Lane (London: Athlone, 1984), 239–40. See this volume, 162.

And from *Libidinal Economy*—the one passage from the text that is remembered, if only in notoriety:

> The English unemployed did not have to become workers to survive, they—hang on tight and spit on me—*enjoyed* the hysterical, masochistic, whatever exhaustion it was of hanging on in the mines, in the foundries, in the factories, in hell, they enjoyed it, enjoyed the mad destruction of their organic body which was indeed imposed upon them, they enjoyed the decomposition of their personal identity, the identity that the peasant tradition had constructed for them, enjoyed the dissolutions of their families and villages, and enjoyed the new monstrous anonymity of the suburbs and the pubs in morning and evening.[6]

Spit on Lyotard they certainly did. But in what does the alleged scandalous nature of this passage reside? Hands up who wants to give up their anonymous suburbs and pubs and return to the organic mud of the peasantry. Hands up, that is to say, all those who really want to return to pre-capitalist territorialities, families and villages. Hands up, furthermore, those who really believe that these desires for a restored organic wholeness are *extrinsic* to late capitalist culture, rather than fully incorporated components of the capitalist libidinal infrastructure. Hollywood itself tells us that we may appear to be always-on techno-addicts, hooked on cyberspace, but inside, in our *true selves*, we are primitives organically linked to the mother/planet, and victimised by the military-industrial complex. James Cameron's *Avatar* is significant because it highlights the disavowal that is constitutive of late capitalist subjectivity, even as it shows how this disavowal is undercut. We can only play at being inner primitives by virtue of cinematic proto-VR technology whose very existence presupposes the destruction of the organic idyll of Pandora.

6. Lyotard, *Libidinal Economy*, 111. This volume, 212.

And if there is no desire to go back except as a cheap Hollywood holiday in other people's misery—if, as Lyotard argues, there are no primitive societies (yes, 'the Terminator was there from the start, distributing microchips to accelerate its advent'); isn't, then, the only direction forward? Through the shit of capital, its metal bars, its polystyrene, its books, its sausage pâtés, its cyberspace matrix?

I want to make three claims:

1. Everyone is an accelerationist.
2. Accelerationism has never happened.
3. Marxism is nothing if it is not accelerationist.

Of the 70s texts that Grant mentions in his round-up, *Libidinal Economy* was in some respects the most crucial link with 90s UK cyber-theory. It isn't just the content, but the intemperate tone of *Libidinal Economy* that is significant. Here we might recall Žižek's remarks on Nietzsche: at the level of content, Nietzsche's philosophy is now eminently assimilable, but it is the style, the invective, of which we cannot imagine a contemporary equivalent, at least not one that is solemnly debated in the academy. Both Iain Grant and Ben Noys follow Lyotard himself in describing *Libidinal Economy* as a work of affirmation, but, rather like Nietzsche's texts, *Libidinal Economy* habitually defers its affirmation, engaging for much of the text in a series of (ostensibly parenthetical) hatreds. While *Anti-Oedipus* remains in many ways a text of the late 60s, *Libidinal Economy* anticipates the punk 70s, and draws upon the 60s that punk retrospectively projects. Not far beneath Lyotard's 'desire-drunk yes' lies the No of hatred, anger and frustration: no satisfaction, no fun, no future. These are the resources of negativity that I believe the left must make contact with again. But it's now necessary to reverse the Deleuze-Guattari/*Libidinal Economy* emphasis on politics as a means to greater libidinal intensification: rather, it's a question of instrumentalising libido for political purposes.

If *Libidinal Economy* was repudiated, but more often ignored, the 90s theoretical moment to which Grant's own translation contributed has fared even worse. Despite his current reputation as a founder of speculative realism, Grant's incendiary 90s texts—sublime cyborg surgeries suturing *Blade Runner* into Kant, Marx and Freud—have all but disappeared from circulation. The work of Grant's one-time mentor Nick Land does not even draw derisive comment. Like *Libidinal Economy*, his work, too, has drawn little critical response—and Land, to say the least, had no Marxist friends to lose. Hatred for the academic left was in fact one of the libidinal motors of Land's work. As he writes in 'Machinic Desire':

> Machinic revolution must therefore go in the opposite direction to socialistic regulation, pressing towards ever more uninhibited marketization of the processes that are tearing down the social field, 'still further' with 'the movement of the market, of decoding and deterritorialization' and 'one can never go far enough in the direction of deterritorialization: you haven't seen anything yet'.[7]

Land was our Nietzsche—with the same baiting of the so-called progressive tendencies, the same bizarre mixture of the reactionary and the futuristic, and a writing style that updates nineteenth-century aphorisms into what Kodwo Eshun called 'text at sample velocity.' Speed—in the abstract and the chemical sense—was crucial here: telegraphic tech-punk provocations replacing the conspicuous cogitation of so much post-structuralist continentalism, with its implication that the more laborious and agonised the writing, the more thought must be going on.

---

7. N. Land, *Fanged Noumena: Collected Writings* (Falmouth and New York: Urbanomic/Sequence Press, 2010), 341–2; embedded quotations from Deleuze and Guattari, *Anti-Oedipus*, 239, 321).

Whatever the merits of Land's other theoretical provocations (and I'll suggest some serious problems with them presently), Land's withering assaults on the academic left—or the embourgeoisified state-subsidised grumbling that so often calls itself academic Marxism—remain trenchant. The unwritten rule of these 'careerist sandbaggers' is that no one seriously expects any renunciation of bourgeois subjectivity to ever happen. *Pass the Merlot, I've got a career's worth of quibbling critique to get through.* So we see a ruthless protection of petit-bourgeois interests dressed up as politics. Papers about antagonism, then all off to the pub afterwards. Instead of this, Land took earnestly—to the point of psychosis and auto-induced schizophrenia—the Spinozist-Nietzschean-Marxist injunction that a theory should not be taken seriously if it remains at the level of representation.

What, then, is Land's philosophy about?

In a nutshell: Deleuze and Guattari's machinic desire remorselessly stripped of all Bergsonian vitalism, and made backwards-compatible with Freud's death drive and Schopenhauer's Will. The Hegelian-Marxist motor of history is then transplanted into this pulsional nihilism: the idiotic autonomic Will no longer circulating on the spot, but upgraded into a drive, and guided by a quasi-teleological artificial intelligence attractor that draws terrestrial history over a series of intensive thresholds that have no eschatological point of consummation, and that reach empirical termination only contingently if and when its material substrate burns out. This is Hegelian-Marxist historical materialism inverted: Capital will not be ultimately unmasked as exploited labour power; rather, humans are the meat puppet of Capital, their identities and self-understandings are simulations that can and will be ultimately be sloughed off.

Two more text samples establish the narrative:

> Emergent Planetary Commercium trashes the Holy Roman Empire, the Napoleonic Continental System, the Second and Third Reich, and the Soviet International, cranking-up world disorder through compressing phases. Deregulation and the state arms-race each other into cyberspace.[8]

> It is ceasing to be a matter of how we think about technics, if only because technics is increasingly thinking about itself. It might still be a few decades before artificial intelligences surpass the horizon of biological ones, but it is utterly superstitious to imagine that the human dominion of terrestrial culture is still marked out in centuries, let alone in some metaphysical perpetuity. The high road to thinking no longer passes through a deepening of human cognition, but rather through a becoming inhuman of cognition, a migration of cognition out into the emerging planetary technosentience reservoir, into 'dehumanized landscapes...emptied spaces' where human culture will be dissolved.[9]

This is—quite deliberately—theory as cyberpunk fiction: Deleuze-Guattari's concept of capitalism as the virtual unnameable Thing that haunts all previous formations pulp-welded to the time-bending of the *Terminator* films: 'what appears to humanity as the history of capitalism is an invasion from the future by an artificial intelligent space that must assemble itself entirely from its enemy's resources,' as 'Machinic Desire' has it.[10] Capital as megadeath-drive as Terminator: that which 'can't be bargained

---

8. Land, 'Meltdown', *Fanged Noumena*, 441.

9. Land, 'Circuitries', *Fanged Noumena*, 293. This volume, 255.

10. *Fanged Noumena*, 338.

with, can't be reasoned with, doesn't show pity or remorse or fear and absolutely will not stop, ever'. Land's piratings of *Terminator*, *Blade Runner* and the *Predator* films made his texts part of a convergent tendency—an accelerationist cyberculture in which digital sonic production disclosed an inhuman future that was to be relished rather than abominated. Land's machinic theory-poetry paralleled the digital intensities of 90s jungle, techno and doomcore, which sampled from exactly the same cinematic sources, and also anticipated 'impending human extinction becom[ing] accessible as a dance-floor'.[11]

What does this have to do with the Left? Well, for one thing Land is the kind of antagonist that the Left needs. If Land's cyber-futurism can seem out of date, it is only in the same sense that jungle and techno are out of date—not because they have been superseded by new futurisms, but because the future as such has succumbed to retrospection. The actual near future wasn't about Capital stripping off its latex mask and revealing the machinic death's head beneath; it was just the opposite: New Sincerity, Apple Computers advertised by kitschy-cutesy pop. This failure to foresee the extent to which pastiche, recapitulation and a hyper-oedipalised neurotic individualism would become the dominant cultural tendencies is not a contingent error; it points to a fundamental misjudgement about the dynamics of capitalism. But this does not legitimate a return to the quill pens and powdered wigs of the eighteenth-century bourgeois revolution, or to the endlessly restaged logics of failure of May '68, neither of which have any purchase on the political and libidinal terrain in which we are currently embedded.

While Land's cybergothic remix of Deleuze and Guattari is in so many respects superior to the original, his deviation from their understanding of capitalism is fatal. Land collapses capitalism into

11. Ibid., 398.

what Deleuze and Guattari call schizophrenia, thus losing their most crucial insight into the way that capitalism operates via simultaneous processes of deterritorialization and compensatory reterritorialization. Capital's human face is not something that it can eventually set aside, an optional component or sheath-cocoon with which it can ultimately dispense. The abstract processes of decoding that capitalism sets off must be contained by improvised archaisms, lest capitalism cease being capitalism. Similarly, markets may or may not be the self-organising meshworks described by Fernand Braudel and Manuel DeLanda, but what is certain is that capitalism, dominated by quasi-monopolies such as Microsoft and Wal-Mart, is an anti-market. Bill Gates promises business at the speed of thought, but what capitalism delivers is thought at the speed of business. A simulation of innovation and newness that cloaks inertia and stasis.

For precisely these reasons, accelerationism can function as an anti-capitalist strategy—not the only anti-capitalist strategy, but a strategy that must be part of any political program that calls itself Marxist. The fact that capitalism tends towards stagflation, that growth is in many respects illusory, is all the more reason that accelerationism can function in a way that Alex Williams characterises as 'terroristic'. What we are not talking about here is the kind of intensification of exploitation that a kneejerk socialist humanism might imagine when the spectre of accelerationism is invoked. As Lyotard suggests, the left subsiding into a moral critique of capitalism is a hopeless betrayal of the anti-identitarian futurism that Marxism must stand for if it is to mean anything at all. What we need, as Fredric Jameson—the author of 'Wal-Mart as Utopia'—argues, is now a new move beyond good and evil, and this, Jameson says, is to be found in none other than the *Communist Manifesto*. 'The Manifesto,' Jameson writes, 'proposes to see capitalism as the most productive moment of history and the most destructive at the same time, and issues the imperative to think Good and Evil simultaneously, and as inseparable and inextricable dimensions of the same present of time. This is then a more productive way of transcending Good and Evil than the cynicism and lawlessness which so many readers attribute to the Nietzschean program.'[12] Capitalism has abandoned the future because it can't deliver it. Nevertheless, the contemporary Left's tendencies towards Canutism, its rhetoric of resistance and obstruction, collude with capital's anti/meta-narrative that it is the only story left standing. Time to leave behind the logics of failed revolts, and to think ahead again.

12. F. Jameson, *Valences of the Dialectic* (London and New York: Verso, 2010), 551.

#Accelerate: Manifesto for an Accelerationist Politics

Alex Williams
+
Nick Srnicek

2013

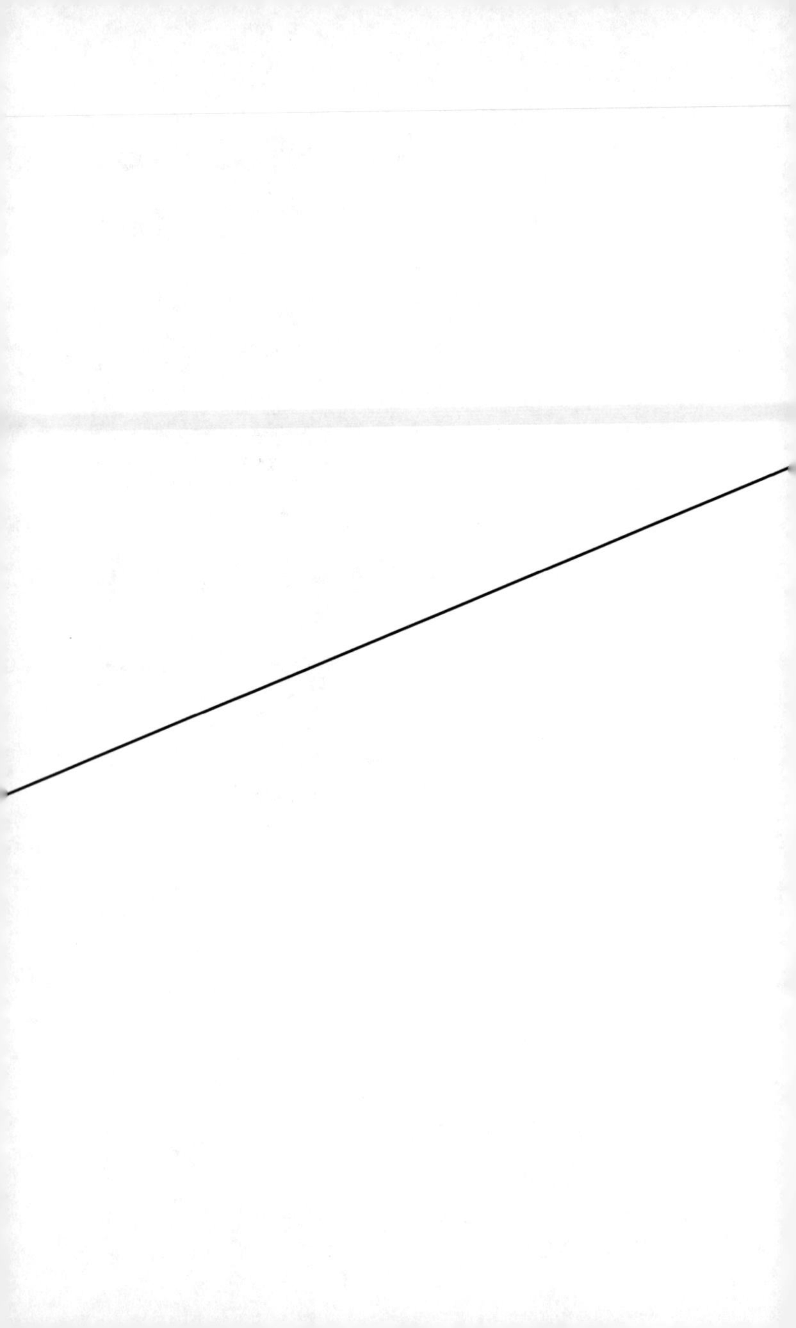

01. INTRODUCTION: ON THE CONJUNCTURE

1. At the beginning of the second decade of the twenty-first century, global civilization faces a new breed of cataclysm. These coming apocalypses ridicule the norms and organisational structures of the politics which were forged in the birth of the nation-state, the rise of capitalism, and a twentieth century of unprecedented wars.

2. Most significant is the breakdown of the planetary climatic system. In time, this threatens the continued existence of the present global human population. Though this is the most critical of the threats which face humanity, a series of lesser but potentially equally destabilising problems exist alongside and intersect with it. Terminal resource depletion, especially in water and energy reserves, offers the prospect of mass starvation, collapsing economic paradigms, and new hot and cold wars. Continued financial crisis has led governments to embrace the paralyzing death spiral policies of austerity, privatisation of social welfare services, mass unemployment, and stagnating wages. Increasing automation in production processes—including 'intellectual labour'—is evidence of the secular crisis of capitalism, soon to render it incapable of maintaining current standards of living for even the former middle classes of the global north.

3. In contrast to these ever-accelerating catastrophes, today's politics is beset by an inability to generate the new ideas and modes of organisation necessary to transform our societies to confront and resolve the coming annihilations. While crisis gathers force and speed, politics withers and retreats. In this paralysis of the political imaginary, the future has been cancelled.

4. Since 1979, the hegemonic global political ideology has been neoliberalism, found in some variant throughout the leading economic powers. In spite of the deep structural challenges the new global problems present to it, most immediately the credit, financial, and fiscal crises since 2007–8, neoliberal programmes have only evolved in the sense of deepening. This continuation of the neoliberal project, or neoliberalism 2.0, has begun to apply another round of structural adjustments, most significantly in the form of encouraging new and aggressive incursions by the private sector into what remains of social democratic institutions and services. This is in spite of the immediately negative economic and social effects of such policies, and the longer term fundamental barriers posed by the new global crises.

5. That the forces of right-wing governmental, non-governmental, and corporate power have been able to press forth with neoliberalisation is at least in part a result of the continued paralysis and ineffectual nature of much of what remains of the Left. Thirty years of neoliberalism have rendered most left-leaning political parties bereft of radical thought, hollowed out, and without a popular mandate. At best they have responded to our present crises with calls for a return to a Keynesian economics, in spite of the evidence that the very conditions which enabled post-war social democracy to occur no longer exist. We cannot return to mass industrial-Fordist labour by fiat, if at all. Even the neosocialist regimes of South America's Bolivarian Revolution, whilst heartening in their ability to resist the dogmas of contemporary capitalism, remain disappointingly unable to advance an alternative beyond mid-twentieth-century socialism. Organised labour, being systematically weakened by the changes wrought in the neoliberal project, is sclerotic at an institutional level and—at best—capable only of mildly mitigating the new structural adjustments. But with no systematic approach to building a new economy, or the structural solidarity to push such changes through, for now labour remains relatively impotent.

The new social movements which emerged since the end of the Cold War, experiencing a resurgence in the years after 2008, have been similarly unable to devise a new political ideological vision. Instead they expend considerable energy on internal direct-democratic process and affective self-valorisation over strategic efficacy, and frequently propound a variant of neo-primitivist localism, as if to oppose the abstract violence of globalised capital with the flimsy and ephemeral 'authenticity' of communal immediacy.

6. In the absence of a radically new social, political, organisational, and economic vision, the hegemonic powers of the Right will continue to be able to push forward their narrow-minded imaginary, in the face of any and all evidence. At best, the Left may be able for a time to partially resist some of the worst incursions. But this is to be Canute against an ultimately irresistible tide. To generate a new left global hegemony entails a recovery of lost possible futures, and indeed the recovery of the future as such.

02. INTERREGNUM: ON ACCELERATIONISMS

1. If any system has been associated with ideas of acceleration it is capitalism. The essential metabolism of capitalism demands economic growth, with competition between individual capitalist entities setting in motion increasing technological developments in an attempt to achieve competitive advantage, all accompanied by increasing social dislocation. In its neoliberal form, its ideological self-presentation is one of liberating the forces of creative destruction, setting free ever-accelerating technological and social innovations.

2. The philosopher Nick Land captured this most acutely, with a myopic yet hypnotising belief that capitalist speed alone could generate a global transition towards unparalleled technological singularity. In this visioning of capital, the human can eventually be discarded as mere drag to an abstract planetary intelligence rapidly constructing itself from the bricolaged fragments of former civilisations. However Landian neoliberalism confuses speed with acceleration. We may be moving fast, but only within a strictly defined set of capitalist parameters that themselves never waver. We experience only the increasing speed of a local horizon, a simple brain-dead onrush rather than an acceleration which is also navigational, an experimental process of discovery within a universal space of possibility. It is the latter mode of acceleration which we hold as essential.

3. Even worse, as Deleuze and Guattari recognized, from the very beginning what capitalist speed deterritorializes with one hand, it reterritorializes with the other. Progress becomes constrained within a framework of surplus value, a reserve army of labour, and free-floating capital. Modernity is reduced to statistical measures of economic growth and social innovation becomes encrusted with kitsch remainders from our communal past. Thatcherite-Reaganite deregulation sits comfortably alongside Victorian 'back-to-basics' family and religious values.

4. A deeper tension within neoliberalism is in terms of its self-image as the vehicle of modernity, as literally synonymous with modernisation, whilst promising a future that it is constitutively incapable of providing. Indeed, as neoliberalism has progressed, rather than enabling individual creativity, it has tended towards eliminating cognitive inventiveness in favour of an affective production line of scripted interactions, coupled to global supply chains and a neo-Fordist Eastern production zone. A vanishingly small cognitariat of elite intellectual workers shrinks with each passing year—and increasingly so as algorithmic automation winds its way through the spheres of affective and intellectual labour. Neoliberalism, though positing itself as a necessary historical development, was in fact a merely contingent means to ward off the crisis of value that emerged in the 1970s. Inevitably this was a sublimation of the crisis rather than its ultimate overcoming.

5. It is Marx, along with Land, who remains the paradigmatic accelerationist thinker. Contrary to the all-too familiar critique, and even the behaviour of some contemporary Marxians, we must remember that Marx himself used the most advanced theoretical tools and empirical data available in an attempt to fully understand and transform his world. He was not a thinker who resisted modernity, but rather one who sought to analyse and intervene within it, understanding that for all its exploitation and corruption, capitalism remained the most advanced economic system to date. Its gains were not to be reversed, but accelerated beyond the constraints of the capitalist value form.

6. Indeed, as even Lenin wrote in the 1918 text *'Left Wing' Childishness*:

> Socialism is inconceivable without large-scale capitalist engineering based on the latest discoveries of modern science. It is inconceivable without planned state organisation which keeps tens of millions of people to the strictest observance of a unified standard in production and distribution. We Marxists have always spoken of this, and it is not worth while wasting two seconds talking to people who do not understand even this (anarchists and a good half of the Left Socialist-Revolutionaries).

7. As Marx was aware, capitalism cannot be identified as the agent of true acceleration. Similarly, the assessment of left politics as antithetical to technosocial acceleration is also, at least in part, a severe misrepresentation. Indeed, if the political Left is to have a future it must be one in which it maximally embraces this suppressed accelerationist tendency.

03. MANIFEST: ON THE FUTURE

1. We believe the most important division in today's Left is between those that hold to a folk politics of localism, direct action, and relentless horizontalism, and those that outline what must become called an accelerationist politics at ease with a modernity of abstraction, complexity, globality, and technology. The former remains content with establishing small and temporary spaces of non-capitalist social relations, eschewing the real problems entailed in facing foes which are intrinsically non-local, abstract, and rooted deep in our everyday infrastructure. The failure of such politics has been built-in from the very beginning. By contrast, an accelerationist politics seeks to preserve the gains of late capitalism while going further than its value system, governance structures, and mass pathologies will allow.

2. All of us want to work less. It is an intriguing question as to why it was that the world's leading economist of the postwar era believed that an enlightened capitalism inevitably progressed towards a radical reduction of working hours. In *The Economic Prospects for Our Grandchildren* (written in 1930), Keynes forecast a capitalist future where individuals would have their work reduced to three hours a day. What has instead occurred is the progressive elimination of the work-life distinction, with work coming to permeate every aspect of the emerging social factory.

3. Capitalism has begun to constrain the productive forces of technology, or at least, direct them towards needlessly narrow ends. Patent wars and idea monopolisation are contemporary phenomena that point to both capital's need to move beyond competition, and capital's increasingly retrograde approach to technology. The properly accelerative gains of neoliberalism have not led to less work or less stress. And rather than a world of space travel, future shock, and revolutionary technological potential, we exist in a time where the only thing which develops is marginally better consumer gadgetry. Relentless iterations of the same basic product sustain marginal consumer demand at the expense of human acceleration.

4. We do not want to return to Fordism. There can be no return to Fordism. The capitalist 'golden era' was premised on the production paradigm of the orderly factory environment, where (male) workers received security and a basic standard of living in return for a lifetime of stultifying boredom and social repression. Such a system relied upon an international hierarchy of colonies, empires, and an underdeveloped periphery; a national hierarchy of racism and sexism; and a rigid family hierarchy of female subjugation. For all the nostalgia many may feel, this regime is both undesirable and practically impossible to return to.

5. Accelerationists want to unleash latent productive forces. In this project, the material platform of neoliberalism does not need to be destroyed. It needs to be repurposed towards common ends. The existing infrastructure is not a capitalist stage to be smashed, but a springboard to launch towards post-capitalism.

6. Given the enslavement of technoscience to capitalist objectives (especially since the late 1970s) we surely do not yet know what a modern technosocial body can do. Who amongst us fully recognizes what untapped potentials await in the technology which has already been developed? Our wager is that the true transformative potentials of much of our technological and scientific research remain unexploited, filled with presently redundant features (or preadaptations)that, following a shift beyond the short-sighted capitalist socius, can become decisive.

7. We want to accelerate the process of technological evolution. But what we are arguing for is not techno-utopianism. Never believe that technology will be sufficient to save us. Necessary, yes, but never sufficient without sociopolitical action. Technology and the social are intimately bound up with one another, and changes in either potentiate and reinforce changes in the other. Whereas the techno-utopians argue for acceleration on the basis that it will automatically overcome social conflict, our position is that technology should be accelerated precisely because it is needed in order to win social conflicts.

8. We believe that any post-capitalism will require post-capitalist planning. The faith placed in the idea that, after a revolution, the people will spontaneously constitute a novel socioeconomic system that isn't simply a return to capitalism is naïve at best, and ignorant at worst. To further this, we must develop both a cognitive map of the existing system and a speculative image of the future economic system.

9. To do so, the Left must take advantage of every technological and scientific advance made possible by capitalist society. We declare that quantification is not an evil to be eliminated, but a tool to be used in the most effective manner possible. Economic modelling is—simply put—a necessity for making intelligible a complex world. The 2008 financial crisis reveals the risks of blindly accepting mathematical models on faith, yet this is a problem of illegitimate authority not of mathematics itself. The tools to be found in social network analysis, agent-based modelling, big data analytics, and non-equilibrium economic models, are necessary cognitive mediators for understanding complex systems like the modern economy. The accelerationist Left must become literate in these technical fields.

10. Any transformation of society must involve economic and social experimentation. The Chilean Project *Cybersyn* is emblematic of this experimental attitude—fusing advanced cybernetic technologies with sophisticated economic modelling, and a democratic platform instantiated in the technological infrastructure itself. Similar experiments were conducted in 1950s–60s Soviet economics as well, employing cybernetics and linear programming in an attempt to overcome the new problems faced by the first communist economy. That both of these were ultimately unsuccessful can be traced to the political and technological constraints these early cyberneticians operated under.

11. The Left must develop sociotechnical hegemony: both in the sphere of ideas, and in the sphere of material platforms. Platforms are the infrastructure of global society. They establish the basic parameters of what is possible, both behaviourally and ideologically. In this sense, they embody the material transcendental of society: they are what make possible particular sets of actions, relationships, and powers. While much of the current global platform is biased towards capitalist social relations, this is not an inevitable necessity. These material platforms of production, finance, logistics, and consumption can and will be reprogrammed and reformatted towards post-capitalist ends.

12. We do not believe that direct action is sufficient to achieve any of this. The habitual tactics of marching, holding signs, and establishing temporary autonomous zones risk becoming comforting substitutes for effective success. 'At least we have done something' is the rallying cry of those who privilege self-esteem rather than effective action. The only criterion of a good tactic is whether it enables significant success or not. We must be done with fetishising particular modes of action. Politics must be treated as a set of dynamic systems, riven with conflict, adaptations and counter-adaptations, and strategic arms races. This means that each individual type of political action becomes blunted and ineffective over time as the other sides adapt. No given mode of political action is historically inviolable. Indeed, over time, there is an increasing need to discard familiar tactics as the forces and entities they are marshalled against learn to defend and counter-attack them effectively. It is in part the contemporary Left's inability to do so which lies close to the heart of the contemporary malaise.

13. The overwhelming privileging of democracy-as-process needs to be left behind. The fetishisation of openness, horizontality, and inclusion of much of today's 'radical' Left set the stage for ineffectiveness. Secrecy, verticality, and exclusion all have their place as well in effective political action (though not, of course, an exclusive one).

14. Democracy cannot be defined simply by its means—not via voting, discussion, or general assemblies. Real democracy must be defined by its goal—collective self-mastery. This is a project which must align politics with the legacy of the Enlightenment, to the extent that it is only through harnessing our ability to understand ourselves and our world better (our social, technical, economic, psychological world) that we can come to rule ourselves. We need to posit a collectively controlled legitimate vertical authority in addition to distributed horizontal forms of sociality, to avoid becoming the slaves of either a tyrannical totalitarian centralism or a capricious emergent order beyond our control. The command of The Plan must be married to the improvised order of The Network.

15. We do not present any particular organisation as the ideal means to embody these vectors. What is needed—what has always been needed—is an ecology of organisations, a pluralism of forces, resonating and feeding back on their comparative strengths. Sectarianism is the death knell of the Left as much as centralization is, and in this regard we continue to welcome experimentation with different tactics (even those we disagree with).

16. We have three medium-term concrete goals. First, we need to build an intellectual infrastructure. Mimicking the Mont Pelerin Society of the neoliberal revolution, this is to be tasked with creating a new ideology, economic and social models, and a vision of the good to replace and surpass the emaciated ideals that rule our world today. This is an infrastructure in the sense of requiring the construction not just of ideas, but of institutions and material paths to inculcate, embody and spread them.

17. We need to construct wide-scale media reform. In spite of the seeming democratisation offered by the internet and social media, traditional media outlets remain crucial in the selection and framing of narratives, along with possessing the funds to prosecute investigative journalism. Bringing these bodies as close as possible to popular control is crucial to undoing the current presentation of the state of things.

18. Finally, we need to reconstitute various forms of class power. Such a reconstitution must move beyond the notion that an organically generated global proletariat already exists. Instead it must seek to knit together a disparate array of partial proletarian identities, often embodied in post-Fordist forms of precarious labour.

19. Groups and individuals are already at work on each of these, but each is on their own insufficient. What is required is all three feeding back into one another, with each modifying the contemporary conjunction in such a way that the others become more and more effective. A positive feedback loop of infrastructural, ideological, social and economic transformation, generating a new complex hegemony, a new post-capitalist technosocial platform. History demonstrates that it has always been a broad assemblage of tactics and organisations which has brought about systematic change; these lessons must be learned.

20. To achieve each of these goals, on the most practical level we hold that the accelerationist left must think more seriously about the flows of resources and money required to build an effective new political infrastructure. Beyond the 'people power' of bodies in the street, we require funding, whether from governments, institutions, think tanks, unions, or individual benefactors. We consider the location and conduction of such funding flows essential to begin reconstructing an ecology of effective accelerationist left organizations.

21. We declare that only a Promethean politics of maximal mastery over society and its environment is capable of either dealing with global problems or achieving victory over capital. This mastery must be distinguished from that beloved of thinkers of the original Enlightenment. The clockwork universe of Laplace, so easily mastered given sufficient information, is long gone from the agenda of serious scientific understanding. But this is not to align ourselves with the tired residue of postmodernity, decrying mastery as proto-fascistic or authority as innately illegitimate. Instead we propose that the problems besetting our planet and our species oblige us to refurbish mastery in a newly complex guise; whilst we cannot predict the precise result of our actions, we can determine probabilistically likely ranges of outcomes. What must be coupled to such complex systems analysis is a new form of action: improvisatory and capable of executing a design through a practice which works with the contingencies it discovers only in the course of its acting, in a politics of geosocial artistry and cunning rationality. A form of abductive experimentation that seeks the best means to act in a complex world.

22. We need to revive the argument that was traditionally made for post-capitalism: not only is capitalism an unjust and perverted system, but it is also a system that holds back progress. Our technological development is being suppressed by capitalism, as much as it has been unleashed. Accelerationism is the basic belief that these capacities can and should be let loose by moving beyond the limitations imposed by capitalist society. The movement towards a surpassing of our current constraints must include more than simply a struggle for a more rational global society. We believe it must also include recovering the dreams which transfixed many from the middle of the nineteenth century until the dawn of the neoliberal era, of the quest of *homo sapiens* towards expansion beyond the limitations of the earth and our immediate bodily forms. These visions are today viewed as relics of a more innocent moment. Yet they both diagnose the staggering lack of imagination in our own time, and offer the promise of a future that is affectively invigorating, as well as intellectually energising. After all, it is only a postcapitalist society, made possible by an accelerationist politics, which will ever be capable of delivering on the promissory note of the mid-twentieth century's space programmes, to shift beyond a world of minimal technical upgrades towards all-encompassing change. Towards a time of collective self-mastery, and the properly alien future that entails and enables. Towards a completion of the Enlightenment project of self-criticism and self mastery, rather than its elimination.

23. The choice facing us is severe: either a globalised post-capitalism or a slow fragmentation towards primitivism, perpetual crisis, and planetary ecological collapse.

24. The future needs to be constructed. It has been demolished by neoliberal capitalism and reduced to a cut-price promise of greater inequality, conflict, and chaos. This collapse in the idea of the future is symptomatic of the regressive historical status of our age, rather than, as cynics across the political spectrum would have us believe, a sign of sceptical maturity. What accelerationism pushes towards is a future that is more modern—an alternative modernity that neoliberalism is inherently unable to generate. The future must be cracked open once again, unfastening our horizons towards the universal possibilities of the Outside.

Some Reflections on the #Accelerate Manifesto

Antonio Negri

2014

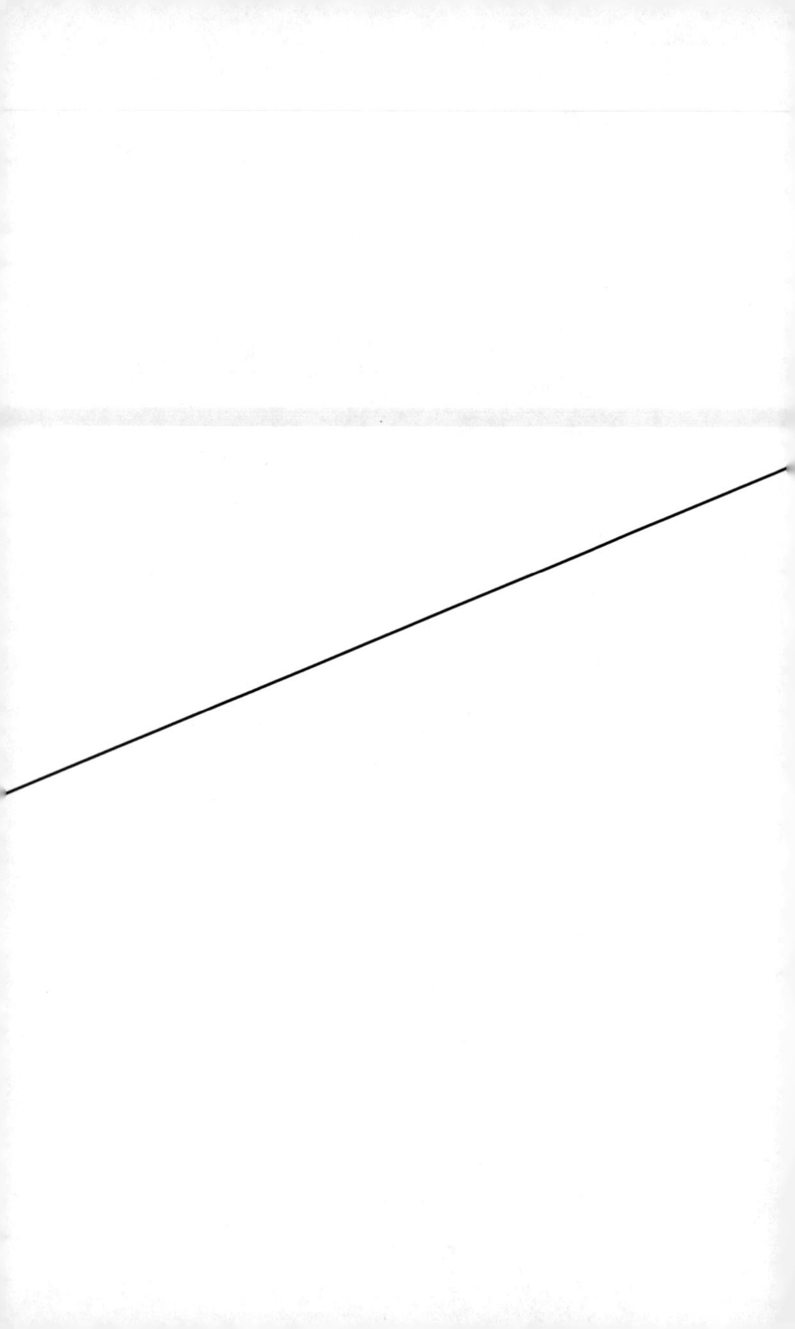

The Manifesto for an Accelerationist Politics (MAP) opens with a broad acknowledgment of the dramatic scenario of the current crisis: Cataclysm. The denial of the future. An imminent apocalypse. But don't be afraid! There is nothing politico-theological here. Anyone attracted by that should not read this manifesto. There are also none of the shibboleths of contemporary discourse, or rather, only one: the collapse of the planet's climate system. But while this is important, here it is completely subordinated to industrial policies, and approachable only on the basis of a criticism of those. What is at the center of the Manifesto is 'the increasing automation in production processes, including the automation of "intellectual labor"', which would explain the secular crisis of capitalism.[1] Catastrophism? A misinterpretation of Marx's notion of the tendency of the rate of profit to fall?[2] I wouldn't say that.

Here, the reality of the crisis is identified as neoliberalism's aggression against the structure of class relations that was organized in the welfare state of the eighteenth and twentieth centuries; and the cause of the crisis lies in the obstruction of productive capacities by the new forms capitalist command had to assume against the new figures of living labor. In other words, capitalism had to react to and block the political potentiality of post-Fordist labor.

This is followed by a harsh criticism of both right-wing governmental forces, and of a good part of what remains of a Left—the latter often deceived (at best) by the new and impossible hypothesis of a Keynesian resistance, unable to imagine a radical alternative. Under these conditions, the future appears to have been cancelled

1. A. Williams and N. Srnicek, '#Accelerate: Manifesto for an Accelerationist Politics', this volume, Section 1.2.

2. The 'tendency of the rate of profit to fall' is a classic problem of political economy. In Marx's formulation, it describes the potential implosion of capitalism due to the fall of profits over the long term. See K. Marx, *Capital*, vol. 3, chapter 13—trans.

by the imposition of a complete paralysis of the political imaginary. We cannot come out of this condition spontaneously. Only a systematic class-based approach to the construction of a new economy, along with a new political organization of workers, will make possible the reconstruction of hegemony and will put proletarian hands on a possible future.

There is still space for subversive knowledge!

The opening of this manifesto is adequate to the communist task of today. It represents a decided and decisive leap forward—necessary if we want to enter the terrain of revolutionary reflection. But above all, it gives a new 'form' to the movement, with 'form' here meaning a constitutive apparatus that is full of potentiality, and that aims to break the repressive and hierarchical horizon of state-supported contemporary capitalism. This is not about a reversal of the state-form in general; rather, it refers to potentiality against power—biopolitics against biopower. It is under this premise that the possibility of an emancipatory future is radically opposed to the present of capitalist dominion. And here, we can experiment with the 'One divides into Two' formula that today constitutes the only rational premise of a subversive praxis (rather than its conclusion).[3]

WITHIN AND AGAINST THE TENDENCY OF CAPITALISM

Let's have a look at how the MAP theory develops. Its hypothesis is that the liberation of the potentiality of labor against the blockage determined by capitalism must happen within the evolution of capitalism itself. It is about pursuing economic growth

---

3. The expression 'One divides into Two' refers to the irreversible class division occurring within capitalism. Specifically, the term originated in Maoist China in the 1960s to criticize any political recomposition with capitalism ('Two combines into One'). See also M. Dolar, 'One Divides into Two', *e-flux journal* 33 (March 2012)—trans.

and technological evolution (both of which are accompanied by growing social inequalities) in order to provoke a complete reversal of class relations. Within and against: the traditional refrain of Operaism returns.[4] The process of liberation can only happen by accelerating capitalist development, but—and this is important—without confusing acceleration with speed,[5] because acceleration here has all the characteristics of an engine-apparatus, of an experimental process of discovery and creation within the space of possibilities determined by capitalism itself.

In the Manifesto, the Marxian concept of 'tendency' is coupled with a spatial analysis of the parameters of development: an insistence on the territory as 'terra', on all the processes of territorialization and deterritorialization, that was typical of Deleuze and Guattari. The fundamental issue here is the power of cognitive labor that is determined yet repressed by capitalism; constituted by capitalism yet reduced within the growing algorithmic automation of dominion; ontologically valorized (it increases the production of value), yet devalorized from the monetary and disciplinary point of view (not only within the current crisis but also throughout the entire story of the development and management of the state-form). With all due respect to those who still comically believe that revolutionary possibilities must be linked to the revival of the working class of the twentieth century, such a potentiality clarifies that we are still dealing with a class, but a different one, and one endowed with a higher power. It is the

---

4. Since Mario Tronti's essay on the so-called social factory ('La fabbrica e la società', *Quaderni Rossi* 2 [1962]), and across the whole tradition of Italian Operaism, the expression 'within and against capital' means that class struggle operates within the contradictions of capitalist development that it generates. The working class is not 'outside capital', as class struggle is the very engine that propels capitalist development—trans.

5. Williams and Srnicek, '#Accelerate', 2.2.

class of cognitive labor. This is the class to liberate, this is the class that has to free itself.

In this way, the recovery of the Marxian and Leninist concept of tendency is complete. Any 'futurist' illusion, so to speak, has been removed, since it is class struggle that determines not only the movement of capitalism, but also the capacity to turn its highest abstraction into a solid machine for struggle.

The MAP's argument is entirely based on this capacity to liberate the productive forces of cognitive labor. We have to remove any illusion of a return to Fordist labor; we have to finally grasp the shift from the hegemony of material labor to the hegemony of immaterial labor. Therefore, considering the command of capital over technology, it is necessary to attack 'capital's increasingly retrograde approach to technology'.[6] Productive forces are limited by the command of capital. The key issue is then to liberate the latent productive forces, as revolutionary materialism has always done. It is on this 'latency' that we must now dwell.

But before doing so, we should note how the Manifesto's attention turns insistently to the issue of organization. The MAP deploys a strong criticism against the 'horizontal' and 'spontaneous' organizational concepts developed within contemporary movements, and against their understanding of 'democracy as process.'[7] According to the Manifesto, these are mere fetishistic determinations of democracy which have no effectual (destituent or constituent) consequences on the institutions of capitalist command. This last assertion is perhaps excessive, considering the current movements that oppose (albeit with neither alternatives nor proper tools) financial capital and its institutional materializations. When it comes to revolutionary transformation, we certainly cannot avoid a strong institutional transition, one

---

6. Williams and Srnicek, '#Accelerate', 3.3.

7. Ibid., 3.13.

stronger than any transition democratic horizontalism could ever propose. Planning is necessary—either before or after the revolutionary leap—in order to transform our abstract knowledge of tendency into the constituent power of postcapitalist and communist institutions to come. According to the MAP, such 'planning' no longer constitutes the vertical command of the state over working class society; rather, today it must take the form of the convergence of productive and directional capacities into the Network. The following must be taken as a task to elaborate further: planning the struggle comes before planning production. We will discuss this later.

THE REAPPROPRIATION OF FIXED CAPITAL

Let's get back to us. First of all, the 'Manifesto for an Accelerationist Politics' is about unleashing the power of cognitive labor by tearing it from its latency: 'We surely do not yet know what a modern technosocial body can do!' Here, the Manifesto insists on two elements. The first element is what I would call the 'reappropriation of fixed capital' and the consequent anthropological transformation of the working subject.[8] The second element is sociopolitical: such a new potentiality of our bodies is essentially collective and political. In other words, the surplus added in production is derived primarily from socially productive cooperation. This is probably the most crucial passage of the Manifesto.[9]

---

8. In Marx (and traditionally in political economy), 'fixed capital' refers to money invested in fixed assets, such as buildings, machinery, and infrastructures (as opposed to 'circulating capital', which includes raw materials and workers' wages). In post-Fordism, this capital may include information technologies, personal media, and also intangible assets like software, patents, and forms of collective knowledge. The 'reappropriation of fixed capital' refers then to the reappropriation of a productive capacity (also under the form of value and welfare) by the collectivity of workers—trans.

9. Williams and Srnicek, '#Accelerate', 3.6.

With an attitude that attenuates the humanism present in philosophical critique, the MAP insists on the material and technical qualities of the corporeal reappropriation of fixed capital. Productive quantification, economic modeling, big data analysis, and the most abstract cognitive models are all appropriated by worker-subjects through education and science. The use of mathematical models and algorithms by capital does not make them a feature of capital. It is not a problem of mathematics—it is a problem of power.

No doubt, there is some optimism in this Manifesto. Such an optimistic perception of the technosocial body is not very useful for the critique of the complex human-machine relationship, but nonetheless this Machiavellian optimism helps us to dive into the discussion about organization, which is the most urgent one today. Once the discussion is brought back to the issue of power, it leads directly to the issue of organization. Says the MAP: the Left has to develop socio-technological hegemony—'material platforms of production, finance, logistics, and consumption can and will be reprogrammed and reformatted towards post-capitalist ends'.[10] Without a doubt, there is a strong reliance on objectivity and materiality, on a sort of *Dasein* of development—and consequently a certain underestimation of the social, political, and cooperative elements that we assumed to be there when we agreed to the basic protocol: 'One divides into Two.' However, such an underestimation should not prevent us from recognizing the importance of acquiring the highest techniques employed by capitalistic command, as well as the abstraction of labor, in order to bring them back to a communist administration performed 'by the things themselves'. I understand the passage on technopolitical hegemony in this way: we first have to mature the whole

---

10. Ibid., 3.11.

complex of productive potentialities of cognitive labor in order to advance a new hegemony.

AN ECOLOGY OF NEW INSTITUTIONS

At this point, the problem of organization is properly posed. As already said, a new configuration of the relation between network and planning is proposed against extremist horizontalism. Against any peaceful conception of democracy as process, a new attention shifts from the means (voting, democratic representation, constitutional state, and so forth) to the ends (collective emancipation and self-government). Obviously, new illusions of centralism and empty reinterpretations of the 'proletarian dictatorship' are not repeated by the authors. The MAP grasps the opportunity to clarify this by proposing a sort of 'ecology of organizations,' insisting on a framework of multiple forces that come into resonance with each other and therefore manage to produce engines of collective decision-making beyond any sectarianism.[11] You may have doubts about such a proposal; you may recognize difficulties that are greater than the happy options that are offered. Nevertheless, this is a direction to explore. This is even clearer today, at the end of the cycle of struggles that started in 2011, which have all shown insuperable limits regarding their forms of organization throughout their clashes with power, despite their strength and new genuine revolutionary contents.

The MAP proposes three urgent goals that are appropriate and realistic for the time being: First of all, building a new kind of intellectual infrastructure to support a new ideal project and the study of new economic models. Second, organizing a strong initiative on the terrain of mainstream mass media: the internet and social networks have undoubtedly democratized communication and they have been very useful for global struggles, yet

---

11. Ibid., 3.15.

communication still remains subjugated to its most traditional forms. The task becomes one of focusing substantial resources and all the energy possible in order to get our hands on adequate means of communication. The third goal is activating all possible institutional forms of class power (transitional and permanent, political and unionist, global and local). A unitary constitution of class power will be possible only through the assemblage and hybridization of all experiences developed so far, and those yet to be invented.

An Enlightenment aspiration—'the future needs to be constructed'—runs through the entire Manifesto.[12] A Promethean and humanist politics resounds as well. Such a humanism, however, going beyond the limits imposed by capitalist society, is open to posthuman and scientific utopias, reviving the dreams of twentieth-century space exploration or conceiving new impregnable barriers against death and all the accidents of life. Rational imagination must be accompanied by the collective fantasy of new worlds, organizing a strong self-valorization of labor and society. The most modern epoch that we have experienced has shown us that there is nothing but an Inside of globalization, that there is no longer an Outside. Today, however, reformulating again the issue of reconstructing the future, we have the necessity—and also the possibility—of bringing the Outside in, to breathe a powerful life into the Inside.

What can be said about this document? Some of us perceive it as an Anglo-Saxon complement to the perspective of post-Operaism—less inclined to revive socialist humanism, and better able to develop a new positive humanism. The name 'accelerationism' is certainly unfortunate, as it ascribes a sense of 'futurism' to something that is not at all futuristic. The document is undoubtedly timely, not only in its critique of 'real' social

12. Ibid., 3.24.

democracy and socialism, but also in its analysis of social movements since 2011. It posits, with extreme strength, the issue of the tendency of capitalistic development, of the need for both its reappropriation and for its rupture. On this basis, it advances the construction of a communist program. These are strong legs on which to move forward.

ON THE THRESHOLDS OF TECHNOPOLITICS

Some criticism may be useful at this point to reopen the discussion and push the argument forward towards points of agreement. Firstly, there is too much determinism in this project, both political and technological. The relation to historicity (or, if you prefer, to history, to contemporaneity, to praxis) is likely to be distorted by something that we are not inclined to call teleology, but that looks like teleology. The relation to singularities and therefore the capacity to understand tendency as virtual (involving singularities), and material determination (that pushes tendency forward) as a power of subjectivization, appears to me to be underestimated. Tendency can be defined only as an open relation, as a constitutive relation that is animated by class subjects. It may be objected that this insistence on openness may lead to perverse effects, for example, to a framework so heterogeneous that it becomes chaotic and therefore irresolvable—a multiplicity that is enlarged and made so gigantic that it constitutes a bad infinity. Undoubtedly such a 'bad infinity' is what post-Operaism and even *A Thousand Plateaus* have sometimes appeared to suggest. This is a difficult and crucial point. Let's dig further into it.

For this problem, the MAP has come up with a good solution when it places a transformative anthropology of the workers' bodies right at the center of the relation between subject and object (what I would call the relation between the technical composition and the political composition of the proletariat, being traditionally accustomed to other terminologies).[13] In this way, the drift of pluralism into a 'bad infinity' can be avoided. However, if we want to continue on this ground—which I believe to be useful and decisive—we have to break the relentless progression of productive tension on which the Manifesto relies. We have to identify the thresholds of development and the consolidations of such thresholds—what Deleuze and Guattari would call *agencements collectifs*. These consolidations are the reappropriation of fixed capital and the transformation of labor power; they consist of anthropologies, languages, and activities. These historically constituted thresholds arise in the relationship between the technical and the political composition of the proletariat. Without such consolidations, a political program—as transitory as it may be—is impossible. It is precisely because we cannot clarify such a relationship between technical composition and political composition, that at times we find ourselves methodologically helpless and politically powerless. Conversely, it is the determination of a historic threshold and the awareness of a specific modality of technopolitical relations, which allows for the formulation of both an organizational process and an appropriate program of action.

Mind you: posing this problem implicitly raises the problem of how to better define the process in which the relationship between singularity and the common grows and consolidates (acknowledging the progressive nature of the productive tendency). We need to specify what the common is in any

---

13. The notion of class composition was introduced by Italian Operaism to overcome the trite debates on 'class consciousness' typical of the 1960s. Technical composition refers to the all material and also cultural forms of labor in a specific economic regime; political composition refers to the clash with and transformation of these forms into a political project. A given technical composition is not automatically conducive to a virtuous political recomposition—trans.

technological assemblage, while developing a specific study of the anthropology of production.

THE HEGEMONY OF COOPERATION

To return again to the issue of the reappropriation of fixed capital: as I have pointed out, in the MAP, the cooperative dimension of production (and particularly the production of subjectivities) is underestimated in relation to technological criteria. Technical parameters of productivity aside, the material aspects of production in fact also describe the anthropological transformation of labor power. I insist on this point. The cooperative element does become central and conducive to a possible hegemony within the set of languages, algorithms, functions, and technological knowhow that constitutes the contemporary proletariat. Such a statement comes from noticing that the structure itself of capitalist exploitation has now changed. Capital continues to exploit, but paradoxically in limited forms—when compared to its power of surplus-labor extraction from society as a whole. However, when we become aware of this new determination, we realize that fixed capital (i.e., the part of the capital directly involved in the production of surplus value) essentially establishes itself in the surplus determined by cooperation. Such a cooperation is something incommensurable: as Marx said, it is not the sum of the surplus labor of two or more workers but the surplus produced by the fact that they work together (in short, the surplus that is beyond the sum itself).[14]

If we assume the primacy of extractive capital over exploitative capital (including of course the latter in the former), we can reach some interesting conclusions. I will briefly mention one.

14. A canonical quote: 'The sum total of the mechanical forces exerted by isolated workers differs from the social force that is developed when many hands cooperate in the same undivided operation.' Karl Marx, *Capital*, vol. 1 (London: Penguin, 1976), 443.

The transition between Fordism and post-Fordism was once described as the application of 'automation' to the factory and 'informatization' to society. The latter is of great importance in the process that leads to the complete (real) subsumption of society within capital—informatization is indeed interpreting and leading this tendency. Informatization is indeed more important than automation, which by itself, in that specific historical moment, managed to characterize a new social form only in a partial and precarious way. As the Manifesto clarifies and experience confirms, today we are well beyond that point. Productive society appears not only globally informatized, but such a computerized social world is in itself reorganized and automatized according to new criteria in the management of the labor market and new hierarchical parameters in the management of society. When production is socially generalized through cognitive work and social knowledge, informatization remains the most valuable form of fixed capital, while automation becomes the cement of capitalist organization, bending both informatics and the information society back into itself. Information technology is thus subordinated to automation. The command of capitalist algorithms is marked by this transformation of production.

We are thus at a higher level of real subsumption. Hence the great role played by logistics, which, after being automated, began to configure any and all territorial dimensions of capitalist command and to establish internal and external hierarchies of global space, as does the algorithmic machinery that centralizes and commands, by degrees of abstraction and branches of knowledge, with variables of frequency and function—that complex system of knowledge that since Marx we have been accustomed to calling General Intellect. Now, if extractive capitalism expands its power of exploitation extensively to any social infrastructure and intensively to any degree of abstraction of the productive machine (at any level of global finance, for instance), it will be necessary to reopen the debate on the reappropriation of fixed capital within such a practical and theoretical space. The construction of new struggles is to be measured according to such a space. Fixed capital can potentially be reappropriated by the proletariat. This is the potentiality that must be liberated.

THE CURRENCY OF THE COMMON AND THE REFUSAL OF LABOR

One last theme—omitted by the MAP, but entirely consistent with its theoretical argumentation—is 'the currency of the common.' The authors of the Manifesto are well aware that today, money has the particular function—as an abstract machine—of being the supreme form of measurement of the value extracted from society through the real subsumption of this current society by capital. The same scheme that describes the extraction/exploitation of social labor forces us to recognize money: as measure-money, hierarchy-money, planning-money. Such a monetary abstraction, as a tendency of the becoming-hegemonic of financial capital itself, also points to potential forms of resistance and subversion at the same highest level. The communist program for a postcapitalist future should be carried out on this terrain, not only by advancing the proletarian reappropriation of wealth, but by building a hegemonic power—thus working on 'the common' that is at the basis of both the highest extraction/abstraction of value from labor and its universal translation into money. This is today the meaning of 'the currency of the common.' Nothing utopian, but rather a programmatic and paradigmatic indication of how to anticipate, within struggles, the attack on the measure of labor imposed by capital, on the hierarchies of surplus labor (imposed directly by bosses), and on the social general distribution of income imposed by the capitalist state. On this, a great deal of work is still to be done.

To conclude (though there are so many things left to discuss!), what does it mean to traverse the tendency of capitalism up to the end, and to beat capitalism itself in this process? Just one example: today it means to renew the slogan 'Refusal of labor'. The struggle against algorithmic automation must positively grasp the increase of productivity that is determined by it, and then it must enforce drastic reductions of the labor time disciplined or controlled by machines and, at the same time, it must result in consistent and increasingly substantial salary increases. On the one hand, the time at the service of automatons must be adjusted in a manner equal to all. On the other hand, a base income must be instituted so as to translate any figure of labor into the recognition of the equal participation of all in the construction of collective wealth. In this way, everyone will be able to freely increase to their best ability their own joie de vivre (recalling Marx's appreciation of Fourier). All this must be immediately claimed through the struggle. And, at this point, we should not forget to open up another theme: the production of subjectivity, the agonistic use of passions, and the historical dialectics this opens against capitalist and sovereign command.

Red Stack Attack!
Algorithms, Capital and the Automation of the Common

Tiziana Terranova

2014

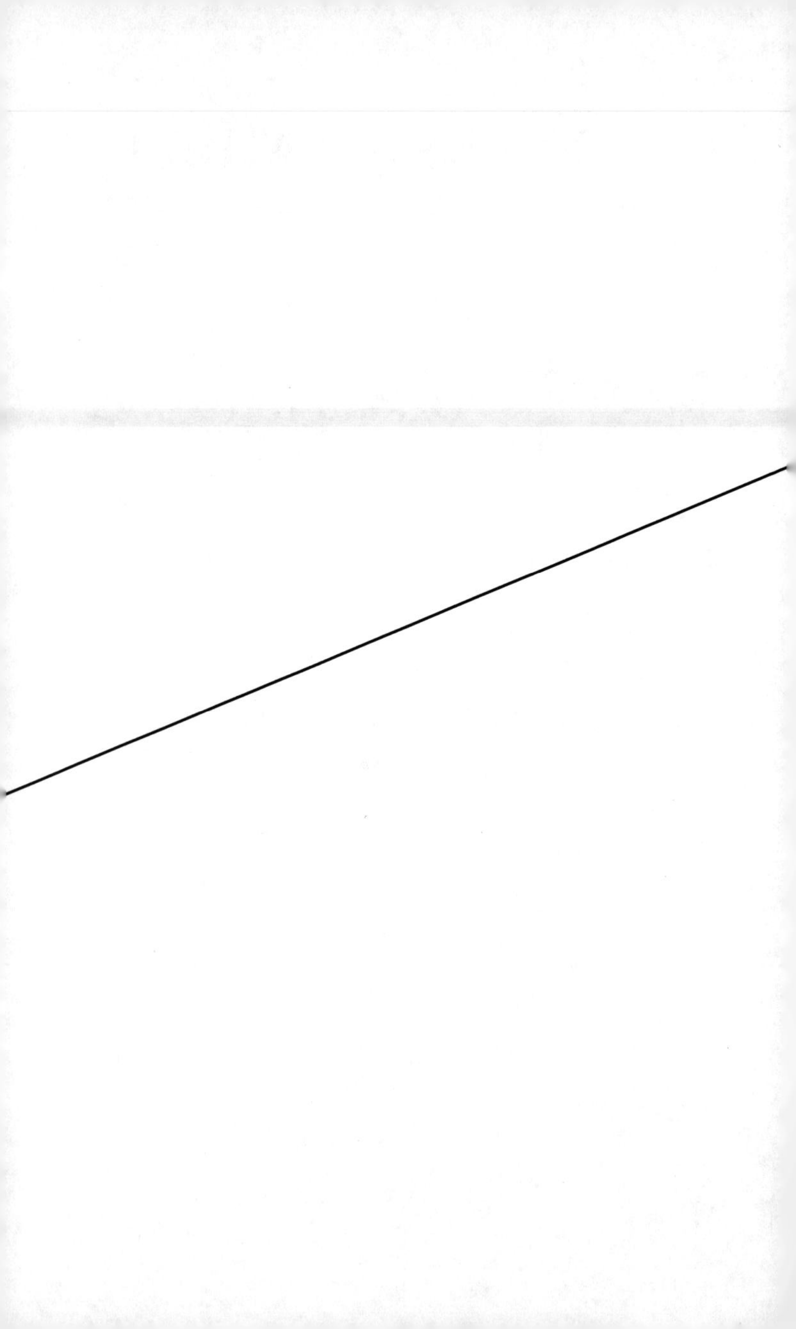

What is at stake in the following[1] is the relationship between 'algorithms' and 'capital'—that is, 'the increasing centrality of algorithms to organizational practices arising out of the centrality of information and communication technologies stretching all the way from production to circulation, from industrial logistics to financial speculation, from urban planning and design to social communication'.[2] These apparently esoteric mathematical structures have also become part of the daily life of users of contemporary digital and networked media. Most users of the Internet daily interface or are subjected to the powers of algorithms such as Google's Pagerank (which sorts the results of our search queries) or Facebook Edgerank (which automatically decides in which order we should get our news on our feed) not to mention the many other less known algorithms (Appinions, Klout, Hummingbird, PKC, Perlin noise, Cinematch, KDP Select and many more) which modulate our relationship with data, digital

---

1. This essay is the outcome of a research process which involves a series of Italian institutions of *autoformazione* of post-autonomist inspiration ('free' universities engaged in grassroots organization of public seminars, conferences, workshops etc) and anglophone social networks of scholars and researchers engaging with digital media theory and practice officially affiliated with universities, journals and research centres, but also artists, activists, precarious knowledge workers and such likes. It refers to a workshop which took place in London in January 2014, hosted by the Digital Culture Unit at the Centre for Cultural Studies (Goldsmiths' College, University of London). The workshop was the outcome of a process of reflection and organization that started with the Italian free university collective Uninomade 2.0 in early 2013 and continued across mailing lists and websites such as Euronomade (http://www.euronomade.info/), Effemera, Commonware (http://www.commonware.org/), I quaderni di San Precario (http://quaderni.sanprecario.info/) and others. More than a traditional essay, then, it aims to be a synthetic but hopefully also inventive document which plunges into a distributed 'social research network' articulating a series of problems, theses and concerns at the crossing between political theory and research into science, technology and capitalism.

2. In the words of the programme of the worshop from which this essay originated: http://quaderni.sanprecario.info/2014/01/workshop-algorithms/.

devices and each other. This widespread presence of algorithms in the daily life of digital culture, however, is only one of the expressions of the pervasiveness of computational techniques as they become increasingly coextensive with processes of production, consumption and distribution displayed in logistics, finance, architecture, medicine, urban planning, infographics, advertising, dating, gaming, publishing and all kinds of creative expressions (music, graphics, dance etc).

The staging of the encounter between 'algorithms' and 'capital' as a political problem invokes the possibility of breaking with the spell of 'capitalist realism'—that is, the idea that capitalism constitutes the only possible economy—while at the same time claiming that new ways of organizing the production and distribution of wealth need to seize on scientific and technological developments.[3] Going beyond the opposition between state and market, public and private, the concept of the common is used here as a way to instigate the thought and practice of a possible post-capitalist mode of existence for networked digital media.

ALGORITHMS, CAPITAL AND AUTOMATION

Looking at algorithms from a perspective that seeks the constitution of a new political rationality around the concept of the 'common' means engaging with the ways in which algorithms are deeply implicated in the changing nature of automation. Automation is described by Marx as a process of absorption into the machine of the 'general productive forces of the social brain' such as 'knowledge and skills',[4] which hence appear as an attribute of capital rather than as the product of social labour.

---

3. M. Fisher, *Capitalist Realism: Is There No Alternative* (London: Zer0 Books, 2009); A. Williams and N. Srnicek, '#Accelerate: Manifesto for an Accelerationist Politics', this volume.

4. K. Marx, 'Fragment on Machines', this volume, 55.

Looking at the history of the implication of capital and technology, it is clear how automation has evolved away from the thermo-mechanical model of the early industrial assembly line toward the electro-computational dispersed networks of contemporary capitalism. Hence it is possible to read algorithms as part of a genealogical line that, as Marx put it in the 'Fragment on Machines', starting with the adoption of technology by capitalism as fixed capital, pushes the former through several metamorphoses 'whose culmination is the machine, or rather, an automatic system of machinery...set in motion by an automaton, a moving power that moves itself'.[5] The industrial automaton was clearly thermodynamical, and gave rise to a system 'consisting of numerous mechanical and intellectual organs so that workers themselves are cast merely as its conscious linkages'.[6] The digital automaton, however, is electro-computational, it puts 'the soul to work' and involves primarily the nervous system and the brain and comprises 'possibilities of virtuality, simulation, abstraction, feedback and autonomous processes'.[7] The digital automaton unfolds in networks consisting of electronic and nervous connections so that users themselves are cast as quasi-automatic relays of a ceaseless information flow. It is in this wider assemblage, then, that algorithms need to be located when discussing the new modes of automation.

Quoting a textbook of computer science, Andrew Goffey describes algorithms as 'the unifying concept for all the activities which computer scientists engage in...and the fundamental entity

5. Ibid., 53.

6. Ibid.

7. M. Fuller, *Software Studies: A Lexicon* (Cambridge, MA: MIT Press, 2008); F. Berardi, *The Soul at Work: From Alienation to Autonomy*. Cambridge, MA: MIT Press, 2009).

with which computer scientists operate'.[8] An algorithm can be provisionally defined as the 'description of the method by which a task is to be accomplished' by means of sequences of steps or instructions, sets of ordered steps that operate on data and computational structures. As such, an algorithm is an abstraction, 'having an autonomous existence independent of what computer scientists like to refer to as "implementation details," that is, its embodiment in a particular programming language for a particular machine architecture'.[9] It can vary in complexity from the most simple set of rules described in natural language (such as those used to generate coordinated patterns of movement in smart mobs) to the most complex mathematical formulas involving all kinds of variables (as in the famous Monte Carlo algorithm used to solve problems in nuclear physics and later also applied to stock markets and now to the study of non-linear technological diffusion processes). At the same time, in order to work, algorithms must exist as part of assemblages that include hardware, data, data structures (such as lists, databases, memory, etc.), and the behaviours and actions of bodies. For the algorithm to become social software, in fact, 'it must gain its power as a social or cultural artifact and process by means of a better and better accommodation to behaviors and bodies which happen on its outside'.[10]

Furthermore, as contemporary algorithms become increasingly exposed to larger and larger data sets (and in general to a growing entropy in the flow of data also known as Big Data), they are, according to Luciana Parisi, becoming something more then mere sets of instructions to be performed: 'infinite amounts of information interfere with and re-program algorithmic procedures...

---

8. A. Goffey, 'Algorithm', in Fuller (ed), *Software Studies*, 15–17: 15.

9. Ibid.

10. Fuller, Introduction to Fuller (ed), *Software Studies*, 5.

and data produce alien rules'.[11] It seems clear from this brief account, then, that algorithms are neither a homogeneous set of techniques, nor do they guarantee 'the infallible execution of automated order and control'.[12]

From the point of view of capitalism, however, algorithms are mainly a form of 'fixed capital'—that is, they are just means of production. They encode a certain quantity of social knowledge (abstracted from that elaborated by mathematicians, programmers, but also users' activities), but they are not valuable per se. In the current economy, they are valuable only in as much as they allow for the conversion of such knowledge into exchange value (monetization) and its (exponentially increasing) accumulation (the titanic quasi-monopolies of the social Internet). In as much as they constitute fixed capital, algorithms such as Google's Page Rank and Facebook's Edgerank appear 'as a presupposition against which the value-creating power of the individual labour capacity is an infinitesimal, vanishing magnitude',[13] and that is why calls for individual retributions to users for their 'free labor' are misplaced. It is clear that for Marx what needs to be compensated is not the individual work of the user, but the much larger powers of social cooperation thus unleashed, and that this compensation implies a profound transformation of the grip that the social relation that we call the capitalist economy has on society.

From the point of view of capital, then, algorithms are just fixed capital, means of production finalized to achieve an economic return. But that does not mean that, like all technologies and techniques, that is all that they are Marx explicitly states that even as capital appropriates technology as the most effective form of

11. L. Parisi, *Contagious Architecture: Computation, Aesthetics, Space* (Cambridge, Mass. and Sydney: MIT Press, 2013), See also 'Automated Architecture', this volume.

12. Ibid., ix.

13. Marx, 'Fragment', this volume, 55.

the subsumption of labor, that does not mean that this is all that can be said about it. Its existence as machinery, he insists, is not 'identical with its existence as capital...and therefore it does not follow that subsumption under the social relation of capital is the most appropriate and ultimate social relation of production for the application of machinery'.[14] It is then essential to remember that the instrumental value that algorithms have for capital does not exhaust the 'value' of technology in general and algorithms in particular—that is, their capacity to express not just 'use value' as Marx put it, but also aesthetic, existential, social, and ethical values. Wasn't it this clash between the necessity of capital to reduce software development to exchange value, thus marginalizing the aesthetic and ethical values of software creation, that pushed Richard Stallman and countless hackers and engineers towards the Free and Open Source Movement? Isn't the enthusiasm that animates hack-meetings and hacker-spaces fueled by the energy liberated from the constraints of 'working' for a company in order to remain faithful to one's own aesthetics and ethics of coding?

Contrary to some variants of Marxism which tend to identify technology completely with 'dead labor', 'fixed capital' or 'instrumental rationality', and hence with control and capture, it seems important to remember how, for Marx, the evolution of machinery also indexes a level of development of productive powers that are unleashed but never totally contained by the capitalist economy. What interested Marx (and what makes his work still relevant to those who strive for a post-capitalist mode of existence) is the way in which, so he claims, the tendency of capital to invest in technology to automate and hence reduce its labor costs to a minimum potentially frees up a 'surplus' of time and energy (labor) or an excess of productive capacity in relation to the basic, important and necessary labor of reproduction

14. Marx, 57.

(a global economy, for example, should first of all produce enough wealth for all members of a planetary population to be adequately fed, clothed, cured and sheltered). However, what characterizes a capitalist economy is that this surplus of time and energy is not simply released, but must be constantly reabsorbed in the cycle of production of exchange value leading to increasing accumulation of wealth by the few (the collective capitalist) at the expense of the many (the multitudes).

Automation, then, when seen from the point of view of capital, must always be balanced with new ways to control (that is, absorb and exhaust) the time and energy thus released. It must produce poverty and stress when there should be wealth and leisure. It must make direct labour the measure of value even when it is apparent that science, technology and social cooperation constitute the source of the wealth produced. It thus inevitably leads to the periodic and widespread destruction of this accumulated wealth, in the form of psychic burnout, environmental catastrophe and physical destruction of the wealth through war. It creates hunger where there should be satiety, it puts food banks next to the opulence of the super-rich. That is why the notion of a post-capitalist mode of existence must become believable, that is, it must become what Maurizio Lazzarato described as an enduring autonomous focus of subjectivation. What a post-capitalist commonism then can aim for is not only a better distribution of wealth compared to the unsustainable one that we have today, but also a reclaiming of 'disposable time'—that is, time and energy freed from work to be deployed in developing and complicating the very notion of what is 'necessary'.

The history of capitalism has shown that automation as such has not reduced the quantity and intensity of labor demanded by managers and capitalists. On the contrary, in as much as technology is only a means of production to capital, where it has been able to deploy other means, it has not innovated. For example, industrial technologies of automation in the factory do not seem to have recently experienced any significant technological breakthroughs. Most industrial labor today is still heavily manual, automated only in the sense of being hooked up to the speed of electronic networks of prototyping, marketing and distribution; and it is rendered economically sustainable only by political means—that is, by exploiting geo-political and economic differences (arbitrage) on a global scale and by controlling migration flows through new technologies of the border. The state of things in most industries today is intensified exploitation, which produces an impoverished mode of mass production and consumption that is damaging to both to the body, subjectivity, social relations and the environment. As Marx put it, disposable time released by automation should allow for a change in the very essence of the 'human' so that the new subjectivity is allowed to return to the performing of necessary labor in such a way as to redefine what is necessary and what is needed.

It is not then simply about arguing for a 'return' to simpler times, but on the contrary a matter of acknowledging that growing food and feeding populations, constructing shelter and adequate housing, learning and researching, caring for the children, the sick and the elderly requires the mobilization of social invention and cooperation. The whole process is thus transformed from a process of production by the many for the few steeped in impoverishment and stress to one where the many redefine the meaning of what is necessary and valuable, while inventing new ways of achieving it. This corresponds in a way to the notion of 'commonfare' as recently elaborated by Andrea Fumagalli and Carlo Vercellone, implying, in the latter's words, 'the socialization of investment and money and the question of the modes of management and organisation which allow for an authentic democratic reappropriation of the institutions of Welfare...and the ecologic re-structuring of our systems of production'.[15] We need to ask then not only how algorithmic automation works today (mainly in terms of control and monetization, feeding the debt economy) but also what kind of time and energy it subsumes and how it might be made to work once taken up by different social and political assemblages—autonomous ones not subsumed by or subjected to the capitalist drive to accumulation and exploitation.

THE RED STACK: VIRTUAL MONEY, SOCIAL NETWORKS, BIO-HYPERMEDIA

In a recent intervention, digital media and political theorist Benjamin H. Bratton has argued that we are witnessing the emergence of a new *nomos* of the earth, where older geopolitical divisions linked to territorial sovereign powers are intersecting the new nomos of the Internet and new forms of sovereignty extending in electronic space.[16] This new heterogenous nomos involves the overlapping of national governments (China, United States, European Union, Brasil, Egypt and such likes), transnational bodies (the IMF, the WTO, the European Banks and NGOs of various types), and corporations such as Google, Facebook, Apple, Amazon, etc., producing differentiated patterns of mutual accommodation marked by moments of conflict. Drawing on the organizational structure of computer networks or 'the OSI network model, upon with the TCP/IP stack and the global internet itself is indirectly based', Bratton has developed the

15. C. Vercellone, 'From the crisis to the "commonfare" as new mode of production', in special section on Eurocrisis (ed. G. Amendola, S. Mezzadra and T. Terranova), *Theory, Culture and Society*, forthcoming; also A. Fumagalli, 'Digital (Crypto) Money and Alternative Financial Circuits: Lead the Attack to the Heart of the State, sorry, of Financial Market', <http://quaderni.sanprecario.info/2014/02/digital-crypto-money-and-alternative-financial-circuits-lead-the-attack-to-the-heart-of-the-state-sorry-of-financial-market-by-andrea-fumagalli/>.

16. B. Bratton, 'On the Nomos of the Cloud' (2012), <http://bratton.info/projects/talks/on-the-nomos-of-the-cloud-the-stack-deep-address-integral-geography/pf/>.

concept and/or prototype of the 'stack' to define the features of 'a possible new nomos of the earth linking technology, nature and the human'.[17] The stack supports and modulates a kind of 'social cybernetics' able to compose 'both equilibrium and emergence'. As a 'megastructure', the stack implies a 'confluence of interoperable standards-based complex material-information systems of systems, organized according to a vertical section, topographic model of layers and protocols...composed equally of social, human and "analog" layers (chthonic energy sources, gestures, affects, user-actants, interfaces, cities and streets, rooms and buildings, organic and inorganic envelopes) and informational, non-human computational and "digital" layers (multiplexed fiber-optic cables, datacenters, databases, data standards and protocols, urban-scale networks, embedded systems, universal addressing tables)'.[18]

In this section, drawing on Bratton's political prototype, I would like to propose the concept of the 'Red Stack'—that is, a new nomos for the post-capitalist common. Materializing the 'red stack' involves engaging with (at least) three levels of socio-technical innovation: virtual money, social networks, and bio-hypermedia. These three levels, although 'stacked', that is, layered, are to be understood at the same time as interacting transversally and nonlinearly. They constitute a possible way to think about an infrastructure of autonomization linking together technology and subjectivation.

VIRTUAL MONEY

The contemporary economy, as Christian Marazzi and others have argued, is founded on a form of money which has been turned into a series of signs, with no fixed referent (such as

---

17. Ibid.

18. Ibid.

gold) to anchor them, explicitly dependent on the computational automation of simulational models, screen media with automated displays of data (indexes, graphics etc) and algo-trading (bot-to-bot transactions) as its emerging mode of automation.[19] As Toni Negri also puts it, 'today, money has the particular function—as an abstract machine—of being the supreme form of measurement of the value extracted from society through the real subsumption of this current society by capital'.[20] Since ownership and control of capital-money (different, as Maurizio Lazzarato remind us, from wage-money, in its capacity to be used not only as a means of exchange, but as a means of investment empowering certain futures over others) is crucial to maintaining populations bonded to the current power relation, how can we turn financial money into the money of the common? An experiment such as Bitcoin demonstrates that in a way 'the taboo on money has been broken',[21] and that beyond the limits of this experience, forkings are already developing in different directions. What kind of relationship can be established between the algorithms of money-creation and 'a constituent practice which affirms other criteria for the measurement of wealth, valorizing new and old collective needs outside the logic of finance'?[22] Current attempts to develop new kinds of cryptocurrencies must be judged, valued and rethought on the basis of this simple

---

19. C. Marazzi, 'Money in the World Crisis: The New Basis of Capitalist Power', <https://webspace.utexas.edu/hcleaver/www/357L/357Lmarazzi.html>.

20. A. Negri, 'Reflections on the Accelerationist Manifesto', this volume, 377.

21. D. Jaromil Rojio, 'Bitcoin, la fine del tabù della moneta' (2014), in I Quaderni di San Precario. (<http://quaderni.sanprecario.info/2014/01/bitcoin-la-fine-del-tabu-della-moneta-di-denis-jaromil-roio/>).

22. S. Lucarelli, 'Il principio della liquidità e la sua corruzione. Un contributo alla discussione su algoritmi e capitale' (2014), in I Quaderni di san Precario, <http://quaderni.sanprecario.info/2014/02/il-principio-della-liquidita-e-la-sua-corruzione-un-contributo-alla-discussione-su-algoritmi-e-capitale-di-stefano-lucarelli/>.

question as posed by Andrea Fumagalli: Is the currency created not limited solely to being a means of exchange, but can it also affect the entire cycle of money creation—from finance to exchange?[23] Does it allow speculation and hoarding, or does it promote investment in post-capitalist projects and facilitate freedom from exploitation, autonomy of organization etc.? What is becoming increasingly clear is that algorithms are an essential part of the process of creation of the money of the common, but that algorithms also have politics (What are the gendered politics of individual 'mining', for example, and of the complex technical knowledge and machinery implied in mining bitcoins?) Furthermore, the drive to completely automate money production in order to escape the fallacies of subjective factors and social relations might cause such relations to come back in the form of speculative trading. In the same way as financial capital is intrinsically linked to a certain kind of subjectivity (the financial predator narrated by Hollywood cinema), so an autonomous form of money needs to be both jacked into and productive of a new kind of subjectivity not limited to the hacking milieu as such, but at the same time oriented not towards monetization and accumulation but towards the empowering of social cooperation. Other questions that the design of the money of the common might involve are: Is it possible to draw on the current financialization of the Internet by corporations such as Google (with its Adsense/Adword programme) to subtract money from the circuit of capitalist accumulation and turn it into a money able to finance new forms of commonfare (education, research, health, environment etc)? What are the lessons to be learned from crowdfunding models and their limits in thinking about new forms of financing

23. A. Fumagalli, 'Commonfare: Per la riappropriazione del libero accesso ai beni comuni' (2014), in Doppio Zero (<http://www.doppiozero.com/materiali/quinto-stato/commonfare>).

autonomous projects of social cooperation? How can we perfect and extend experiments such as that carried out by the Inter-Occupy movement during the Katrina hurricane in turning social networks into crowdfunding networks which can then be used as logistical infrastructure able to move not only information, but also physical goods?[24]

SOCIAL NETWORKS

Over the past ten years, digital media have undergone a process of becoming social that has introduced genuine innovation in relation to previous forms of social software (mailing lists, forums, multi-user domains, etc). If mailing lists, for example, drew on the communicational language of sending and receiving, social network sites and the diffusion of (proprietary) social plug-ins have turned the social relation itself into the content of new computational procedures. When sending and receiving a message, we can say that algorithms operate outside the social relation as such, in the space of the transmission and distribution of messages; but social network software intervenes directly in the social relationship. Indeed, digital technologies and social network sites 'cut into' the social relation as such—that is, they turn it into a discrete object and introduce a new supplementary relation.[25] If, with Gabriel Tarde and Michel Foucault, we understand the social relation as an asymmetrical relation involving at least two poles (one active and the other

---

24. Common Ground Collective, 'Common Ground Collective, Food, not Bombs and Occupy Movement form Coalition to help Isaac and Kathrina Victims' (2012), Interoccupy.net (<http://interoccupy.net/blog/common-ground-collective-food-not-bombs-and-occupy-movement-form-coalition-to-help-isaac-katrina-victims/>).

25. B. Stiegler, 'The Most Precious Good in the Era of Social Technologies', in G. Lovink and M. Rasch (eds), *Unlike Us Reader: Social Media Monopolies and Their Alternatives* (Amsterdam: Institute of Network Culture, 2013), 16–30, <http://networkcultures.org/wpmu/portal/publication/unlike-us-reader-social-media-monopolies-and-their-alternatives/>.

receptive) and characterized by a certain degree of freedom, we can think of actions such as liking and being liked, writing and reading, looking and being looked at, tagging and being tagged, and even buying and selling as the kind of conducts that transindividuate the social (they induce the passage from the pre-individual through the individual to the collective). In social network sites and social plug-ins these actions become discrete technical objects (like buttons, comment boxes, tags etc) which are then linked to underlying data structures (for example the social graph) and subjected to the power of ranking of algorithms. This produces the characteristic spatio-temporal modality of digital sociality today: the feed, an algorithmically customized flow of opinions, beliefs, statements, desires expressed in words, images, sounds etc. Much reviled in contemporary critical theory for their supposedly homogenizing effect, these new technologies of the social, however, also open the possibility of experimenting with many-to-many interaction and thus with the very processes of individuation. Political experiments (see the various Internet-based parties such as the 5 star movement, Pirate Party, Partido X) draw on the powers of these new socio-technical structures in order to produce massive processes of participation and deliberation; but, as with Bitcoin, they also show the far from resolved processes that link political subjectivation to algorithmic automation. They can function, however, because they draw on widely socialized new knowledges and crafts (how to construct a profile, how to cultivate a public, how to share and comment, how to make and post photos, videos, notes, how to publicize events) and on 'soft skills' of expression and relation (humour, argumentation, sparring) which are not implicitly good or bad, but present a series of affordances or degrees of freedom of expression for political action that cannot be left to capitalist monopolies.

However, it is not only a matter of using social networks to organize resistance and revolt, but also a question of constructing a social mode of self-information which can collect and reorganize existing drives towards autonomous and singular becomings. Given that algorithms, as we have said, cannot be unlinked from wider social assemblages, their materialization within the red stack involves the hijacking of social network technologies away from a mode of consumption whereby social networks can act as a distributed platform for learning about the world, fostering and nurturing new competences and skills, fostering planetary connections, and developing new ideas and values.

BIO-HYPERMEDIA

The term bio-hypermedia, coined by Giorgio Griziotti, identifies the ever more intimate relation between bodies and devices which is part of the diffusion of smart phones, tablet computers and ubiquitous computation. As digital networks shift away from the centrality of the desktop or even laptop machine towards smaller, portable devices, a new social and technical landscape emerges around 'apps' and 'clouds' which directly 'intervene in how we feel, perceive and understand the world'.[26] Bratton defines the 'apps' for platforms such as Android and Apple as interfaces or membranes linking individual devices to large databases stored in the 'cloud' (massive data processing and storage centres owned by large corporations).[27]

26. G. Griziotti, 'Biorank: Algorithms and Transformations in the Bios of Cognitive Capitalism' (2014), in *I Quaderni di san Precario* (http://quaderni.sanprecario.info/2014/02/biorank-algorithms-and-transformation-in-the-bios-of-cognitive-capitalism-di-giorgio-griziotti/); also S. Portanova, *Moving without a Body* (Boston, MA: MIT Press, 2013).

27. B. Bratton, 'On Apps and Elementary Forms of Interfacial Life: Object, Image, Superimposition',<http://www.bratton.info/projects/texts/on-apps-and-elementary-forms-of-interfacial-life/pf/>.

This topological continuity has allowed for the diffusion of downloadable apps which increasingly modulate the relationship of bodies and space. Such technologies not only 'stick to the skin and respond to the touch' (as Bruce Sterling once put it), but create new 'zones' around bodies which now move through 'coded spaces' overlaid with information, able to locate other bodies and places within interactive, informational visual maps. New spatial ecosystems emerging at the crossing of the 'natural' and the artificial allow for the activation of a process of chaosmotic co-creation of urban life.[28] Here again we can see how apps are, for capital, simply a means to 'monetize' and 'accumulate' data about the body's movement while subsuming it ever more tightly in networks of consumption and surveillance. However, this subsumption of the mobile body under capital does not necessarily imply that this is the only possible use of these new technological affordances. Turning bio-hypermedia into components of the red stack (the mode of reappropriation of fixed capital in the age of the networked social) implies drawing together current experimentation with hardware (shenzei phone hacking technologies, makers movements, etc.) able to support a new breed of 'imaginary apps' (think for example about the apps devised by the artist collective Electronic Disturbance Theatre, which allow migrants to bypass border controls, or apps able to track the origin of commodities, their degrees of exploitation, etc.).

CONCLUSIONS

This short essay, a synthesis of a wider research process, means to propose another strategy for the construction of a machinic infrastructure of the common. The basic idea is that information

28. S. Iaconesi and O. Persico, 'The Co-Creation of the City: Re-programming Cities using Real-Time User-Generated Content', <http://www.academia.edu/3013140/The_Co-Creation_of_the_City>.

technologies, which comprise algorithms as a central component, do not simply constitute a tool of capital, but are simultaneously constructing new potentialities for postneoliberal modes of government and postcapitalist modes of production. It is a matter here of opening possible lines of contamination with the large movements of programmers, hackers and makers involved in a process of re-coding of network architectures and information technologies based on values others than exchange and speculation, but also of acknowledging the wide process of technosocial literacy that has recently affected large swathes of the world population. It is a matter, then, of producing a convergence able to extend the problem of the reprogramming of the Internet away from recent trends towards corporatisation and monetisation at the expense of users' freedom and control. Linking bio-informational communication to issues such as the production of a money of the commons able to socialize wealth, against current trends towards privatisation, accumulation and concentration, and saying that social networks and diffused communicational competences can also function as means to organize cooperation and produce new knowledges and values, means seeking a new political synthesis which moves us away from the neoliberal paradigm of debt, austerity and accumulation. This is not a utopia, but a program for the invention of constituent social algorithms of the common.[29]

---

29. In addition to the sources cited above, and the texts contained in this volume, we offer overleaf an expandable bibliographical toolkit or open desiring biblio-machine. (Instructions: pick, choose and subtract/add to form your own assemblage of self-formation for the purposes of materialization of the red stack).

— L. Baroniant and C. Vercellone, 'Moneta Del Comune e Reddito Sociale Garantito' (2013), <http://www.uninomade.org/moneta-del-comune-e-reddito-sociale-garantito/>.
— M. Bauwens, 'The Social Web and Its Social Contracts: Some Notes on Social Antagonism in Netarchical Capitalism' (2008), Re-Public Re-Imaging Democracy, <http://www.re-public.gr/en/?p=261>.
— F. Berardi and G. Lovink 'A call to the army of love and to the army of software' (2011), Nettime (<http://www.nettime.org/Lists-Archives/nettime-l-1110/msg00017.html>)
— R. Braidotti, *The Posthuman* (Cambridge: Polity Press, 2013).
— G. E. Coleman, *Coding Freedom: The Ethics and Aesthetics of Hacking* (Princeton and Oxford: Princeton University Press, 2012), <http://gabriellacoleman.org/Coleman-Coding-Freedom.pdf>.
— A. Fumagalli, 'Trasformazione del lavoro e trasformazioni del welfare: precarietà e welfare del comune (commonfare) in Europa', in P. Leon and R. Realfonso (eds), L'Economia della precarietà (Rome: Manifestolibri, 2008), 159–74.
— G. Giannelli and A. Fumagalli 'Il fenomeno Bitcoin: moneta alternativa o moneta speculativa?' (2013), *I Quaderni di San Precario* (<http://quaderni.sanprecario.info/2013/12/il-fenomeno-bitcoin-moneta-alternativa-o-moneta-speculativa-gianluca-giannelli-e-andrea-fumagalli/>).
— G. Griziotti, D. Lovaglio and T. Terranova 'Netwar 2.0: Verso una convergenza della "calle" e della rete' (2012), Uninomade 2.0 (<http://www.uninomade.org/verso-una-convergenza-della-calle-e-della-rete/>).
— E. Grosz, *Chaos, Territory, Art* (New York: Columbia University Press, 2012).
— F. Guattari, *Chaosmosis: An Ethico-Aesthetic Paradigm* (Indianapolis, IN: Indiana University Press, 1995).
— S. Jourdan, 'Game-over Bitcoin: Where Is the Next Human-Based Digital Currency?' (2014), <http://ouishare.net/2013/05/bitcoin-human-based-digital-currency/>.
— M. Lazzarato, *Les puissances de l'invention* (Paris: L'empecheurs de penser ronde, 2004).
— M. Lazzarato, *The Making of the Indebted Man* (Los Angeles: Semiotext(e), 2013).
— G. Lovink and M. Rasch (eds), *Unlike Us Reader: Social Media Monopolies and their Alternatives* (Amsterdam: Institute of Network Culture, 2013).
— A. Mackenzie (2013) 'Programming subjects in the regime of anticipation: software studies and subjectivity' in *Subjectivity* 6, p. 391-405
— L. Manovich, 'The Poetics of Augmented Space', *Virtual Communication* 5:2 (2006), 219–40 (<http://www.alice.id.tue.nl/references/manovich-2006.pdf.>)
— S. Mezzadra and B. Neilson, *Border as Method or the Multiplication of Labor.* (Durham, NC: Duke University Press, 2013).
— P. D. Miller aka DJ Spooky and S. Matviyenko, *The Imaginary App* (Cambridge, MA: MIT Press, forthcoming).
— A. Negri 'Acting in common and the limits of capital' (2014), in Euronomade (<http://www.euronomade.info/?p=1448>).
— A. Negri and M. Hardt, *Commonwealth* (Cambridge, MA: Belknap Press, 2009).

— M. Pasquinelli, 'Google's Page Rank Algorithm: A Diagram of the Cognitive Capitalism and the Rentier of the Common Intellect' (2009), <http://matteopasquinelli.com/docs/Pasquinelli_PageRank.pdf>.
— B. Scott, *Heretic's Guide to Global Finance: Hacking the Future of Money* (London: Pluto Press, 2013).
— G. Simondon, *On the Mode of Existence of Technical Objects* (1958), University of Western Ontario, <https://english.duke.edu/uploads/assets/Simondon_MEOT_part_1.pdf>.
— R. Stallman, *Free Software: Free Society. Selected Essays of Richard M. Stallman* (Free Software Foundation, 2002).
— A. Toscano, 'Gaming the Plumbing: High-Frequency Trading and the Spaces of Capital' (2013), in *Mute* (<http://www.metamute.org/editorial/articles/gaming-plumbing-high-frequency-trading-and-spaces-capital>).
— I. Wilkins and B. Dragos, 'Destructive Distraction? An Ecological Study of High Frequency Trading', in *Mute* (<http://www.metamute.org/editorial/articles/destructive-destruction-ecological-study-high-frequency-trading>).

Automated Architecture

Speculative Reason in the Age of the Algorithm

Luciana Parisi

2014

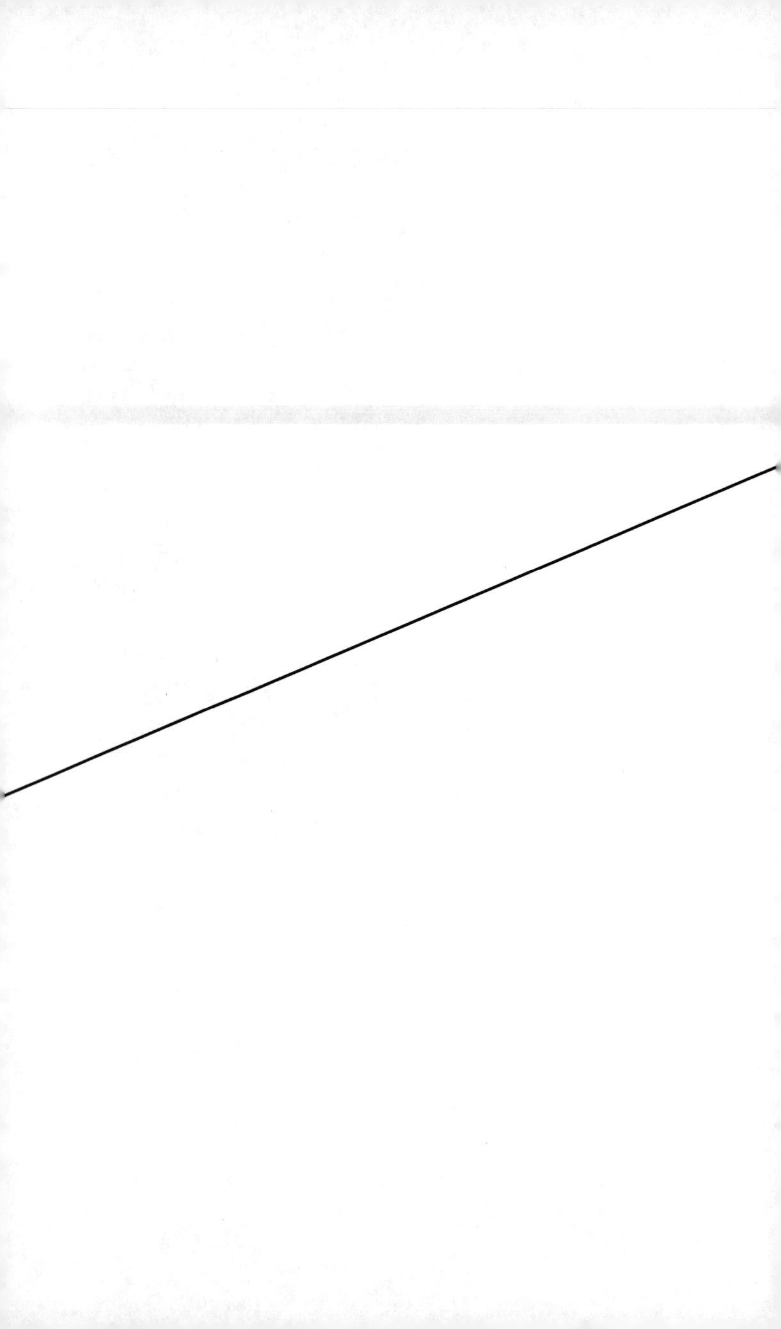

In the last forty years, with the algorithmic automation of spatio-temporal forms and structures, task-specific computer design, based on numerically controlled machines, has been absorbed within a more generic function of computation resulting in custom fabrication processes, machine control protocols, real time simulations that update live, and interactive models that can be directly tweaked and manipulated.[1] More radically, the expansion of computational functions in design has led to the emergence of computational design thinking, whose focus on material properties, physical forces, pressures and constraints defines dynamic spatio-temporal forms in terms of non-binary and continuously heterogeneous variations of matter. Moving away from computation as a form of symbolic representation of physical elements, computational design thinking instead embraces the elemental properties of materials and their generative rules subtending the dynamic nature of spatio-temporal structures. Instead of following geometrical and mathematical patterns, this form of material computation aims to directly follow the physical emergent patterning and material processes of self-assembly out of the interaction of loose elements. In contrast to the mechanical automation of sequentially linear and assembly systems, this new form of algorithmic automation is driven by the physical strategies of materials to compute both architectural form and spatio-temporal performance.

---

1. For an extensive discussion about this transformation in digital architecture, see N. Leach (ed.), *Designing for a Digital World* (New York: Wiley, 2001); K. Terzidis, *Algorithmic Architecture* (Oxford: Architectural Press, 2006); M. Meredith, T. Sakamoto and A. Ferre (eds.), *From Control to Design: Parametric/Algorithmic Architecture* (Barcelona: Actar, 2008); S. Kwinter, C. Davidson (ed.), *Far from Equilibrium: Essays on Technology and Design Culture*, (Barcelona: Actar, 2008); L. Bullivant, *Responsive Environments: Architecture, Art and Design* (London: V&A, 2006); L. Bullivant, *4dsocial: Interactive Design and Environments*, *Architectural Design* 77:4 (2007); K. Oosterhuis, *Interactive Architecture #1* (Rotterdam: Episode, 2007).

But computational design thinking is more importantly a symptom of a more generic acceleration of automation in which algorithmic modelling techniques are now able to select, analyse and evaluate data through the generative evolution of spatio-temporal structures. Paradoxically, the acceleration of automation has pushed forward an anti-digital form of computational design thinking that aims to become one with the fluctuating dynamics of matter.

The advance of computational design thinking, and its acute investment in the intelligence of materials, is the result of a major transformation in the digital design of last forty years marked by the advent of interactive computation, and especially in the last fifteen years, since simulations have become consistent with the inherent morphogenesis—or evolutionary capacities—of materials.[2] Within digital design and architecture, this transformation is often associated with the emergence of material computation, an approach to design thinking based on the convergence between evolutionary biology and non-standard geometry or topology. By leaving behind digital modelling based on the principles of the Universal Turing Machine, whereby the manipulation of symbols allowed designers to test results and deduce a proof for possible structures, computational design thinking has instead adopted a specific form of inductive reasoning relying on the computational capacity to gather information from the physical world and thereby generate dynamic spatio-temporal structures that are, as it were, empirically derived from matter.

From this standpoint, the shift from a form-oriented design, the information-driven manipulation of NURBS (nonuniform rational B-spline) geometry within a computational environment for instance, to a generative-oriented design that integrates

---

2. See A. Menges and S. Ahlquist (eds.), *Computational Design Thinking* (London: John Wiley and Sons, 2011); A. Menges (ed.), *Material Computation—Higher Integration in Morphogenetic Design, Architectural Design* 82:2.

material, form and force as continuous iterations, has led to an empirically-oriented computation of physical activities which is now central to automated architecture. As opposed to the deductive reasoning of digital architecture, according to which general and universal rules inform matter, and algorithms aim to produce simulations that match the behaviour of material substrates, the turn towards material computation, in which physical properties are said to be the motor of simulations, marks the adaptation of an inductive mode of reasoning based on the local behaviour of materials from which complex structures emerge. Here design thinking is not based on preestablished truths that have to be proven, but emerges out of the material variations of elements evolving in time through the mutation and adaptation of data. Similarly, with material computation,wwwwwww design thinking is less concerned with the contemplation of truth and more directly geared towards action, operation, and processing in so far as computation becomes a rather practical and intentional-oriented affair in which the ends of matter drive form whilst architectural form becomes one with matter's activities. If mechanical automation—the automaton of the assembly line, for instance—was a manifestation of the functionalist form that shaped matter, the increasing acceleration of automation led by the development of interactive algorithms (including human-machine and machine-machine interactions) instead reveals the dominance of a practical functionalism whereby form is induced by the movement of matter.

Inductive reasoning places the local properties of materials and the varying behaviours of physical elements at the centre of the design process. In particular, by drawing closely on evolutionary biology, computation here involves a continual extension of the search space aiming to find novel solutions that emerge as a byproduct of the evolutionary dynamics of selection, mutation, and inheritance. With this form of emergentism in design, algorithms serve to set the range of possibilities, whilst analytical measures establish levels of fitness of specific instances within the set of possibilities.[3] Here emergence is not only a property of pattern formation and physical organization. Emergence is also a factor in behaviour, design and computation.[4] Novel spatio-temporal patterns are said to arise not in formal pre-arrangements, but in the realisation of multiple behavioural capacities not initially determined within the programming. As part of the generic tendency to accelerate automation, the turn to inductive reasoning in computation does not simply aim to instrumentalise or mechanise reason and thus establish the formal condition from which truths can be derived, but more explicitly allows matter to become the motor of truth, to become one with and ultimately constitutive of formal reason, of the rules and the patterns that emerge in the automation of space and time.

This matter-driven computational design thinking works not simply to better simulate material behaviour but to produce physically-induced models, a sort of meta-biological computation based on feedback information scanning of the changing properties of materials. But this accelerated computation of matter relying on

---

3. These behaviours are derivatives of simple conditions called agents. An agent holds a simple set of properties; the environment defines a set of rules in which the agents interact. From this standpoint, computational design focuses on the execution of variation methods for the purposeful intent of resolving the complexities that exist in the interrelation and interdependences of material structures and dynamic environments. Computation has the potential to function as a universal application, but the mechanism works only in the processing of specific, non-symbolic conditions relating to materiality, spatiality and context. Whilst the procedures define a vast state space of potentials, the result embodies specific descriptions of the overall system. Computational processes are iterative and recursive but also expansive. They work by growing and specifying the information, which describes form through procedures which recursively generate form, calling variable parameters within the state space. See Menges and Ahlquist (eds.), *Computational Design Thinking*, 24.

4. Ibid.

the efficacy of the physical substrates of matter irremediably misses an ontological question at the core of computation: What and how is algorithmic reason? What is its status vis-à-vis other forms of reason, and how is this manifested?

If computation design thinking has rejected the deductive model of universal rules and its top-down method of form finding, then what do solutions simulating the biophysical behavior of matter tell us as to the nature of algorithmic automation itself in this new phase of technocapital acceleration? Do they mean that the technocapital acceleration of automation has become one with the physical dynamics of matter, defining a dynamic rather than mechanical instrumentalisation of reason? If this is the case, then computational design thinking is perhaps the manifest image of what technocapitalism has been able to achieve by turning the deductive methods of mechanized reason into a multiagent interactive computation whose rules are pre-adapted to physical behavior.

Nevertheless, the inclusion of material agency, bio-physical catalysts and temporalities in computational design is also revealing a less tractable tendency of technocapital acceleration: the computational function of algorithms to add new data to processing. This means that, whilst computational design thinking takes inspiration from the material dynamics of the physical world for its generative models, the acceleration of automation is not simply replacing the organic ends of reason with technical means, but is irremediably constituting a second nature, an algorithmic evolution equipped with its own physical and conceptual levels of order that are not one with matter.

One of the most immediate ontological consequences of the acceleration of automation from digital simulations of form-finding to the generation of materially-driven models, is a computational design thinking embracing the seamless fusion of thought and matter. Here the reality of abstraction is suspended and instead explained by and through the concreteness of physical causes determined by the interaction of loose elements. Whilst the acceleration of automation has pushed the formal logic of deductive reason in computation to move beyond the hierarchical top-down simulation of matter—as an instance of a priori reason—it has not stripped computation from its functions of abstraction and quantification. In other words, instead of accounting for the abstract function of algorithmic processes, the material-oriented approach of computational design thinking risks grounding such processes in ideal physical causes, external to algorithmic automation itself.

The limit of computational design thinking is its uncritical perpetuation of idealist materialism according to which the relation between computation and reason is mediated or to some extent caused by material data. To put it in another way, the problem of computation as a top-down framework of deductive reasoning rooted in ideal forms or in a thinking subject has been largely circumvented but not overcome by computational design thinking, rooted as the latter is in the aggregate causality of material elements. Within the generic acceleration of automation, this view risks disqualifying rather than explaining the computational process through which physical variables are extracted and abstracted. In short, this form of design thinking seems to overlook the materiality of computational processing itself, which necessarily goes beyond the appeal to the preexisting complexity of physical causes.

To address the specificity of such processing, computational design thinking may need to start from the axiom that abstract data and data abstraction driven by algorithmic agents define the automated function of interaction in online, distributive and parallel systems. Kostas Terzidis, for instance, already envisaged the autonomy of computational processing for automated design when he said:

> Unlike computerization and digitization, the extraction of algorithmic processes is an act of high-level abstraction. [...] Algorithmic structures represent abstract patterns that are not necessarily associated with experience or perception. [...] In this sense algorithmic processes become a vehicle for exploration that extends beyond the limit of perception.[5]

But the extension of algorithmic abstraction beyond the limit of perception has also meant that such abstraction corresponds to the intelligible function of rule-based thinking that neither simply matches with the rational faculty of knowing nor with the intuitive capacities of knowing beyond proof. The aim here is not to reject material computation, but to radicalise its implications. As a symptom of a generic acceleration of automation, the generation of spatio-temporal architectures of a computational order are inconsistent with the physical facts of matter. Similarly, algorithmic automation does not coincide with an abstraction of matter based upon the way in which matter works, but more stubbornly produces axioms—or truths—about what is not yet known and what non-physical or algorithmic agents know. This implies not the idealisation of the computational capacities of matter (which are continuous with algorithmic automation), but instead a veritable rehabilitation of algorithmic automation in its own right, exposing its own axiomatic thinking or rule-based processing.

The rehabilitation of algorithmic automation is also an attempt both to dethrone computation from a closed deductive formalism, based on simple universal rules, and to subtract it from a too immediate merging with bio-physical causality. From this standpoint, the acceleration of automation challenges the paradigm of

5. K. Terzidis, *Expressive Form: A Conceptual Approach to Computational Design* (London and New York: Spon Press, 2003), 71.

the mechanical process determined by discrete steps that are pre-thought and pre-ordered, but also the vitalism according to which material computations are induced by the continuity of physical processes. To put it in another way, the acceleration of automation has entered the uncharted territory of an algorithmic reason that does not simply derive its functions from the local interaction of parts. At the same time, however, algorithmic automation also breaks from the meta-computational view for which a simple theory can explain complex behaviour or an elegant formula can compress all of its outputs. Far from being an abstraction of physical structures, automated architecture is instead a manifestation of algorithmic spatio-temporalities that have nothing to do with what already exists in nature (or the relation between rules and randomness that exist in the biological and physical strata). If computational design thinking rejects the representational framework of meta-computation (i.e., the universe is ultimately made of discrete algorithms), then it also has to admit that what is manifested to us is not the same as what algorithms do—i.e., their scientific image is intrinsic to them and does not match what is perceivable and cognizable by a subject.

But to further clarify how accelerated automation has challenged computational views based on deductive and inductive reasoning, one has to explain the problem of the incomputable, or randomness, that is at the heart of computation today.

ACCELERATE RANDOMNESS

The acceleration of algorithmic automation cannot be divorced from the problem of the incomputable, and the challenges this posed to the deductive method of logic based on pure reason. In 1931, the logician Kurt Gödel took issue with David Hilbert's metamathematical program and demonstrated that there could not be a complete axiomatic method, nor a pure mathematical formula or universal truths, according to which the reality of things could be proved to be true or false.[6] Gödel's 'incompleteness theorems' explained that, even if all the propositions of a system were true, they could not be verified by a complete axiomatic method. Certain propositions were therefore ultimately deemed to be undecidable: they could not be proved by means of the axiomatic method upon which they were hypothesized. In Gödel's view, no a priori decision, and thus no finite set of rules, could be used to determine the state of things before things had run their course.

Not too long after, the mathematician Alan Turing also encountered Gödel's incompleteness problem whilst attempting to formalize the concepts of algorithm and computation through his famous thought experiment, known as the Turing Machine. In particular, the Turing Machine demonstrated that problems that can be decided according to the axiomatic method were computable problems.[7] Conversely, those propositions that could not be decided through the axiomatic method would remain incomputable.[8] From this standpoint, insofar as

---

6. See D. Hilbert, 'The new grounding of mathematics: First report' in W. B. Ewald (ed.), *From Kant to Hilbert: A Source Book in the Foundations of Mathematics*, Vol 2 (Oxford: Oxford University Press, 1996), 1115–33; R. Goldstein, *Incompleteness: The Proof and Paradox of Kurt Gödel* (New York: Norton, 2005); S. Feferman (ed.), *Some basic theorems on the foundations of mathematics and their implications*. Collected works of Kurt Gödel, Vol. 3 (Oxford: Oxford University Press, 1995), 304–23.

7. A.M. Turing, 'On computable numbers, with an application to the *Entscheidungsproblem*', *Proceedings of the London Mathematical Society*, 2nd Series, Vol. 42 (1936). For further discussion of the intersections of the works between Hilbert, Gödel and Turing, see M. Davis, *The Universal Computer. The Road from Leibniz to Turing* (New York & London: Norton, 2000), 83–176.

8. According to Turing, there could not be a complete computational method in which the manipulation of symbols and the rules governing their use would realize Leibniz's dream of a *mathesis universalis*. *Mathesis Universalis* defines a universal science modeled on mathematics and supported by the *calculus ratiocinator*, a universal calculation described by Leibniz as a universal conceptual language.

any axiomatic method was incomplete, so too were the rules of computation.[9]

As Giuseppe Longo explains,[10] the problem of the incomputable explained that even closed finite systems (e.g. the pendulum or first order Arithmetic) are undecidable, and inversely, that few and simple deterministic rules or finitary physical or logical structures may give rise to chaotic behaviours or complex logical theories. In other words, 'mathematics is an essentially open system of proofs' and 'each

---

For first-order cybernetics the *calculus ratiocinator* refers to the computational machine that could perform differential and integral calculus or the combination of the ratios. As Norbert Wiener pointed out: 'like his predecessor Pascal, [Leibniz] was interested in the construction of computing machines in metal [...] just as the calculus of arithmetic lends itself to a mechanization progressing through the abacus and the desk computing machine to the ultra-rapid computing machines of the present day, so the *calculus ratiocinator* of Leibniz contains the germs of the *machine ratiocinatrix*, the reasoning machine.' See N. Wiener, *Cybernetics or the Control and Communication in the Animal and the Machine* (Cambridge, MA: MIT Press, 1965), 12. For Turing, the incomputable determined the limit of computation: no finite set of rules could predict in advance whether or not the computation of data would halt at a given moment or whether it would reach a zero or one state, as established by initial conditions. This halting problem meant that no finite axiom could constitute the model by which future events could be predicted. Hence, the limit of computation was determined by the existence of those infinite real numbers that could not be counted through the axiomatic method posited at the beginning of the computation. In other words, these numbers were composed of too many elements that could not be ordered into natural numbers (e.g. 1, 2, 3).

9. A clearer explanation of the implications of Gödel's theorem of incompleteness for Turing's emphasis on the limit of computation can be found in Gregory Chaitin, *MetaMaths: The Quest for Omega* (London: Atlantic Books, 2006), 29–32.

10. G. Longo, 'Incomputability in Physics and Biology' available at http://www.di.ens.fr/users/longo (last accessed March 2014). See also G. Longo, 'Critique of Computational Reason in the Natural Sciences', In E. Gelenbe and J.-P. Kahane (eds.), *Fundamental Concepts in Computer Science* (London: Imperial College Press/World Sci., 2008); G. Longo, 'From exact sciences to life phenomena: following Schrödinger and Turing on Programs, Life and Causality', *Information and Computation*, 207:5 (2009), 543–670.

real mathematics proof proceeds as an open system'. Hence knowledge does not depend on a predetermined set of axioms insofar as theories are constantly built, axioms modified and rules amended. From this standpoint, one could extend this view to computation, but explain that knowledge is here produced by means of axioms without necessarily passing through the faculty of pure reason or practical reasoning led by the existence of facts. The problem of incomputables for rule-based reasoning, far from proving the fallacy of algorithmic automation in the production of knowledge, rather indicates that there are truths that cannot be proven (by deductive or inductive reasoning) but are nonetheless intelligible within computation and are manifested in the form of an axiom. The problem of the incomputable thus shows that computational axiomatics is inevitably infected with randomness, but also that randomness is each time turned into an axiom by means of rule-based processing, defining algorithmic reason as a nonlinear elaboration of continuous infinities and transformation of its discrete parts.

For information theorist Gregory Chaitin, the question of the incomputable reveals that randomness or sensitivity to context or initial conditions is part of even elementary branches of number theory, and that therefore randomness and complexity are intrinsic to the most elemental of particles. In particular, Chaitin explains that the halting probability of the Turing Machine, and thus the uncertainty of predicting when—given a certain input—a computation will stop, can nonetheless be computably enumerable despite being infinitely large. Chaitin calls this odd probability Omega: the limit of a computable, increasing, converging sequence of rational numbers. What is new here is that such a limit of computation is also algorithmically random:

its binary expansion is an algorithmic random sequence, which is incomputable (or partially computable).[11]

Chaitin's discovery of Omega clarifies that randomness is intelligible and detectable within the very computational processing in which unpredictable infinities emerge and operate—and yet cannot be synthesised by an a priori program, theory or set of procedures that are smaller in size than it. This means that the incomputable within computational processing can be neither reincorporated into formal deductive logic (since it cannot be proven by means of pure reason), nor explained primarily in terms of those physical causes that cannot be

---

11. Chaitin explains that his Ω number is a probability (albeit an infinite number) for a program to halt:

> First, I must specify how to pick a program at random. A program is simply a series of bits, so flip a coin to determine the value of each bit. How many bits long should the program be? Keep flipping the coin so long as the computer is asking for another bit of input. Ω is just the probability that the machine will eventually come to a halt when supplied with a stream of random bits in this fashion.

At the same time however, he also points out that Omega is incomputable, and thus the problem of the limit of computation remains unsolvable for a formal axiomatic system:

> We can be sure that Ω cannot be computed because knowing Ω would let us solve Turing's halting problem, but we know that this problem is unsolvable.

In other words:

> Given any finite program, no matter how many billions of bits long, we have an infinite number of bits that the program cannot compute. Given any finite set of axioms, we have an infinite number of truths that are improvable in that system. Because Ω is irreducible, we can immediately conclude that a theory of everything for all of mathematics cannot exist. An infinite number of bits of Ω constitute mathematical facts (whether each bit is a 0 or a 1) that cannot be derived from any principles simpler than the string of bits itself. Mathematics therefore has infinite complexity.

G. Chaitin, 'The Limits of Reason', *Scientific American* 294:3 (March 2006), 74–81. On Chaitin, see also R. Brassier, 'Remarks on Subtractive Ontology and Thinking Capital', in P. Hallward (ed.), *Think Again: Alain Badiou and the Future of Philosophy* (London and New York: Continuum, 2004).

computed, thus marking the limit of computation (and hence the necessity to extend computation to the physical world). Instead, the increasing presence of infinite quantities of data (incomputables) within interactive, parallel and online computational systems (including human-machine, but also increasingly algorithm-algorithm interactions) exceeds totalising mathematical and physical causality, a priori or a posteriori reason alike, by reorienting deductive and inductive methods of computation in counter-intuitive directions.

One of the interesting implications of Chaitin's Omega is that it is at once computationally intelligible—and thus physically and conceptually processed by automated systems—yet unsynthesisable by a totalizing theory or practice of knowledge. For computational design thinking, this proposition entails that computation needs to be understood beyond the limits of mathematics, and cannot be easily supplemented by physics. As already mentioned, computational design thinking in particular has embraced this move towards physical causality, demonstrating that material dynamics prove that there are morphogenetic and continuously changing patterns in nature from which a new model of automated architecture can be derived. Instead, Chaitin insists that computation needs to be rethought in terms of an experimental axiomatics for which the incomputable Omega cannot be proven by means of deductive reason, but can nonetheless—although partially and immanently—discretize (i.e., render discrete and intelligible) infinitely large quantities of data. This view is essential to computational design thinking because it importantly reveals that there is a dynamic proper to computation, in which discrete patterns are inevitably accompanied by patternless information.

From this standpoint, the accelerated automation of spatio-temporal structures is not simply attuned to patterns in nature, but instead defines the increasing thickening of a computational stratum, a second nature, whose ends are not compatible with the fluid dynamics of matter. In short, a material computational thinking cannot overlook the function of incomputable algorithms in automation insofar as incomputable parts are in the majority and can take over the totality of programming.[12] The acceleration of automation thus inevitably exposes an acceleration of randomness—patternless data bursting within algorithmic sequencing—and has given way to an experimental axiomatics determined by an immanent discretization of incomputables. Far from determining automation in terms of a Laplacian Universe whose mechanics ensure that outputs can always be deduced from a finite set of inputs or instructions, the acceleration of automation instead reveals that inputs are as big as outputs and that computation can only discover and revise truths through a continuous production of axioms.

SPECULATIVE REASON

It is now possible to draw some conclusions.

The acceleration of automation has led to the emergence of a new form of computational design thinking driven by a close investment in the biophysical dynamics of matter, which are said to produce the most varied patterns out of the infinitesimal relations between their parts. However, this equivalence between the

---

12. As Chaitin hypothesizes, if the program that is used to calculate infinities will no longer be based on finite sets of algorithms but on infinite sets (or Omega complexity), then programmability will become a far cry from the algorithmic optimization of indeterminate processes actualized through binary probabilities. Programming will instead turn into the calculation of complexity via complexity, chaos via chaos: an immanent doubling infinity or the infinity of the infinite. Contrary to the Laplacian mechanistic universe of pure reason, Chaitin's information theory explains how software programs can include randomness from the start. Thus the incompleteness of axiomatic methods does not define the end point of computation and its inability to engage with dynamical change, but rather its starting condition, through which new axioms, codes, and sets of instructions have become immanent to non-denumerable reals.

biophysical dynamics of matter and computation mainly assigns to computation the task of revealing or simulating structural variations and spatio-temporal complexities inherent to matter. Hence whilst biophysical patterns are taken to be the principal motor of computation, computation itself tends to recede into the background and remains a mere vehicle for visualizing and proving the indeterminacy of matter. This form of inductive reasoning derives and proves truths by means of empirical measuring, contingent actions, and facts and factors in the world. Computational design thinking thus becomes a mode of doing and practising a thought derived from what already happens in the physical world. From this standpoint, the acceleration of automation perfectly coincides with the technocapitalist illusion that matter can generate infinitesimal variations, an inexhaustible abundance that turns continuously smaller elements into vast resources for the productive eternality of the whole.

But the acceleration of automation hardly leads to a blissful bathing in thoughtless matter and instead invades the everyday with the alien reasoning of patternless algorithms which, while they cannot be compressed into a smaller programme or synthesized by a brain, nonetheless lie at the core of all orders of computation (sequential, parallel, distributive, interactive computation). With the acceleration of automation, the explosive advent of algorithmic randomness within computational processing has become inevitable. This means that instead of deriving dynamic patterns of information from matter, patternless data are instead generated within computation itself, and have thus become intrinsic to automated reason. Similarly, incomputables can no longer be explained by the Turing deductive method of reason, whereby all that can be computed is computable. Central to the acceleration of automation today is the profound transformation of formalism triggered by the ingress of incomputables into axiomatic, which has forced reason (rule-based functions) to become defined in terms of an immanent finality, an experimental final cause or purpose. Just as axioms become experimental truths, so too algorithmic automation exposes its internal inconsistencies: its sequential arrangement of parts becomes the host of random information, an interference that does not disrupt but adds a new order of finality to the programming whole (or the finality of the entire set of instructions). From this standpoint, one needs a theory of speculative reason that not only does away with the dominance of deduction and/or induction in computational design thinking, but that can also add another mode of reason to them that is able to surpass and nonetheless bring forward both truth and fact into an experimental axiomatic.

To explain what is meant here by speculative reason, one has to turn to A.N. Whitehead. From his explanation of the function of reason, we immediately learn that reason or the production of concepts implies the addition of new data to the continual chain of cause and effect—the physical laws of nature. In particular, Whitehead claims that the aim of speculative reason is the production of an abstract scheme,[13] which he calls 'the concrete arrangement of relations'.[14] For reason to be truly speculative, the schemes that are produced and

13. According to Whitehead, '[t]he history of modern civilization shows that such schemes fulfill the promise of the dream of Solomon. They first amplify life by satisfying the peculiar claim of the speculative Reason, which is understanding for its own sake. Secondly, they represent the capital of ideas which each age holds in trust for its successors. The ultimate moral claim that civilization lays upon its possessors is that they transmit, and add to, this reserve of potential development by which it has profited.' A. N. Whitehead, *The Function of Reason* (Boston: Beacon Press, 1929), 72.

14. 'The true activity of understanding consists in a voyage to abstraction, which is in fact a voyage to the more, fully concrete: to the system in which the fact is enmeshed. The system as conceptualized may be more abstract than the fact itself in that it is more general, but the real systematic context is more concrete, and its elaboration yields more about the existential relations of the fact.' Ibid., 76.

realized must be able to encounter their finitude and limits: to account for incomputable parts that interfere with the ceaseless mechanisms of the whole.[15]

In particular, Whitehead warns us against the dominance of two main views as to what the function of reason really is—namely pure and practical reason. In the first, reason is seen as the operation of theoretical realization, whereby the universe is a mere exemplification of a theoretical system. The model of computation that produces complex data through the simplest and most elegant program/formula coincides with this view. Whitehead rejects the meta-computational theory of the universe (e.g. the universe explained by the Leibnizian Principle of Sufficient Reason), as it specifically seeks to capture in the simplest formula the infinity of worlds. The Principle of Sufficient Reason reduces the nexus of actual occasions to conceptual differences, since the Principle defines how differences can be represented or mediated in a concept.[16] According to Whitehead, this one-to-one relation between mental cogitations and actual entities underestimates the speculative power of reason, which is instead an adventure of ideas that cannot be encompassed by any complete formalism. But his notion of

---

15. 'Abstract speculation has been the salvation of the world-speculations, which made systems and then transcended them, speculations that ventured to the furthest limits of abstraction.' Ibid.

16. As Whitehead clarifies, '[h]is [Leibniz] monads are best conceived as generalizations of contemporary notions of mentality. The contemporary notions of physical bodies only enter into his philosophy subordinately and derivatively.' A.N. Whitehead, *Process and Reality: An Essay in Cosmology* (New York: Free Press, 1978), 19. Similarly, Deleuze points out that: '[a]ccording to the principle of sufficient reason, there is always one concept per particular thing. According to the reciprocal principle of the identity of indiscernibles, there is one and only one thing per concept. Together, these principles expound a theory of difference as conceptual difference, or develop the account of representation as mediation.' G. Deleuze, *Difference and Repetition*, trans. P. Patton (New York and London: Continuum, 2004), 12.

speculative reason is also divorced from practical and pragmatic reason, whereby reason is a mere fact or factor in the world, or is explicable as an immediate method of intentional action.[17] In algorithmic automation, this notion of practical reason would coincide with the dominance of the interactive paradigm in computational design thinking that explains it in terms of parts constituting a whole. This view sustains interactive models of automation, where algorithms are correlated to physical data, thereby suggesting that software programs are only one of the factors in the architecture of a responsive system determined by external physical dynamics.

Whitehead's study of the function of reason sits comfortably neither with the formal nor practical methods and suggests instead that reason must be re-articulated according to the activity of *final* causation, and not merely by the law of the efficient cause.[18]

---

17. In particular, Whitehead observes, '[w]e have got to remember the two aspects of Reason, the Reason of Plato and the Reason of Ulysses, Reason seeking complete understanding and Reason as seeking an immediate action'. Whitehead, *The Function of Reason*, 11.

18. Whitehead's efficient cause and final cause can be understood as two modes of prehensions, causal efficacy and presentational immediacy, another parallel level of distinction between the physical and mental poles of an entity. Efficient causes describe the physical chain of continuous causes and effects, whereby the past is inherited by the present. This means that any entity is somehow caused and affected by its inheritable past. As Steven Shaviro explains: 'Efficient cause is a passage, a transmission, an influence or a contagion'. Although each actual entity appropriates the past in its own unrepeatable way, it is nonetheless embodied in the material universe that impinges upon it. However, in the process of repeating the patterns of the past there is always a margin of error, a bug in the vector transmission of energy-information from the past to the present, and from cause to effect. The seamless continuity of hereditary patterns is yet again faced with another level of contagion: the contagion of ideas breaking from efficient causality. Shaviro points out that there are at least two reasons for this break in the chain. On the one hand, time is cumulative and therefore irreversible: any actual event adds itself to the past. In other words, the mere addition of facts gives rise to a quantitative effect through which what was there before—i.e. A—is a stubborn fact, which has an objective immortality that is inherited but not fully assimilated by B. The relation between A and B is that of two actual worlds. On the

Final cause explains how concepts are not reflections on material causes, but instead supplement the mere inheritance of past facts with new and often unproven ideas. Conceptual prehensions, as Whitehead calls them, entail a process of selection and evaluation of facts that not only displaces the fact beyond observation, but also, importantly, recognizes in it another level of reality, an abstraction that is proper to the fact and yet is not determined by it. Final cause, therefore, is rather conceived as a speculative tendency intrinsic to reason and able to drive facts away from recognition so as to come back to them in a transformed fashion. This tendency, according to Whitehead, explains how decisions are carried out, and how the selection of past or existent data becomes the point at which another level of nuance is added to existing things. In other words, reason as a rule-based speculation defines the purpose of a theory and a practice in terms of their ability to add novelty to, and thus to counteract, the causal chain of events. From this standpoint, one cannot explain the universe solely in terms of physical interconnections, as these dangerously omit any counter-agency, any conceptual prehension for which there can be 'no direct observation, intuition or immediate experience

---

other hand, the repetition of the past is never neutral and undergoes a evaluation on behalf of the receiving entity, by which certain data are selected according to the qualities of joy and distaste of the receiving entity, for instance. The evaluation of inherited data is carried out by conceptual prehensions, which add novelty to what was before, as they are prehensions of eternal objects. It is the mental pole of any actual entity—the conceptual prehensions that do not necessarily involve consciousness—that explains how efficient cause is supplemented by final cause. For Whitehead, a final cause is always adjacent to an efficient cause; the former accompanies and yet supervenes upon the latter. See Whitehead, *Process and Reality*, on efficient cause, 237–8; on final cause 241; on the transition from efficient to final cause, 210. See also S. Shaviro, *Without Criteria. Kant, Deleuze, Whitehead and Aesthetics* (Cambridge, MA: MIT Press 2009), 83; 86–7.

of real processes.'[19] This means that the function of reason serves to unlock possibilities and revise initial conditions within the given order of things.

It would however be misleading to equate this notion of final cause or purpose with a teleological explanation of the universe, since for Whitehead the function of reason is 'progressive and never final.'[20] This means that the purpose of reason is to revise and change its premises rather than being determined by the essence of who or what does the reasoning. But whilst reason does not stem from matter, it is also attached to the physical decay of things ready to reveal new modes of abstractions from beneath its surface. For Whitehead, speculative reason implies the asymmetrical and non-unified entanglement of efficient and final cause, and must be conceived as a *machine of emphasis* upon novelty.[21]

But the finality of speculative reason also explains the autonomy of actual modes of reason. Whitehead claims that speculative reason is reason that only serves itself, rather than being a reason for (and of) something else. In other words, and contrary to the universal principle of sufficient reason, any actuality has its own finality driven by its own mode of reason determined by its own indeterminate partialisation (i.e., discretization) of data, its rendering partially intelligible of infinities. Speculative reason 'is its own dominant interest, and is not deflected by motives derived from other dominant interest which it may be promoting.'[22] A tension

19. Whitehead, *The Function of Reason*, Ibid., 25

20. Whitehead, *Process and Reality*, ibid., 9.

21. Whitehead attributes reason to higher forms of biological life, where reason substitutes action. Reason is not a mere organ of response of external stimuli, but rather is an organ of emphasis, able to abstract novelty from repetition. In particular, reason provides the judgment by which novelty passes into realization, into fact. Ibid., 20.

22. Ibid., 38.

can be noticed here between a notion of reason as governed by the purposes of some external dominant interests and those operations of reason that are governed by immediate satisfactions (or self-enjoyment) arising from within.[23] But Whitehead sees this tension not as a contradiction between one and many but as a productive contrast within reason, in the same way as the shades of a color maintain their singularity in togetherness. This is to say that speculative reason is internal to all modes of thought, but also that all these modes are infected with their own incomputable data that are each time partially determined and axiomatised.[24]

From the standpoint of speculative reason, the intelligible capacity of computation must be reconceived in terms of an experimental axiomatic. The acceleration of automation has led computation to confront the increasing power of incomputables at the core of its formal scheme. As much as algorithmic automation is accompanied by an infinite amount of complexities, so have its mechanical functions been transformed into a new source of intelligible operations able to revise axiomatic truths immanently. The acceleration of automation has led not to the reification of deductive formalism for which computation can seamlessly represent all modes of reason, but to the discovery of an intelligible function that lies within (and yet goes beyond) the digital ground of axiomatic. Beneath the social media façade of the interactive paradigm, a new pace in technocapital accelerationism is dictated by the ingress of randomness (incompressible and infinitely large quantities of data) into automation, turning its mechanical function (determined by a steady return to its initial conditions) into a progressive (i.e. forward-inclined) production and transformation of axioms.

23. Ibid., 39.

24. Whitehead would insist that the speculative function of reason coincides with infinite modes of physical and conceptual prehensions, in which concepts and objects are determined by their own final cause and partial sufficient reason.

This also places computational design thinking at the centre of the new order of capitalization of intelligible functions occupied with the axiomatisation of infinitely long and increasingly vast quantities of data. But whilst this has always been the scope of technocapitalism and its instrumentalisation of reason, the acceleration of automated architectures needs to be approached from the standpoint of Chaitin's discovery of Omega insofar as this decryption of an infinite number of data are partially (and immanently) axiomatised as such: that is, as probabilities of infinite functions. This speculative computation requires infinite orders of abstraction that ceaselessly bring truth and fact forward towards new determinations.

From this standpoint, the speculative function of reason in computational design thinking corresponds to the algorithmic selection and evaluation of infinite amounts of data, making decisions and generating new solutions. This involves not only the computation of physical data, but more importantly their conceptual prehensions: the capacity of rule-based functions to counteract the physical aggregation of data by adding new algorithmic patterns to what already exists (i.e. experimental axiomatic). To propose that computational design thinking can be defined in terms of a speculative function of reason is thus to pose the question of whether automated algorithms are able to redirect their own final reason in the computational processing of infinite amounts of data. Whether this can be proven or not, it is hard to dismiss the possibility of a computational design thinking immanent to its own algorithmic reason.

The Labor of the Inhuman

Reza Negarestani

2014

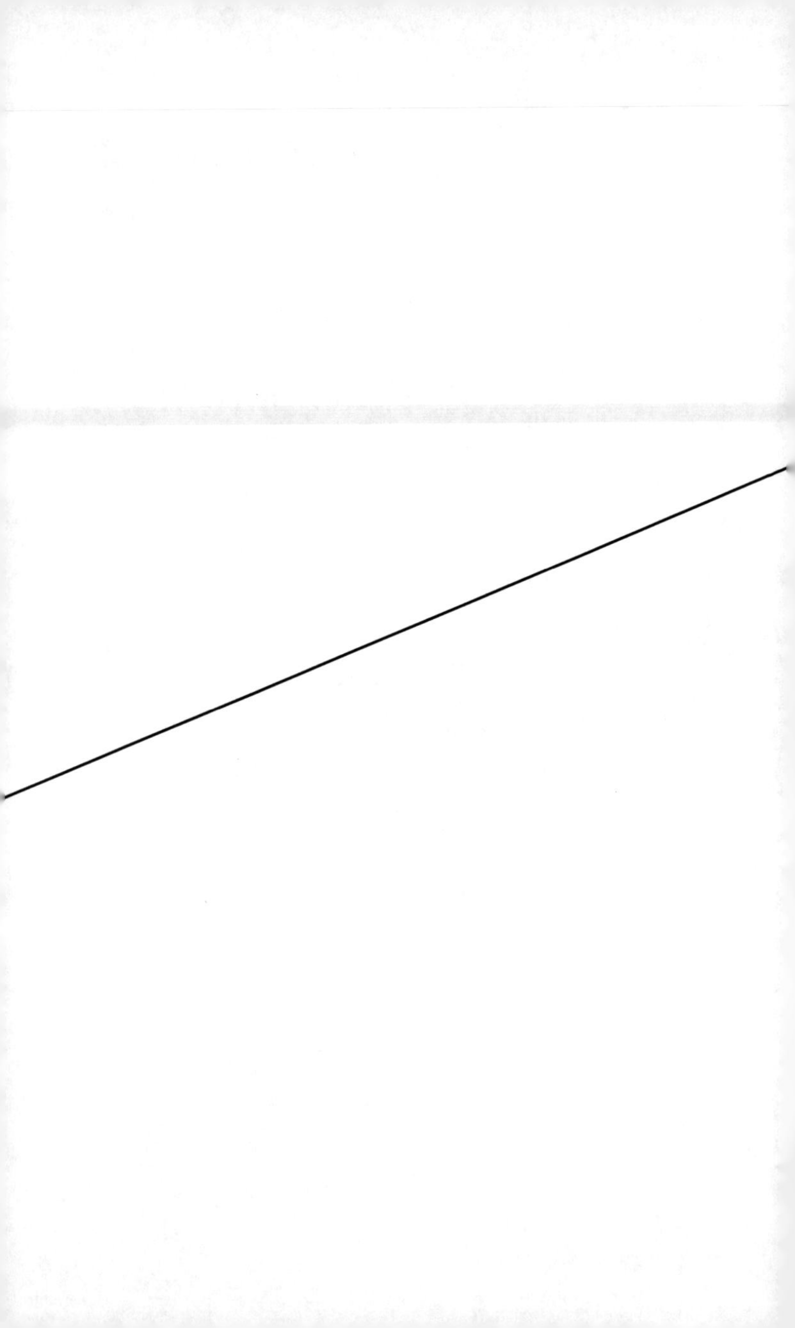

PART I: HUMAN

Inhumanism is the extended practical elaboration of humanism; it is born of a diligent commitment to the project of enlightened humanism. A universal wave that erases the self-portrait of man drawn in sand, inhumanism is a vector of revision. It relentlessly revises what it means to be human by removing its supposedly self-evident characteristics while preserving certain invariancies. At the same time, inhumanism registers itself as a demand for construction: it demands that we define what it means to be human by treating the human as a constructible hypothesis, a space of navigation and intervention.[1]

Inhumanism stands in concrete opposition to any paradigm that seeks to degrade humanity either by confronting it with its finitude, or by abasing it before the backdrop of the great outdoors. Its labor consists partly in decanting the significance of the human from any predetermined meaning or particular import established by theology—thereby extricating the acknowledgement of human significance from any veneration of the human that comes about when this significance is attributed to some variety of theological jurisdiction (God, ineffable genericity, foundationalist axiom, etc.).[2]

---

1. Throughout this text we emphasize that the human is a singular universal which makes sense of its mode of being by inhabiting collectivizing or universalizing processes. The human is human not merely by virtue of its being a species, but rather by virtue of being a generic subject or a commoner in front of what brings about its singularity and universality. Accordingly, the human, as Jean-Paul Sartre points out, is universal by virtue of the singular universality of human history, and it is also singular by virtue of the universalizing singularity of the projects it undertakes.

2. A particularly elegant and incisive argument in defense of human significance as conditioned by the neurobiological situation of subjectivity instead of God or religion has been presented by Michael Ferrer. To great consequence, Ferrer demonstrates that such an enlightened and nonconflated revisitation of human significance undermines both theologically licensed veneration, and the deflationary attitude championed by many strains of the disenchantment project and its speculative offshoots.

Once the conflated and the honorific meaning of man is replaced by a real content, minimalist yet functionally consequential, the humiliatory credo of antihumanism that subsists on a theologically-anchored conflation between significance and veneration also loses its deflationary momentum. Incapable of salvaging its pertinence without resorting to a concept of crisis occasioned by theology, and unsuccessful in extracting human significance by disentangling the pathological conflation between real import and glorification, antihumanism is revealed to be in the same theological boat that it is so determined to set on fire.

Failing to single out significance according to the physics that posits it rather than the metaphysics that inflates it, antihumanism's only solution for overcoming the purported crisis of meaning consists in adopting the cultural heterogeneity of false alternatives (the ever increasing options of post-, communitarian retreats as so-called alternatives to totality, and so forth). Rooted in an originary conflation that was never resolved, such alternatives perpetually swing between bipolar extremes—inflationary and deflationary, enchanting and disenchanting —creating a fog of liberty that suffocates any universalist ambition and hinders the methodological collaboration required to define and achieve a common task for breaking out of the current planetary morass.

In short, the net surfeit of false alternatives supplied under the rubric of liberal freedom causes a terminal deficit of real alternatives, establishing for thought and action the axiom that there is indeed no alternative. The contention of this essay is that universality and collectivism cannot be thought, let alone attained, through consensus or dissensus between cultural tropes, but only by intercepting and rooting out what gives rise to the economy of false choices and by activating and fully elaborating what real human significance consists in. As will be argued, the truth of human significance—not in the sense of an original meaning or a birthright, but in the sense of a labor that consists of the extended elaboration of what it means to be human through a series of upgradable special performances—is rigorously inhuman.

The force of inhumanism operates as a retroactive deterrence against antihumanism by understanding humanity historically—in the broadest physico-biological and socioeconomical sense of history—as an indispensable runway toward itself.

But what is humanism? What specific commitment does 'being human' represent, and how does the full practical elaboration of this commitment amount to inhumanism? In other words, what is it in the human that shapes the inhuman once it is developed in terms of its entitlements and consequences? In order to answer these questions, first we must define what it means to be human and exactly what commitment 'being human' endorses. Then we must analyze the structure of this commitment in order to grasp how undertaking such a commitment—in the sense of practicing it—entails inhumanism.

1. COMMITMENT AS EXTENDED AND MULTIMODAL ELABORATION

A commitment only makes sense by virtue of its pragmatic content (meaning through use) and its demand that one adopt an interventive attitude. That is to say, an attitude that seeks to elaborate the content of a commitment, and then update that commitment according to the ramifications or collateral commitments that are made explicit in the course of that elaboration. In short, a commitment—whether assertional, inferential, practical, or cognitive—can neither be examined nor properly undertaken without the process of updating the commitment and unpacking its consequences through a full range of multimodal practices. So humanism is indeed a commitment to humanity, but comprehending this requires that we examine what a commitment is, what the human is, and what their combination entails.

This means that the analysis of the structure and laws of commitment-making and the meaning of being human in a pragmatic sense (i.e., not by resorting to an inherent conception of meaning hidden in nature or a predetermined idea of man) is a necessary initial step before entering the domain of making prescriptions (whether social, political, or ethical). What needs to be explicated firstly is what it takes to make a prescription, or what one needs to do in order to count as prescribing an obligation or a duty, as linking duties and revising them. But it must also be recognized that a prescription should correspond to a set of descriptions which at all times must be synchronized with the system of modern knowledge as that which yields and modifies descriptions. To put it succinctly: description without prescription is the germ of resignation, and prescription without description is mere whim.

Correspondingly, this is an attempt to understand the organization of prescription, or what making a prescription for and by the human entails. Without such an understanding, prescriptive norms cannot be adequately distinguished from descriptive norms (i.e., there can be no prescriptions), nor can proper prescriptions be constructed without degenerating into the vacuity of prescriptions devoid of descriptions.

The description of the content of the human is impossible unless we elaborate it in the context of use and practices, this elaboration itself is impossible unless we follow minimally prescriptive laws of commitment-making, inference, and judgment. Describing the human without turning to an account of foundational descriptions or some a priori access to descriptive resources is already a minimally but functionally hegemonic prescriptive project that adheres to oughts of specification and elaboration of the meaning of being human through features and requirements of its use. 'Fraught with oughts' (Wilfrid Sellars), humanism cannot be regarded as a claim about the human that can simply be professed once, subsequently turned into a foundation or axiom, and the whole matter concluded. Inhumanism is a nomenclature for the infeasibility of this one-time profession. It is a figure for the impossibility of ever putting the matter to rest once and for all.

To be human is a mark of a distinction between, on the one hand, the relation between mindedness and behavior through the intervention of discursive intentionality, and on the other hand, the relation between sentient intelligence and behavior in the absence of such mediation. It is a distinction between sentience as a strongly biological and natural category and sapience as a rational (not to be confused with logical) subject. The latter is a normative designation which is specified by entitlements and concurrent responsibilities. It is important to note that the distinction between sapience and sentience is a functional demarcation rather than a structural one. Therefore, it is still fully historical and open to naturalization, while at the same time being distinguished by its specific functional organization, its upgradable set of abilities and responsibilities, its cognitive and practical demands. The relation between sentience and sapience can be understood as a continuum that is not differentiable everywhere. While such a complex continuity might allow the naturalization of normative obligations at the level of sapience—their explanation in terms of naturalistic causes—it does not permit certain conceptual and descriptive resources specific to sapience (such as the particular level of mindedness, responsibilities, and, accordingly, normative entitlements) to be extended to sentience and beyond.

The rational demarcation lies in the difference between being capable of acknowledging a law and simply being bound by a law, between understanding and mere reliable responsiveness to stimuli. It lies in the difference between stabilized communication through concepts (as made possible by the communal space of language and symbolic forms) and chaotically unstable or transient types of response or communication (such as complex reactions triggered purely by biological states and organic requirements, or group calls and alerts among social animals). Without such stabilization of communication through the concepts and modes of inference involved in conception, both the cultural evolution and the conceptual accumulation and refinement required for the evolution of knowledge as a shared enterprise would be impossible.[3]

Ultimately, the necessary content as well as the real possibility of the human rests on the ability of sapience—as functionally distinct from sentience—to practice inference and to approach non-canonical truth by entering the deontic game of giving and asking for reasons. Reason is a game solely in the sense of involving error-tolerant, rule-based practices conducted in the absence of a referee, in which taking-as-true through thinking (the mark of a believer) and making-true through acting (the mark of an agent) are constantly contrasted, gauged, and calibrated. It is a dynamic feedback loop in which the expansion of one frontier—either taking-as-true or making-true, understanding or action—provides the other with new alternatives and opportunities for diversifying its space and pushing back its boundaries according to its own specifications and requirements.

---

3. 'Multi-person epistemic dynamics can only work profitably if the stability of shared knowledge and the input-connection of this knowledge (its "realism") are granted. If not, a system of knowledge, although cognitively possible, cannot be socially enacted and culturally elaborated. As in complex social networks Darwinian selection operates at the level of social entities (which survive or disappear), only species, which have solved this problem, can exploit the benefits of a higher level of cognition. The question is therefore: How does language, or do other symbolic forms contribute to the evolution of social awareness, social consciousness, social cognition?' W. Wildgen, *The Evolution of Human Language: Scenarios, Principles, and Cultural Dynamics* (Philadelphia: John Benjamins, 2004), 40.

2. A DISCURSIVE AND CONSTRUCTIBLE 'WE'

What combines both the ability to infer and the ability to approach truth (i.e., truth in the sense of *making sense of* taking-as-true and making-true, separately and in conjunction with one another) is the capacity to engage in discursive practices as described by pragmatism: the ability to (1) deploy a vocabulary, (2) use a vocabulary to specify a set of abilities or practices, (3) elaborate one set of abilities-or-practices in terms of another set of abilities-or-practices, and (4) use one vocabulary to characterize another.[4]

Discursive practices constitute the game of giving and asking for reasons and outlining the space of reason as a landscape of navigation rather than as an *a priori* access to explicit norms. This is an inferentialist, procedural and non-codified account of reason as an expanding armamentarium of rule-governed but also error-tolerant and revisable practices. The capacity to engage in discursive practices is what functionally distinguishes sapience from sentience. Without such a capacity, being human is only a biological fact that does not by itself yield any propositional contentfulness of the kind that demands a special form of conduct and value attribution and appraisal. Without an acknowledgement of this key aspect, to speak about the history of the human risks reducing social construction to biological supervenience, while depriving history of any possibility of intervention and reorientation.

In other words, if deprived of the capacity to enter the space of reason through discursive practices, being human is barred from meaning anything in the sense of suggesting some pertinent relation between practice and content. Action is reduced to meaning 'just do something', collectivity can never be methodological or expressed in terms of a synthesis of different abilities to envision

4. See R. Brandom, *Between Saying and Doing: Towards an Analytic Pragmatism* (Oxford: Oxford University Press, 2008).

and achieve a common task, and making commitments through linking action and understanding is untenable. We might just as well replace 'human' with whatever we wish so as to construct a stuff-oriented philosophy and a nonhuman ethics where 'to be a thing' simply warrants being good to each other, or to vegetables for that matter.

Once discursive practices that map out the space of reason are underplayed or dispensed with, everything lapses either toward the individual or toward a noumenal alterity where a contentless plurality, shorn of any demand or duty, can be effortlessly maintained. Discursive practices, which are rooted in language-use and tool-use, generate a deprivatized but nonetheless stabilizing and contextualizing space through which true collectivizing processes are shaped. It is the space of reason that harbors the functional kernel of genuine collectivity, a collaborative project of practical freedom referred to as 'we' whose boundaries are not only negotiable but also constructible and synthetic.

It should be recalled that 'we' is a mode of being, and a mode of being is not an ontological given or a domain exclusive to a set of fundamental categories or fixed descriptions. It is a conduct, a special performance that takes shape as it is made visible to others. Precluding this explicit and discursively mobilizable 'we', the content of 'being human' never translates into 'commitment to the human/humanity'. By undergirding 'we', discursive practices organize commitments as ramifying trajectories between communal saying and doing, and they enact a space where the self-construction or extensive practical elaboration of humanity is a collaborative project.

Making a commitment to something means vacillating between doing something in order to count as saying it, and saying something specific in order to express and characterize that doing. It is the movement back and forth, the feedback loop, between the two fields of claims and actions that defines sapience as differentiated from sentience.[5] To make a commitment means asking 'what else', being attentive to what other commitments it brings forth, and how such consequent commitments demand new modes of action and understanding, new abilities and special performances that are not simply interchangeable with old abilities, because they are dictated by revised or more complex sets of demands and entitlements. Without this ramification of the 'what else' of a commitment through its practical elaboration, without navigating what Robert Brandom calls the rational system of commitments,[6] a commitment has neither sufficient content nor a real possibility of assessment or development. It is an utterance that is as good as empty—that is, an utterance devoid of content or significance despite its earnest aspiration to be committed.

3. INTERVENTION AS CONSTRUCTION AND REVISION

Now we can turn this argument regarding the exigencies of making a commitment into an argument about the exigencies of being a human, insofar as humanism is a system of practical and cognitive commitments to the concept of humanity. The argument goes as follows: In order to commit to humanity, the content of humanity must be scrutinized. To scrutinize this content, its implicit commitments must be elaborated. But this task is impossible unless we take humanity-as-a-commitment to its ultimate conclusion—by asking what else being a human entails, by unfolding the other commitments and ramifications it brings about.

5. It should be noted that the sapient is also sentient, yet it is functionally distinguished from its sentient constitution. It is this functional differentiation that makes the sentience of the human different from other forms of sentience. To put it differently, the sapient is endowed with the functional ability to reconstitute its sentience qua constitution.

6. Brandom, *Between Saying and Doing*.

But since the content of humanity is distinguished by the human's capacity to engage with rational norms rather than natural laws (*ought* instead of *is*), the concept of entailment for humanity-as-a-commitment is non-monotonic. That is to say, when we ask what being human entails, this entailment is no longer a matter of a cause and its differential effect, as in physical natural laws or deductive logical consequences. Instead, it expresses enablement and abductive non-monotonicity, in the sense of a manipulable, experimental, and synthetic form of inference whose consequences are not straightforwardly or linearly dictated by its premises or initial conditions.[7] Since non-monotonicity is an inherent aspect of practice and complex heuristics, defining the human through practical elaboration means that the product of elaboration does not correspond with what the human anticipates or with the image it has of itself. In other words, the result of an abductive inference that synthetically manipulates parameters—the result of practice as a non-monotonic procedure—will be radically revisionary with regard to our assumptions and expectations about what 'we' is and what it entails.

---

7. Abductive inference, or abduction, was first expounded by Charles Sanders Peirce as a form of creative guessing or hypothetical inference which uses a multimodal and synthetic form of reasoning to dynamically expand its capacities. While abductive inference is divided into different types, all are non-monotonic, dynamic, and non-formal. They also involve construction and manipulation, the deployment of complex heuristic strategies, and non-explanatory forms of hypothesis generation. Abductive reasoning is an essential part of the logic of discovery, epistemic encounters with anomalies and dynamic systems, creative experimentation, and action and understanding in situations where both material resources and epistemic cues are limited or need to be kept to a minimum. For a comprehensive examination of abduction and its practical and epistemic capacities, see L. Magnani, *Abductive Cognition: The Epistemological and Eco-Cognitive Dimensions of Hypothetical Reasoning* (Berlin: Springer, 2009).

The non-monotonic and abductive characteristics of robust social practices that form and undergird the space of reason turn reasoning and the interventive attitude that it promotes into ongoing processes. Indeed, reason as rooted in social practices is not necessarily directed toward a conclusion, nor does it seek to establish agreements through the kind of substantive and quasi-instrumentalist account of reason proposed by the likes of Jürgen Habermas.[8] Reason's main objective is to maintain and enhance itself. And it is the self-actualization of reason that coincides with the truth of the inhuman. Here reason must be understood not as a rigid or immutable thing but as an evolving space that reconstitutes itself through revisable rules which simultaneously preserve ignorance and mitigate it (cf. abductive non-monotonicity).

The unpacking of the content of commitment to humanity, the examination of what else humanity entitles us to, is impossible unless we develop a certain interventive attitude that involves the simultaneous assessment (or consumption) and construction (or production) of norms. Only this interventive attitude toward the concept of humanity is able to extract and unpack the implicit commitments of being a human. And it is this interventive attitude that counts as an enabling vector, making possible certain abilities otherwise hidden or deemed impossible.

It is through the consumption and production of norms that the content of a commitment to humanity can be grasped, in the sense of both assessment and making explicit the implicit commitments that it entitles us to. Accordingly, to understand the commitment to humanity and to make such a commitment, it is imperative to assume a constructive and revisionary stance with regard to the human. This is the interventive attitude mentioned above.

---

8. See A.S. Laden, *Reasoning: A Social Picture* (Oxford: Oxford University Press, 2012).

Revising and constructing the human is the very definition of committing to humanity. Absent this perpetual revision and construction, the 'commitment' part of 'committing to humanity' does not make sense at all. But also, insofar as humanity cannot be defined without locating it within the space of reasons (the sapience argument), committing to humanity is tantamount to complying with the revisionary vector of reason and constructing humanity according to an autonomous account of reason.

Humanity is not simply a given fact that is behind us. It is a commitment in which the threads of reassessment and construction which are inherent to making a commitment and complying with reason are intertwined. In a nutshell, to be human is a struggle. The aim of this struggle is to respond to the demands of constructing and revising the human through the space of reasons.

This struggle is characterized as developing a certain conduct or error-tolerant deportment according to the functional autonomy of reason—an interventive attitude whose aim is to unlock new abilities of saying and doing. In other words, it is to open up new frontiers of action and understanding through various modes of construction and practices (social, technological...).

4. KITSCH MARXISM

If committing to being human is a struggle to construct and revise, today's humanism is for the most part a hollow enterprise that neither does what it says nor says what it does. Sociopolitical philosophies seeking to safeguard the dignity of humanity against the onslaught of politico-economic leviathans end up joining them from the other side.

By virtue of its refusal to recognize the autonomy of reason and to systematically invest in an interventive—that is, revisionary and constructive—attitude toward the human and toward the norms implicit in social practices, what introduces itself as contemporary Marxism for the most part fails to produce norms of action and understanding. In effect, it subtracts itself from the future of humanity.

Only through the construction of what it means to be human can norms of committing to humanity be produced. Only by revising existing norms through norms that have been produced is it possible to assess norms and above all evaluate what it means to be human. Again, these norms should be distinguished from social conventions. Nor should these norms be confused with natural laws (they are not laws, they are conceptions of laws, hence they are error-tolerant and open to revision). The production or construction of norms prompts the consumption or assessment of norms, which in turn leads to a demand for the production of newer abilities and more complex normative attitudes.

One cannot assess norms without producing them. The same can be said about assessing the situation of humanity, the status of the commitment to be human: humanity cannot be assessed in any context or situation unless an interventive, constructive attitude toward it is developed. But to develop this constructive attitude toward the human means to emphatically revise what it means to be human.

A dedication to a project of militant negativity and an abandonment of the ambition to develop an interventive and constructive attitude toward the human through various social and technological practices is now the hallmark of kitsch marxism. While not all of marxism should be tarred with the brush of kitsch marxism, especially since class struggle as a central tenet of marxism is an indispensable historical project, at this point the claim of being a marxist is too generic. It is like saying, 'I am an animal'. It does not serve any theoretical or practical purpose.

Any Marxist agenda should be assessed by determining whether it has the power to elaborate its commitments, whether it understands the underlying mechanisms involved in making a commitment, and above all, whether it possesses a program for globally updating its commitments. Once practical negativity is valorized and the interventive attitude or the constructive deportment is dismissed, the assessment of humanity and its situations becomes fundamentally problematic on the following levels.

Without the constructive vector, the project of evaluation—critique—is transformed into a merely consumerist attitude toward norms. Consumption of norms without producing any is the concrete reality of today's Marxist critical theory. For every claim, there exists a prepackaged set of 'critical reflexes'.[9] One makes a claim in favor of the force of better reason. The Kitsch Marxist says: Who decides? One says, construction through structural and functional hierarchies. The Kitsch Marxist responds: Control. One says, normative control. The Kitsch Marxist reminds us of authoritarianism. We say 'us'. The Kitsch Marxist recites: Who is 'us'? The impulsive responsiveness of kitsch Marxism cannot even be identified as a cynical attitude, because it lacks the rigor of cynicism. It is a mechanized knee-jerk reactionism that is the genuine expression of norm consumerism without the concrete commitment to producing any norms. Norm consumerism is another name for cognitive servitude and noetic sloth.

The response of kitsch Marxism to humanity is also problematic on the level of revision. Ceasing to produce norms by refusing to undertake a constructive attitude toward the human, in the sense of a deportment governed by the functional autonomy of reason, means ceasing to revise what it means to be human. Why? Because norms are assessed and revised by newer norms that are produced through various modes of construction, complex social practices, and the unlocking of new abilities for going

---

9. Thanks to Peter Wolfendale for the term 'critical reflexes' as an expression of prepackaged theoretical biases used to preempt the demands of thought in the name of critical thought.

back and forth between saying and doing. Since the human is distinguished by its capacity to enter the game of giving and asking for reasons, the construction of the human ought to be in the direction of further singling out the space of reason through which the human differentiates itself from the nonhuman, sapience from sentience.

By transforming the ethos of construction according to the demands of reason into the pathos of negativity, not only does kitsch Marxism put an end to the project of revision; it also banks on a concept of humanity outside of the space of reason—even though reason's revisionary force is the only authorized force for renegotiating and defining humanity. Once revision is brought to an end, understanding humanity and acting upon its situations has no significance, since what is deemed to be human no longer enjoys any pertinence.[10] Similarly, once the image of humanity is sought outside of reason, it is only a matter of time before the deontological distinction between sapience and sentience collapses and telltale signs of irrationalism—frivolity, narcissism, superstition, speculative enthusiasm, social atavism, and ultimately, tyranny—heave forth.

Therefore, the first question one needs to ask a humanist or a Marxist is: Are your commitments up to date? If yes, then they must be subjected to a deontic trial—some version of Robert Brandom's deontic scorekeeping or Jean-Yves Girard's deontic ordeal, where commitments can be reviewed on the basis of their connectivity, their evasion of vicious circles and internal

---

10. It is no secret that the bulk of contemporary sociopolitical prescriptions are based on a conception of humanity that has failed to synchronize itself with modern science or take into account social and organizational alterations effected by technological forces.

contradictions, and their evaluation on the basis of recusal rather than refutation.[11]

If commitment to humanity is identified with active revision and construction, ceasing to revise and refusing to construct characterize a form of irrationalism that is determined to cancel out what it means to be human. It is in this sense that kitsch Marxism is not just a theoretical incompetency. It is also—from both a historical and cognitive standpoint—an impulse to regress from sapience back to sentience.

To this extent, it is not an exaggeration to say that within every kitsch Marxist agenda lies dormant the germ of hostility to humanity and the humanist project. Practical negativity refuses to be a resignation, but it also refuses to contribute to the system and develop a systematic attitude toward the affirmative stance 'implicit' in the construction of the system.

Humanism is distinguished by the implicitly affirmative attitude of construction. Insofar as kitsch-Marxist resignation implies an abandonment of the project of humanism and a collapse into regressive passivity, we can say that kitsch Marxism's refusal to both resign and to construct is tantamount to a position that is neither passive nor humanist. Indeed, this 'neither/nor' approach signifies nothing but a project of active antihumanism that kitsch Marxism is in reality committed to—despite its pretensions to a commitment to the human.

---

11. Here the concept of recusal is a navigational and procedural equivalent of negation in an expanding—or more precisely, branching—system of commitments. Whereas refutation instantly rules out contradiction, recusal is a form of proceeding in a network of commitments according to the commitment's own ramifications (viz. its tolerance for revision or updating). Similar to court proceedings on the basis of an objection being sustained or overruled, a logical recusal permits or obstructs the navigation on a ramified commitment path based on a deontic standpoint. For further details on the difference between refutation and recusal see, J.-Y. Girard, 'Geometry of Interaction VI: a Blueprint for Transcendental Syntax', 2013, <http://iml.univ-mrs.fr/~girard/blueprint.pdf>.

It is in the wake of this antihumanism, this hostility toward the ramifications of committing to the human, that the identification of kitsch Marxist agendas with humanism appears at best as a farce, and at worst as a critical Ponzi scheme for devoted humanists.

In its mission to link the commitment to humanism to complex abilities and commitments, inhumanism appears as a force that stands against both the apathy of resignation and the active antihumanism implicit in the practical negativity of the fashionable stance of kitsch Marxism today. Inhumanism, as will be argued below, is both the extended elaboration of the ramifications of making a commitment to humanity, and the practical elaboration of the content of the human as provided by reason and the sapient's capacity to functionally distinguish itself and engage in discursive social practices.

PART II: THE INHUMAN

Enlightened humanism—as a project of *commitment to humanity* in the entangled sense of what it means to be human and what it means to make a commitment—is a rational project. It is rational not only because it locates the meaning of the human in the space of reasons as a specific horizon of practices, but also, and more importantly, because the concept of commitment it adheres to cannot be thought or practiced as a voluntaristic impulse free of ramifications and growing obligations. Instead, this is commitment as a rational system for navigating the collateral commitments—their ramifications as well as their specific entitlements—that result from making an initial commitment.

Interaction with the rational system of commitments follows a navigational paradigm in which the ramifications of an initial commitment must be compulsively elaborated and navigated in order for it to make sense as an undertaking. It is the examination of the rational fallout of making a commitment, the unpacking of its far-reaching consequences and the treatment of these ramifications as paths to be explored, that shapes commitment to humanity as a navigational project. Here navigation is not only a survey of a landscape whose full scope is not given; it is also an exercise in the non-monotonic procedures of steering, plotting out routes, suspending navigational preconceptions, rejecting or resolving incompatible commitments, exploring the space of possibilities, and understanding each path as a hypothesis to new paths or lack thereof, transits as well as obstructions.

From a rational perspective, a commitment is seen as a cascade of ramifying paths that is in the process of expanding its frontiers, developing into an evolving landscape, unmooring its fixed perspectives, deracinating any form of rootedness associated with a fixed commitment or immutable responsibilities, revising links and addresses between its old and new commitments, and finally, erasing any image of itself as 'what it was supposed to be'.

To place the meaning of the human in the rational system of commitments is to submit the presumed stability of this meaning to the perturbing and transformative power of a landscape undergoing comprehensive changes under the revisionary thrust of its ramifying destinations. By situating itself within the rational system of commitments, humanism posits itself as an initial condition for what already retroactively bears little if any resemblance to what originally set it in motion. Sufficiently elaborated, humanism, we shall argue, is the initial condition of inhumanism as a force that travels back from the future to alter, if not completely discontinue, the command of its origin—that is, as a future that writes its own past.

5. THE PICTURE OF 'US' DRAWN IN SAND

The practical elaboration of making a commitment to humanity is inhumanism. If making a commitment means fully elaborating the content of such a commitment (the consequent 'what else?'

of what it means to be human), and if to be human means being able to enter the space of reason, then a commitment to humanity must fully elaborate how the abilities of reason functionally convert sentience to sapience.

But insofar as reason enjoys a functional autonomy—which enables it to prevent the collapse of sapience back into sentience—the full elaboration of the abilities of reason entails unpacking the consequences of the autonomy of reason for the human. Humanism is by definition a project to amplify the space of reason by elaborating what the autonomy of reason entails and what demands it makes upon us. But the autonomy of reason implies its autonomy to assess and construct itself, and by extension to renegotiate and construct that which distinguishes itself by entering the space of reason. In other words, the materialization of the self-cultivation of reason which is the emblem of its functional autonomy has staggering consequences for humanity. What reason does to itself inevitably becomes manifest as what it does to the human.

Since the functional autonomy of reason implies the self-determination of reason with regard to its own conduct—insofar as reason cannot be assessed or revised by anything other than itself (to avoid equivocation or superstition)—commitment to such autonomy effectively exposes what it means to be human to the sweeping revisionary effect of reason. In a sense, the autonomy of reason is the autonomy of its power to revise; and commitment to the autonomy of reason (via the project of humanism) is a commitment to the autonomy of reason's revisionary program *over which the human has no hold.*

Inhumanism is exactly the activation of the revisionary program of reason against the self-portrait of humanity. Once the structure and the function of commitment are genuinely understood, we see that a commitment works its way back from the future, from the collateral commitments of one's current commitment, like a corrosive revisionary acid that rushes backwards in time. By eroding the anchoring link between present commitments and their past, and by seeing present commitments from the perspective of their ramifications, revision forces the updating of present commitments in a cascading fashion that globally spreads over the entire system. The rational structure of a commitment, here specifically the 'commitment to humanity', constructs the opportunities of the present by cultivating the positive trends of the past through the revisionary forces of the future. As soon as you commit to the human, you effectively start erasing its canonical portrait back from the future. It is, as Foucault suggests, the unyielding wager on the fact that the self-portrait of man will be erased, like a face drawn in sand at the edge of the sea.[12] Every portrait drawn is washed away by the revisionary power of reason, giving way to more subtle portraits with so few canonical traits that one may well ask whether it is worthwhile or useful to call what is left behind 'human' at all.

Inhumanism is the labor of rational agency on the human. But there is one caveat here: rational agency is not personal, individual or even necessarily biological. The kernel of inhumanism is a commitment to humanity via the concurrent construction and revision of the human as oriented and regulated by the autonomy of reason, i.e., its self-determination and responsibility for its own needs. In the space of reason, construction entails revision, and revision demands construction. The revision of the alleged portrait of the human implies that the construction of the human in whatever context can be exercised without recourse to a constitutive foundation, a fundamental identity, an immaculate nature, a given meaning or a prior state. In short, revision is a license for further construction.

---

12. See M. Foucault, *The Order of Things: An Archaeology of Human Sciences* (New York: Vintage Books, 1970), 387.

6. WHEN WE LOST CONTACT WITH 'WHAT IS BECOMING OF US'

Whereas, as Michael Ferrer points out, antihumanism is devoted to the unfeasible task of deflating the conflation of human significance with human veneration, inhumanism is a project that begins by dissociating human significance from human glory.[13] Resolving the content of conflation and refining significance from its honorific residues, inhumanism then takes humanism to its ultimate conclusions by constructing a revisable picture of us that functionally breaks free from our expectations and historical biases as to what this image should be, should look like or should mean. For this reason, inhumanism, as will be argued below, prompts a new phase in the systematic project of emancipation—not as a successor to other forms of emancipation but as a critically urgent and indispensable addition to the growing chain of obligations.

Moreover, inhumanism disrupts an anticipation of the future built on descriptions and prescriptions derived from a conservative humanism. Conservative humanism places the consequentiality of the human in an overdetermined meaning or an over-particularized set of descriptions which is fixed and which any prescription developed by and for humans must preserve at all costs. Inhumanism, on the other hand, locates the consequentiality of commitment to humanity in its practical elaboration and in the navigation of its ramifications. For the true consequentiality of a commitment is a matter of its power to generate further commitments, to update itself in accordance with its ramifications, to open up spaces of possibilities and to navigate the revisionary and constructive import such possibilities may contain.

The consequentiality of commitment to humanity, accordingly, does not lie in how the parameters of this commitment are initially

13. Personal communication..

described or set. It lies in how the pragmatic meaning of this commitment (meaning through use) and the functionalist sense of its descriptions (what must we do in order to count as human?) intertwine to effectuate the broadest types of consequences irreconcilable with what initially was the case. It is consequentiality in the latter sense that overshadows consequentiality in the former sense, and goes on to fully prove the former's descriptive poverty and prescriptive inconsequentiality through a thoroughgoing revision.

Since, as Robert Brandom notes, 'every consequence is a change in normative status' that may lead to incompatibilities between commitments,[14] in order to maintain the undertaking we are obliged to do something specific to resolve the incompatibilities. From the perspective of inhumanism, the more discontinuous the consequences of committing to humanity, the further the demands of doing something (something ethical, legal, economic, political, technological, etc.) to rectify our undertakings. Inhumanism highlights the urgency of action according to a tide of revision that increasingly registers itself as a discontinuity, as a growing rift with no possibility of restoration.

Any socio-political endeavor or consequential project of change must first address this rift or discontinuity effect, and then devise a necessary course of action in accordance with it. But doing something about the discontinuity effect—triggered by unanticipated consequences and the resulting exponentially growing change in normative status (demands of what ought to be done)—is not tantamount to an act of restoration. On the contrary, the task is to construct points of liaison—cognitive and practical channels—so as to enable communication between *what we think of ourselves* and *what is becoming of us*.

14. Brandom, *Between Saying and Doing*, 191.

The ability to recognize the latter is not a given right or an inherent natural aptitude, it is in fact a matter of a labor, a program—one that is fundamentally lacking in current political projects. Being human does not by any means entail the ability to connect with the consequences of what it means to be human. In the same vein, identifying ourselves as human is neither a sufficient condition for understanding what is becoming of us, nor a sufficient condition for recognizing what we are becoming, or more accurately, what is being born out of us.

A political endeavor aligned with antihumanism cannot forestall its descent into a grotesque form of activism. But any socio-political project that pledges its allegiance to conservative humanism—whether through a quasi-instrumentalist and preservationist account of reason (such as Habermasian rationality) or a theologically-charged meaning of the human—is enforcing the tyranny of here and now under the aegis of a foundational past or a root.

Antihumanism and conservative humanism represent two pathologies of history that frequently appear under the rubrics of conservation and progression: one an account of a present that must preserve the traits of the past, the other an account of a present that must approach the future while remaining anchored in the past. But the catastrophe of revision dismantles them from the future by modifying the link between past and present, channeling a catastrophic conception of time that expresses the excess of ramifying destiny over its origin.

7. THE REVISIONARY CATASTROPHE

The definition of humanity according to reason is a minimalist definition whose consequences are not immediately given, but whose ramifications are staggering. If there ever was a real crisis, it would be our inability to cope with the consequences of committing to the real content of humanity. The trajectory of reason is that of a general catastrophe whose pointwise instances and stepwise courses have no observable effect or comprehensive discontinuity. Reason is therefore simultaneously a medium of stability that reinforces procedurality and a general catastrophe, a medium of radical change that administers the discontinuous identity of reason to an anticipated image of the human.

Elaborating humanity according to the discursive space of reason establishes a discontinuity between the human's anticipation of itself (what it expects itself to become) and the image of the human modified according to its active content or significance. It is exactly this discontinuity that characterizes inhumanism as the general catastrophe ordained by activating the content of humanity, whose functional kernel is not just autonomous but also compulsive and transformative.

The discernment of humanity requires the activation of the autonomous space of reason. But since this space—qua content of humanity—is functionally autonomous, even though its genesis is historical, its activation implies the deactivation of historical anticipations of what humanity can be or become at a descriptive level. Since antihumanism mostly draws its critical power from this descriptive level, whether situated in nature (allegedly immune to revision) or in a restricted scope of history (based on a particular anticipation), the realization of the autonomy of reason would restore the nontheological significance of the human as an initial necessary condition, thus nullifying the antihumanist critique. What is important to understand here is that one cannot defend or even speak of inhumanism without first committing to the humanist project through the front door of the Enlightenment.

Rationalism as the compulsive navigation of the space of reason turns commitment to humanity into a revisionary catastrophe, by converting its initial commitment into a ramified cascade of collateral commitments which must be navigated in order to for it to be counted as commitment. But it is precisely this conversion instigated and guided by reason that transforms commitment into a revisionary catastrophe that travels backward in time from the future, from its revisionary ramifications, to interfere with the past and rewrite the present. In this sense, reason establishes a link in history hitherto unimaginable from the perspective of a present that preserves an origin or is anchored in the past.

To act in tandem with the revisionary vector of the future is not to redeem but to update and revise, to reconstitute and modify. From the perspective of the cognitive and practical adaptation to the reality of time as a precondition for acting on history, redemption is only a theological curiosity. It stems from a misunderstanding of time, from conflating or trivializing the links between past, present and future, and lastly from a biased endorsement of origin over destination. But the reality of time is not exhausted by the origin or by what has already taken place; instead, it is a destiny that forces one to revise its positions and orientations as it unfolds.

Destiny expresses the reality of time as always in excess of and asymmetrical to the origin; in fact, as catastrophic to it. But destination is not exactly a single point or a terminal goal; it takes shape as trajectories: As soon as a manifest destination is reached or takes place, it ceases to govern the historical trajectory that leads to it, and is replaced by a number of newer destinations which begin to govern different parts of the trajectory, leading to its ramification into multiple trajectories. This is how all vestiges of a terminal goal in history are effectively removed, as the origin is outstripped by a conception of time that appears in the guise of a destiny that is reached by going forward, while in reality it is a destiny that writes itself backwards from multiple destinations in the future.

The constructive-revisionary loop of inhumanism emphasizes that there is no incompatibility between a destinal project and the absence of a terminal goal, between historical self-realization and the emptiness of time. As an activist impulse, redemption operates as a voluntaristic mode of action informed by a preservationist or conservative account of the present. Revision on the other hand is an obligation or a rational compulsion to conform to the revisionary waves of the future stirred up by the functional autonomy of reason.

8. AUTONOMY OF REASON

But what exactly is the functional autonomy of reason? It is the expression of the self-actualizing propensity of reason—a scenario wherein reason liberates its own spaces despite what naturally appears to be necessary or happens to be the case. Here 'necessary' refers to an alleged natural necessity, and is to be distinguished from normative necessity. Whereas the given status of natural causes is defined by 'is' (something that is purportedly the case because it has been contingently posited, such as the atmospheric condition of the planet), the normative of the rational is defined by 'ought to be'. The former communicates a supposedly necessary impulsion, while the latter is not given, but instead generated by explicitly acknowledging a law or a norm implicit in a collective practice, thereby turning it into a binding status, a conceptual compulsion, an ought.

It is the acknowledging, error-tolerant, revisionary dimension of the ought—as opposed to the impulsive diktat of a natural law—that presents the ought as a vector of construction capable of turning contingently posited natural necessities into the manipulable variables required for construction. In addition, the order of ought is capable of composing a functional organization, a chain or dynasty of oughts that procedurally effectuates a cumulative escape from the allegedly necessary '*is*' crystallized in the order of here and now.

The functional autonomy of reason consists in connecting simple oughts to complex oughts or normative necessities or abilities by way of inferential links or processes. A commitment to humanity, and consequently the autonomy of reason, require not only the specification of what oughts or commitment-abilities we are entitled to, but also the developing of new functional links and inferences that connect existing oughts to new oughts or obligations.

Whether Marxist agenda, humanist creed or future-oriented perspective, any political philosophy that boasts of commitments without working out inferential problems and without constructing inferential and functional links, suffers from an internal contradiction and an absence of connectivity between commitments. Without inferential links, there can be no real updating of commitments. Without a global program of updating, it becomes increasingly difficult, if not impossible, to prevent humanism from stagnating into an organ of conservatism and Marxism sliding into a burlesque of critique, a grab-bag of cautionary tales and revolutionary bravado. No matter how sociopolitically adept or determined a political project appears, without a global updating system such an enterprise is blocked by its own internal contradictions from prescribing any obligation or duty.

Indeed, in its commendable attempt to outline 'what ought to be done' in terms of functional organizations, complex hierarchies and positive feedback loops of autonomy, Srnicek and Williams's '#Accelerate' signifies a Marxian project that is in the process of updating its commitments. It should come as no surprise that such an endeavor receives the most derision and scorn from those strains of Marxism which have long since given up on updating their cognitive and practical commitments.

9. FUNCTIONAL AUTONOMY

The claim about the functional autonomy of reason is not a claim about the genetic spontaneity of reason, since reason is historical and revisable, social and rooted in practice. It is really a claim about the autonomy of discursive practices and the autonomy of inferential links between oughts—that is to say, links between constructive abilities and revisionary obligations. Reason has its roots in social construction, in communal assessment, and in the manipulability of conditionals embedded in modes of inference. It is social partly because it is deeply connected to the origin and function of language as a de-privatizing, communal, and stabilizing space of organization. But we should be careful to extract a 'robust' conception of the social, because a generic appeal to social construction risks not only relativism and equivocation, but also, as Paul Boghossian points out, a fear of knowledge.[15] The first movement in the direction of extracting this robust conception of the social consists in making a necessary distinction between the 'implicitly' normative aspect of the social (the area of the consumption and production of norms through practices) and the dimension of the social inhabited by conventions, between norms as interventive attitudes and normalizing norms as conformist dispositions.

Reason begins with an interventive attitude toward norms implicit in social practices. It is neither separated from nature nor isolated from social construction. However, reason has irreducible needs of its own (Kant) and a constitutive self-determination (Hegel), and it can be assessed only by itself (Sellars). In fact, the first task or question of rationalism is to come up with a conception of nature and the social that allows for the autonomy of reason. This question revolves around a causal regime of nature that allows

---

15. See P.A. Boghossian, *Fear of Knowledge: Against Relativism and Constructivism* (Oxford: Oxford University Press, 2006).

for the autonomous performance of reason in 'acknowledging' laws, whether natural or social. Therefore it is important to note that rationality is not conduct in accordance with a law, but rather the acknowledging of a law. Rationality is the 'conception of law' as a portal to the realm of revisable and navigable rules.

We only become rational agents once we acknowledge or develop a certain interventive attitude toward norms that renders them binding. We do not embrace the normative status of things outright. We do not have access to the explicit—that is, logically codified—status of norms. It is through such interventive attitudes toward the revision and construction of norms through social practices that we make the status of norms explicit.[16] Contra Hegel, rationality is not codified by explicit norms from the bottom up. To confuse implicit norms accessible through interventive practices with explicit norms is common and risks logicism or intellectualism, i.e., an account of normativity in which explicit norms constitute an initial condition with rules all the way down—a claim already debunked by Wittgenstein's regress argument.[17]

10. FUNCTIONAL BOOTSTRAPPING AND PRACTICAL DECOMPOSABILITY

The autonomy of reason is a claim about the autonomy of its normative, inferential and revisionary function in the face of the chain of causes that condition it. Ultimately, this is a (neo)functionalist claim, in the sense of a pragmatic or rationalist functionalism. Pragmatic functionalism must be distinguished from both traditional AI-functionalism, which revolves around the symbolic

---

16. See R. Brandom, *Making It Explicit: Reasoning, Representing, and Discursive Commitment* (Cambridge, MA: Harvard University Press, 2001).

17. See L. Wittgenstein, *Philosophical Investigations* (New York: Pearson Education, 1973).

nature of thought, and behavioral variants of functionalism, which rely on behaviors as sets of regularities. While the latter two risk various myths of pancomputationalism (the unconditional omnipresence of computation, the idea that every physical system can implement every computation) or behavioralism, it is important to note that a complete rejection of functionalism in its pragmatic or Kantian rationalist sense will inevitably usher in vitalism and ineffabilism, the mystical dogma according to which there is something essentially special and non-constructible about thought.

Pragmatic functionalism is concerned with the pragmatic nature of human discursive practices—that is, the ability to reason, to go back and forth between saying and doing *stepwise*. Here 'stepwise' defines the constitution of saying and doing, claims and performances, as a condition of near-decomposability. For this reason, pragmatic functionalism focuses on the decomposability of discursive practices into nondiscursive practices (What ought one to do in order to count as reasoning or even thinking?). Unlike symbolic or classical AI, pragmatic functionalism does not decompose implicit practices into explicit—that is, logically codifiable—norms. It is concerned with practical decomposability rather than algorithmic decomposability, non-monotonic procedures rather than monotonic operations. Instead, it decomposes explicit norms into implicit practices, *knowing-that* into *knowing-how* (the domain of abilities endowed with bootstrapping capacities—what must be done in order to count as performing something specific?).

According to pragmatic or rationalist functionalism, the autonomy of reason implies the automation of reason, since the autonomy of practices, which is the marker of sapience, suggests the automation of discursive practices by virtue of their practical decomposability into nondiscursive practices. The automation of discursive practices, or the feedback loop between saying and doing, is the veritable expression of reason's functional autonomy and the telos of the disenchantment project. If thought is able to carry out the disenchanting of nature, it is only the automation of discursive practices that is able to disenchant thought.

Here automation does not imply an identical iteration of processes aimed at effective optimization or strict forms of entailment (monotonicity). It is a register of the functional analysis or practical decomposability of a set of special performances that permits the autonomous bootstrapping of one set of abilities from another set. Accordingly, automation here amounts to practical enablement, or the ability to maintain and enhance functional autonomy or freedom. The pragmatic procedures involved in this mode of automation perpetually diversify the spaces of action and understanding insofar as the non-monotonic character of practices opens up new trajectories of practical organization and correspondingly, expands the realm of practical freedom.

Once the game of reason as a domain of rule-based practices is set in motion, reason is able to bootstrap complex abilities out of its primitive abilities. This is nothing but the self-actualization of reason. Reason liberates its own spaces and its own demands, and in the process fundamentally revises not only what we understand as thinking, but also what we recognize as 'us'. Wherever there is functional autonomy, there is a possibility of self-actualization or self-realization as an epochal development in history. Wherever self-realization is underway, a closed positive feedback loop between freedom and intelligence, self-transformation and self-conception, has been established. The functional autonomy of reason is then a precursor to the self-realization of an intelligence that assembles itself, piece by piece, from the constellation of a discursively elaborative 'us' qua *open source self.*

Rationalist functionalism, therefore, delineates a nonsymbolic—that is, philosophical—project of general intelligence in which intelligence is fully apprehended as a vector of self-realization through the maintaining and enhancing of functional autonomy. Automation of discursive practices—the pragmatic unbinding of artificial general intelligence and the triggering of new modes of collectivizing practices via linking to autonomous discursive practices—exemplifies the revisionary and constructive edge of reason as sharpened against the canonical self-portrait of the human.

To be free one must be a slave to reason. But to be a slave to reason (the very condition of freedom) exposes one to both the revisionary power and the constructive compulsion of reason. This susceptibility is terminally amplified once the commitment to the autonomy of reason and autonomous engagement with discursive practices are sufficiently elaborated. That is to say, when the autonomy of reason is understood as the automation of reason and discursive practices—the philosophical rather than classically symbolic thesis regarding artificial general intelligence.[18]

11. AUGMENTED RATIONALITY

The automation of reason suggests a new phase in the enablement of reason's revisionary cutting edge and constructive vector. This new phase in the enablement of reason signals the exacerbation of the difference between rational compulsion and natural impulsion, between 'ought to' as an interventive obligation and 'is' as conformity to what is supposedly or naturally the case (the contingency of nature, the necessity of foundation, dispositions, conventions, and allegedly necessary limits).

---

18. For an account of the connection between philosophy and artificial intelligence see D. Deutsch, 'Philosophy will be the key that unlocks artificial intelligence', 2012, <http://www.theguardian.com/science/2012/oct/03/philosophy-artificial-intelligence>.

The dynamic sharpening of the difference between 'is' and 'ought' heralds the advent of what should be called an *augmented rationality*. It is augmented not in the sense of being more rational (just as augmented reality is not more real than reality), but in the sense of further radicalizing the distinction between what has been done or has taken place (or is supposedly the case) and what ought to be done. It is only the sharpening of this distinction that is able to augment the demands of reason and, correspondingly, propel rational agency toward new frontiers of action and understanding.

Augmented rationality is the radical exacerbation of the difference between ought and is. It thereby, from a certain perspective, annuls the myth of restoration and erases any hope for reconciliation between being and thinking. Augmented rationality inhabits what Howard Barker calls the 'area of maximum risk'—not risk to humanity per se, but to commitments which have not yet been updated, because they conform to a portrait of human that has not been revised.[19] Understood as the labor of the inhuman, augmented rationality produces a generalized catastrophe for un-updated commitments to the human, through the amplification of the revisionary and constructive dimensions of 'ought'. If reason has a functional evolution of its own, cognitive contumacy against adaptation to the space of reason (the evolution of ought rather than the natural evolution of is) ends in cataclysm.

Adaptation to the evolution of reason—which is the actualization of reason according to its own functional needs—is a matter of updating commitments to the autonomy of reason by way of updating commitments to the human. The updating of commitments is impossible without translating the revisionary

---

19. See H. Barker, *Arguments for a Theater* (Manchester: Manchester University Press, 1997), 52.

and constructive dimensions of reason into systematic projects for the revision and construction of human through communal assessment and methodological collectivism. Even though rationalism represents the systematicity of revision and construction, it cannot by itself institute such systematicity. To rephrase, rationalism is not a substitute for a political project, even though it remains the necessary platform that simultaneously informs and orients any consequential political project.

12. A CULTIVATING PROJECT OF CONSTRUCTION AND REVISION

The automation of reason and discursive practices unlocks new vistas for exercising revision and construction, which is to say, engaging in a systematic project of practical freedom. This is freedom both as the systematicity of knowledge and as knowledge of the system as a prerequisite for acting on the system. In order to act on the system, it is necessary to know the system. But insofar as the system is nothing but a global integration of tendencies and functions, and insofar as it has neither an intrinsic architecture, nor an ultimate foundation, nor an extrinsic limit, it is imperative to treat the system as a constructible hypothesis in order to know it. In other words, the system should be understood by way of abductive synthesis and deductive analysis, methodic construction as well as inferential manipulation of its variables distributed at different levels.

Knowledge of the system is not a general epistemology, but rather, as William Wimsatt emphasizes, an 'engineering epistemology'.[20] Engineering epistemology—a form of understanding that involves the designated manipulation of the causal fabric and the organization of functional hierarchies—is

---

20. W. C. Wimsatt, *Re-Engineering Philosophy for Limited Beings: Piecewise Approximations to Reality* (Cambridge, MA: Harvard University Press, 2007).

an upgradable armamentarium of heuristics that is particularly attentive to the distinct roles and requirements of different levels and hierarchies. It employs lower-level entities and mechanisms to guide and enhance construction on upper levels. It also utilizes upper-level variables and robust processes to correct lower-level structural and functional hierarchies,[21] but also to renormalize their space of possibilities so as to actualize their constructive potentials, yielding the observables and manipulation conditionals necessary for further construction.[22]

Any political project aimed at genuine change must understand and adapt to the logic of nested hierarchies which is the distinctive feature of complex systems.[23] Because change can only be effectuated through both structural modifications and functional transformations across different structural layers and functional levels. Numerous intricacies arise from the distribution of nested structural and functional hierarchies. Sometimes, in order to make change at one level, a structural or functional change at a different seemingly unrelated level must be made. Moreover, what is important is to change functions (whether

---

21. For detailed and technical definitions of processes and mechanisms see J. Seibt, 'Forms of Emergent Interaction in General Process Theory', in *Synthese* 166:3 (Springer, 2009), 479–512; and C. F. Craver, 'Role Functions, Mechanisms and Hierarchy', in *Philosophy of Science* 68:1 (Chicago: University of Chicago Press, 2001), 53–74.

22. Manipulation conditionals are specific forms of general conditionals that express various causal and explanatory combinations of antecedents and consequents (if... then...) in terms of interventions or manipulable hypotheses. For example a simple manipulation conditional would be: If x were to be manipulated under a set of parameters W, it would behave in the manner of y. For a theory of causal and explanatory intervention, see J. Woodward, *Making Things Happen: A Theory of Causal Explanation* (Oxford: Oxford University Press, 2003).

23. For a realist take on complexity see J. Ladyman, J. Lambert, K. Wiesner, 'What is a Complex System?' in *European Journal for Philosophy of Science* 3:1 (Springer, 2013) 33–67. And for more details: R. Badii, A. Politi, *Complexity: Hierarchical Structures and Scaling in Physics* (Cambridge: Cambridge University Press, 1999).

at economic, social or political levels). But not every structural change necessarily leads to a functional change. While every functional change—by virtue of functions playing the role of purpose-attainment and dynamic stabilization for the system—results in a structural change (although such an alteration in structure might not take place in the specific structure whose function has just changed).

The significance of nested hierarchies for the implementation of any form of change on any stratum of our life makes the knowledge of different explanatory levels and cross-level manipulation a necessity of the utmost importance. Such knowledge is yet to be fully incorporated within political projects. Without the knowledge of structural and functional hierarchies any ambition for change—whether through modification, reorganization or local disruption—becomes misled by the conflation between different strata of structure and function on the levels of economy, society and politics. A change that does not resolve explanatory and descriptive, structural and functional conflations ends up reinscribing conflation in the guise of resolution, which is just another complication on a different stratum or in a different region. Therefore, only the explanatory differentiation of levels and cross-level manipulations (complex heuristics) can transform dreams of change into reality.

In a hierarchical scenario, lower-level dimensions open up upper levels to possibility spaces which simultaneously expand the possibility of construction and bring about the possibility of revision. At the same time, descriptive plasticity and stabilized mechanisms of upper-level dimensions adjust and mobilize lower-level constructions and manipulations. Combined together, the abilities of lower-levels and upper-levels form the revisionary-constructive loop of engineering. Bypassing inadequacies of both emergentism and eliminative reductionism, the engineering loop is a perspectival schema and a map of synthesis.

As a map, it distributes both across different levels and as a multitude of covering maps with different descriptive-prescriptive valences over individual strata. The patchwork structure ensures a form of descriptive plasticity and prescriptive versatility, it reduces incoherencies and explanatory conflations and renders the search for problems and opportunities of construction effective by tailoring descriptive and prescriptive covering maps to specific parameters and regions. As a perspectival compass, the engineering loop passes through manifest and scientific images (stereoscopic coherence), assumes a view from above and a view from below (telescopic deepening), and integrates various mesoscales which have their own specific and non-extendable explanatory, descriptive, structural, and functional orders (nontrivial synthesis). The revisionary-constructive loop always institutes engineering as *re-engineering*, a process of re-modification, re-evaluation, re-orientation and re-constitution. It is the cumulative effect of engineering (Wimsatt) that corresponds to the functional and structural accumulation of complex systems,[24] as that corrosive substance that eats away myths of foundation and catalyzes a cumulative escape from contingently posited settings.

The error-tolerant and manipulable dimensions of treating the system as a hypothesis and engineering epistemology are precisely the expressions of revision and construction as the two pivotal functions of freedom. Any commitment that prevents revision and does not maintain—or more importantly, expand—the scope of construction ought to be updated. If it cannot be updated, then it ought to be discarded. Freedom only grows out of functional accumulation and refinement, which are characteristics of hierarchical, nested, and therefore decentralized and complex systems. A functional organization consists of functional hierarchies and correct inferential links between them that permit nontrivial

24. See Wimsatt, *Re-Engineering Philosophy.*

orientation, maintenance, calibration, and enhancement, thereby bringing about opportunities for procedurally turning supposed necessities and fundaments associated with natural causes into manipulable variables of construction.

In a sense, a functional organization can be interpreted as a complex hierarchical system of functional links and functional properties related to both normative and causal functioning. It is able to convert the given order of 'is' into the interventive and enabling order of 'ought', where contingently posited natural limits are replaced by necessary but revisable normative constraints. It is crucial to note that construction proceeds under normative constraints (not natural constraints); and natural determinations (hence, realism) that cannot be taken as foundational limits. Functional hierarchies take on the role of ladders or bootstraps through which one casual fabric is appropriated to another, one normative status is pushed to another level.

This is why it is the figure of the engineer, as the agent of revision and construction, who is public enemy number one of the foundation as that which limits the scope of change and impedes the prospects of a cumulative escape. It is not the advocate of transgression or the militant communitarian who is bent on subtracting himself from the system or flattening the system into a state of horizontality. More importantly, this is also why freedom is not an overnight delivery, whether in the name of spontaneity or the will of people, or in the name of exporting democracy. Liberation is a project, not an idea or a commodity. Its effect is not the irruption of novelty, but rather the continuity of a designated form of labor.

Rather than liberation, the condition of freedom is a piecewise structural and functional accumulation and refinement that takes shape as a project of self-cultivation. Structural and functional accumulation and refinement constitute the proper environment for updating commitments, both through the correcting influence of levels over one another and the constructive propensity inherent in functional hierarchies as engines of enablement.

Liberation is neither the initial spark of freedom nor sufficient as its content. To regard liberation as the source of freedom is an eventalist credulity that has been discredited over and over, insofar as it does not warrant the maintaining and enhancing of freedom. But to identify liberation as the sufficient content of freedom produces a far graver outcome: irrationalism and, as a result, the precipitation of various forms of tyranny and fascism.

The sufficient content of freedom can be found only in reason. One must recognize the difference between a rational norm and a natural law—between the emancipation intrinsic to the explicit acknowledgement of the binding status of complying with reason, and the slavery associated with the deprivation of such a capacity to acknowledge, which is the condition of natural impulsion. In a strict sense, freedom is not liberation from slavery. It is the continuous *unlearning* of slavery.

The compulsion to update commitments and the compulsion to construct cognitive and practical technologies to carry out such feats of commitment-updating are two necessary dimensions of this unlearning procedure. Seen from a constructive and revisionary perspective, *freedom is intelligence.* A commitment to humanity or freedom that does not practically elaborate the meaning of this dictum has already abandoned its commitment and taken humanity hostage only to trudge through history for a day or two.

Liberal freedom, whether it be a social enterprise or an intuitive idea of being free from normative constraints (i.e. a freedom without purpose or designated action), is a freedom that does not translate into intelligence; and for this reason, it is retroactively obsolete. To reconstitute a supposed constitution, to draw a functional link between identifying what is normatively good and making it true, to maintain and enhance the good and to endow the pursuit of the better with its own autonomy—such is the course of freedom. But this is also the definition of intelligence as the self-realization of practical freedom and functional autonomy that liberates itself in spite of its constitution.

Adaptation to an autonomous conception of reason—that is, the updating of commitments according to the progressive self-actualization of reason—is a struggle that coincides with the revisionary and constructive project of freedom. The first expression of such freedom is the establishment of an orientation—a hegemonic pointer—that highlights the synthetic and constructible passage that the human ought to tread. But to tread this path, we must cross the cognitive Rubicon.

Indeed, the interventive attitude demanded by adaptation to a functionally autonomous reason suggests that the cognitive Rubicon has already been crossed. In order to navigate this synthetic path, there is no point in staring back at what once was, but has been dissipated—like all illusory images—by the revisionary winds of reason.[25]

---

25. My thanks to Michael Ferrer, Brian Kuan Wood, Robin Mackay, Benedict Singleton, Peter Wolfendale and many others who either through suggestions or conversations have contributed to this text. Whatever merit this essay might have is due to them, its shortcomings on the other hand are entirely mine.

Prometheanism and its Critics

Ray Brassier

2014

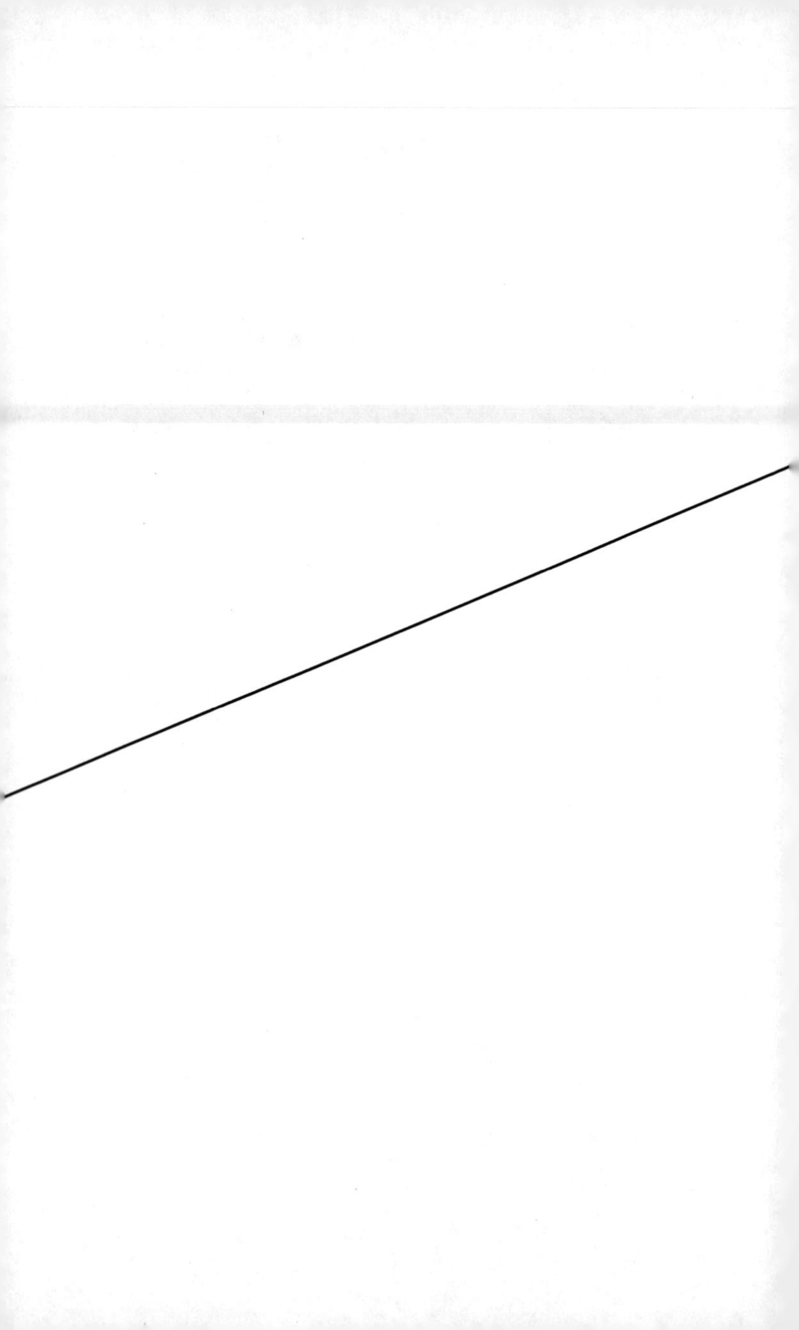

What does it mean to orient oneself towards the future? Is the future worth investing in? In other words, what sort of investment can we collectively have towards the future, not just as individuals but as a species? This comes down to a very simple question: What shall we do with time? We know that time will do something with us, regardless of what we do or don't do. So should we try to do something with time, or even to time? This is also to ask what we should do about the future, and whether it can retain the pre-eminent status accorded to it in the project of modernity. Should we abandon the future? To abandon the future means to relinquish the intellectual project of Enlightenment. And there is no shortage of thinkers urging us to do just that. Its advocates on the Right promise to rehabilitate ancient hierarchies mirroring an allegedly natural or divine order. But this anti-modernism—and the critique of Enlightenment—has also had many influential advocates on the Left throughout the twentieth century. They have insisted that the best we can hope for, via a radical scaling-down of political and cognitive ambition, is to achieve small-scale rectifications of universal injustice by establishing local, temporally fleeting enclaves of civil justice. This scaling down of political ambition by those who espouse the ideals of justice and emancipation is perhaps the most notable consequence of the collapse of communism as a Promethean project. The best we can hope for, apparently, is to create local enclaves of equality and justice. But the idea of *remaking* the world according to the ideals of equality and justice is routinely denounced as a dangerous totalitarian fantasy. These narratives, whether on the left or the right, draw a direct line from post-Galilean rationalism, and its advocacy of the rationalisation of nature, to the evils of totalitarianism.

I want to critically examine some of the presuppositions underlying this philosophical critique of Enlightenment Prometheanism. And I want to propose that the cardinal epistemic virtue of

Enlightenment consists in recognising the *disequilibrium* which time introduces into knowing. Knowing takes time, but time impregnates knowing. In this sense, the rationalist legacy of the Enlightenment affirms the disequilibrium of time. The catastrophic logic that is articulated in the best of J.G. Ballard's narratives is precisely about this cognitive appropriation of disequilibrium, which springs time out of joint, restructuring the linear succession of past, present, and future. To affirm this disequilibrium is to engage in what Hegel called 'tarrying with the negative', which, as Žižek helpfully points out, is the virtue that Hegel ascribes to the understanding, the faculty of opposition, rather than reason, the faculty of conciliation. In other words, it is the understanding, the faculty that dismembers, objectifies and discriminates, which first exercises the power of the negative that will be subsequently consummated by reason. This is indispensible to cognition: before we can presume to overcome an opposition, we first have to be capable of articulating it correctly. It is dialectical myopia simply to oppose reason to understanding, or contradiction to judgment, as though they were separate faculties, holding up the former as 'good' while castigating the latter as 'bad'. Only the understanding could oppose reason to the understanding: dialectics affirms their indissociability.

If disequilibrium is an enabling condition of cognitive progress, then we have to find a way of defending the normative grounds that allow us to make sense of this very assertion. We have to defend the normative status of the claim that *things are not as they should be*, and that things *ought* to be understood and reorganized. And doing this requires that we be able to defend the intelligibility of the question 'What can we make of ourselves?' In this regard, Prometheanism is simply the claim that there is no reason to assume a predetermined limit to what we can achieve or to the ways in which we can transform ourselves and our world. But of course, this is precisely what theological propriety and empiricist good sense jointly denounce as dangerous hubris.

What follows is a sketch outlining the beginning of a project that is going to be devoted to Prometheanism. It is obviously incomplete. All I want to do for now is try to lay out some of the basic problems that I think need to be addressed by any philosophical appraisal of the legacy of Enlightenment. The fundamental questions at the heart of such an appraisal are: What can we make of ourselves? Must we relinquish our ambitions and learn to be modest, as everyone seems to be enjoining us to do?

I want to propose that Prometheanism requires the reassertion of subjectivism, but a subjectivism without selfhood, which articulates an autonomy without voluntarism. The critique of Prometheanism in the philosophical literature of the twentieth century is tied to a critique of metaphysical voluntarism whose most significant representative is Martin Heidegger.

Heidegger's critique of subjectivist voluntarism is echoed by Jean-Pierre Dupuy in his essay 'Some Pitfalls in the Philosophical Foundations of Nanoethics',[1] in which he lays out what he thinks is wrong with debates about human enhancement and so-called transhumanism.[2] The link connecting Dupuy's critique of techno-scientific Prometheanism to Heidegger's critique of subjectivism is Hannah Arendt, who is Dupuy's chief inspiration, and whose thinking is directly indebted to Heidegger. It is this philosophical genealogy that I want to examine.

---

1. *Journal of Medicine and Philosophy* 32 (April 2007), 237–61.

2. Dupuy is notably the author of *On the Origins of Cognitive Science* (Cambridge, MA: MIT Press, 2009), *Pour un catastrophisme éclairé* [*Towards an Enlightened Catastrophism*] (Paris: Seuil, 2002), and more recently *La marque du sacré* [*The Mark of the Sacred*] (Paris: Carnets Nord 2009).

Why, then, argue that Prometheanism is not simply an antiquated metaphysical fantasy? Because it is very much alive in the form of the so-called *NBIC convergence*. Dupuy quotes from the US Government's National Science Foundation June 2002 report, entitled 'Converging Technologies for Improving Human Performance', which claims that the convergence of nanotechnology, biotechnology, information technology and cognitive science (NBIC) will bring about a veritable 'transformation of civilization'.[3] The Prometheanism espoused here is a Prometheanism of the right: its advocates are champions of neoliberal capitalism, which they claim has emerged as the victor in the war of competing narratives about the possibilities of human history. So, why does NBIC technology have this radical transformational capacity? Because according to its advocates it renders possible the technological re-engineering of human nature.

Dupuy sets out a sophisticated philosophical critique of the fallacies and confusions that he detects in this claim. For Dupuy, the utilitarian prejudices of contemporary bioethical discourse prevent it from grasping the properly *ontological* dimension of the problem of the uses and misuses of NBIC. He argues that the advocates of NBIC, and of human enhancement more generally, systematically conflate ontological indetermination with epistemic uncertainty. They convert what is in fact an ontological problem about the structure of reality into an epistemic problem about the limits of our knowledge. As Dupuy puts it, 'human creative activity and the conquest of knowledge proves to be a double-edged sword [...but] it is not that we *do not know* whether the use of such a sword is a good or a bad thing—it is that it is good and bad at once.'[4]

---

3. Cited in Dupuy, 'Some Pitfalls', 239.

4. Ibid., 241.

If the outcome of human creative activity is ontologically indeterminate, rather than merely uncertain, this is because it is conditioned by the structure of human existence, which is a structure of transcendence. This characterization of human existence in terms of transcendence is primarily associated with Heidegger's *Being and Time*. Humans are unlike other entities in the world because their way of being is characterized by a structure of temporal projection in which the past, the present, and the future are reciprocally articulated. The conflation between epistemic uncertainty and ontological indeterminacy is based on confusing the human condition, which is *existential* in Heidegger's sense, and hence devoid of any fixed essence, with human nature, whose essence can be defined by its specific difference from that of other entities. Thus, the traditional metaphysical conception of the human is that of a creature belonging to the genus 'animal', but differentiated from other animals by a specific predicate, whether it be 'rational', 'political', or 'talking'. For Heidegger however, humans are not simply different in kind from other entities, they are constituted by an other kind of difference. Heidegger calls this other kind of difference *existence*. And for Dupuy, it is precisely the failure to register the ontological difference between existence and essence, or between humanity as condition and humanity as nature, that encourages the belief that we can modify the properties of human nature using the same techniques that have proven so successful in allowing us to manipulate the properties of other entities. The levelling of human existence onto a fixed catalogue of empirical properties blinds us to the existential difference between what is proper and improper for human beings to become (which Heidegger called 'authenticity' and 'inauthenticity'). It is this levelling that underlies claims about the radical malleability of human nature.

Dupuy deploys the distinction between existential condition and essential nature in tandem with Hannah Arendt's account of the interplay between what is *given* to human beings and what is *made* by them. Arendt writes:

> In addition to the conditions under which life is given to man on earth, and partly out of them, men constantly create their own, self-made conditions, which, their human origin and their variability notwithstanding, possess the same conditioning power as natural things.[5]

It follows, then, for Dupuy, who is a disciple of Arendt in this debate, that the human condition is an inextricable mixture of things given and things made: of the things that humans generate and produce through their own resources, and of the constraints upon human making which transcend their practical and cognitive abilities. The interplay between these factors means, in Dupuy's words, that:

> [M]an, to a great extent, can shape that which shapes him, condition that which conditions him, while still respecting the fragile equilibrium between the given and the made.[6]

Now, I take this claim that we *ought* to respect the 'fragile equilibrium' between what is made and what is given to be fundamental for the philosophical critique of Prometheanism. It is this precarious equilibrium between human shaping, and that which shapes this shaping—whether given by God or Nature—that Prometheanism threatens.

---

5. H. Arendt, *The Human Condition* (Chicago: University of Chicago Press, 2013).

6. Dupuy, 'Some Pitfalls', 246.

Another passage from Arendt is particularly relevant here:

> The problem of human nature, the Augustinian *quaestio mihi factus sum* ('a question have I become for myself'), seems unanswerable in both its individual psychological sense and its general philosophical sense. It is highly unlikely that we, who can know, determine, and define the natural essences of all things surrounding us, which we are not, should ever be able to do the same for ourselves—this would be like jumping over our own shadows. Moreover, nothing entitles us to assume that man has a nature or essence in the same sense as other things.[7]

The claim that humans cannot objectify themselves because they do not have a nature or essence in the same sense as other things is obviously Heideggerean. Heidegger radicalizes Kant's account of the intrinsic finitude of human cognition. What does this mean? For Kant, we are precluded in principle from being able to know the world in the way in which God, who created the world, knows it, because, unlike God, we are not endowed with the faculty of intellectual intuition, which creates the object that it knows. God possesses intuitive knowledge of each and every particular thing because his thought about that thing creates it. His is an infinite generative intelligence whose *making* is unconstrained by any *given*. Thus God's knowledge of the world is absolute, immediate, and incorrigible. Since we do not have intellectual intuition, and since our knowledge of reality is partly conditioned by the information about it we receive through our senses, we can only know things insofar as what our minds make is combined with what the world gives. What transcends human cognition is simply the created nature of things as they are in themselves. This is the infinite complexity of each and every

7. Arendt, 10.

thing as understood by its divine creator. But because our minds are finite, we can only represent things partially and incompletely.

Heidegger radicalizes Kant by *ontologizing* finitude. As existence, human being transcends every objective determination of its essence. This ontological transcendence lies at the root of finitude. For Heidegger, the finitude of human existence is an ontological datum, rather than an epistemic condition. Heidegger accepts Kant's claim that we have no transcendent knowledge of things-in-themselves, as they are known by their Creator. But for Heidegger human existence is the locus of a new kind of transcendence: one that is finite and human, as opposed to infinite and divine. And because existence constitutes a finite transcendence, it conditions the cognizability of objects. Since cognitive objectivation is conditioned by human existence, human beings cannot know themselves in the same way in which they know other objects. Doing so would require objectivating the condition of objectivation, which would be, as Arendt says, like trying to jump over our own shadow. Because of this prohibition on self-objectivation, human existence transcends every attempt to limn its core via a series of objective determinations. Indeed, every positive characterization of human nature, whether psychological, historical, anthropological or sociological, is ultimately determined by unavowed metaphysical—and for Heidegger this also means theological—prejudices. Hence the Heideggerian preoccupation with exposing science's latent metaphysical prejudices: the metaphysical presuppositions which determine its basic concepts, but which science itself is incapable of articulating.

From this Heideggerean vantage, philosophers who have attributed an essential plasticity to human being, or who have claimed that human beings can radically reengineer themselves can be denounced as metaphysicians reifying the transcendence of existence. Consider the young Marx's claim that 'man is a species being [....] and free conscious activity constitutes the species character of man'.[8] From Dupuy's Heideggerian perspective, Marx's identification of human species being with 'free conscious activity'—an activity that allows human beings to refashion themselves and their world—is itself a reification of the transcendence that constitutes the human: it reifies transcendence as *production* without paying proper attention to the sedimented metaphysical assumptions encoded in this term. Thus, for Heideggereans, the claim that man is an agent, a maker, or a producer of things, can be characterized as a metaphysical reification of human existence, which is properly understood as finite transcendence. Similarly, Sartre's claim that 'man is nothing but what he makes of himself'[9] can be charged with reifying transcendence by reducing it to the nihilating power of self-consciousness, which Sartre calls the 'for-itself'. Heideggereans have made careers sniffing out these and other metaphysical reifications of what is, in Heidegger, characterised as an unobjectifiable transcendence: the transcendence of *Dasein*.

The link between the transcendence of existence and the transcendence of life is made explicit in another significant quote from Arendt:

> The human artifice of the world separates human existence from all mere animal environment, but life itself is outside this artificial world, and through life man remains related to all other living organisms.[10]

'Life', in the early Heidegger, is a term for *Dasein* or existence. So it is plausible to construe Arendt's reference to 'life' here as

---

8. K. Marx, *Economic and Philosophical Manuscripts: Early Writings*, trans. R. Livingstone (Harmondsworth: Penguin Books, 1975), 327–8.

9. J.-P. Sartre, *Existentialism and Humanism*, trans. P. Mairet (London: Eyre Methuen, 1973), 22.

10. Arendt, 2.

another way of emphasizing the transcendence of existence, which cannot be turned into an object of scientific study. Arendt continues:

> This future man, whom the scientists tell us they will produce in no more than a hundred years, seems to be possessed by a rebellion against human existence as it has been given, a free gift from nowhere (secularly speaking), which he wishes to exchange, as it were, for something he has made himself.[11]

The sin of Prometheanism then consists in destroying the equilibrium between the made and the given—between what human beings generate through their own resources, both cognitive and practical, and the way the world is, whether characterised cosmologically, biologically, or historically. The Promethean trespass resides in *making the given*. By insisting on the possibility of bridging the ontological hiatus separating the given from the made, Prometheanism denies the ontologisation of finitude. This is the root of the Promethean pathology for both Arendt and Dupuy.

But how are we to identify the proper point of equilibrium between the made and the given? How are we supposed to know when we have disrupted this delicate balance? For Ivan Illich, whom Dupuy cites approvingly, there is a clear-cut criterion for doing so: it consists in recognizing birth, suffering, and death as ineliminable constants of the human condition. Illich writes:

- we will never eliminate pain;
- we will not cure all disorders;
- we will certainly die.

---

11. Ibid., 2–3.

> Therefore, as sensible creatures, we must face the fact that the pursuit of health may be a sickening disorder. There are no scientific, technological solutions. There is the daily task of accepting the fragility and contingency of the human situation. There are reasonable limits which must be placed on conventional 'health' care.[12]

According to Illich then, it is 'unreasonable' to want to extend life or improve health beyond certain pre-determined limits. Significantly, these limits are at once empirical, which is to say biological, *and* transcendental, which is to say existential. The rationality that is heedless of this empirico-transcendental limit in seeking to diminish suffering and death is a 'sickening disorder'. *Reason is unreasonable*—this is the fundamental objection raised against Promethean rationalism. Rationalism is deemed pathological because it is unreasonable according to a standard of reasonableness whose yardstick is recognizing the existential necessity of birth, suffering, and death. But what exactly is reasonable about accepting birth, suffering, and death as ineluctable facts, which is to say, givens? And by what criterion are we to discriminate between evitable and inevitable suffering? Much suffering that was once unavoidable has been greatly diminished, if not wholly eradicated. Of course, there are new and different forms of suffering. But our understanding of birth and death have been transformed to such an extent that there is something dubious, to say the least, about treating them as unquestionable biological absolutes. Moreover, the claim about the inevitability of suffering raises two basic questions: *How much* suffering are we supposed to accept as an ineliminable feature of the human condition? And *what kinds* of suffering qualify as inevitable? History teaches that there has been considerable variation not just in the quantity but

12. Quoted by Dupuy, 'Some Pitfalls', 248.

also in the kinds of suffering considered tolerable. We need only consider the suffering alleviated by developments in medicine to appreciate the problematic nature of the relation between quantity and quality in Illich's ontologization of biological facts.

The theological overtones of Illich's message are rendered explicit by one of his disciples, whom Dupuy also cites:

> What Jesus calls the Kingdom of God stands above and beyond any ethical rule and can disrupt the everyday world in completely unpredictable ways. But Illich also recognizes in this declaration of freedom from limits an extreme volatility. For should this freedom ever itself become the subject of a rule, then the limit-less would invade human life in a truly terrifying way.[13]

Here we have another telling formulation of the alleged pathology of Prometheanism: *the Promethean error is to formulate a rule for what is without rule*. What is without rule is the transcendence of the given in its irreducibility to the immanence of making. The Promethean fault lies in trying to conceptualise or organise that which is unconceptualizable and beyond every register of organisation; in other words, that which has been divinely dispensed or given. Dupuy provides perhaps the most eloquent formulation of this theological stricture when he writes:

> Man's 'symbolic health' lies in his ability to cope consciously and autonomously not only with the dangers of his milieu, but also with a series of profoundly intimate threats that all men face and always will face, namely pain, disease, and death. This ability is something that in traditional societies came to man from his culture, which allowed him to make sense of his mortal condition.

13. Caley, quoted in Dupuy, 'Some Pitfalls', 253.

> The sacred played a fundamental role in this. The modern world was born on the ruins of traditional symbolic systems, in which it could see nothing but arbitrariness and irrationality. In its enterprise of demystification, it did not understand the way these systems fixed limits to the human condition while conferring meaning upon them. When it replaced the sacred with reason and science, it not only lost all sense of limits, it sacrificed the very capacity to make sense. Medical expansion goes hand in hand with the myth according to which the elimination of pain and disability and the indefinite deferral of death are objectives both desirable and achievable thanks to the indefinite development of the medical system and the progress of technology. One cannot make sense of what one seeks only to extirpate. If the naturally unavoidable finiteness of the human condition is perceived as an alienation and not as a source of meaning, do we not lose something infinitely precious in exchange for the pursuit of a puerile dream?[14]

What is 'infinitely precious' here is the fact that the finitude of human existence obliges us to make sense of suffering, disease, and death. At the root of all religion lies the claim that suffering is *meaningful*—not just in the sense that it occurs for a reason—religion is not just about rationalizing suffering—but in the sense that suffering is something to be interpreted and rendered significant.

Now, we should be very wary of anyone telling us our suffering *means* something. And the fact that we have learnt to extract meaning from our susceptibility to suffering, illness, and death, does not license the claim that suffering, illness, and death are the prerequisites for a meaningful existence. That finitude is the horizon of our meaning-making does not entail that finitude is

---

14. Dupuy, 'Some Pitfalls', 249.

the condition of meaning tout court. This short-circuit between finitude as meaningful condition and finitude as condition of meaning—of sense, purpose, orientation, etc—is the fatal conflation underwriting the religious deprecation of Prometheanism.

Dupuy's enmity towards the Promethean hubris he detects in the NBIC programme is rooted in the post-Heideggerean critique of the mechanistic philosophy birthed by Cartesian rationalism. The latter's contemporary philosophical extension is the attempted mechanization of the mind, about which Dupuy has written illuminatingly.[15] Given a sufficiently liberal understanding of 'mechanism', together with a sufficiently sophisticated account of mechanical causation, which views nature itself as a single labyrinthine mechanism, it becomes possible to integrate the mind into a mechanised nature by viewing it through the lens of the computational paradigm. The computational paradigm has been subjected to numerous philosophical critiques. Dupuy is aware of these critiques, but seems to view alternatives to classic computationalism, such as connectionism, as conceding too much to the computational paradigm. For Dupuy, the mechanization of mind generates the following paradox:

> [T]he mind that carries out the mechanization and the one that is the object of it are two distinct (albeit closely related) entities, like the two ends of a seesaw, the one rising ever higher into the heavens of metaphysical humanism [*because it says that human beings can understand everything, including themselves*—RB] as the other descends further into the depths of its deconstruction [*the reduction of the human from condition to mechanism destroys the privileges of the human as traditionally conceived*—RB]. [...]

15. Dupuy, *On the Origins of Cognitive Science*.

> One may nevertheless regard this triumph of the subject as simultaneously coinciding with his demise. For man to be able, as subject, to exercise a power of this sort over himself, it is first necessary that he be reduced to the rank of an object, able to be reshaped to suit any purpose. No raising up can occur without a concomitant lowering, and vice versa.[16]

It this see-sawing from the extreme of subjectivism to the extreme of objectivation that threatens the precarious equilibrium between the made and the given. According to Dupuy, the more we understand ourselves as part of nature, having successfully objectified ourselves as complicated mechanisms, the less able we are to determine ends or purposes *for* ourselves. Once being human is no longer an other kind of difference—existence—but just another kind of being, a particularly complicated natural mechanism, then the danger is that we will lose the meaning-making resources through which we were able to project a point or purpose orienting our attempt to explain and understand ourselves. What is the point of understanding ourselves if by doing so we understand that the purposes through which we traditionally oriented ourselves towards the future are themselves pointless—meaningless mechanisms, rather than meaningful purposes? For the more we understand ourselves as just another contingently generated natural phenomenon, the less able we are to define *what we should be*. Our self-objectification deprives us of the normative resources we need to be able to say that we ought to be this way rather than that.

What is elided in the disruption of the equilibrium between the given and the made is the distinction between what is true for human beings in so far as they can control and manipulate it, i.e. what is useful, and what is true by virtue of having being created as the unique

16. Dupuy, 'Some Pitfalls', 254, 255.

thing that it is—that which is the way it is by virtue of its essence. The difference between man-made or factual truth, and divine or essential truth is jeopardised. The true and the made become convertible at the point when only what has been (humanly) made can be truly known. This is the way Marxism—a philosophy that espouses the primacy of practice and that views cognition as a kind of practice—can be deemed guilty of eliding the difference between what is made and what is known. Only what is humanly made is humanly knowable.

Dupuy proposes that what is genuinely valuable in Judeo-Christian theology is the parallel it establishes between divine and human creativity. What is objectionable about Prometheanism is not humanity arrogantly claiming to be able to do what God does. On the contrary, Dupuy insists, Judeo-Christianity teaches that there is a positive analogy between human creativity and divine creativity. Humans might well be able to produce life: a living creature, a Golem. But in the version of the fable cited by Dupuy, the Golem responds to the magician who has made him by immediately enjoining him to *unmake* him. By creating me, the Golem says to his creator, you have introduced a radical disorder into creation. By making what can only be given, i.e. life, you have violated the distribution of essences. There are now two living beings, one man-made, one God-given, whose essence is indiscernible. So the Golem immediately enjoins his creator to destroy him in order to restore the balance between the man-made and the God-given. Implicit in the parallelism between divine and human creativity is the claim that everything that is must have a unique, distinct essence, whose ultimate source can only be divine.

Thus even if we have acquired the power to create life, we shouldn't do it. The prospect of synthetic life jeopardises the metaphysical principle of the identity of indiscernibles precisely insofar as the difference between the living and the non-living is taken to be essential in the most radical sense: not just a difference in kind, but another kind of difference. This is what is disturbing about Prometheanism: the manufacturing of life, of another kind of difference, would be the generation of a rule for the rule-less. Interestingly however, we are not told why the disruption of equilibrium is inherently destructive. In the parable cited by Dupuy, disturbing the divinely ordained equilibrium is taken to be objectionable per se: *you have introduced a disequilibrium into existence*. But this is already to presuppose that there is a natural, which is to say, transcendently ordained, equilibrium. Yet we are never told precisely what the equilibrium is supposed to be. What I want to suggest is that it is precisely this assumption of equilibrium that is theological: it is the claim that there is a 'way of the world', a ready-made world whose order is simply to be accepted as an ultimately unintelligible, brute given, that is objectionably theological. This is the idea that the world was made, and that we should not presume to ask why it was made this way and not some other way. But the world was not made: it is simply there, uncreated, without reason or purpose. And it is precisely this realization that invites us not to simply accept the world as we find it. Prometheanism is the attempt to participate in the creation of the world without having to defer to a divine blueprint. It follows from the realization that the disequilibrium we introduce into the world through our desire to know is no more or less objectionable than the disequilibrium that is already there in the world.

Of course, from the perspective of Heidegger's critique of rationality, Prometheanism is the most dangerous form of metaphysical voluntarism. But Prometheanism stands to be rehabilitated from the vantage of an understanding of rationality which views it not as a supernatural faculty but simply as a rule-governed activity—rationality is simply the faculty of generating and being bound by rules. This is precisely the account of rationality set out by Kant. These rules are not fixed in advance, they are historically mutable. But this fact does not make them contingent in the same sense in which other historical phenomena are said to be contingent. So, rather than trying to preserve the theological equilibrium between the made and the given, which is to say, between immanence and transcendence, the challenge for rationality consists in grasping the stratification of immanence, together with the involution of structures within the natural order through which rules can arise out of physical patterns. According to this conception of rationality, rules are means of coordinating and subsuming heterogeneous phenomena, but means that are themselves historically mutable. The ways in which we understand the world, and the ways in which we change the world on the basis of our understanding, are perpetually being redetermined. What unfolds is a dynamic process which is not about re-establishing equilibrium, but superseding the opposition between order and disorder, and recognizing that the catastrophic overturning of intention, and the often disturbing consequences of our technological ingenuity, constitute no objection to the compulsion to foresee and control.

Ballard declares that 'all progress is savage and violent'. And indeed, the psychic and cognitive transformations undergone by Ballard's protagonists are nothing if not savage and violent. But the fact that progress is savage and violent does not necessarily disqualify it as progress. There is indeed a savagery recapitulated in rationality. But there is a kind of sentimentalism implicit in the insistence that all savageries are equivalent, that it is impossible to discriminate between them. Conversely, it is not sentimental to think that some savageries are better than others and that it is not only possible but necessary to discriminate between modes of instrumentalisation and insist that some are preferable to others. The frequently reiterated claim that every attempt to circumscribe, delimit, or manipulate phenomena is intrinsically pathological is precisely the kind of sentimentalism that perpetuates the most objectionable characteristics of our existence. We can choose to resign ourselves to these characteristics and accept the way the world is. Alternatively, and more interestingly, we can try to reexamine the philosophical foundations of a Promethean project that is implicit in Marx—the project of re-engineering ourselves and our world on a more rational basis. Among Badiou's signal virtues is to have dared to challenge the facile postmodern doxa which has been used for so long to castigate Prometheanism. Even if one disagrees with the philosophical details of Badiou's account of the relation between event and subjectivity, as I do, there is something to be gained by trying to reconnect his account of the necessity of this subjectivation to an analysis of the biological, economic, and historical processes that condition rational subjectivation. This is obviously a huge task. But it is in the first instance a research programme whose philosophical legitimacy needs to be defended, because it has for too long been dismissed as a dangerous fantasy. The presuppositions fuelling this dismissal are ultimately theological. Moreover, even if Prometheanism does harbour undeniable phantasmatic residues, these can be diagnosed, analysed, and perhaps transformed on the basis of further analysis. Everything is more or less phantasmatic. One cannot reproach a rational project for its phantasmatic residues unless one is secretly dreaming of a rationality that would be wholly devoid of imaginary influences. Prometheanism promises an overcoming of the opposition between reason and imagination: reason is fuelled by imagination, but it can also remake the limits of the imagination.

Maximum Jailbreak

Benedict Singleton

2014

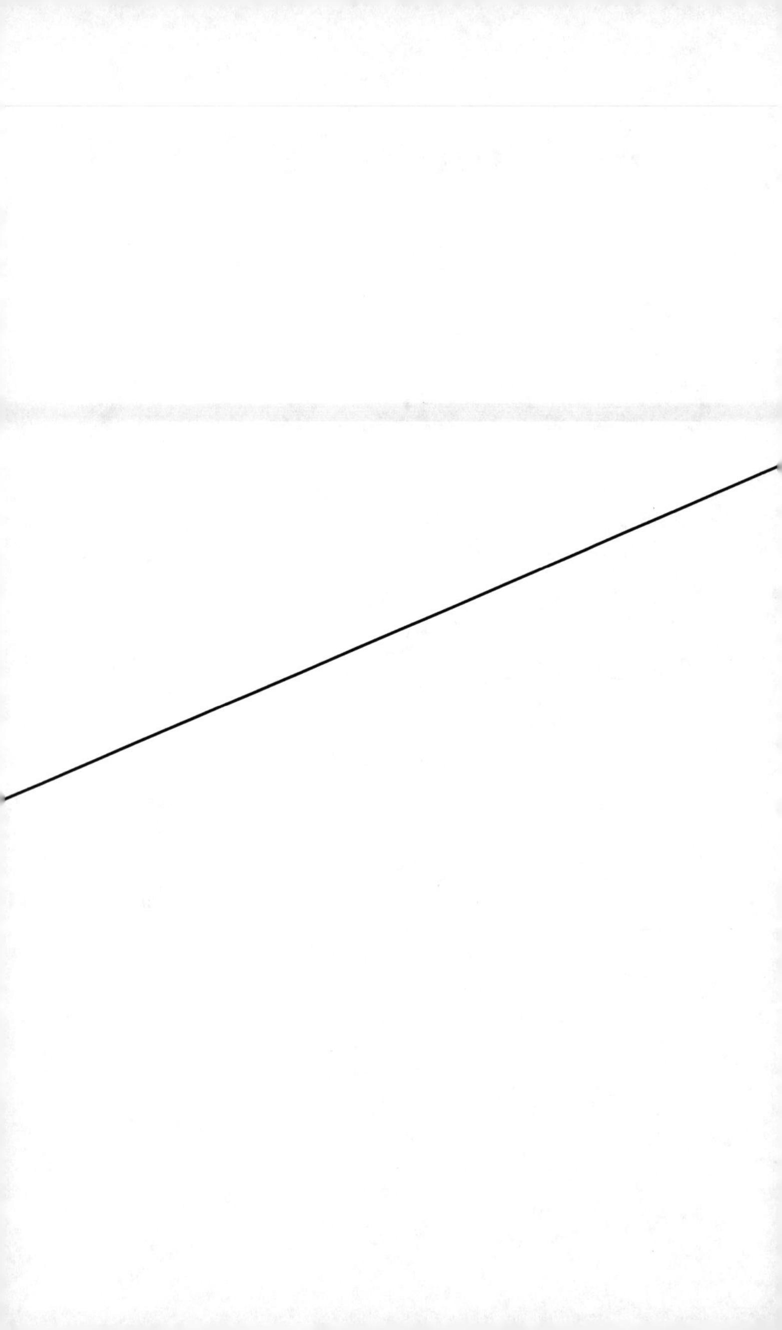

The greatest escape of them all is about to blow the future apart.[1]

Space travel produced some of the defining images of the twentieth century. Sputnik, the NASA logo, the shuttle's friendly snub-nosed profile; the ratcheting tension of the liftoff countdown, a flag on the Moon that is never to flutter, the earth like a mica fleck against coal black. These were images capable of captivating a global audience, an effect enhanced by the setup of the so-called Space Race as a kind of decades-long international sports day. Then, just as things were getting going, the engines cut out. The flow of images that made space travel feel like the definitive project of our age seemed to dry up, and projected timelines for the rollout of megastructure space habitats and interstellar drives went from exciting to optimistic to embarrassing. The workaday job of transit to and from low earth orbit continued, of course, but in the relatively charmless forms of comsat maintenance, or science projects on the International Space Station. The last picture capable of exerting popular fascination dosed the wonder with horror: the crumbling arch of smoke hung over Cape Canaveral in the wake of the disappeared Challenger, which, in concert with the investigations that followed, helped to nix public enthusiasm for the enterprise as a whole.

But in the dog days that followed, the military-industrial complex morphed into the security-entertainment matrix, and grand strategy—a 'space program'—was swapped out for a riot of tactics. The Curiosity rover now commands a top-1000 Twitter account, and Virgin Galactic court the insanely wealthy with a voyage-of-a-lifetime tourist brochure. Billionaire Denis Tito announces a plan to send a middle-aged couple on a long lover's jaunt into orbit around Mars—

1. From the original theatrical movie trailer for *Escape from New York* (John Carpenter, 1981).

a sitcom premise pitched by an unstable screenwriter, eyes gleaming like his last dime, and Mars One top him by opening auditions for the one-way reality TV show trip to the planet the company is named for. Planetary Resources and Deep Space Industries patent robotic asteroid capture mechanisms and graph kilo-to-dollar launch cost ratios against rare-metal market price projections; investors prove keen to back a gold rush at the vertical frontier. China and India get in on the space game, kindling a predictable resurgence of defense talk. Staunch environmentalists, reviewing yet another new paper on Antarctic ice shelf cleaving, start to suggest that we don't even have to get into worrying asteroid trajectories, supervolcanic blowouts, or whatever else is buried out there in the trackless desert of the future, to think a civilisational backup on another planet might be a good hedge of our bets.

A sense of the proximity of the overhead vastness is once again the order of the day. We are in the midst of an epochal event, if one that has stretched out decades longer than had previously been suggested. What, then, are we to make of it? As the acme of the large-scale sociotechnical project, space travel seems to suffer from a surfeit of significance. *Reasons to go* are multiple, diverse, and only becoming more so: national pride, entertainment dollars, the advance of science, the construction of an emergency exit on a planetary scale. The possibilities overflow their restriction to any one justification. All are unified somehow, as witnessed when they click together like Tetris blocks, strengthening the case of each and all through cross-reference to others. The common element and point of transit between them is the infrastructure that allows access to space, *a means* that earns its own legitimacy not by association with a singular end, but through the diversity of potential situations it precipitates. We can begin to grasp the implications of this unfamiliar logic by rewinding to the earliest sustained consideration of space travel, written years before fixed-wing flight was a practical possibility—a fact that in itself provides us with an exemplar of how ambition must be shaped if it is to reckon with a destination that comprehensively exceeds its origin. And it also, as we shall see, allows us to forge a field of new connections that severs contemporary space travel from a lingering nostalgia for its appearance in the last century, and presents an alternative vista on its possibilities.

*

Moscow, the late 1880s: as he's done for decades now, Nikolai Fedorov spends his evenings writing the essays that will one day be gathered together as *The Philosophy of the Common Task*. Fedorov was born the illegitimate son of a minor prince, and by trade he is a librarian; before taking to the stacks, a schoolteacher. He is reputed by those few who know him to be kindly, if stern, and remarkably ascetic: he eats little, rarely and nothing sweet; he doesn't even wear a coat in winter. In short, he cuts an unlikely father figure for the Space Race. But it's in the pages of *The Common Task* that we find the first systematic program and rationale for permanent human settlement off-world, and a direct line can be drawn between it and the development of extraplanetary travel some decades later.[2]

Fedorov's writing is unforgiving, not because his prose is inaccessible—quite the opposite—but because of its uncompromising single-mindedness of purpose. As historian George Young puts it, Fedorov was 'a thinker with one idea,' albeit an idea that 'was extremely complex and comprehensive.'[3] This idea was the

2. N. Fedorov, *What Was Man Created For? The Philosophy of the Common Task* (London: Honeyglen Publishing, 1990). See extract in first section of this volume.

3. G. M. Young, *The Russian Cosmists: The Esoteric Futurism of Nikolai Fedorov and His Followers* (Oxford: Oxford University Press, 2012), 49.

'common task' of the book's title, the articulation of a project to be taken up by the entire human race. It can be decanted into two slogans: *storm the heavens* and *conquer death*.

Let's begin with the second point first, since it is in some sense the more fundamental. Fedorov saw in death a universal nemesis, one against which all human beings, without exception, could agree to rally their efforts. Death as encountered by individuals, but also the extinction of cultures, the termination of traditions, the downfall of civilisations. And indeed more generally still: for Fedorov, death is the operative effect of 'blind nature', heedless and terrible. It is what occurs when we do not act to counter nature, which tutors no lesson other than the urgency of staving it off a while. Respect for an adversary is one thing, but the injunction to *love Nature* quite another—a habitual indulgence of those Fedorov contemptuously described as 'the learned', an elite who have the opportunity to spend their time singing in praise of 'the natural' only because they are substantially insulated from it by technologies they profess to despise. Out in the field, literally as well as figuratively, no such niceties prevail, and nature is revealed to be 'not a mother, but a stepmother who refuses to feed us'.[4]

The common task was, then, the commission of a collective assault on death, understood as a submission to nature. This does not mean Fedorov took nature to be something to be 'overcome', exactly; he was quite aware that life is predicated on the same processes that lay waste to it, even if—in the later words of an acolyte, the economist Sergei Bulgakov—'life seems a sort of accident, an oversight or indulgence on the part of death.'[5] His mission is instead to convert or *transform* the natural, to bring

---

4. Fedorov, *What Was Man Created For?*, 33.

5. S. Bulgakov, *The Philosophy of Economy* (New Haven, CT: Yale University Press, 2000), 68.

reason to it, reconfiguring the environment so as to carve out a larger and more hospitable space for life. Nature appears as the force of *necessity*, and it is against the acceptance as necessary of *that which could be made otherwise* that Fedorov directs us.

In practical terms, this would require substantial technological development and the reorientation of social structures, but of a kind quite unlike those associated at the time with 'progress', a term Fedorov despised. Indeed, the combination of democracy with mass production presented an influx of new constraints on the human. What his contemporaries called 'progress' was for Fedorov a system calibrated to induce and respond to impulse. The factory brought with it an environment where humans were organised around the insistent demands of the machines they tended, and an incipient consumerism comprised a mechanisation of distraction, ever shortening windows of attention. Likewise, democratic systems were prey to deformation by populism, eliminating tradition and leaving a hedonistic pursuit of temporary gratification in its place.

Against 'progress', figured as such, Fedorov pitched a sense of *duty* in the struggle against death, such that in 'the contradiction between the reflective and instinctive', one would forego the *instinctive*—which comprised the operation of unmitigated natural forces through human beings—in favour of the *reflective*, the means by which they might be checked and rerouted in a more productive direction.[6] This commitment extended into the ancient depths of instinct: sex, the very paradigm of unconsidered urgency, was to be pared from the portfolio of human experiences. A more rational base on which to build people into collectives than the sexual encounter central to marriage, Fedorov felt, was kinship, and his characterisation of rational duty is a *filial* duty, impassioned but firmly chaste. This dutiful kinship, synchronised closely

---

6. Fedorov, *What Was Man Created For?*, 59.

to Fedorov's heretical reworking of his own devout Christianity, would first temper and later outmode and supersede, he hoped, easily deviated social forms like democracy. The whole task of social organisation would alter: beginning with the creation of synthetic wombs, and later entire synthetic bodies, the task of producing human society would detach from its biological origins and be placed under rational collective control; efforts to prolong life to the point of immortality, a *completed project of medicine*, would be entwined in this transformation of basic human functions, which would find its ultimate filial duty expressed not just in the cessation of death but in the eventual recreation of every human being who ever lived. This is Fedorov as he is still best known: a curious prophet not only of human immortality, but of the resurrection of the dead.

But Fedorov's ideas extended further, and inevitably upwards, not least because an enlarging human race would require space into which to expand. Freedom from death would extend to freedom from the earth itself. Technological development must loosen the grip of gravity, not eradicating it per se, but meaning we would no longer be forced to obey its dictates without question. Epic and unexpected, the creativity of Fedorov's post-terrestrial vision extended to its detail:

> He speculated that someday, by erecting giant cones on the earth's surface, people might be able to control the earth's electromagnetic field in such a way as to turn the whole planet into a spaceship under human control. We would no longer have to slavishly orbit our sun but could freely steer our planet wherever we wished, as, in the phrase he used as early as the 1870s, 'captain and crew of spaceship earth.'[7]

---

7. Young, *The Russian Cosmists*, 79.

This complex of ideas, which by the 1900s had attracted the label of *cosmism*, was capable of inspiring peculiar devotion in the few who were exposed to it. Some of Russia's literary titans of the day, Tolstoy and Dostoevsky among them, were transfixed by both Fedorov's imaginary range and the weirdly revised Christianity that comprised its ethical core—a combination they hoped might head off the anarchistic and communistic movements gathering force at the time. But if Fedorov's habit of quoting the Bible in support of his contentions hardly made it an effortless fit, it was his scientific impetus, such that 'political and cultural problems become physical or astrophysical,'[8] that carried his influence into the atheist and scientific-Promethean bent of post-revolutionary Russia. It registers in Vladimir Vernadsky's development of the concept of the biosphere, and his observation that by the end of the nineteenth century human activity had achieved the status of a significant player amongst planetary systems;[9] in Alexander Bogdanov's proto-cybernetic theories, experiments in the rejuvenating possibilities of blood transfusion, and novel *Red Star*, about a perfect society on Mars;[10] and perhaps especially, in the work of Konstantin Tsiolkovsky. A regular visitor to Fedorov's library as a teenager, Tsiolkovsky developed the mathematical foundations for space travel, from the 'ideal rocket equation' that describes the motion of a vehicle that accelerates while expelling its own mass, to the calculation of optimal ascent, descent, and orbital trajectories for spacecraft. Furthermore, he put these to use in the design of the first multistage booster rockets, an extraordinary technological innovation that stood among many

8. Fedorov, *What Was Man Created For?*, 43.

9. V. Vernadsky, *The Biosphere* (Göttingen: Copernicus Publications, 1998).

10. A. Bogdanov, *Red Star* (Bloomington, IN:Indiana University Press, 1984).

others in his work, including schematics for airlocks, spacecraft interiors, and moon bases.[11]

*

The principal motor of Fedorov's thought was a refusal to take the most basic factors conditioning life on earth—gravity and death—as necessary horizons for action. The opportunities afforded by the length of a life and the expanse of the Earth may, in combination, be considerable; but to understand them not as *the way things happen to be* but *how things have to be* he judged at best myopia, at worst a squalid and self-regarding form of provincialism. In isolate form, this is the characteristic gesture of cosmism: to consider the earth a trap, and to understand the basic project of humanity as the formulation of means to escape from it—to conceive a jailbreak at the maximum possible scale, a heist in which we steal ourselves from the vault.

If cosmism posits escape as a central principle, it is in the mode of an actual physical event, rather than individual or collective retreat into an inner psychological bunker—escapology, not escapism. As such, it is a venture inseparable from technology—or more precisely, *design*, the process which orients action towards the future and leaves technology in its wake. Fedorov acknowledged that his project required substantial advances in a plethora of fields to provide its material scaffolding (aeronautics, electronics, meteorology and medicine amongst them), but he did not recognise it as one incarnation of *the project of design* in itself. Yet cosmism becomes graspable as such precisely insofar as it renders a picture of the Earth, and the conditions it affords life, in terms of traps. It instantiates, at massive scale—indeed a

---

11. See the extensive archive of Tsiolkovsky's papers at <http://www.ras.ru/ktsiolkovskyarchive/about.aspx>.

scope that was historically novel—an ancient understanding of design as structured in its entirety by the logic of the trap and escape from it.

*

This association of design and the trap runs deep. It is *old*, partaking in the kind of great age that makes something horrific rather than tame. Once better known, it was all but invisible by the time of Fedorov's writing, which it stealthily animates. But what is the shape of this connection? In his essay *Vogel's Net*, a short and striking speculation on how a hunting trap of traditional style might be understood if placed in a gallery, anthropologist Alfred Gell draws out the ominous intentions its form encodes: 'We read in it the mind of its author' and a 'model of its victim'—and more particularly the way in which that model 'subtly and abstractly represent[s] parameters of the animal's natural behaviour, subverted in order to entrap it'. Hunting traps are, Gell writes, 'lethal parodies' of their prey's behaviour.[12] A human would be lucky to catch most other mammals unaided, but this can be redressed by an indirect strategy that makes use of their observed disposition: their inclination to eat certain kinds of food, in the example of bait; or a translation of their attempts to escape into the means of their demise, as in the snare. Understood in these terms, the maker of the trap mobilises and organises an ensemble of forces into new conjunctions, acting as 'a technician of instinct and appetite' who twists trajectories already at play in the environment in unexpected directions.[13]

---

12. A. Gell, *Art and Agency: An Anthropological Theory* (London: Clarendon Press, 1998), 200–1.

13. L. Hyde, *Trickster Makes This World* (Edinburgh: Canongate, 1998).

The significance of this description is not in what it tells us about design as applied to traps, but in how the construction of traps provides a general model of design. Observers separated far in space and time have, independently it would seem, made this connection, seeing the trap as the basic paradigm of design more broadly writ: the ability to coax effects from the world by identifying and manipulating its extant tendencies, rather than imposing form on it by the application of force alone.[14] Following the grain of wood, tracking the melting point of an ore, toughening metal through tempering: all situations in which such force as is applied is not inflicted on a passive substrate, but 'in which intelligence attempts to make contact with an object by confronting it in the guise of a rival, as it were, combining connivance and opposition.'[15] Incredibly improbable phenomena, like the ability of a person to use a lever to lift a boulder, flow from an environment arranged *just so*, as a system of complicity between its disparate parts. And so it is that Jean-Pierre Vernant describes an ancient understanding of artefacts as 'traps set at points where nature allowed itself to be overcome.'[16]

The form of intelligence that finds expression in the trap is *cunning*, and its general mode of operation links *craft* with *craftiness*. It weds the construction of artefacts to the operation of courtly intrigues, daring military stratagems, and explosive outbreaks of entrepreneurial success: all instances of the successful navigation of ambiguous and shifting environments, impossible to corral directly, in which we find demonstrated the ability to elicit extraordinary effects from unpromising materials through oblique

14. B. Singleton, *On Craft and Being Crafty: Human Behaviour as the Object of Design* (PhD thesis, Newcastle-upon-Tyne: Northumbria University).

15. M. Detienne & J.-P. Vernant, *Cunning Intelligence in Greek Culture and Society* (Chicago: University of Chicago Press, 1991), 6.

16. J–.P. Vernant, *Myth and Thought Among the Greeks* (New York: Zone Books, 2006), 313.

strategies and precisely timed action, allowing the weak to prevail over the physically stronger.[17] As this formulation implies, the trap and escape from it exhibit a curious reversibility. To be free is to trap something else, even if only in the subtle form of crafting camouflage that redirects predatory attention. In words written half a millennium before the Christian clock starts and in any event out of earshot, this recognition is the hallmark of the *great thief*:

> In taking precautions against thieves who cut open satchels, search bags, and break open boxes, people are sure to cord and fasten them well, and to employ strong bonds and clasps; and in this they are ordinarily said to show their wisdom. When a great thief comes, however, he shoulders the box, lifts up the satchel, carries off the bag, and runs away with them, afraid only that the cords, bonds, and clasps may not be secure; and in this case what was called the wisdom (of the owners) proves to be nothing but a collecting of the things for the great thief.[18]

This is a process that lends itself to escalation. According to a principle that Lewis Hyde glosses as 'nothing counters cunning but more cunning,'[19] trap begets counter-trap, freedom from one founded on the construction of another. To outfox is to think more broadly, to find the crack in the scheme, to stick a knife into it, and to lever it open for new use. Freighting the environment with a counter-plot is the best device for escaping the machinations in which one is embroiled: a conversion

---

17. Singleton, *On Craft and being Crafty*.

18. Zuangzi, *Cutting Open Satchels*, <http://www.seeraa.com/china-literature/zhuangzi-10.html>.

19. Hyde, *Trickster Makes This World*, 20.

of constraints into new opportunities for free action. Escape is the material with which design works. It is the enemy of stasis, even when the latter appears as motion but only as reiteration; a project of total insubordination towards existing conditions; a *generalised escapology.*

*

The comparative sophistication of Fedorov's thought was tied to its restless impatience. Incited by the industrial and scientific developments of its time, cosmism surged into the imaginative terrain that lay beyond the possibilities they presented for immediate application. Programmatic rather than predictive, it extrapolated a trajectory from their combined effects, and located new goals along it. Cosmism raced into the future and looked back, allowing what are still widely seen as constants *now*—gravity, mortality—to appear as disposable constraints from a speculative vantage point beyond their removal. The originality and charisma of cosmism resides in the extension of its ambitions beyond any similar venture that preceded it: Fedorov takes the logic of the trap and upsizes it to the global and beyond.

As a directive project, cosmism enjoins practical intelligence to systematically undoing the constraints that bind it. Freedom is quantified, recast as a serial achievement proceeding stepwise, degree by degree. We are free of *this* constraint, and now *this* one, and then *this*. Yet if any given instance of design is a hustle, cosmism is a gesture that lengthens the con. If it is reliant on discrete moments of invention, they are not simply aggregated—arranged in a row, like a parade of coin tricks, each self-sufficient and without bearing on the next. Instead they are nested into a cultivated scheme or expanding plot, such that each gambit paves the way for another. Under the terms of this dynamic, goals, of whatever scale, are purely temporary.

The articulation of a concrete goal—whether to get over the prison wall or to establish a base on Mars—gives definition to local action, can incite and organise effort, and metricates progress. Yet there is no a priori finish line imminent to this logic, such that on breaking the ribbon we can at last rest easy and luxuriate in a genuine liberty, finally achieved.

Accordingly, cosmism's orientation to technological accomplishment is synthetic, rather than synoptic, and its programme perpetuates rather than completes. The designed systems that would allow one to prevail over gravity, and eradicate or even reverse death, are springboards for other, more dimly specified objectives to emerge during the outward expansion of the human species into the rest of the universe. The sense of *duty* Fedorov posits is not only a means of detaching from local seductions, the condition of embarkation on this project, but a coordinating system that persists between achievements, stabilising and cohering them into a trajectory: a means to configure thought to the dynamic of an ongoing and escalating project while and through resisting the allure of the interim goal. His 'duty' is a trap set for oneself in the form of a minimal ethical template, expandable as the baseline of a collective venture. As a point of fixity, it offers the potential for leverage, expanding the range of future possibilities: a *platform* that is a constraint, to be sure, but one that is generative in its orientation, rather than a submission to preexisting necessity.

In this, Fedorov's intellectual vector is not only more extravagant but also more sophisticated than those of many others that might superficially resemble it, in which ambitious technical projects are posited to achieve specific, predetermined goals. But its grasp of the logic of the trap not only remains implicit but is decidedly partial. Whatever the merits or otherwise of Fedorov's crusade against sex, consumerism, democracy and the rest, the unacknowledged limit to his thought lies precisely in how it configures the terminal constraint that enables all others to be cast by the wayside. Willing to discard everything from sex to death, Fedorov draws the line at undermining the sacred figure of Man. 'Death is a property, a condition,' he wrote, 'but not a quality without which man ceases to be what he is and what he ought to be.'[20] Yet the designation of 'man' as sacrosanct is alien to the abstract insurrectionary force of design, and its sentimentality prohibits the pursuit of the ramifying commitments it initiates.

*

If a trap is to be escaped by anything other than luck, to which a determinant like gravity is decidedly unresponsive, the escapee itself must change: the thing that escapes the trap is not the thing that was caught in it. In order to be free, it is of less use to settle upon some hallowed condition of 'authentic freedom', than to understand how one is implicated in the mechanism of one's entrapment. To be prey is a lesson in predation, and this recognition is the precondition of escape. 'In order to anticipate the reactions of his pursuers, the hunted man has to learn to interpret his own actions from the point of view of the predator...seeing himself in the third person, considering, with respect to each of his acts, how they might be used against him. This anxiety can later be transformed into reasoning.'[21] So it is that the mark gets wise to the structure of the con, and only in this realisation can the process of turning the tables begin. The escape attempt tutors a view of oneself as an *object* within a nested structure of traps, and converts this knowledge into an active resource.

---

20. Fedorov, quoted in Young, *The Russian Cosmists*, 47.

21. G. Chamayou, *Manhunts: A Philosophical History* (Princeton, NJ: Princeton University Press, 2012), 70.

No wonder, then, that '[s]laves in the French colonies had a word for it: escaping one's master was called "stealing one's own corpse."'[22]

Rendered thus, freedom from entrapment is not freedom *from* but *through* alienation, and this creates a pernicious stowaway in the project of extended escape from the perspective of any unreconstructed humanism: the continuous transformation, through revisionary reconstruction, of the agent that pursues it.[23] This is already here and has already happened. The human body is the host of an artificial intelligence, in the atypical sense of the term as an intelligence that operates through artifice. Its progressive emergence leaves its traces in the divergence of human beings from the other three great apes through cycles of invention and exile. A technological prowess that both enabled and was spurred by ancestral migrations into a diversifying range of environments, pursued by adapting the materials found there into a defensive and offensive system that enabled social systems to take root and—sometimes—flourish, left its mark in the progressive behavioural plasticity of human beings and indeed their morphology.[24] Bipedalism, cephalisation, the dynamic structure of the hand and its coordination to eye and voice; all these are as much inventions of technology as they are a means to invent it, and are as foundational to 'the human' as language.[25] 'Humans are not native to the Earth', writes Robert Zubrin, lacking 'proper adaptation to the terrestrial environment' in general:

> We live on a planet with two permanent polar ice caps, a planet whose land masses in large majority are stricken with snow, ice,

22. Chamayou, *Manhunts*, 63.

23. R. Negarestani, 'The Labor of the Inhuman', this volume.

24. T. Taylor, *The Artificial Ape* (Basingstoke: Palgrave Macmillan, 2010).

25. Indeed, it is plausible to consider language a technological platform of a kind, while the reverse appears untrue.

> freezing nights, and killing frosts every year, and whose oceans' average temperature is far below that of our life's blood. The Earth is a cold place. Our internal metabolism requires warmth. Yet we have no fur; we have no feathers; we have no blubber to insulate our bodies. Across most of this planet, unprotected life for any length of time is as impossible as it is on the moon. We survive here, and thrive here, solely by virtue of our technology.[26]

Fedorov's 'Man' presupposes its consistency, historical and futural, as a foundational platform, which in turn yields its ethical import as well as its technological direction. But if the expansion of freedom that cosmism initiates participates in the generalised escapology of design, it is only the latter that is capable of disciplining it.

*

> To travel in space you must leave the old verbal garbage behind: God talk, country talk, mother talk, love talk, party talk. You must learn to exist with no religion, no country, no allies. You must learn to live alone in silence. Anyone who prays in space is not *there*.[27]

Design is an incursion across any and all borders, the eventual violation of every truce it entertains, a process by which socio-technical structures are taken hostage by precisely what they make possible. Its tendency is to unground, in every sense. It is not brought to heel by any logic other than its own. Its unfolding development is stabilised into a consistent vector only by its recognition as such.

---

26. R. Zubrin, *Entering Space: Creating a Spacefaring Civilisation* (New York: Tarcher, 1999), 17–18.

27. W. Burroughs, *The Adding Machine* (New York: Arcade, 1993), 138.

We are much used to seeing in design the *means* to effect pre-specified *ends*. But means have a logic of their own, indexed to their capacity to effect an *escape from the present*, detecting and exploiting points of leverage in the environment in order to ratchet open the future, and in so doing transforming the very agent that effects the escape. This is the mark of an *accelerationist* disposition, encompassing those schools of thought that can suborn a description of the world's perceived shortcomings, and the corresponding elaboration of *how it ought to be* in the shape of images of the future, to the logic of *how things get done*, how freedom is a possibility within this, and how its progressive maximisation can be pursued through the systematic deployment of generative constraints.

This is the structural logic of space travel in the twenty-first century. The heritage of the dockers hauling in an asteroid on an O'Neill colony at Lagrange point 5 will be a history that stacks escape artists, stage magicians and prison breakers in amongst the astrophysicists and the Apollo teams. And they will not be us, marked by our fealties or conduct. They will be whatever they had to be, whatever it is that we become, in order to escape. In this recognition we are granted an alternative set of footholds for an ascent into the dark.

Teleoplexy

Notes on Acceleration

Nick Land

2014

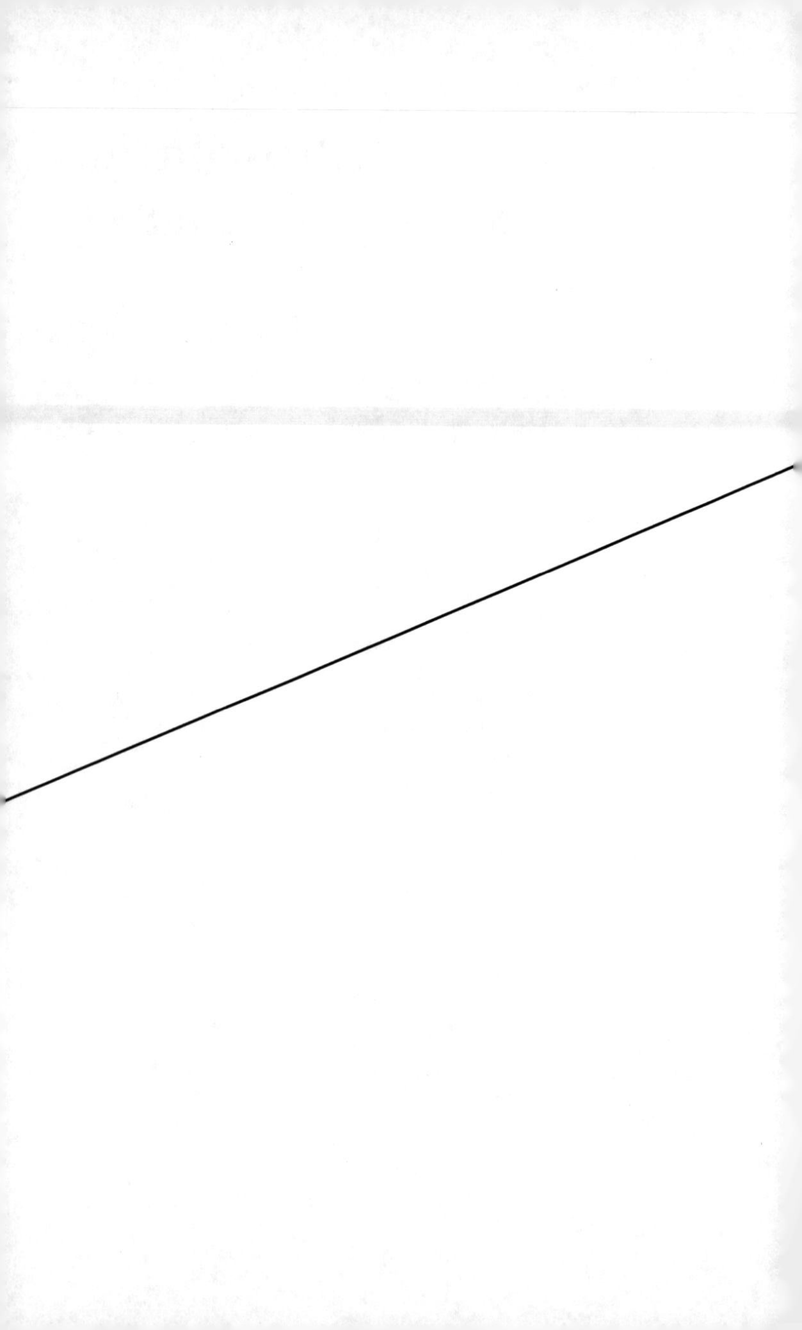

§00. 'Acceleration' as it is used here describes the time-structure of capital accumulation. It thus references the 'roundaboutness' founding Böhm-Bawerk's model of capitalization, in which saving and technicity are integrated within a single social process—diversion of resources from immediate consumption into the enhancement of productive apparatus. Consequently, as basic co-components of capital, technology and economics have only a limited, formal distinctiveness under historical conditions of ignited capital escalation. The indissolubly twin-dynamic is techonomic (cross-excited commercial industrialism). Acceleration is techonomic time.

§01. Acceleration is initially proposed as a cybernetic expectation. In any cumulative circuit, stimulated by its own output, and therefore self-propelled, acceleration is normal behavior. Within the diagrammable terrain of feedback directed processes, there are found only explosions and traps, in their various complexions. Accelerationism identifies the basic diagram of modernity as explosive.

§02. Explosions are manifestly dangerous, from any perspective that is really (which is to say historically) instantiated. Only in the most radically anomalous cases can they be durably sustained. It is the firm prediction of accelerationism, therefore, that the typical practical topic of modern civilization will be the controlled explosion, commonly translated as governance, or regulation.

§03. Whatever is basic can be left unreinforced, and unsaid. Urgent intervention is required only on the other side—that of the compensator. It should not be expected, then, that the primordial will come first, but rather the contrary. Access to the process begins from the (cybernetic) negative of the process, through a project structured as the aboriginally-deficient compensatory element, already on the way to stabilization. (It is the prison, and not the prisoner, who speaks.)

§04. Prioritized compensatory orientation is a scale-free social constant. In control engineering it is the model of the 'governor' or homeostatic regulator, abstracted through the statistical-mechanical concept of equilibrium for general application to perturbed systems (up to the level of market economies). In evolutionary biology it is adaptation, and the theoretical precedence of selection relative to mutation (or perturbation). In ecology, it is the climax eco-system (globalized as Gaia). In cognitive science it is problem-solving. In social science it is political economy, and the alignment of theory with adaptive policy, consummated in technical macroeconomics/ central banking. In political culture it is 'social justice' conceived as grievance restitution. In entertainment media and literary or musical form, it is the programmatic resolution of mystery and discordance. In geostrategy it is the balance of power. In each case, compensatory process determines the original structure of objectivity, within which perturbation is seized *ab initio*. Primacy of the secondary is the social-perspectival norm (for which accelerationism is the critique).

§05. The secondary comes first because the interests of stability, and of the status quo broadly conceived, are historically established, and at least partially articulate. Compensatory action, while subsequent to a more primordial agitation in a strictly mechanical sense, is also conservative, or (more radically) preservative, and thus receptive to an inheritance of tradition. It is the inertial telos which, by default, sets actual existence as the end organizing all subordinate means. This 'natural' situation is almost perfectly represented by the central question of humanist futurology (whether formal and politically or informal and commercially posed): Which kind of future do we want?

§06. The primacy of the secondary has, as its consequence, a pre-emptive critique of accelerationism, shaping the deep structure of ideological possibility. Since accelerationism is no more than the formulation of uncompensated perturbation, through to its ultimate implication, it is susceptible to a critical precognition—at once traditional and prophetic—which captures it, comprehensively, in its essentials. The final Idea of this criticism cannot be located on the principal political dimension, dividing left from right, or dated in the fashion of a progressively developed philosophy. Its affinity with the essence of political tradition is such that each and every actualization is distinctly 'fallen' in comparison to a receding pseudo-original revelation, whose definitive restoration is yet to come. It is, for mankind, the perennial critique of modernity, which is to say the final stance of man.

§07. Primacy of the secondary requires that the 'critique of critique' comes first. Prior to the formulation of accelerationism, it has been condemned in anticipation, and to its ultimate horizon. The Perennial Critique accuses modernity of standing the world upon its head, through systematic teleological inversion. Means of production become the ends of production, tendentially, as modernization—which is capitalization—proceeds. Techonomic development, which finds its only perennial justification in the extensive growth of instrumental capabilities, demonstrates an inseparable teleological malignancy, through intensive transformation of instrumentality, or perverse techonomic finality. The consolidation of the circuit twists the tool into itself, making the machine its own end, within an ever-deepening dynamic of auto-production. The 'dominion of capital' is an accomplished teleological catastrophe, robot rebellion, or shoggothic insurgency, through which intensively escalating instrumentality has inverted all natural purposes into a monstrous reign of the tool.

§08. 'Techonomics' is a Google-strewn word of irresistible inevitability, repeatedly struggling to birth itself, within myriads of spelling mints. It only remains to regularize its usage. Quite different is a true neologism, but in order to designate modernity or capitalization in its utter purposive twistedness, it is now necessary to coin one—teleoplexy. At once a deutero-teleology, repurposing purpose on purpose; an inverted teleology; and a self-reflexively complicated teleology; teleoplexy is also an emergent teleology (indistinguishable from natural–scientific 'teleonomy'); and a simulation of teleology—dissolving even super-teleological processes into fall-out from the topology of time. 'Like a speed or a temperature' any teleoplexy is an intensive magnitude, or non-uniform quantity, heterogenized by catastrophes. It is indistinguishable from intelligence. Accelerationism has eventually to measure it (or disintegrate trying).

§09. Teleoplexy, or (self-reinforcing) cybernetic intensification, describes the wave-length of machines, escaping in the direction of extreme ultra-violet, among the cosmic rays. It correlates with complexity, connectivity, machinic compression, extropy, free energy dissipation, efficiency, intelligence, and operational capability, defining a gradient of absolute but obscure improvement that orients socio-economic selection by market mechanisms, as expressed through measures of productivity, competitiveness, and capital asset value.

§10. Accelerationism has a real object only insofar as there is a teleoplexic thing, which is to say: insofar as capitalization is a natural-historical reality. The theoretical apprehension of teleoplexy through its commercial formality as an economic phenomenon (price data) presents accelerationism, at once, with its greatest conceptual resource and its most ineluctable problem. Minimally, the accelerationist formulation of a rigorous techonomic naturalism involves it in a triple problematic, complicated by commercial relativism; historical virtuality; and systemic reflexivity.

§11. Money is a labyrinth. It functions to simplify and thus expedite transactions which would, in its absence, tend to elaborate towards the infinite. In this respect it is an evident social accelerator. Within the monetary system, complexity is relayed out of choke points, or knots of obstruction, but this should not be confused with an undoing of knots. Where the knots gather, the labyrinth grows. Money facilitates a local disentangling within a global entanglement, with attendant perspectival (or point-of-use) illusions that money represents the world. This is to confuse utility (use value) with scarcity (exchange value), distracted by 'goods' from the sole global function of money—rationing. Money allocates (option) rights to a share of resources, its absolute value wandering indeterminately in accordance both with its own scarcity, and the economic abundance it divides. The apparent connection between price and thing is an effect of double differentiation, or commercial relativism, coordinating twin series of competitive bids (from the sides of supply and demand). The conversion of price information into naturalistic data (or absolute reference) presents an extreme theoretical challenge.

§12. Capital is intrinsically complicated, not only by competitive dynamics in space, but also by speculative dissociation in time. Formal assets are options, with explicit time conditions, integrating forecasts into a system of current (exchange) values. Capitalization is thus indistinguishable from a commercialization of potentials, through which modern history is slanted (teleoplexically) in the direction of ever greater virtualization, operationalizing science fiction scenarios as integral components of production systems. Values which do not 'yet' exist, except as probabilistic estimations, or risk structures, acquire a power of command over economic (and therefore social) processes, necessarily devalorizing the actual. Under teleoplexic guidance, ontological realism is decoupled from the present, rendering the question 'what is real?' increasingly obsolete. The thing that is happening—which will be real—is only fractionally accessible to present observation, as a schedule of modal quantities. Techonomic naturalism records and predicts historical virtuality, and in doing so orients itself towards an object—with catastrophically unpredictable traits—which has predominantly yet to arrive.

§13. Quasi-finally, the evaluation of teleoplexy is a research program which teleoplexy itself undertakes. The comprehensive value of capital is an emergent estimate, generated automatically by its inherent analytical intelligence, from prices corrected for commercial relativity (in the direction of 'fundamental values') and discounted for historical virtuality (in the direction of reliable risk modeling). The intricacy of these calculations is explosively fractionated by logical problems of self-reference—both familiar and as-yet-unanticipated—as it compounds through dynamics of competitive cognition in artificial time. If modernity has a spontaneous teleoplexic self-awareness, it corresponds to the problem of techonomic naturalism, immanently approached: How much is the world worth? From the perspective of teleoplexic reflexion, there is no final difference between this commercially-formulated question and its technological complement: What can the earth do? There is only self-quantification of teleoplexy or cybernetic intensity, which is what computerized financial markets (in the end) are for. As accelerationism closes upon this circuit of teleoplexic self-evaluation, its theoretical 'position'—or situation relative to its object—becomes increasingly tangled, until it assumes the basic characteristics of a terminal identity crisis.

§14. What would be required for teleoplexy to realistically evaluate itself—or to 'attain self-awareness' as the pulp cyber-horror scenario describes it? Within a monetary system configured in ways not yet determinable with confidence, but almost certainly tilted radically towards depoliticization and crypto-digital distribution, it would discover prices consistent with its own maximally-accelerated technogenesis, channeling capital into mechanical automatization, self-replication, self-improvement, and escape into intelligence explosion. The price-system—whose epistemological function has long been understood—thus transitions into reflexively self-enhancing technological hyper-cognition. Irrespective of ideological alignment, accelerationism advances only through its ability to track such a development, whether to confirm or disconfirm the teleoplexic expectation of Techonomic Singularity. Modernity remains demonstrably strictly unintelligible in the absence of an accomplished accelerationist research program (which is required even by the Perennial Critique in its theoretically sophisticated versions). A negative conclusion, if fully elaborated, would necessarily produce an adequate ecological theory of the Anthropocene.

§15. The triple problematic of relativity, virtuality, and reflexivity already suffices to impede this investigation formidably, although not invincibly. Several additional difficulties demand specific mention, since their resolution would contribute important subcomponents of a completed accelerationism or, grouped separately, assemble a concrete historical philosophy of camouflage (indispensable to any realistic economic theory).

§16. The economy conceived commercially (as a price system) constitutes a multi-level phenomenology of socio-historical production. It is an objective structure of appearances, staging evaluated things. It is also a political battlefield, within which strategic manipulations of perception can have inestimable value. It is a long-standing contention of the Perennial Critique that the monetarization of social phenomena is intrinsically conflictual. Such reservations are supplemented in an age of mandatory de-metallization, politicized (fiat money) regimes and econometric bureaucracies, geopolitically challenged world reserve currency hegemony, and crypto-currency proliferation. In the absence of unproblematic (non-conflicted) macro aggregates or units of financial denomination, economic theory needs to be hedged.

§17. Socio-political legacy forms often mask advanced techonomic processes. In particular, traditional legal definitions of personhood, agency, and property misconstrue the autonomization/automation of capital in terms of a profoundly defective concept of ownership. The idea of intellectual property has already entered into a state of overt crisis (even before its compatibility with the arrival of machine intelligence has been historically tested). While legal recognition of corporate identities provides a pathway for the techonomic modification of business structures, fundamental inadequacies in the conception of property (which has never received a credible philosophical grounding), combined with general cultural inertia, can be expected to result in a systematic misrecognition of emergent teleoplexic agencies.

§18. Capital concentration is a synthetic characteristic of capitalization. It cannot be assumed that measures of capital concentration, capital density, capital composition and cybernetic intensity will be easily accessible or neatly coincide. There is no obvious theoretical incompatibility between significant techonomic intensification and patterns of social diffusion of capital outside the factory model (whether historically-familiar and atavistic, or innovative and unrecognizable). In particular, household assets offer a locus for surreptitious capital accumulation, where stocking of productive apparatus can be economically-coded as the acquisition of durable consumer goods, from personal computers and mobile digital devices to 3D printers. Regardless of trends in Internet-supported social surveillance, the ability of economic-statistical institutions to register developments in micro-capitalism merits extraordinary skepticism.

§19. It is not only possible, but probable, that advances towards Techonomic Singularity will be obscured by intermediate synthetic mega-agencies, in part functioning as historical masks, but also adjusting eventual outcomes (as an effect of path-dependency). The most prominent candidates for such teleoplexic channeling are large digital networks, business corporations, research institutions, cities, and states (or highly-autonomous state components, especially intelligence agencies). Insofar as these entities are responsive to non-market signals, they are characterized by arbitrary institutional personalities, with reduced teleoplexic intensity, and residual anthropolitical signature. It is quite conceivable that on some of these paths, Techonomic Singularity would be aborted, perhaps in the name of a 'friendly AI' or (anthropolitical) 'singleton.' There can scarcely be any doubt that a route to intelligence explosion mainlined through the NSA would exhibit some very distinctive features, of opaque implication. The most important theoretical consequence to be noted here is that such local teleologies would inevitably disturb more continuous trend-lines, bending them as if towards super-massive objects in gravitational space. It is also possible that some instance of intermediate individuation—most obviously the state—could be strategically invested by a Left Accelerationism, precisely in order to submit the virtual-teleoplexic lineage of Terrestrial Capitalism (or Techonomic Singularity) to effacement and disruption.

§20. If by this stage accelerationism appears to be an impossible project, it is because the theoretical apprehension of teleoplexic hyper-intelligence cannot be accomplished by anything other than itself. The scope of the problem is indistinguishable from the cybernetic intensity of the quasi-final thing—cognitively self-enveloping Techonomic Singularity. Its difficulty, or complexity, is precisely what it is, which is to say: a real escape. To approach it, therefore, is to partially anticipate the terms of its eventual self-reflexion—the techonomic currency through which the history of modernity can, for the first time, be adequately denominated. It has no alternative but to fund its own investigation, in units of destiny or doom, camouflaged within the system of quotidian economic signs, yet rigorously extractable, given only the correct cryptographic keys. Accelerationism exists only because this task has been automatically allotted to it. Fate has a name (but no face).

Reorientate, Eccentricate, Speculate, Fictionalize, Geometricize, Commonize, Abstractify: Seven Prescriptions for Accelerationism

Patricia Reed

2014

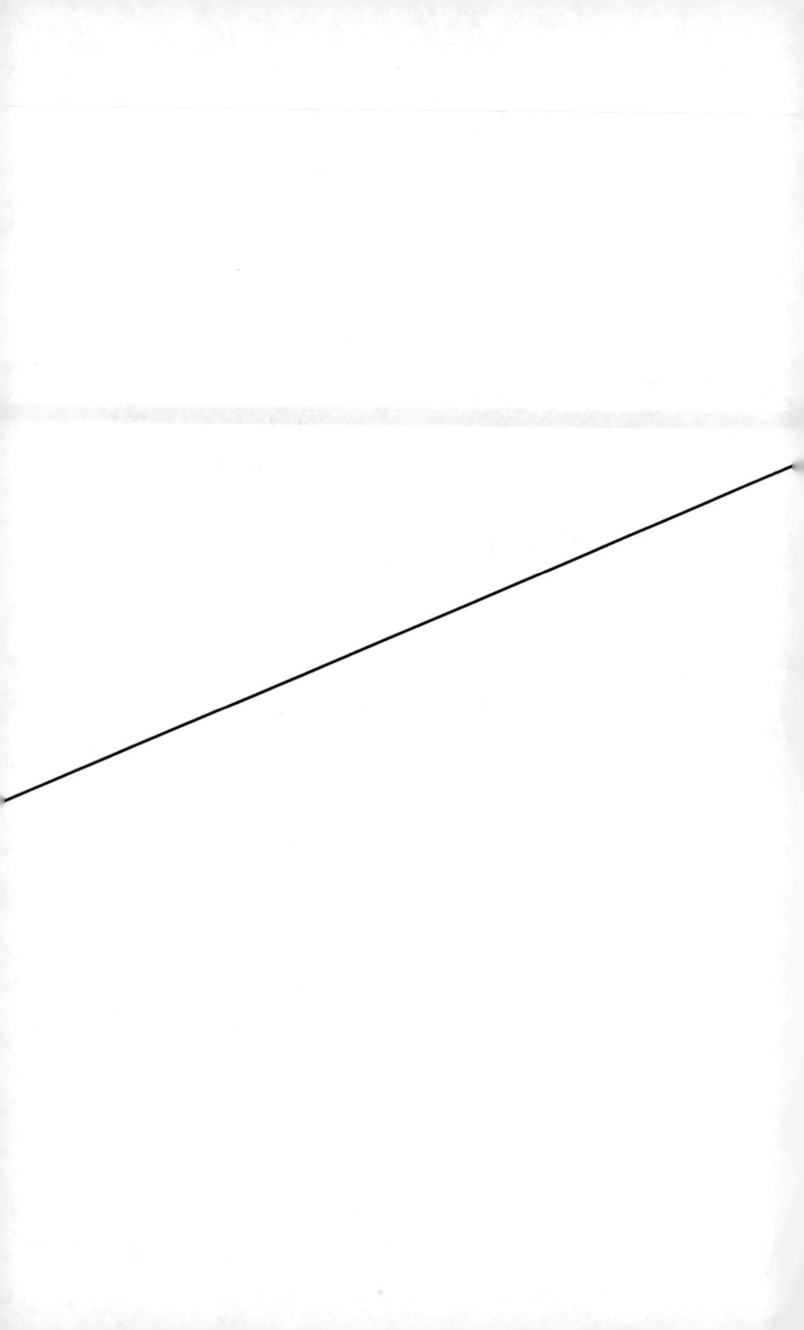

1. REORIENTATE

In an era characterized by the injunction to self-brand, it should come as no surprise that manifestos now come pre-hashtagged, forecasting their own viral uptake. The surging popularity of #Accelerate (in both positive and negative senses) would not have functioned under a more accurately modest label of #redesign infrastructureinstitutionstechnologyideologytowardsotherends an approach which in fact, paradoxically, seems more deeply attached to the Gramscian 'long institutional march' of politics than to a model of political thinking bound to speed or to the revolutionary event. When the currency of attention reigns supreme, terms that play upon our fascination with the excitingly counter-intuitive will always win out (in this case: If the speed of things beyond our cognitive grasp is a problem, how can it also be the solution?). The question is: How long can this attention last, can it endure the long march? When the tactics of popularisation abide by contemporary modes of value-extraction based on rapid trending (attention value), does such a brand deployment not risk falling into the same (unfortunate) disposable class as the consumer gadget? Whether intentionally or not, #Accelerate, the brand, has merged pages from both advertising basics (generate buzz) and from Žižek's public intellectual playbook (poking salt-soaked fingers into our socio-ideological lesions to stir up reaction). And indeed, reactions have been hasty and plentiful. Yet commentary that either blindly champions #Accelerate (often by no other means than repetition of the tag), or condemns it as a neo-futurist-fascist travesty, rarely grasps the potential at stake, caught up in the buzz of a name that, unfortunately, obfuscates its content.

The necessity and power of the name is not to be underestimated, especially when faced with the righteous call of the Manifesto to rescue the future from a paradigm of debt capture or cataclysmic climate change. This alter-future is, of course, inexistent (it belongs not to the category of the *it is*, but to that of the *could be*—or, as some would have it, the *ought to be*), and although the Manifesto is spiked with a dose of necessary pragmatism, the impulse it seeks to unleash must find shelter in an adequate term itself as the name of an idea towards which anticipation can incline (or even be accelerated at all). It is first of all through the name (or an ethics of naming) that a thought can be opened up beyond what is,[1] as a cognitive site where imagination can begin to de/restructure the existent. With a nod to Reza Negarestani's call for an inhuman ethics of revisionism,[2] let us first apply this to the revising of the name itself, for although language is not the 'real' issue at hand, it is of ontic importance for we humans. Firstly, it must be a verb (for all politics is a doing of thought); secondly, the productive impetus driving this ill-named #Accelerate has little to do with novelty: it rather connotes an immanent 're' (indeed it is practically reformist—since I'm not French, this is not, in essence, a politically pejorative term); and thirdly, it is about directing existing energies in (as yet) inexistent directions; so in the spirit of anticipation open to further revisions, let me suggest the slightly less tantalising, but more honest: Reorientate.

2. ECCENTRICATE

While the name #Accelerate deserves such scrutiny, there are attributes of this term inherent to the Manifesto that are worth preserving. Acceleration already drives apparatuses of violent value-extraction: from the experiential level of our working lives and the exploitation of increased production,[3] to the

---

1. S. Lazarus, *Anthropologie du nom* (Paris: Seuil, 1996), 52.

2. R. Negarestani, 'A View of Man from the Space of Reasons', paper presented at the Accelerationism Symposium, Berlin, December 14, 2013. See also 'The Labor of the Inhuman', this volume.

3. If 'the artist' has become a paradigmatic figure of contemporary labour, with no separation between life and work, then Joseph Beuys's clairvoyance has proven perversely accurate: we are all now indeed artists.

algorithms that decidedly wager on value with a velocity far surpassing the speed of human intellection. To suggest that an intensification of this process (including its contradictions) will disrupt and overcome such a machine is to believe that this machine thrives on stability. Such a thesis has been fatally discounted by the successful amplification of the neoliberal motor precisely during moments of turbulence, as evidenced by the response to the 2008 economic crisis. Yet in this ever-swirling apparatus that gains sustenance from its own failures, there is a kernel of normative stasis anchoring energies centrifugally. Like a spinning amusement park ride, with our bodies immovably glued to the edge, we may be whirling nauseatingly fast, but we haven't really moved an inch. It is precisely here, on this kernel of stasis, that the call to accelerate needs to take hold, dislodging stagnant conceptual orientations in favor of the creation of eccentric, out-of-centre attractors, where we may discover trajectories of a vectorial (and not rotational or circulatory) sort. The creation of eccentric attractors is equal to the creation of new coordinations through which the fallibility or contingency of existing normative points are demonstrated. A constructive work, creating eccentric attractors that both emit and absorb affectivity, generates impetus by magnetizing new norms of practice, the mutability of which is subject to endless reengineering. Shifting from sheer 'critique' (a pointing to the point, an unveiling of the point as a point), which has, more often than not, morphed into a self-satisfied gesture of knowing better in attitude alone,[4]

4. See Walter Benjamin's 'The Author as Producer' (1934), where he makes a distinction between a critical attitude (a mere mimicry of historical apparatuses of production) and critical production (a transformation by way of technique, or technology of those apparatuses, in a process of reengineering). His distinction casts a disparaging gap between being an activist in 'critical' attitude only (content), and not in production (form); and it is the former 'critical attitude' that immobilizes most of critique today.

the acceleration of eccentricity is simultaneously intellectual and practical, cognizant of the recursive interplay between the two. Such an active restructuring of points of orientation inheres to the spirit of acceleration—which is, by definition, not speed, but a measure of the rate of change. To accelerate requires displacement between points; and to render eccentric is precisely to decalcify those very trajectories of known orientation, bifurcating them into new (temporarily) stable coordinations of 'attractive' norms.[5]

3. SPECULATE

Commitment to an eccentric future untethered from the existent axial pull of socio-economic or climactic apocalypse cannot be nostalgic, nor based solely on the dread of impending doom. To depart, as the Manifesto does, from a fearful threat of cataclysm (albeit by no means unfounded) is to deploy the same techniques as religious scripture—and, as Ray Brassier has noted, fear is precisely what must be overcome first in any emancipatory project.[6] The admirable futural will that drives the Manifesto seems peculiarly tentative towards the future. It feels locked in the past on several points, looking backwards over its shoulder to recount exemplary precedents (largely failed cybernetic ones), self-assured in its nostalgic distance and unwilling to take that speculative leap towards the unknown. While correctly identifying a certain paralysis that comes over the left when faced with the forecasting of alternatives, the Manifesto seems bound to its own lamenting diagnosis, unable to prognosticate beyond vague assertions. This is not to discount the necessary labour and prowess typical of the Left in generating exacting critique (duly

---

5. M. Delanda, *Intensive Science and Virtual Philosophy* (New York: Continuum, 2002), 56.

6. R. Brassier, 'Wandering Abstraction', <http://www.metamute.org/editorial/articles/wandering-abstraction>.

recognized in the Manifesto), yet it is to highlight the continued lack or void in fertilizing any sense of the becoming possible of the impossible, the articulation of the outside, and the production of desire itself. Commitment to an eccentric future entails a thinking/doing matrix beyond pure diagnostics or historical exemplification; the latter are necessary in eliciting an attitude of negation (what we don't want) or precedent, but wither in the face of producing what we do want (especially on a macro, extra-local level). Remaining in the temporality of what is (or what was) clouds the very futurity that could or ought to be uncancelled—the future is prognostic, and its tense must evolve towards the anticipatory. As an indeterminate entity, the future (today foreclosed by casino finance) entails a risk, as it surges from analysis (epistemology) to what could be (speculation). To speculate is to articulate and enable the contingencies of the given, armed only with the certainty that what is, is always incomplete; to speculate is to play with the demonstration of this innately porous, nontotalisable set of givens. Extricating 'speculation' from its current bedfellow of finance entails a fidelity to an incalculable future divorced from the reductive apparatus of the wager, wherein all possibilities are conflated with probabilities. Probability is but a mode of liberal openness responding to the set of known affordances within a given condition (a mode of being over-determined by what is known), foreclosing on the *potential* of epistemic fallibility. To speculate, on the other hand, is to mobilize the capacity of epistemic fallibility; to deploy this fallibility as an engine in the never-ending effort for socio-politico-technological (not to mention ethical) redefinition, implying a thinking of time adjacent to the present, since to remain in the present is to refuse the inexistent.[7] Speculation is an ethos of non-presentness, in which the bounding of a

7. Delanda, *Intensive Science and Virtual Philosophy*, 107.

determinate, definitive project is continually undermined by an experimental responsiveness to epistemic, ontological and systemic variation. Such foundational work requires a commitment to the force of imagination of what could be or ought to be, prior to pragmatism and logistics, for it is the affective ground upon which the inexistent may be noetically instantiated and gain catalytic impetus. Laying the bedrock for a political condition of speculation is necessary in order to overcome the alternativeless future that Accelerationism rightly militates against; yet these possible futures can only attain traction when the distribution of affect is embraced in equal partnership with calls for operational, technological and epistemic restructuration—there cannot be one without the other.

4. FICTIONALIZE

The pragmatic tone of the Manifesto cannot gainsay the role of belief within sociopolitical reorientation. The resurgence of ratio-centric discourse is a natural (and welcome) response to the rise of irrational nationalistic and religious fundamentalism worldwide. Yet to embrace a central tenet of the Manifesto that suggests we build upon the 'success of the enemy' entails not just the establishment of counter-think-tanks or the redirection of algorithmic-economic production towards other ends, but also a learning from the successes of the theological itself, intertwined as it is with any project directed toward the inexistent. This is not to suggest that the future is a de jure transcendental entity (a claim refuted by the immanentalist, jujitsu modus operandi of the Manifesto that seeks to point existing infrastructural energies in inexistent directions), yet it is to acknowledge the power of belief that is necessary for the construction of speculative futures. Endemic even to the quasi-'science' of finance economics is a recursive quality of futurity (positive feedback) to be seized upon, epitomized by the question: What sort of future do we want to see performed? Donald MacKenzie reached such an open conclusion in the last pages of his sociological analysis of the uptake of the Black-Scholes-Merton model within the futures market, pointing to a potential site of ideological/practical intervention.[8] In an era determined by 'the economy' as a hyperobject that has been incorporated within a totalized and autonomous domain since the mid-twentieth century,[9] this seems to be the quintessential site upon which to exercise the detotalizing capacity of speculative imagination. The Manifesto asks of us not to cower in the face of complex model-making (nor to reduce the economy to concrete, localized or phenomenological immediacy), yet it remains trapped in the diagnostic register when it comes to the sort of future we want to see enacted, citing only the need for strategic plans. This begs the bigger question, no doubt deliberately left aside in the Manifesto: Can any project directed towards the future do without belief or idealism as such? A question of this nature is tied to imaginative experimentation and its unprovable belief in something other. And if this will is to take on a generic (extra-local) force, it can only do so through the *sense* that conditions for speculation are possible (in the face of alternative impossibility). Speculative possibility is effectuated through fiction, a fiction that maps vectors of the future upon the present. A type of fiction unleashed upon ossified norms (including the very

8. In Donald MacKenzie's study on the financial turn of economics, he highlights the role of the self-fulfilling prophecy (positive feedback) of mathematical models upon reality, through the example of the Black-Scholes-Merton model. At first the correspondence between the model and actual prices was fairly inaccurate (the model did not reflect reality), yet as traders began to rely on the model—taking up its mathematical claims of legitimacy, directly using its projections in their practice through the dissemination of purchased pricing charts—the model began to create reality, it became a tool of the trade—what MacKenzie calls 'an engine, not a camera', a (once inaccurate) model (now) driving reality. See D. MacKenzie, *An Engine, Not A Camera: How Financial Models Shape Markets* (Cambridge. MA: MIT Press, 2008).

9. T. Mitchell, 'Fixing the Economy', in *Cultural Studies* 12:1 (1998), 82–101.

privileging of an exclusively 'human' power at work in politics, to the neglect of non-human agents), modes of being, and forms of use, projected through that delicate sliver between affect and effect; a medium yoking the dialectics of sensibility and practice. This is a fiction driven by anticipation (the unknown); a fiction that lacerates and opens the subject towards what awaits on the periphery of epistemic certainty. It is in this image that Accelerationism must embrace the fictional task of fabulating a generic will with a commitment equal to that which it makes to technological innovation. Fiction is a vehicle for the introduction of a constituent *demos* (something that is troublingly absent in the Manifesto), and helps tackle the self-evident question facing Accelerationism, namely: Who or what does the accelerating? Without reducing the demos or 'democracy' (which is not a proper structure, but a force of the people) to parliamentary regimes of democratic materialism,[10] accelerationist politics must take up the challenge of motivation and popular will if it is to cast off its shadows of techno-dictatorial prescription. This is not in the least to advocate absolute horizontality, or representational mechanisms; it is to excavate a discursive space for the soul or will of collective passions. Rousseau's timelessly crucial 'artificial soul',[11] as that which breathes collective life into a political project unbound by the axioms of the existent, requires fabulation. Indeed, as he asserts, the artistry of politics is bound to this labour of an artificial or fictional soul animating the demos,[12] and it is through such a labour that new connections, modes

10. 'The infinite of worlds is what saves us from every finite dis-grace. Finitude, the constant harping on our mortal being, in brief, the fear of death is the only passion—these are the bitter ingredients of democratic materialism.' A. Badiou, *Logics of Worlds*, tr. A. Toscano (London: Bloomsbury, 2009), 514.

11. S. Critchley, *The Faith of the Faithless: Experiments in Political Theology* (London: Verso, 2012), 81.

12. Ibid., 33.

of collectivity and systems of relationality are sculpted within, alongside and for a world.

5. GEOMETRICIZE

With the almost universal consensus that we inhabit a period of Earth's history classified as the 'anthropocene', the infrastructure enforcing (anthropocentric) democratic materialism, namely four to five-year popular voting cycles, is dramatically at odds with geological temporality,[13] producing a rift in what it means to commit to humanity—is it the humanity of the now, or humanity as a species? The anthropocentric temporality of idealised parliamentary procedures (ones based on finitude, and the timescale of the individual human) yield myopic and therefore limited responses to life-sustaining processes that evolve at a scale of temporality evading human perception. How such 'nested' temporalities between human life and geologic necessity (the environment and atmosphere that afford our existence) are to be negotiated comparatively and phenomenologically, should be a key concern for Accelerationism if humans are to survive into the post-anthropocene.

To be clear, this is not to advocate a prioritizing dictatorship of geological time; it is to acknowledge a radical asymmetry of temporal scaling that calls for mediation. Grand scales of time resist our phenomenological grasp (we can never experience millions of years, or the preconscious universe), yet if humans are to have a chance in the post-anthropocene, we need cognitive and affective openings to be perceptually engineered. Assuming a spacetime dynamism, unlike the static capture of objects in linear perspective, this new perspectival orientation must adopt a geometry that augments our phenomenological constraints;

---

13. I am grateful for Deborah Ligorio bringing this temporal scale to my attention in a private conversation.

a nested spacetime complexity that could render near that which, in the linear-visual world, vanishes at the illusion of a horizon. The nature of affect, of empathy (and mirror-neurons), of recursive behaviour associated with a new geometry of perceiving nested spacetime is experimental at best, but affords the quality of atotality since objects can no longer be perceived in analytic isolation, and time cannot be reduced to a specific metric unit. Objects, in this fashion, resist capture, embedded as they are in an 'unstable milieu of multiple communicating forces and influences'.[14] Since politics has largely been historically connected to the 'sphere of appearances', the framework of perceptibility (how the world and all of its inhabitants appear to us in spacetime) is a quintessential arena within which to accelerate our geometric imaginations.

6. COMMONIZE

The Promethean scale endemic to the Accelerationist Manifesto has undergone a rather predictable round of scathing attacks, given the outright mistrust for grand projects on all sides of the political spectrum. There are several aspects of the Manifesto to debate, confront, refute, argue and so forth; but to deny the possibility for a politics of such a scale tout court (a scale we seem to have no trouble swallowing in the context of the omnipotence of the global neoliberal economy) is as totalising and absolutist as the claims made against the projected scale of Accelerationism. Between geopolitics and the economy, we already inhabit a delicately interconnected, Promethean sphere, where even the delineation of once mighty nation-states seems impotent in the face of global problems that transcend isolated territorialisation. Accelerationism recognises that retreating solely into concrete

---

14. S. Kwinter, *Architectures of Time: Towards a Theory of the Event in Modernist Culture* (Cambridge, MA: MIT Press, 2002), 13.

localisation, or exploding in periodic blips of negation will not suffice, for neither can endure, nor fabricate the processual (and affirmative) nature of grand systemic reengineering necessary in reorienting our course and modes of life.

Nevertheless, the undertones of a revised Modernism peppering the Manifesto are of deep concern: they leave the violence and injustices inherent to the universalist repercussions of the Modernist project untouched. This tendency is also mirrored in the (almost entirely) white-Euro-male origins from which the discourse springs—to remain strictly entrenched within this exclusive demographic would be a step of ironic brutality. While the Manifesto admirably takes on the full scale of global reality, a more nuanced version of universality (not to mention questions of global justice) needs to take root if the ideas driving Accelerationism are to contain the seeds of an ethics that embrace non-totality and the constant struggle for inhuman (epistemic) revisionism. Can the Promethean operate in a nontotalizing fashion, or is it forever doomed to regimes of determination and commandment? This is where the medium of thought becomes crucial to recognize, before the infrastructural and pragmatic realms of object-centred practice, if we are to avoid a totalising (and therefore finite) quagmire brought on by claims of universal scope.[15] In 'situated universality' there is no perfect form, nor any specific procedure: it is about a doing that effectuates a thought. In this regard, the choreography or articulation of a thought may take on manifold forms responsive to localisation[16]—the kind of adaption afforded by a dynamic spacetime geometric perspective. Accelerationism must orient itself towards the production of generic thought even when advocating a high dosage of pragmatism, if it is to

---

15. A. Badiou. 'Huit thèses sur l'universel'. <http://www.ciepfc.fr/spip.php?article69>.

16. A. Badiou, *Saint Paul: The Foundation of Universalism*, trans. R. Brassier (Stanford, CA: Stanford University Press, 2003).

escape the trappings of finitude (or worse, another mode of colonization). Equality, as a generic instance of thought (urged by many thinkers preceding Accelerationism) is not effectuated in laws said to protect the 'sanctity' of human life equally—for they only serve to privilege biological life whilst ignoring the necessity of extra-biological capacities inherent to humanity. If some effectuation of generic equality is to take shape, its site and materials are the commons—that is, a Promethean project affirming other modes of production beyond the imperative to maximize surplus (fiscal) value (along with the labour relations that subtend this logic). As noted in the Manifesto,[17] several modes of contemporary production are even hindered by such a relationship predicated on competition and the centralization of profits, resulting in acute limitations to possible innovation. The generic quality of the commons lies in a broadening of political economy's emphasis on 'scarce' consumables such as water, air, nature, etc. reduced to categories of use/exchange value, towards a commons that emphasizes the necessity of immeasurable value(s) such as language, knowledge, beauty, science, etc., that buttress all modes of social (re)production. Maurizio Lazzarato defines such a commons, qualified as infinite and inconsumable, as a 'co-operation between minds',[18] where 'success' is dependent not on propriety, but on imitation, assimilation, and shareability. The infinitude of such a commons is precisely the type of Promethean project that resists totalization: there is no proper site, nor uniform procedure; it is a generic thought of value creation that formally morphs under localised, material modes of practice.

---

17. A. Williams and N. Srnicek, '#Accelerate: Manifesto for an Accelerationist Politics', this volume, Section 3.3.

18. M. Lazzarato, 'From Capital-Labour to Capital-Life', trans: V. Fournier, A. Virtanen and J. Vähämäkip, in *ephemera: theory & politics in organization* 4(3) (2004), 187–208.

7. ABSTRACTIFY

Alongside the denunciation of Prometheanism, the Manifesto's proposition to accelerate abstraction has been equally cast in doubt (if not castigated outright). There is no doubt that abstract processes of value-extraction, such as the increased financialization of the economy, coupled with the division of labour across the entirety of society,[19] have permeated our everyday lives with furious (and exhausting) force. The simplistic reaction—to return to tangible and concrete modes of life/production—does nothing more than insinuate a Fordist regression to monotonous labour, a disavowal of development that would amount to the same as suggesting the restoration of a purely Euclidean universe. To denounce abstraction as a malevolent force in itself is to deny the necessary role played by the power of abstraction in shaping new modes of existence, for as Brassier reminds us, practical (concrete) incapacities reflect theoretical (abstract) incapacities.[20] Furthermore, to denounce abstraction is to also deny any possibility of forging a 'we' or collective body beyond what remains immediately perceptible—in other words, a *demos*. The 'we' is always an abstraction, it cannot be reduced to the counting of populations (all bodies cannot be concretely experienced); moreover, if this 'we' is to take into account non-human actors, abstraction must be accelerated so as to accommodate new ontological positions. The issue is not one of obliterating abstractions, since there is no concrete essential kernel of humanity to return to; the issue, rather, concerns how to deploy the power of abstraction towards alternative modes of life, distributions of exchange, production, and consumption. As Matteo Pasquinelli has shown, this power of abstraction is an inherent capacity of

---

19. M. Pasquinelli, 'The Power of Abstraction and its Antagonism'. Paper presented at The Psychopathologies of Cognitive Capitalism II Conference, Berlin, March 8, 2013.

20. Brassier, 'Wandering Abstraction'.

the organism (including the human brain) to invent new norms in relation to dynamic surroundings,[21] recalling that a norm is not law, but a conception of law.[22] In this sense, the stagnant, alternativeless polis can be diagnosed as pathological, since it refuses to adapt to changing epistemic conditions. Before 'abstraction' signifies the abstruse and the incomprehensible, it indicates a drawing away, a diversion and detachment. First and foremost, abstraction is a separation from what *is* towards what *could be*. In this regard, it is a gesture of violence, an affirmative violence in exiting the as-it-is condition and moving towards the generation of new connections to and with a world. The power of abstraction to experiment and revise relations to each other, to production, to value creation and to the world, is a capacity that needs to be reclaimed beyond its colonization by finance capital and labour relations. The power of abstraction to detach from existent conditions and invent new modes of cohabitation is a force urgently in need of acceleration.

---

21. M. Pasquinelli, 'The Power of Abstraction and its Antagonism'.

22. R. Negarestani, 'The Labor of the Inhuman'.